Laurette Taylor,
American Stage Legend

# Laurette Taylor, American Stage Legend

LYNN KEAR

McFarland & Company, Inc., Publishers
*Jefferson, North Carolina, and London*

ALSO BY LYNN KEAR
AND FROM MCFARLAND

*Evelyn Brent: The Life and Films
of Hollywood's Lady Crook* (2009)

*The Complete Kay Francis Career Record: All Film,
Stage, Radio and Television Appearances* (2008)

*Kay Francis: A Passionate Life and Career* (2006)

**Frontispiece:** Laurette Taylor in a promotional photograph for the play *Happiness* (1917).

LIBRARY OF CONGRESS CATALOGUING-IN-PUBLICATION DATA

Kear, Lynn.
　　Laurette Taylor, American stage legend / Lynn Kear.
　　　　p.　　cm.
　　Includes bibliographical references and index.

　　**ISBN 978-0-7864-5922-3**
　　softcover : 50# alkaline paper ∞

　　1. Taylor, Laurette, 1884–1946.　2. Actors — United States — Biography.　I. Taylor, Laurette, 1884–1946. Dying wife.　II. Title.
PN2287.T25K43　　2010
792.0'28092 — dc22　　　　　　　　　　　　　2010034802
[B]

British Library cataloguing data are available

©2010 Lynn Kear. All rights reserved

*No part of this book may be reproduced or transmitted in any form or by any means, electronic or mechanical, including photocopying or recording, or by any information storage and retrieval system, without permission in writing from the publisher.*

Cover image: Laurette Taylor publicity photograph (courtesy of Mary Pearsall)

Manufactured in the United States of America

*McFarland & Company, Inc., Publishers
　Box 611, Jefferson, North Carolina 28640
　　www.mcfarlandpub.com*

To Buster

# Acknowledgments

Rick McKay's brilliant film inspired me to write this book. I can't thank him enough for making *Broadway: The Golden Age, By the Legends Who Were There*.

I especially want to thank Jon Mirsalis and Mark Henne for putting me in touch with Laurette's family. Meg Courtney, Audrey Wallace-Taylor, Peter Wallace, Mary Pearsall, and Kathy Starr graciously agreed to speak to me. Their insights into Laurette Taylor were key to my choosing a direction for the book. In addition, Meg, Mary, Kathy, and Jon also generously supplied many of the photographs and illustrations.

Carl A. Rossi was eager to help in any way he could. I'm also much appreciative of Carolyn Gage's enthusiasm and quick responses to my requests for information.

As usual, Kevin Brownlow was a joy. He patiently answered my questions and encouraged me to write about Laurette.

I'd also like to thank John Rossman for helping me with the research in the early stages of this project. Archivist G.D. Hamann helped immeasurably in locating obscure articles on Laurette. Georgia Perimeter College's Eileen Kramer often went the extra mile for me and provided helpful advice. Thanks also to the Mountain Park branch of the Gwinnett County Library for helping with interlibrary requests.

Others who deserve a tip of the hat include David Menefee, James Robert Parish, Eleanor Knowles Dugan, Bill Cramer, James King, Ray Paradez, Katrina Callahan, and Michelle Vogel.

My friend David C. Tucker helped keep me sane and made great suggestions. Finally, I want to thank Kimber Herndon for reading the manuscript and offering valuable support and advice.

# Table of Contents

*Acknowledgments* .................................... vi
*Preface* .................................................. 1

1. La Belle Laurette ................................ 5
2. Charles Taylor .................................... 9
3. J. Hartley Manners ............................ 20
4. *Peg o' My Heart* ................................ 42
5. After *Peg* ........................................... 77
6. Laurette in Hollywood ..................... 112
7. After Hollywood .............................. 154
8. The Longest Wake ............................ 170
9. *Outward Bound* ............................... 184
10. *The Glass Menagerie* ....................... 196
11. Afterlife ........................................... 216

*Appendix I: Filmography* ......................... 229
*Appendix II: Selected Stage Appearances* ... 231
*Appendix III:* The Dying Wife *by Laurette Taylor* ............ 240
*Chapter Notes* ....................................... 243
*Bibliography* .......................................... 265
*Index* .................................................... 269

# Preface

*"I sometimes forget a face, but I never forget a back!"*[1]

Laurette Taylor became the biggest star of her day in 1912, when the stage play *Peg o' My Heart* opened. Highly sought after to enter films, she appeared in three silent films between the years 1922 and 1925. Her career declined and her personal fortunes dwindled after her husband, playwright J. Hartley Manners, died in 1928. Following years of alcoholism and erratic performances, Laurette made a comeback in the 1939 revival of *Outward Bound* and then regained her fame with a memorable performance in *The Glass Menagerie* in 1944.

New York poet Charles Hanson Towne once wrote a column devoted to Laurette. He told a story about sitting next to an unnamed actress while watching Laurette perform. "As the scene went on, I heard this great actress gasp with astonishment and delight. She turned to me. 'Ah, she has the rhythm of the theater as no one else today has it. She is always in tune. She cannot make a mistake. She is marvelous.' She meant by that that if Laurette Taylor so much as stoops to pick up a bit of paper, she does it with a certain inborn grace, an intuitive sense of how the simple act should be accomplished. All the dramatic schools in the world couldn't teach her that. It is part of her genius."[2]

While directing his documentary *Broadway: The Golden Age, By the Legends Who Were There*, Rick McKay discovered that Laurette Taylor had influenced an entire generation of actors. Ben Gazzara made it clear that "all he ever really wanted to be was Laurette Taylor when he grew up.... 'How can someone laugh and cry in the same breath?... She changed acting.... I think we've all been striving to be her one way or another.'"

Many of the legendary actors said she was the greatest actor they'd ever seen. Gena Rowlands said, "She was mesmerizing. She was ... powerful." According to Uta Hagen, "She was unforgettable." A moment later, Hagen, thinking about Laurette in *Outward Bound*, was overcome with emotion. Charles Durning admitted, "I thought they pulled her off the street. She was so natural." Martin Landau said, "Laurette Taylor was almost like this woman that found her way into the theatre through the stage door and was sort of wandering around the kitchen."

Kaye Ballard saw Laurette in *The Glass Menagerie* and thought, "Ah, she's not so good. She's just like everybody you see on the street. I didn't realize it took a lifetime to get to be that good." Patricia Neal said of *The Glass Menagerie* "That was the greatest performance I have ever seen in all my life." Hal Prince added, "I knew when I watched it and I sat in the balcony, you'll never see greater acting as long as you live." Marian Seldes saw *The Glass Menagerie* before it opened. "And then I saw it three more times. I had to see her. I just had to see her again.... She was anything she wanted to be." Fred Ebb saw *The Glass Menagerie* seven times. "Laurette Taylor turned around and pulled down her girdle, and I have never been that affected by a stage action in my whole life. It made me weep." Maureen Stapleton said, "Oh boy ... I can't describe what she did or how she did it, but boy...." Nanette Fabray saw her in *The Glass Menagerie* and said, "This, we must preserve this. It never happened."

I had heard of Laurette Taylor before seeing Rick McKay's documentary, but my interest was captured after seeing the film. At the time I was working on two Kay Francis books, and I put any thoughts of researching Taylor on the back burner. Finally, after completing my work on Kay Francis, I was looking for a new project.

I looked in vain for a video or DVD copy of any of Laurette's three silent films. Finally, I purchased a DVD of silent film trailers and eagerly settled in to see a trailer for Laurette's first film, *Peg o' My Heart*. This trailer sealed the deal for me. She was fresh, original, charming, and gorgeous. If that weren't enough to convince me, the following night I was half-listening to a 1940s music station on the satellite. As I listened more closely, I suddenly realized that the song playing was "Peg o' My Heart." Being a firm believer in signs, I realized I had just been given one.

This book makes no attempt to be a full-scale biography of Laurette Taylor. Marguerite Courtney wrote the definitive biography of her mother. Titled *Laurette: The Intimate Biography of Laurette Taylor*, it is indeed that. Courtney's remarkable book, written pre–Internet, is a masterful work that covers a lot of ground.

The purpose of this book, instead, is to discover how Laurette Taylor became an acting genius, the most celebrated performer of her time, still revered decades after her death. I viewed the film *Peg o' My Heart* and read hundreds of contemporary newspaper and magazine articles to understand how Laurette's style evolved. I also read long-forgotten memoirs and autobiographies written by her peers, which provided a more candid look at Laurette. One of the most valuable things I did was read many of Hartley Manners's plays to get an idea of how he viewed his wife as woman and performer.

The book also contains a filmography and information on selected stage appearances. The appendix includes her only published play, *The Dying Wife*, which provides an interesting view of Laurette's writing styles and themes.

## Chapter 1

# La Belle Laurette

*"When I was a little girl, I was a fearful liar, because it was so easy to think of things that pleased me far better than the plain facts.... I turned from a liar into an actress and there isn't much change inside."*[1]

Laurette Taylor was an imaginative, creative child who preferred make-believe to the real world. She lived in her head. Her mother thought her a gifted storyteller. Her father thought her a horrible liar especially when she told people she was the illegitimate daughter of a Spanish count. Years later, husband Hartley Manners wrote these lines for her in *Happiness*: "I can be a queen in me mind ... and I am a queen lots o' times, in my thoughts. Lots o' times. It doesn't cost me nothin' an' it don't hurt the queen." This was no doubt a description of a young Laurette. Her imaginative ability, encouraged by her mother, helped her become an actress.

Years later, Laurette described how important imagination is to an actor. "Imagination is the heart of acting. Eight times a week, for two hours each time, you throw yourself away and turn into somebody else. It is the greatest release anybody could hope for."[2]

She also came to believe that charisma and physical attractiveness were weak substitutes for an active imagination. "It isn't beauty or personality or magnetism that makes a really great actress. It is imagination, though these other qualities are useful.... We create in the imagination, the character we wish to express. If it is real and vital to us in imagination we will be able to express it with freedom and surety.... [Y]ou might get along without the slightest beauty and little or no personal magnetism if you were generously endowed with the imaginative mind."[3]

As a youngster Laurette liked drama. If there was none, she created it. "One Sunday I was walking through a deserted street in Harlem. Nothing stirred. The dead silence was too much for me. The only living thing besides myself was a horse tied to a post. I untied him, gave him a switch, and yelled 'Runaway horse!' Instantly the whole street swarmed with people. The horse was caught, no harm was done, and I went home satisfied."[4]

"I'm Irish—100 per cent,"[5] she liked to say. Both parents were indeed Irish, though Loretta Cooney, later named Laurette, was born in the Harlem section of New York City on April Fools Day in 1884. Laurette's birth was unusual and auspicious. A caul, part of the amniotic sac, was wrapped around her face and head. According to superstition, this meant two things: she would never drown, and she would grow up to enjoy a rich, great life. Both turned out to be true.

Laurette had two younger siblings, Elizabeth, known as Bessie, and Edward. However, her parents' focus was always on her. In fact, Laurette's daughter Marguerite Courtney explained that her mother commanded center stage in her childhood. "[B]oth parents seemed singularly indifferent to the two younger children."[6]

When Laurette was born, Harlem, located on New York City's Upper East Side, was home to immigrants and small businesses. Her mother, Elizabeth Dorsey Cooney, was the family's breadwinner. A talented seamstress and ambitious businesswoman, she'd converted a two-story house at 52 West 125th Street[7] into a millinery, where she made dresses and other clothing with the assistance of several hired assistants.

James Cooney, Laurette's father, was not as ambitious, though unlike Elizabeth, who was illiterate, he was a great reader and lover of books. He helped in Elizabeth's business, but his main preoccupation was reading and visiting local taverns. He was also the sterner parent of the two, and most of his punishment was reserved for headstrong Laurette. If her mother was guilty of indulging and encouraging Laurette's flair for drama and fantasy, then James was guilty of trying to dominate his daughter. He often punished her with a whip that he kept hanging at the ready for any offense Laurette might commit. Laurette stoically handed it to him when she misbehaved. One time she defiantly tied a pink bow on the whip.

Laurette also loved to torment grandmother Bridgett Dorsey. She later saw similarities between her two most famous roles, Peg and Amanda, and herself. "Peg was a scold and so is Amanda, and come to think of it, I was quite a scold myself as an infant around the house.... I took considerable pleasure bedeviling my grandmother, who was intensely religious. For instance, as a six-year-old, I'd [ease] up to her gently and then [ask], 'How do you explain the Trinity? How can three be one?' Once when I got off this particular piece of juvenile impudence she called angrily for my mother to come and give me the proper what for. Mother quietly called me into the kitchen and showed me five pennies in one hand and nickel in the other and said, 'Now, dear, aren't they the same? That's the way it is with the Trinity. Do you understand?' 'Yes,' I said, 'but come explain it to Gramma.'"[8]

Most young artists begin by imitating others. It's part of the path to one's unique style. Sure enough, Laurette became an excellent mimic. It's likely she mimicked her Ireland-born grandmother, but her early repertoire was more extensive than just family members. "In those days I used to imitate somebody all the time, or play a part that pleased me better than my own. When I went to a different school where the children did not know me, I pretended to be a foreigner and talked with a strange accent. Some of the boys were much impressed till one day the accent fell off and broke."[9]

Elizabeth and James disagreed about their eldest child's show business ambition. James bitterly opposed it for religious reasons and wanted his daughter to attend business school. Elizabeth, however, encouraged her daughter, for she, too, had once wanted to go into show business. According to Laurette, "Mother was always a little stage-struck, and she must have had some prescience that I was destined for the theater when she gave me such a flossy name as Laurette, instead of Elizabeth, or something else conventional. My father ... hated the theater, being a devout churchman. But mother and I would sneak off to the Harlem Opera House, where we could sit in the gallery for 25 cents, and see such stars as Richard Mansfield. When I saw Mansfield do *Dr. Jekyll and Mr. Hyde*, I fainted — thereby proving my right to be an actress."[10]

An early disagreement occurred when Elizabeth paid for dancing and singing lessons with former vaudeville performer Ida Whittington. Laurette, then around 12, wasn't a good student, and James considered the tuition a waste of money. Elizabeth ignored him and even teamed up with Ida, also known as Miss Whitty, to find Laurette a job. Together, they sent out flyers heralding "La Belle Laurette." According to Laurette, "My singing teacher urged my mother on, so we had some stationery printed, advertising my act—'La Belle Laurette' in imitation of Anna Held, George M. Cohan, Maggie Mitchell and other stars."[11]

They received only one positive

**An early publicity phototograph of Laurette (courtesy of Mary Pearsall).**

response. It was from a nickelodeon in Lynn, Massachusetts. Laurette performed there for about a week. Her act consisted of her imitation of Anna Held singing "You're Just a Little Nigger but You're Mine All Mine" and a recitation of "How Salvador Won." The theatre manager told mother and daughter they were out of their league and should get out of show business. "Neither of you know anything about the stage ... and I think you had better try something else."[12]

The Cooneys returned to Harlem, only momentarily discouraged. Another company, this one in Gloucester, Massachusetts, asked for "La Belle Laurette." Elizabeth and Laurette packed and went back to Massachusetts, where Laurette sang.

> It was there on a summer evening,
> On a night I'll ne'er forget
> I was caught by the wile of the sunny smile
> Of my own little pet Laurette.[13]

The show was so bad Laurette took a pay cut. "The manager said it was not worth twenty-five dollars and gave me twenty."[14] The young performer was open to advice and learned crowd-pleasing antics such as teasing the audience with glimpses of her petticoat. She learned this bit of stagecraft from the Bernard Sisters, a mother-daughter act who'd been in show business long enough to know what customers wanted.

Elizabeth wasn't sure that this was what she wanted for her daughter. However, when Laurette was kicked out of high school and her father insisted she go to business school to learn a trade, Elizabeth decided to give Laurette another chance. Once again she teamed up with Miss Whitty and had Laurette audition at Keith's vaudeville. This time Laurette's act included the Anna Held imitation as well as a song that featured Laurette in blackface. Still, the effort resulted in no offers. Disillusioned, Laurette began to wonder if she was really meant for show business.

She soon received another offer, this one from Boston to perform at the Athenaeum for a week. Her new opportunity led to a family break-up. "Father was furious — said he'd walk out of the house, never to return, if I repeated the experiment.... [F]ather did walk out. He never returned, because my mother locked the door on him. I think she had only been waiting for the chance."[15] Elizabeth shipped off Laurette's two siblings to relatives and left for Boston with her daughter. Indeed, this was the last straw for James. He left, and Laurette didn't see him again until her mother's funeral years later.

Laurette was already adept at living in imaginary worlds and mimicking those around her; her next big step was hooking up with the man who tremendously influenced her career and ultimately married her.

## *Chapter 2*

# CHARLES TAYLOR

*"[Y]ou have to be open to all things. You have not to be afraid. Of anything."*[1]

One day in 1901, while Laurette was jumping rope with neighborhood children, a stranger asked her where Ida Whittington lived. Laurette directed him to her teacher and later found out that he was Charles Taylor, an old friend of Ida's. Born (perhaps) in 1864, Taylor was a playwright and producer. He'd been married twice and had a young son who traveled with him. He was also 20 years older than Laurette. Dwight Taylor later described his father as "an extremely handsome man.... Tall and well-proportioned, with high cheekbones like an Indian's.... He had a thin, aquiline nose, a thin-lipped, rather large mouth, and arresting gray eyes beneath black brows."[2]

Laurette, sensing this might be her big break, got up her nerve and set out to find Taylor to ask for a job. He promptly sent the teen back home. However, in Boston, Taylor caught one of her performances and immediately offered her a 40-week contract in *King of the Opium Ring*. Elizabeth, a shrewd woman, informed Taylor that her teenage daughter would need a chaperone and promptly got hired to help with costumes.

*King of the Opium Ring* was set in Chinatown in 1890 and featured an exciting police raid. Marguerite Courtney called it "the worst kind of claptrap but very much what the audience demanded in the popular theatre of the day."[3] Laurette had a small part as a street urchin.

Taylor requested Laurette's services for his next show, and Elizabeth successfully orchestrated her daughter's marriage. She needed to return home to care for her other children and strongly hinted to Taylor that this might be a good time for him to marry her 16-year-old daughter. It probably seemed like a good idea to the overwhelmed Elizabeth, but Taylor was 36 and not great husband material. He promised Laurette that he'd make her star. It wasn't difficult to convince this teenage girl that her future would be romantic and rosy. Dwight later described his father as controlling. "He had a possessive, almost annoying, way of handling people, making them do exactly what he wanted them to do."[4] Laurette and Taylor married in 1901.

Taylor, a prolific writer of melodramatic plays, immediately wrote a play for his wife. Laurette and Taylor's troupe went on tour for some 40 weeks in the aptly titled *Child Wife*. This wasn't successful, however, and the company ended its tour in Seattle.

Guthrie McClintic, who later married Katharine Cornell, grew up in Seattle and recalled attending performances by Taylor's company. He quickly realized that there was something special about Laurette: "[L]ong blond curls framed a face of peculiar loveliness, with great, deep-blue eyes that reflected her Irish moods and a radiant smile that seemed to give the lie to the haunting melancholy of her voice. She had for me an inexplicably disturbing appeal.... She was different."

Taylor's leading lady on stage at that time was Ailleen May. She was a beauty in the style of a Gibson girl and certainly a much more experienced actress than Laurette. She was a fan favorite but a definite contrast to Laurette. According to McClintic, "Miss May was winsome, with a bleached blond pompadour that never varied no matter what part she was playing — and an off-stage wardrobe of big hats with waving ostrich plumes and dresses with peekaboo tops (very daring), mostly in baby blue, that made the stage-door mob gasp when she came out after the matinees. She spoke to all of them and they followed her up the hill to her hotel. She was a great favorite. Mrs. Taylor was not so popular, perhaps because she was concerned more with her acting than with hobnobbing with the customers. For me, magic hovered over her like a halo."[5]

After May left the company, lured away by a rival producer, Laurette took over her roles. McClintic noticed that Laurette played May's roles with a different style. For example, he'd seen May in *Stolen by Gypsies*, a typically overheated melodrama. In the play the mother's soul travels into the daughter's body, affording the actor the opportunity to play both mother and daughter. "As I recall Miss May's entrance down a painted rock runway, her bleached-blond hair was exquisitely marcelled, her make-up was impeccably pink-and-white, her costume of red china silk was jingling with Chinese yen, and her gold sandals were immaculate, a great tribute to the roads over which she had traveled — she obviously had not run, even from her dressing room. Her first request was for a drink of water, of which she took two dainty sips from the miner's dipper that eager hands had rushed to her; and then one of the miners, removing his hat, asked the name of the wee bairn. Miss May, grasping the prop papoose, vocalized thus: 'I call her Lone Star because she is the only star' — and left it at that, while the miner wiped away a tear."

Laurette took the part in an entirely new direction. "Laurette Taylor's performance was as different as chalk from cheese. On her entrance, you saw a dark hand grasp a rock for support as slowly she pulled herself into view.

The rocks became real. Her natural blond curls were obscured by dark hair that had been in wind and rain. Her clothes were torn and soiled; her sandals revealed feet that were dirty and bloody. She literally collapsed. Her speech was incoherent. (No dressing-room trek, this.) When she got her drink of water it was as if a thirsty plant was absorbing it and gradually showing signs of life. And when she was asked the name of the child, she looked at the prop she was holding and it became active. You felt her heart beat faster as she held it close. She transformed that 'Lone Star' speech into something that was motherhood and longing and desperation. The actors around her, with their assumed Western accents, were forgotten. We were in the presence of a dimensional person wracked with emotion, her great eyes haunted with the image of what was to be her destiny — her husband and the knife! That moment Laurette Taylor opened my eyes to the facts of acting."[6]

Laurette was no longer simply mimicking other actors. While many young actors might have tried to imitate Ailleen May, she was taking chances, trying different techniques, and continuing to use her imagination. What would the character do in this situation, she'd ask herself? How can I make this character more real? "The imaginative actress builds a picture, using all her heart and soul and brain. She builds this picture not alone for the people out in front but for herself. She believes in it and she makes the people across the footlights believe in it. Unless she has done this she has failed. She must stimulate the imagination of the audience. An actress should not only be able to play a part; she should be able to play *with* it. Above all, she should not allow anything to stand between her and the thing she is expressing."[7]

Sometimes, early in her career, Laurette didn't take the plays seriously. According to Marguerite Courtney, "The imp got the better of her and she would play them for laughs. Charlie lectured her. You believed completely in what you were saying and doing, and made the audience believe, no matter how silly it seemed. 'Believe it, and the audience will believe it.' She learned the lesson well."[8]

Unfortunately business wasn't good, and when Laurette became pregnant the decision was made to return to New York. Taylor, who probably could have become a successful attorney if show business wasn't his passion, seemed to know every important technicality of the law. For example, he found out about a law stipulating that no hotel could refuse food service to a pregnant woman. He had Laurette order enough food to her room to feed the cast members. He also found a law decreeing that no one could lay a hand on a pregnant woman. Laurette spent a good amount of time on top of their trunk, which held just about everything they owned, as they beat a hasty retreat out of town to avoid creditors.

Dwight Oliver Taylor, Laurette's son, was born on January 1, 1902, in New York. Laurette, through sheer will power, waited to have the baby until she heard the announcement of the new year. In her mind, 1901 had been a bad year, and she felt the baby would have a better chance being born in 1902. The birth was not a sign that the marriage was a happy one. Early on, Laurette realized that Taylor was a philanderer and had little understanding of her emotional needs. Like her father, he was controlling and often grew impatient with her.

Taylor's next production was *Queen of the Highway*, which toured in 1902. At first, Taylor's sister, Helen Hunter, played Jess Miller, but Laurette eventually felt well enough to return to play the lead. Taylor also produced *Through Fire and Water* and *The White Tigress of Japan*, but *From Rags to Riches* was his most popular play during this period. Written for child actor Joseph Santley, it marked Laurette's Broadway debut when it premiered on August 31, 1903.

According to Dwight Taylor, "All his [Charles Taylor's] plays had one thing in common: mother was in almost constant mortal danger from the time the curtain rose until it fell. I saw her pursued by Indians, cowboys, Chinamen and, above all, by a man with a black mustache.... The titles of these plays will give some indication of their nature: *The White Tigress of Japan*, *Through Fire and Water*, *Queen of the White Slaves*, *Escapes from the Harem*, *The Derby Mascot*, *Queen of the Highway*, *The Female Detectives*, *King of the Opium Ring*, and *From Rags to Riches*. This latter, written in three weeks, was one of the biggest money-makers of the day and my father's *chef d'oeuvre*. In the last act mother was entombed in a dungeon by a mad Chinese doctor, there to be set upon by wild dogs."[9]

Ward Morehouse called it an "overwrought and lachrymose drama,"[10] which is a pretty good description of all of Charles Taylor's melodramas. Still, despite a lack of critical appeal, he was popular with audiences. Taylor's fortunes improved to the point that he purchased a comfortable house in Mount Vernon, New York, when Laurette became pregnant again in 1904. Despite the material trappings, Laurette continued to be unhappy. Not only were she and her husband mismatched, but for her domesticity equated boredom.

Their daughter Marguerite was born in August 1904 while *From Rags to Riches* was still on Broadway. The Taylors lived for a time in Mount Vernon before again hitting the road with *Queen of the Highway* in 1905. Later that year, they sold the Mount Vernon house and its furnishings and relocated to Seattle, where they enjoyed some success at the Third Avenue Theatre.

This time would prove to be the key to Laurette's artistic development. "The Seattle company played in a theatre at which the price of admission was the familiar ten, twenty, and thirty scale. Performances were given seven nights a week, with four matinees, and there was, of course, a change of bill weekly.... [T]he company played every conceivable sort of play which could be obtained without having recourse to the annoying necessity of paying any royalty to the authors."[11] According to Dwight Taylor, the building was a "ramshackle, two-story affair, its gloomy exterior relieved only by the colorful posters with which my father had plastered its sides."[12]

Laurette liked to tell people her time in Seattle didn't help her career. "People talk of the advantages of hardship and disappointment. I don't see that those years helped me any. The plays were melodramas with no chance for truth in expression."[13]

A childhood photograph of Marguerite and Dwight Taylor (courtesy of Meg Courtney).

In fact, these early experiences were crucial for her later development. It didn't matter which plays Laurette was in. Make no mistake about it, the melodramas written and produced by her husband were bad. Dwight Taylor wrote about a poster for *The Queen of the Highway*: "With the aid of a magnifying glass, I see that she is clad in buckskin, standing in a position of delightful insouciance, her left hand on her waist, and with the other flourishing a revolver in the general direction of heaven. This play was one of my father's most successful ventures, and like everything else he wrote, had enough plot and situation to make a dozen television plays.... The plot, like all my father's plots, is so involved that to embark upon it is somewhat like entering a maze in an amusement park...."[14]

What mattered was that Laurette was on stage in front of an audience over and over again, learning her craft. This belies the popular myth that Laurette "wasted herself" on inferior plays. For example, *Time* wrote, "One of Laurette's mistakes as an actress was that she used herself up on plays written by her husbands."[15] In fact, every performance Laurette gave, regardless of the quality of the play, provided a learning experience for her.

Her time in Seattle also provided her with the practice necessary to master her profession. According to Malcolm Gladwell's book *Outliers: The Story of Success*, "The idea that excellence at performing a complex task requires a critical minimum level of practice surfaces again and again in studies of expertise. In fact, researchers have settled on what they believe is the magic number for true expertise: ten thousand hours."[16] Let's say Laurette averaged four hours a day, seven days a week of either rehearsing or acting. If she did this for seven years, she would have exceeded 10,000 hours of practice. Interestingly, Laurette was with Charlie Taylor for around seven years.

Gladwell quotes Daniel Levitin, who said, "The emerging picture...is that ten thousand hours of practice is required to achieve the level of mastery associated with being a world-class expert — in anything.... In study after study, of composers, basketball players, fiction writers, ice skaters, concert pianists, chess players, master criminals, and what have you, this number comes up again and again.... It seems that it takes the brain this long to assimilate all that it needs to know to achieve true mastery."[17] It stands to reason that this would be true for actors too. Of course, it's not enough just to do the 10,000 hours. Many actors have been in the business long enough to log the hours but come nowhere near the mastery of Laurette. According to researcher Sheena Iyengar, "If you want to improve, you must continuously observe and critically analyze your performance: What did you do wrong? How can you do it better?... [P]ractice doesn't always make perfect, but it can help you cultivate genuine expertise if you go about it in the right way."[18] Laurette's quick mind lent itself to just this kind of critical analysis.

While appearing in *The Great John Ganton* on Broadway in 1909, Laurette reflected on the importance of her Seattle experience. "My real experience ... I gained in a stock company, playing Camille one week and Topsy the next.... I spent two years in Seattle, working hard, never shirking, looking upon its quantity and its quality. When the play called for a fencing bout, I had it delayed until I could acquit myself at least creditably.... For *Carmen* I clicked castanets for three weeks, keeping them going as I ate, as I studied, even the last thing as I fell asleep.... I learned to dance, to sing 'La Paloma'.... After two years of this, while playing in Rider Haggard's *She*, I had nervous prostration. As that is always a sort of diploma for a leading woman, I regarded my education as finished, and went to New York."[19]

Marguerite Courtney explained that Seattle was also where Laurette developed the rehearsal method that she used the rest of her life. Rather than memorizing the lines, Laurette "worked instead to get the general sense of each scene, achieve a consistent character, and let the words fall where they would. Mumbling the gist of a speech, feeling out 'business,' watching the other plays, seeming more intent upon their parts than her own, she was establishing a relationship — a very real relationship — between the character she played and those which were contingent upon it.... Then at the last minute, if necessary, she would sit up all night and work away at the actual lines as though she were finishing off the last details of an edifice already solidly standing on its foundation."[20] This method would later drive directors, producers, and fellow actors crazy, but it worked for Laurette.

Although her husband's material offered her few meaty roles, Laurette was learning much about acting, and, more important, developing her own unique style. Laurette's style was no longer derived from other stage stars. In fact, she saw few theatrical shows other than the ones she was in. Instead, her technique was based on observations, instinct, and imagination. "By herself she was evolving an approach to characterization which combined both head and heart. She drew her material from the people she knew, a passerby on the street, a brief but all-inclusive glance at another human being: this was stored in her memory, and then brought out at the appropriate moment to become refined or embellished by her imagination. And, incredibly, she was able to instill the warm pulse of life into her husband's wooden stage characters."[21]

The key word is *evolving*. Laurette realized, perhaps unconsciously, that a career for any actor, as for any artist, is based on evolution. "Play-acting, like the rest of living, means learning and growing all the time. That is why I don't like to do one piece too long, or to keep doing the same kind of plays and parts.... It seems to me better to play role after role, each in a different key, till the public learns to count on your unexpectedness. Then people will never tire of you and never leave you as you grow older."[22]

Laurette continued to believe that imagination was important. This was no longer childhood daydreams but a method of imagining that helped make a performance more real. "Too few actresses follow their instinct. I think instinct is the direct connection to the truth. It is not enough to know just what you are to do yourself in the action of a piece; you must know also the exact relation you must bear to every other character in the play. For instance, take the business of dying. You must in your imagination realize not only the fact that you are dying but the effect which your death will have on every character related to your part. You know that you are not dying and the audience knows it, but in your imagination you must really believe you are. The business of dying becomes actual to you; also, you compel the audience to believe in you by the very sincerity of your attitude."[23]

Great instinct develops only after years of practice. Writer Frank Carrington often asked Laurette to explain her process of acting. She usually demurred. One day, however, she finally gave him his answer. "'Frank, dear, we either make magic or we don't."[24] However, the magic didn't happen without years of practice. She told another interviewer, "I don't know how I act. I just act, that's all, after I have absorbed the part."[25]

Laurette explained the importance of observation in an article she wrote in 1914 for *The Green Book Magazine*. "The artist looks for the unusual. She watches everyone, always searching for the unusual in clothes, in manner, in gesture.... The most interesting thing to me in acting is the working out of the character itself, the finding of that which is uncommon and the small, seemingly insignificant trait which will unconsciously make an appeal to the audience and establish the human appeal."[26] She also wrote about observation in *The Greatest of These*—. "People supply *me* with a new outlook. Personalities give me material for my work on the stage. My own kind thrill me — make me laugh sometimes, hurt me at others, but, they always thrill me! *Out of contact I* [italics in the original] acquire the thousand little things that are of use to me."[27]

An argument could be made that Laurette became Laurette while in Seattle. She still had a long way to go to before she became a subtle, nuanced performer, but she was honing a distinct style, different from anyone else's. It wasn't Charles Taylor who made Laurette, but he literally provided the stage for her to do so.

In *Blood-and-Thunder*, Dwight Taylor listed the plays produced by Charles in 1907 alone. The season began in mid–May and ended in late December. Laurette appeared in 27 plays, ranging from hokie Taylor melodramas to *Faust* to *Carmen*. He may have been a bad husband and a mediocre writer, but Charles Taylor's influence stayed with Laurette throughout her career. Without that mind-numbing, relentless work, it's unlikely she would have achieved her success on Broadway just a few years later.

While there's no question the roles provided variety, it's no wonder that she eventually revolted. She was tired of bad plays and felt stuck. Laurette was Charlie's partner at the Third Street Theatre, and that meant that in addition to her acting duties, she also helped with selling tickets, making curtains and sets, and anything else that needed to be done. Unfortunately, Taylor didn't always include her in the business decisions, and his blunders eventually ended up hurting the company financially.

In Seattle, Laurette also learned to think quickly on her feet. She had to because something was always going wrong. Indeed, if Laurette could survive Seattle, there was a good chance she'd reach stardom. At times it seemed a big "if." Laurette often told stories that, while humorous, illustrated the dangers of performing in plays where the props were often the stars. "Once we did a play called *The Bridge Tender's Daughter*,[28] or something like that.... I was little Nell, the brave and fearless daughter of the old man who was the guardian of the railroad bridge in the Rocky Mountains. This particular bridge, as I remember it, spanned a yawning chasm which was distinctly stated to be 7,000 feet deep. The villain, who had a grudge against someone who was about to cross this bridge as a passenger on the Western Mail, loosened the railroad track, planning to send the train and all on board hurtling to the depths below. It was my mission to foil this dastardly plot by forcing the rail back into position, and I was supposed to finish the job too late to make my way to safety by running to either side. I was called upon, therefore, to swing myself over the side of the bridge and to hang from the ends of the ties while the train thundered past. That was the finish of the act. At one performance everything went off according to plan until it came time for the train to put in an appearance. I was hanging over the side of the bridge with my feet about a foot off the floor of the stage. Something had gone wrong with that train. The rays from the headlight were dancing on the bridge and the puffing of the locomotive could be plainly heard off stage, but something had happened to delay its appearance. I raised myself until my head was above the level of the tracks and turned to peer into the wings to find out what was the matter. Just at that moment the difficulty was adjusted and the train shot across the bridge. Of course, it was just a painted piece of canvas, but it was reinforced at the front with a heavy piece of wood to hold it in position, and this struck me with a terrible blow on the head, knocking me unconscious and releasing my hold on the ties. I dropped to the stage behind a piece of scenery painted to represent a projecting rock. So far as the play was concerned I fell to the bottom of the chasm 7,000 feet below. Inasmuch as there was another act in which I had to be infolded in the heroes [sic] arms, I naturally had to appear again. But no one seemed to mind it. I received a severe cut on my head, but the only sign of damage visible to the audience after my 7,000-foot fall was a bandage wound round my head."[29]

According to Dwight, Laurette thought the property man was a genius. "Ingenious he may have been, and resourceful as well, but why Mother continued to hold him in such high regard, when so many of his devices and inventions nearly cost her her life, remains a mystery."[30] He wrote that in *She*, "Mother was almost electrocuted in full view of the audience, and was forced to retire from the part for several days."[31]

Laurette told another story where her dignity suffered damage. Playing a sultan's wife, she was supposed to jump from a tower onto an elephant in order to make her escape. "The property man faked up the body ... and two supers played the front and hind legs. This scheme worked beautifully for the first few days, or seemed to, but I was to learn that rank treason was developing in the hind legs. On the occasion of the fourth or fifth performance, just as I landed on the elephant's back, I heard the hind legs mutter to his companion in front: 'This is my last night for this stunt, bo. She came down on my neck like a pile-diver.' My sense of humor got the best of me and I burst out laughing. The hind legs man heard me and reared backward, thereby dislodging me from my position and sending me sprawling on the stage. The movement also unsettled his own balance and he toppled over, to the huge delight of the audience. He scrambled to his feet, and the disjointed elephant ran off the stage, while I followed on foot."[32]

Laurette stayed about two years in Seattle before deciding, not surprisingly, she'd had enough. She packed up the children and went back to New York. Some reports suggested she had a nervous breakdown. She didn't, but she probably felt like she had. Years later, Laurette reflected back on the experience. "It is usually the custom for people who have attained a certain measure of success in life always to wind up by saying that their struggling days were the happiest ... but that's a pose. I'm far happier right at the present moment [March 1918], winding up my second consecutive season on Broadway, than I ever was in the early days of my career, and, believe me, I speak from the depths of a profound conviction when I say that lounging around in this dressing room is a darned sight pleasanter than trying to keep clean and warm in the little old closet that served that purpose in the old Third Avenue Theatre in Seattle."[33]

Still, there is no question that Laurette's stock experience was invaluable. These were the key experiences that eventually made her the toast of Broadway in *Peg o' My Heart* and then later in *The Glass Menagerie*. Lynn Fontanne explained, "Laurette had played so many years with stock companies in the west and she was accustomed to handling quickly every unexpected situation that might occur during a performance. She showed me how to exploit my resources and how to work spontaneously and not be all tensed up inside. You see, what there was about her was she could be absolutely free about expressing her emotions on stage. She hadn't any fear of doing anything she wanted to do and saying anything she wanted to say. So I saw how you must come to feel completely at home on stage and then you would forget it was a stage."[34]

Laurette left Charles Taylor in 1907 and later divorced him. For the rest of her life she'd pretend he'd died, that she was, in fact, widowed and not divorced. It was a combination of her disdain for Charlie as well as the fact that divorce was considered immoral. Dwight wrote about a melancholy time following the divorce. His father dropped him off after one visit, and Laurette was waiting to pick him up. She stiffly asked Charles how he was doing. "'All right,' said my father. 'I'm planning a big revival of *From Rags to Riches*. You could play the end of it now.'" My mother looked back at him a moment without saying anything, then turned and led me toward the cab."[35]

Dwight told Laurette on the way back about the stories his father had told him. Most of them concerned a woman, and he was convinced it was her. "I was conscious of the new smell of luxury that had come into our life— of flowers and furs and a faint perfume. 'You have too much imagination,' she said. 'Like he has. None of those women were me.... That was the trouble.'"[36]

After leaving Taylor and returning to New York, Laurette enlisted her mother to care for her children. She was now even more determined to become a stage success.

*Chapter 3*

# J. Hartley Manners

*"Hartley and I are joined in 'holy deadlock' and as a wife I have a right to look to him for his love, honour, obedience and plays."*[1]

Some credit long-forgotten Howard Jacott, assistant to producer Lee Shubert, with discovering Laurette. When she was just 16 Laurette was rehearsing in New York City's Seventh Regiment Armory for a Charles Taylor production. It was an unbearably hot summer day. Doors had been thrown open in an attempt to create even a small breeze. As a result, Jacott was able to hear a remarkable actor. "A closed door would have bottled up this voice. But now it issued forth — strong, penetrating, dramatic. It was climbing the scales of high emotion. One had the impression its owner was actually living tragedy.... The voice it developed, belonged to a mere girl in her teens, a graceful slip of an Irish lass, with blonde hair and big blue eyes.... The play was deep-dyed melodrama of the ten-twenty-thirty variety. The third act was on and Laurette Taylor was dying — dying so realistically and so horribly that even the veteran Jacott was affected."[2] Jacott dutifully reported the discovery to Shubert and concluded, "I've found a real actress." It would be a few years before Shubert took Jacott's advice.

When Laurette returned to New York, she lived with her mother and children. Jobs, however, were not easy to come by. Laurette admitted, "I was shabby, I was anxious — and an actress should never look either."[3] Despite badly needing a job, Laurette was still defiant. She auditioned for a role in Molnar's *The Devil* and was told to attend the current New York production and mimic exactly what the actress did. Laurette thought the woman was awful and decided to take the role in a different direction. The director, however, insisted Laurette imitate the actress and implied that her job depended on it. Laurette watched the actress again. "At the next rehearsal every sigh, every droop of despair was in her performance, an exact take-off. The cast howled with laughter. Laurette was promptly fired."[4]

Laurette had the last laugh, however, because a rival producer hired her for the same part. The play opened in November 1908 in Chicago. Burns

Mantle noted that she "made the model literally true rather than sympathetic, reaping her last scene well."⁵ Another critic, not knowing Laurette's audition story, suggested that the other actress attend Laurette's performance to learn how to do the part correctly. Unfortunately, the production closed after five days because money had run out.

Soon after, Charles Taylor arrived, intent on reconciling with her. Not having any other job prospects, she reluctantly agreed to appear in his 1908 New York production of *Yosemite* (it was also called *Stolen by the Gypsies*). The four-act play was a lulu. Described as a "play of the great outdoors, a romantic love story laid in bewitching California before the days of the discovery of gold,"⁶ the script featured reincarnation and lavish scenery. It opened in Buffalo on December 8, 1908.

Laurette quickly became infamous because her costume didn't cover her legs. In fact, the production was considered scandalous, and Laurette was unhappy when most of her press pieces were about the scantiness of her costumes. "[A]las, the critics, while they praised my acting, gave so much attention to my bare feet and the dress made of leaves I wore that instead of fame I achieved notoriety."⁷ Laurette tired of it and asked that the production be closed. *Yosemite* closed in Washington, D.C., in the first part of 1909, and Charles Taylor, who never wrote another play, wandered off to parts unknown.

The stage was set for the improbable romance between Laurette Taylor and Hartley Manners. Laurette showed up at Shubert's office one day, again frantic for work. "The receptionist in Mr. Shubert's outer office wouldn't give her the time of day. Outraged by these continual rebuffs, she ... lost control of her good Irish temper, telling the receptionist in no uncertain terms her opinion of her. At that moment Hartley Manners arrived

**Hartley Manners and Laurette Taylor married in 1912 (photograph courtesy of Meg Courtney).**

to see Mr. Shubert by appointment.... [H] said, 'There's an attractive young woman outside who has the fire and spirit for that third-act scene of *The Great John Ganton* (Manners' play, which they were then casting). Shubert said, 'Let's have her in' and buzzed for the receptionist, who said the lady had left but she would try to get her. The office boy was sent scurrying after her, and returned triumphantly with Miss Taylor in tow. She was signed immediately; and that was the beginning of the partnership of Laurette Taylor and Hartley Manners."[8] In the year that they met Laurette turned 25, and Hartley was close to 40.

*The Great John Ganton* was about a successful Chicago meatpacker. It opened on Broadway in April 1909 with George Fawcett playing Ganton. The drama critic for *Life* liked the play — "one of the strongest plays seen this season" — and raved about Laurette. "Miss Laurette Taylor brought a new and charming personality to our stage, and showed a rare combination of girlish sweetness and womanly strength."[9] Critics were already noticing that she wasn't typical. Alas, the play ran less than two months, closing in June.

Laurette candidly told a reporter that she preferred parts like the one in *Yosemite* to the one in *The Great John Ganton*. "She would much rather dress in the skins of wild animals, or in some other unusual attire, and play the role of a wild, carefree gipsy, than trail satin robes across the stage, as she does at present."[10] As for the much-needed job, Laurette admitted, "I am grateful, even though it is not what I like to play best. The fashionably gowned, marcelled heroines hold no charm for me. But I feel that I have one foot on the bottom rung of the ladder of fame, and, although it is as wobbly as the water wagon, I hope to persist. After all, the person born to wealth and fame misses all the fun of getting there, and loses the capacity for keen relish of their successes through the bitterness of past failures."[11]

During the play's run, to her great distress, Laurette noticed that Manners was taking another actress, Jane Peyton, to lunch virtually every day. She casually mentioned it to Peyton, who told her the lunches weren't the least bit romantic. She was, Peyton told Taylor, simply an old friend of Hartley's, and besides, Hartley "really didn't care much about women."[12] Laurette later received a box of flowers from Manners on opening night and thought it was a sign of his romantic interest until she learned that all cast members had received the same gift. Nevertheless, eventually Manners came around, and the couple married in 1912 when *Peg o' My Heart* was in rehearsals.

"He is an Irishman, educated in England, who made his money in America."[13] This is how Taylor described J. Hartley Manners. In some ways, Hartley was an odd choice for Laurette. He was strait-laced whereas Laurette was definitely a free spirit. According to Noël Coward, "Hartley was a charming man, but his spirit seemed to be shut up permanently inside a sort of 'iron virgin' of moral principles. This, as far as I was concerned, made any lengthy conversations difficult. I had to tread lightly, and in the few literary discussions that we had, I soon learned not to allow enthusiasm to carry me too far, and to hop aside, nimbly, from any anti-social, anti-religious, or remotely sexual allusion. Laurette, on the other hand, was frequently blunt to the point of embarrassment. She was naïve, intolerant, lovable, and entirely devoid of tact."[14]

Laurette often explained that she and Hartley were more different than alike. "I prefer tennis, my husband golf. I tell my troubles to everyone, my husband keeps his to himself. I have little tact, and he is

Hartley Manners as a young man (photograph courtesy of Mary Pearsall).

very diplomatic. I lose my temper on a moment's notice; he always has his under control. I have no sense of order and he is very methodical. I'm all imagination; he is all reason and analysis. I fall in love with every handsome movie star I see in pictures; he is amazingly constant, but for all differences we get along splendidly together. Probably it is very old fashioned to be so happily married ... but it is very comfortable and satisfying."[15]

One of the biggest differences between Laurette and Hartley was their temperaments. Laurette had first been warned by her mother and then Hartley to control her temper. "'Count ten before you lose your temper!' admonished Elizabeth one day, slapping her daughter smartly on the cheek. 'Count it yourself before you lose your own!' answered Loretta, holding her aching jaw.'"[16] On the eve of their visit to England to present *Peg o' My Heart*, Hartley warned, "You have an Irish tongue, Laurie.... Speak in haste to the English and you'll repent in solitude." Like her mother, he also begged her to count ten before she spoke. "If I stop to count ten ... nothing seems worth saying."[17] It is unlikely that anyone ever asked Hartley to control his temper.

Laurette discussed their working life as collaboration but agreed they were opposites. "Often we fuss about the very things each admires in the other. I respect his sense of form but I hate his working so long over one piece. I want him to go ahead and finish things as fast as they come to him. On his side, he thinks I'm too easily affected by impulse and mood."[18] She added, "He has given me ... a sense of the fitness of things — a sense of proportion."[19]

Hartley was a nineteenth-century writer writing in the twentieth. His style was old-fashioned and in many ways a reaction to anything modern. Still, there is no doubt that he was popular and successful with audiences, as antimodern artists often strike a chord with certain audiences. Hartley, who had once been an actor, provided an interesting view on playwriting when interviewed in 1912. "In England ... the public tries to keep up with its dramatists, who lead; in America, the dramatists scramble to keep up with the public.... The Englishman would be a prophet; the American would have profit." In this interview he also attacked George Bernard Shaw as "a sham and a humbug.... Shaw is the modern quack among dramatists and dramatic writers." He also made a prediction. "Personally, I have no faith in the realists.... I'll venture a prophecy: future ages will call George Meredith — not Thackeray or Dickens — the great novelist of the Victorian era."[20] Oops.

Producer George C. Tyler was one of the few who admitted liking Hartley's plays. He called them "grand plays that gave her [Laurette] unquestioned genius every opportunity to blaze up and show her as the really great actress she is.... In some ways Laurette Taylor was unparalleled. I always insisted that Manners try to work into each play a long story for her to tell, because she could hold an audience tense through a long narrative better than anybody since James A. Herne — that was her specialty, like [James] O'Neill's staircase."[21]

Most, however, didn't think Hartley was a great or even good playwright. Many believed that it was a testament to Laurette's talent that she was able to make so many of his plays successes. "That Laurette's performances transcended Manners' material was regarded as one of the miracles of the age. Fellow actors grudgingly admitted that the Taylor magic could make anything seem better than it was. Even the dialogue and plots of Hartley Manners."[22]

Hartley's female characters were sentimental, naïve, and childlike beings who bore little resemblance to modern women of the 1920s. They represented nostalgic views of women who neatly fit into the stereotypical categories of child, wife, and mother.

An interviewer once asked Hartley at what age women become most interesting. His answer is revealing. "The most interesting age is from fifteen to eighteen years, when the first call of youth comes with all its imaginings. There is nothing so pure, so high, so free from the taint of selfishness of the world as the dreams of a young girl. Castles in Spain are lovely places in which to live, with rose vines trellised to their windows and the soft thrum of music echoing through their shining halls.... The most interesting age of woman is from eighteen to twenty-one years, when romance enters in and the world takes on a different tinge. In birdland we might call this age the mating age. Not every girl finds her mate during those three prescient years. At this time she realizes the full meaning of love. Romance grips her. The love affairs of her friends are fascinating chapters in the book of life. Cupid is her patron saint, a bow and arrow her talisman. A magic age.... The most interesting age of woman is when the realization of perfect womanhood crystallizes in the wife and mother. Surely there is no one so biased on the subject of marriage as to deny that wifehood adds immeasurably to the sum total of perfect womanhood. Marriage is a part of the Great Universal Plan. Wifehood must be that humanity may continue onward and upward. A world without wives would be a decadent, doomed world. I shouldn't care for it. Most unhappy sort of place. Mothers! No man will deny their blessed interest. It is as a mother the woman reaches the very pinnacle of her womanhood. It is now she has fulfilled her mission as a woman. She has paid her debt to man and God. She has made the supreme sacrifice. Admirable age, the age of wife and mother.... Above all, a woman is most interesting when, as a complete woman, she wields the full power of effort and influence and shares in the destiny not only of her family but of her country.... I never realize the value of a good woman so much as when I see her in the midst of her family, using her mature mother influence to secure for her family the greatest possible amount of success and happiness.... I might say never so much with but one exception — and that is when she has renounced even her hunger of motherhood and placed on the altar of country her very heart's blood — her husband, father, brother, sweetheart and last and greatest of all, her sons. A magnificent age, the age of completed motherhood.'"[23] That was Hartley. So, of course, he promptly went out and chose a woman who was like none of the examples he provided, except perhaps for the teenager.

In some ways, he kept Laurette childlike, insisting on taking care of finances, making career decisions, and getting her out of scrapes caused by immature behavior. Many of his plays featured her in roles where she was much younger than her actual age. For her part, Laurette was an eager participant in this dynamic. She didn't want to grow up. She'd been indulged by her mother and now looked to Hartley to pat her on the head, chuckle at her antics, and make things right. Charles Taylor had attempted to control Laurette in her first marriage. Though he certainly had a different style and personality, Hartley also tried to do the same. According to Marguerite, "The primary force of his influence on Laurette was toward temperateness in both her personal and artistic life."[24] Hartley had his work cut out for him.

Laurette began a tradition of appearing in only her husband's plays. Although she was sometimes criticized for this, especially by critics who weren't impressed with Hartley's writing skills, Laurette was fiercely loyal to her husband and expressed disgust with anyone who couldn't see his genius.

Hartley provided stability for Taylor as well as good advice. "One of the things he taught me," she said, "was not to take advice from too many people. Young actors sometimes spoil their work by trying to please everybody; they listen and do this to satisfy one person and that to satisfy another. Pretty soon they can't act."[25] Laurette didn't listen to a lot of people, but Hartley was someone she trusted.

Laurette and Hartley talked and lived theatre. They may have had different personalities and interests, but they were great collaborators who shared an obsession with plays and acting. For example, they observed audiences together. According to Laurette, "I used to make little peep holes in the scenery and study the audience, to see the effect as it showed upon individual faces. And I would call Mr. Manners to do the same thing. There were spots where dozens of people always began to look around at their neighbors or study their programs. When this happened several times in the same place, we knew that the scenes were too long and that certain speeches had to be eliminated. A line was cut out here and another there, quickening the action."[26]

After the couple married, they first lived in an apartment on West End Avenue; later, in the fall of 1922, they moved into a mansion at the corner of 77th Street and Riverside Drive. Among the many celebrity guests who came to the house was Noël Coward, who described it as "an odd demi–Gothic edifice.... This house possessed one enormous room below stairs, with an open fireplace, much tortured woodwork, and stained-glass windows, and, upstairs, many small rooms on different levels, varying in décor from Laurette's gilt and belaced bedroom and a formal mahoganied dining-room, to the correct and rather heavy-handed virility of Hartley's study, with its sports trophies, pipe-racks, and sturdy writing-table."[27]

Fifty Riverside Drive was an impressive place from which to conduct interviews. One writer who visited her after her first trip to Hollywood to make *Peg o' My Heart* described meeting her in the drawing room, "furnished with sculpture by Clare Sheridan[28] and Chesterfields deeply upholstered in velvet."[29] "In the midst of this homespun simplicity sat Miss Taylor, with a heavily aromatic cigarette between her fingers. She was swathed in costly furs, for in the interest of honesty let it be recorded that the great log fire was not burning cheerily—it was smoking dismally, and furs were comfortable. To complete the homelike atmosphere, a taxicab was outside clicking off dimes every four minutes that Miss Taylor delayed her departure for the Ritz, where Douglas Fairbanks and Mary Pickford—simple souls!—were awaiting her arrival for tea."[30]

Alexander Woollcott glanced up at the monstrosity one day while on a walk. Not knowing who was leasing it, he mentioned to his companion, "'There's a vile bourgeois ostentation for you!' At which point Laurette and dog Michael emerged through the front door bundled up in identical sweaters and looking about as bourgeois as two circus performers on their way to the tanbark."[31]

Years later Coward wrote the play *Hay Fever*, which he claimed was based on Laurette Taylor and her family. "On Sunday evenings up on Riverside Drive we had cold supper and played games, often rather acrimonious games, owing to Laurette's abrupt disapproval of any guest (whether invited by Hartley, Marguerite, Dwight or herself) who turned out to be self-conscious, nervous, or unable to act as an adverb or an historical personage with proper abandon. There were also, very often, shrill arguments concerning rules. These were waged entirely among the family, and frequently ended in all four of them leaving the room and retiring upstairs, where, later on, they might be discovered, by any guest bold enough to go in search of them, amicably drinking tea in the kitchen. It was inevitable that someone should eventually utilise [sic] portions of this eccentricity in a play, and I am only grateful to Fate that no guest of the Hartley Manners thought of writing *Hay Fever* before I did."[32]

What was Laurette's reaction to Coward's portrayal of her family? She was hurt, but not for the obvious reasons. According to her daughter, "After seeing the play in New York she found it hard to forgive him; the addlepated group of rugged individualists whom he depicted were not her family at all. 'None of us,' she declared emphatically, 'is ever unintentionally rude.'"[33]

Some of Laurette's coactors

**Dwight and Marguerite Taylor (photograph courtesy of Meg Courtney).**

might have begged to differ. According to Jared Brown, "Taylor had no patience with actors she considered to be inferior. After a rehearsal a group of actors might be invited to the Taylor-Manners home for a party, but if Manners suggested an actor whose ability Taylor disdained should be invited, she would loudly and tactlessly shout, 'My God, I have to suffer with him for three hours on the stage, isn't that enough?'"[34]

Leslie Howard, a frequent house guest, echoed Coward's description in a letter to his wife. "The Hardly-any-Manners atmosphere [is] very prominent. Laurette *means* well, of course, but you know being a guest in that household is not so amusing as it sounds."[35]

According to daughter Marguerite, "You couldn't sit still with Laurette and just talk peacefully. You had to 'do something.' She'd always pick on her women guests. She once savagely criticized Ethel Barrymore in front of other people and Miss Barrymore never again came to the house."[36]

Lynn Fontanne was another guest who didn't enjoy playing games at the Riverside house and paid the price. One time Fontanne thought Laurette was successfully reading people's minds. Laurette later laughed and told her the set-up had all been pre-arranged. Everyone was in on it but Fontanne. "Are you above games now that you are a star?"[37] Laurette scolded. Laurette's teasing became so cruel that Fontanne's husband, Alfred Lunt, finally refused to attend her gatherings. Eventually, Fontanne, too, had had enough and ended their friendship.

Laurette was famous — or perhaps infamous — for her parties. According to Jessie Royce Landis, "Some of Laurette's dinner parties really were fantastic. I don't think Laurette was ever down to greet her guests. You would arrive and be shown into the huge sunken living-room, beautifully decorated with dark, rich colours, old Italian furniture, and a tremendous fireplace, over which hung a lifesize portrait of Laurette as 'Peg' with her dog. The lighting was very soft so that the room had an old mellow look — even a bit musty. The guests would arrive and, finding no host, would introduce themselves. Cocktails would be served, and then Hartley would appear. Finally, Laurette would make her entrance — and it was an *entrance!*"[38]

Laurette knew how to liven things up when one of her parties turned dull. According to Landis, "One night, during one of her dinner parties (which was not going very well), Laurette had an idea that everyone should tell his most embarrassing moment. I knew her well enough to realize she was doing it only to 'loosen up' or shock two very stuffy people who, in some miraculous way, had been invited. I think it was A.E. Matthews who told of a big New Year's Eve party he had gone to at the Ritz in Boston. One of the guests became very 'tight' so they had taken his clothes away from him and locked

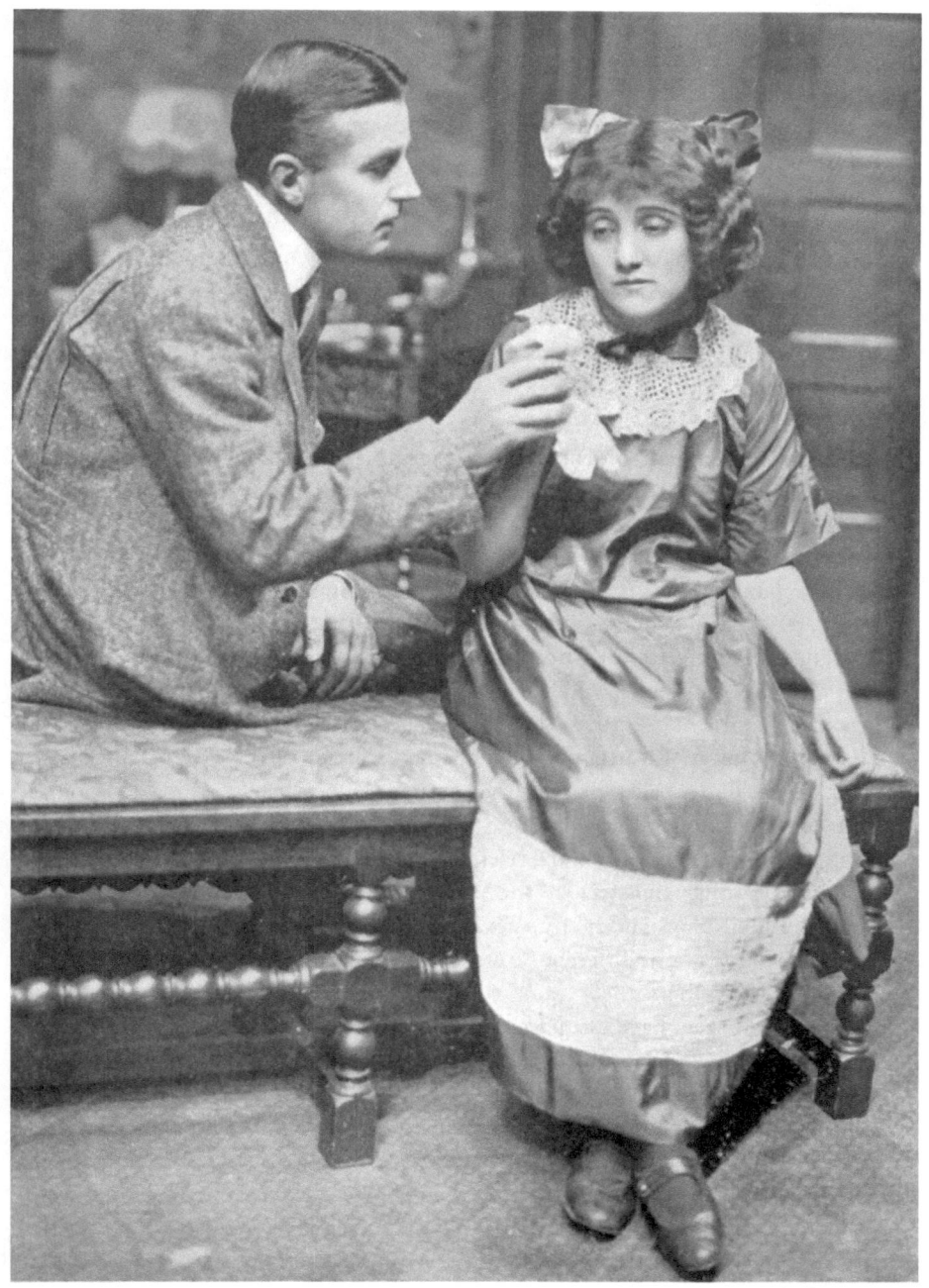

Matthews and Laurette in *Peg o' My Heart* (1921).

him in his room, which was on the fourth floor. A little later, when Matty and some of the party were going down in the lift, it stopped at the fourth floor — and there, confronting them, was said drunk, completely nude, save for his cane and silk hat! And before the stuffy guest could catch their breaths, Laurette chirped up: 'Was it on his head?' Even they couldn't hold out any longer."[39]

Leslie Howard was one of several British actors who often attended parties at the Manners' household. "At many of these Leslie would find Jack Buchanan and Gertrude Lawrence, Freddie Lonsdale, Ethel Barrymore, and A.E. Matthews. If Ruth [Leslie's wife] did not come to New York, he would sometimes end up in Hartley Manners' bed at 5 A.M. Conversation seemed to have been as varied and odd as the cocktails. Leslie remarked after one session that it had 'ranged from abortions to Queen Anne chairs,' and that at another Laurette Taylor had informed the gathering that 'Christ was a modern, a European, had written the Bible and the Ten Commandments and other interesting and previously unknown facts!'"[40]

Laurette could also be a terror on the set. Sometimes she would take over directing duties from Hartley during rehearsals. She'd criticize the performers, offer advice, and generally create such a disturbance that Hartley threatened to cancel the rehearsal or throw Laurette out.

Some observers viewed the marriage as more of a business partnership than a romantic one. It seemed to some that Hartley and Laurette led separate lives. Marguerite Courtney explained that Hartley continued for the most part to live like a bachelor after the marriage. They had separate bedrooms. "Laurette had her suite of bedroom, sitting room and bath at one end of the long corridor which formed the backbone of the shallow house, while Hartley occupied similar quarters at the other end."[41] Most of their discussions involved their plays and the theatre. Other than that, they had little in common. They even kept different hours. Hartley preferred to write at night after everyone had gone to sleep.

Some writers have suggested that Laurette was a lesbian. According to Axel Madsen, "Alla Nazimova taught Laurette Sapphic love and how to hold out for great roles."[42] He also wrote that Laurette was sexually involved with Tallulah Bankhead and Dorothy Arzner, though he offered no evidence.[43] In fact, Nazimova and Taylor were friends. According to Nazimova's biographer Gavin Lambert, "Nazimova had a unique range of friends and acquaintances, from Chekhov to Rudolph Valentino, Ellen Terry to Stanislavsky, Eugene O'Neill to Noël Coward, Laurette Taylor to Marlene Dietrich, D.W. Griffith to George Cukor, Emma Goldman to Nancy Reagan."[44]

Diana McLellan also wrote that Nazimova and Laurette were lovers.

According to her, the two met at the home of lesbian agent Elisabeth (Bessie) Marbury and her partner interior decorator Elsie de Wolfe. "At Bessie and Elsie's salon, Alla met not only the brilliant and beautiful stage stars of the day, but an ever-widening circle of their rich women admirers, including Anne Morgan, daughter of financier J.P. Morgan, and Anne Vanderbilt ... Alla, between heterosexual flings, flew into many of the stage's most celebrated smooth white arms. One of her most gossiped-about early conquests was Laurette Taylor, the toast of Broadway in the comedy *Peg o' My Heart*."[45]

Leslie Davis wrote that Laurette was part of the "sewing circle." According to Davis, "The phrase 'sewing circles' ... allegedly coined by actress Alla Nazimova to describe discreet gatherings of Hollywood lesbians, became a common way of referring to lesbian and bisexual actresses of that era. Many actresses of the 1930s, 1940s, and 1950s participated in the 'sewing circles'.... Tallulah [Bankhead] participated.... While in Hollywood, she was often a guest at Nazimova's 'Garden of Alla.' Her lesbian partners included Katharine Cornell, Laurette Taylor, also a lover of Nazimova and director Dorothy Arzner, Sybil Thorndyke and Beatrice Lillie. Lillie had affairs with Eva Le Gallienne, Cornell and Judith Anderson. It just gets so confusing."[46] It sure does.

Laurette became a regular at parties held at an apartment shared by Beatrice Lillie and Gertrude Lawrence. The two performers, who many believed to be bisexual or lesbian, were appearing in *Charlot's Revue* which had opened on Broadway in late 1925. According to Lawrence, "Bea and I took a duplex apartment together in a converted house on West Fifty-fourth Street and this soon became a rendezvous for a gay crowd. Many of those who came there were connected, in one way or another, with the theater. There were composers, writers of lyrics, playwrights, and newspapermen. They would drop in at all hours, and it seemed to make no difference to them at all whether Bea or I was there. If we weren't, they would immediately make themselves comfortable and wait for one or the other of us to turn up.... Our steady salonites included such grand people as Neysa McMein, Dorothy Parker, Jeanne Eagels, Bob Sherwood, Richard Barthelmess, Laurette Taylor ... Oscar Hammerstein, Howard Dietz, Arthur Schwartz, Jerome Kern, Irene Castle, Fanny Brice, June Walker, Estelle Winwood, Lenore Ulric ... Rodgers and Hart, George and Ira Gershwin, Irvin Berlin ... Clifton Webb, Prince Dmitri, Schuyler Parsons, Jascha Heifetz, Alexander Woollcott, and Eddie Goulding."[47]

Infamous lesbian Mercedes de Acosta hosted an event that brought together several famous actresses. According to Diana McLellan, "It happened that 1927 was a banner year on Broadway, with some 268 attractions on the boards. By now Mercedes had collected enough of their stars to try a daring social experiment. She would toss an all-woman, all-star dinner — 'a cat party.' She invited the cream of the season to the handsome five-story house that she and Abram [Poole] had filled with fine English furniture, set an extravagant table, and welcomed her guests. Katharine Cornell, the toast of Broadway again for her role in *The Letter*, swept in. So did Nazimova, currently a sensation as Madame Ranevsky in Eva Le Gallienne's new production of *The Cherry Orchard*, Eva herself declined, but there was the English actress Mrs. Patrick Campbell, internationally famous for her role a dozen years earlier as the first Eliza Doolittle in Shaw's *Pygmalion*; Constance Collier, a smash in *An Ideal Husband*; Helen Hayes, another smash in *Coquette*; Elsie Ferguson, the star of *House of Women*; and two greats currently resting between hits, Alla's seducee Laurette Taylor of *Peg o' My Heart*, and Doris Keane of the almost equally long-running *Romance*. Even Jeanne Eagels, star of *Her Cardboard Lover* and Mercedes's frequent charge, arrived. The 'cat party' was chic, amusing, and ambitious in the planning. In reality, it was a catastrophe. Each guest was dumbstruck at being jostled by so many other scene-stealers. Most, wondering who else had been bedded by the hostess, who had loved whom among the others, and who now hated whom, thought that Mercedes was playing some kind of trick. Only Mrs. Patrick Campbell, the senior (and probably un-seduced) star, got up the steam to talk, and she was both bitchy and patronizing."[48]

Not surprisingly, de Acosta's version of the party was a little different. "I gave a strange dinner party that winter that taught me there can be only one lion on occasions of this sort. What made me give this dinner I will never know! Fearlessly I invited the guests I wanted and the place cards read like the all-star cast of a benefit performance: Mrs. Patrick Campbell, Doris Keane, Jeanne Eagels, Alla Nazimova, Elsie Ferguson, Constance Collier, Laurette Taylor, Helen Hayes, Helen Menken and Katharine Cornell. Needless to say, each one of these marvelous women could glitter and shine in her own right, but together they eyed each other almost dumbly — all except Mrs. Pat Campbell, whom no one could ever silence. She was especially well known for her biting remarks to other women. On this occasion she decided to direct them at Doris Keane. Doris had been playing with great success for many years in *Romance*, by Edward Sheldon. Actually I believe she had played it for over nine years and she had played with as much applause in London as in New York, and everyone knew it. Mrs. Campbell addressed her across the dinner table. 'Doris, darling, why don't you go to London with your little play *Romance*?' Laurette took up Doris's defense with her Irish forthrightness: 'Don't play the cat, Mrs. Pat. You know perfectly well that Doris has had a raving success in London — or perhaps you don't read about other actresses' successes? Maybe you just try to forget them.' The dinner was definitely *not* the happy event I had hoped it would be."[49] Indeed, McLellan concluded, "Mercedes learning her lesson that night: A star expects center stage; to mingle your star lovers courts disaster."[50]

Laurette was a hero to Eva Le Gallienne, who compared her to Alla Nazimova, with whom she'd had a love affair. Le Gallienne said Laurette had an "attractive, charming magnetism."[51] She was thrilled when Laurette and friend Constance Collier asked her to join their dancing club in the early part of 1915. Le Gallienne's biographer Helen Sheehy reported Le Gallienne to have said, "'They have accepted me as a member which is a great honor as only people who dance very well are allowed,' Eva said. The club met several afternoons a week, from four to six. 'It is splendid for me as I meet all the stage people there & get to know them well,' Eva wrote. 'You bet I shall be there every time.' At the club, she danced with Elsie Janis, with Constance, with actress Marie Lohr, and with Laurette Taylor ('a genius,' Eva thought), who was in London playing in *Peg o' My Heart*."[52]

Le Gallienne found Taylor different from most American women whom she described as "'henroosty.'" In contrast, she found Taylor "'dear, so sweet & unaffected.'"[53] Le Gallienne's friendship with Taylor came in handy when she was asked to play an Irish lass in *The Melody of Youth*. "The brogue didn't pose a problem — Laurette Taylor coached her, and since Eva had seen *Peg o' My Heart* a dozen times in London, she merely imitated Taylor's speech and pitched her voice into a higher register."[54]

In contrast to this view of Laurette, Marguerite Courtney described her mother as a prude. One of Laurette's favorite sayings was "I get my sex between bedcovers, not book covers." In fact, Laurette reacted violently to lesbian-themed literature. "The play, *The Captive*, in which the symbol for lesbian love was a bunch of violets, spoiled her love of that flower for years; and a fit of prolonged morbidity after reading *The Well of Loneliness*, a novel on the same subject, was dissipated only by the laugh she got when Hartley pointed melancholically at his toilet one morning and sighed, 'Ah, *there's* the well of loneliness.'"[55]

Maurice Zolotow suggested that Laurette didn't particularly like women. "Laurette was jealous of other women. She had only two women friends, the actress Jane Peyton, who married Samuel Hopkins Adams, and Lynn [Fontanne]. Laurette competed with every other woman, even, at times, with these two. She wanted to be the only woman in a world of men."[56]

In her autobiography, gossip columnist Hedda Hopper claimed that Laurette confided to her that she didn't like women. "She used to say to me darkly,

Laurette as the charming Peg in *Peg o' My Heart* (1921).

'Don't trust 'em, Hedda; they'll double-cross you every time.' Then she'd add with a laugh. 'Don't trust me either. I'm Black Irish — we love you one minute and turn on you the next.'"[57]

As a mother, Laurette was a mess. She had no patience for children, and hers were alternately neglected and smothered. According to Dwight, "The relationship between my mother and myself— at least in my more cognizant years — was not really like that of a mother and son at all. I think this was partly due to her reluctance, perhaps even inability, to sustain the responsibilities of the conventional relationship and at the same time fulfill the demands of her profession."[58] In other words, Laurette was a child herself and when asked to choose between raising her children and building her career she chose her profession.

Her children were possessions and showpieces. "My mother demanded wit rather than obedience,"[59] Dwight wrote. He also wrote, "It was characteristic of her, throughout her life, to neglect some friend or loved one for long periods, and then suddenly shower him with a flood of love and generosity. The giving of presents seemed to hold for her a tremendous, almost portentous, significance, as it does with children. She was an unusually inarticulate person when it came to trying to express her love directly. Her gifts were often a form of hieroglyphics, whereby the presents, together with the times when they were delivered, were supposed to impart a message which she was unable to convey in any other way."[60]

Hartley neither volunteered nor chose to help with the children. Although he and Dwight and Marguerite grew closer during his final illness, he was never a father figure to them. However, in some ways he was a father figure to Laurette. After working together on *The Great John Ganton*, Laurette next appeared in *The Ringmaster* in the summer of 1909. This was one of the last plays in which Hartley exerted no influence over Laurette. *The New York Times* described it as a "play that needs a large blue pencil and a pruning knife." They added, "Miss Laurette Taylor was a pleasant, self-contained heroine, agreeable to looks and manner...."[61] It ran for only 32 performances and closed in September.

Laurette and Hartley became better acquainted when she appeared in his play *The Girl in Waiting* in 1910. Originally titled *Miss Brown, Burglar*, the play, based on a novel by Archibald Eyre, was purchased by Cohan and Harris for Laurette and produced first in Philadelphia and then in New York, Chicago, and Boston. Hartley's play was described as a "delightful and farcical comedy," and Laurette was described as "the newest and daintiest dramatic star."[62] It's a clever, funny play that featured Laurette in a part that was reminiscent of Peg. She played Lillian Turner, daughter of an alcoholic member of Parliament, who ends up pretending to be a burglar named Miss Brown. Read today, it's easy to see how Lillian was the genesis of Peg, a charming, good-natured girl full of mischief. It's also one of Hartley's most delightful plays and shows his strength was writing comedy.

On April 19, 1910, *The Girl in Waiting* opened in Philadelphia, and then was in Chicago in the fall of 1910 at the Olympic. A reviewer described the play as an "instantaneous hit." Though the critic thought Laurette was quite good, he also pointed out that she seemed nervous. "Miss Taylor won her way into the hearts of Chicago theater goers.... As a hoyden Miss Taylor is perfection, except that at times she showed distressing symptoms of what might be termed 'near stage fright.'"[63] The stage fright resulted from Cohan and Harris billing her as a star. Laurette didn't feel she was ready and knew she gave a poor performance. "I have only a confused recollection of that first night. Nerves that were jangled, feeling of nausea, and an hysterical laugh. My wits went wool gathering."[64]

She felt so bad, in fact, that she apologized at the end of her performance. According to Percy Hammond, "In the course of the proceedings at the Olympic last evening Miss Laurette Taylor, the principal person involved, stepped to the footlights and made the suggestion which stifles, if it does not altogether choke, the words of criticism which otherwise we should utter. This suggestion, expressed in the frank and engaging manner so characteristic of Miss Taylor, was to the effect that she was quite overcome with agitation at the glaring prospect of her name electrically emblazoned in the façade of the theater and therefore was somewhat uncertain that she had done the things she ought to do and had left undone the things which she ought not."[65] Percy Hammond agreed that her performance was awful. "[S]he forgets instinct and intelligence and relies entirely, and one regrets to say with some success, on personality." Still, Hammond believed, even at this early stage, that Laurette was a rare talent, and that the failure was only a blip. "The fact that *The Girl in Waiting* retards her is of little consequence, since such things must be expected, as we learn from biography."

The play closed before it came to New York. Laurette felt she'd let down the audience, critics, and Hartley, but resolved to succeed. "I am going to make them say all those lovely things about me some day without any buts. Of course, I have all the ambition in the world. I have made the plunge, and after the first shock, the water is fine."[66]

Laurette's next role was in Washington, D.C., in Kate Jordan's *Mrs. Dakon*. A reviewer remarked that "Laurette Taylor's work was one of the best examples of good acting we have to record this season."[67] Laurette was apparently such a force as the 16-year-old Ruth Dakon that the title was changed

**Two views of Laurette Taylor. These were included in a 1915 publicity booklet for *Peg o' My Heart*.**

to *Dakon's Daughter* when it opened in New York. Dorothy Dorr, who played Mrs. Dakon, couldn't have been happy. The play closed before it made it to New York.

Laurette's first real hit was in 1910 in *Alias Jimmy Valentine*, written by Paul Armstrong and based on the O. Henry story, "A Retrieved Reformation." Taylor earned $200 a week from producer Liebler & Company playing Rose Lane. Ward Morehouse wrote that Taylor "played charmingly as the heroine."[68] According to the *New York Times*, her part was "capitally acted."[69] *Life* found the play "stirring and interesting" and mentioned that Laurette acted "piquantly" though with a "certain 'flipness' and lack of elegance."[70]

Interestingly, critic James O'Donnell Bennett pointed out as early as this 1910 performance the mannerisms that came to define Laurette decades later. "Audiences follow her maneuvers with intense interest for she exercises in an almost uncanny way the faculty of riveting attention upon herself; and observation is constantly rewarded by the disclosure of fleeting bits of detail, swift changes of mood, little quizzical touches of emphasis and tricks of facial play that are unexpected as they are right and charming.... It has been suggested that perhaps this actress has not yet acquired a method.... But when you note the excellence of her pauses ... or when you listen with her while she listens with an eloquence more illuminating than a dozen sentences would be — then you are constrained to believe that here is either an extraordinarily subtle method or an intuitive gift for expression that amounts to genius."[71]

In February 1911 Laurette appeared at the Lyceum with Charles Cherry in *The Seven Sisters*. Cherry was a matinee idol described by one writer as "attractive [and] manly."⁷² Laurette played Mici, a rebellious but sweet young lady who is forced to dress much younger than her age. It wasn't the lead role, but Laurette thought it the choice role — and she was right. Daniel Frohman recalled trouble with *The Seven Sisters*. In particular, Laurette and Frohman's stage manager were feuding. According to Frohman, "They constantly quarreled and the stage manager notified me that Miss Taylor had neither charm, ability, nor suitability for the part. I could not agree with her, because I knew what Miss Taylor could do. Finally the stage manager complained that she could not get on with Miss Taylor in the leading role." Laurette was adamant that a particular scene be played with subtlety. Refusing to budge, she wrote a letter of resignation to Frohman: "I'm home and penitent, simply because you're so courteous and considerate — I feel a very small person indeed to make a scene — but — believe me, the most serious, tender, passionate love scenes are those that are played and projected over the footlights through suggestion, without actual contact, and because a small band of unimaginative everyday people can't see it, no reason why it should be changed and brought down to their level — a man mauling a woman on the stage is a subject for laughter from the old roués and a matter of regret from the nice men — Hungarian or not!!! The greatest love scenes in the world are played [apart] from physical contact — Shakespeare realized it, and the two greatest lovers in the world played a scene, the acme of tenderness, on the balcony and ground, respectively. Just as she pictures innocence and unsophistication as an indiscriminate mass of gurgles, giggles and clapping of hands — and hips, so she pictures a love scene — a blurred mass of defiance and actual wrestling between two people — I'm sorry we can't agree."⁷³

Laurette continued, "Unless I am vitally wrong and ruining the chances of your play succeeding, tell her to leave me alone ... or, if she must correct me, to stop remarking on my 'lack of temperament, my conventional manner,' etc. That's a matter of opinion purely — and it is her misfortune that she had such a cold, commonplace, un–Hungarian person like myself thrust upon her. I don't know what's wrong, she seems to annihilate the only quality that holds anger at bay — 'my sense of humor.' Don't think that I'm a shrew — and if it had been plaint to me earlier that the author considered I lacked the real warmth needed for the part, I should have saved her any unpleasantness by withdrawing. I am sorry and I do hope you understand."⁷⁴

Before he received Laurette's letter, Frohman had already dropped the stage manager. "I preferred Miss Taylor as the leading actress to the stage manager as the director."⁷⁵ Who wouldn't?

*Seven Sisters* is about a mother's efforts to marry off her seven daughters.

In perhaps one of the biggest understatements by a critic, Franklin Fyles wrote, "Laurette has not had much stage experience, but managers are inclined to look for big things from her, and in this role she has begun to satisfy expectations.... I wouldn't wonder if she fulfilled expectation, but maybe, like many another find of genius, she will be lost to fame. She is young, pretty, and facile."[76] As for the play, he found it charming. "It is outright farce, but smoothed like comedy by the acting, and made a polite entertainment."

The *New York Times* singled out Laurette for praise. "Miss Laurette Taylor, with limited opportunities, was ... the shining light of the performance. To begin with, she is an actress with a most engagingly fresh and different personality. To this she adds the values of a method of playing unlike that of any one else. In her hands Mici became a fascinating little hoyden, arch, saucy, irresponsible, and yet always delightfully feminine and appealing."[77]

*Lola* opened in March. The play bombed, and Laurette was criticized as well. According to the *New York Tribune*, "*Lola* is not much of a play. But Miss Taylor saw an opportunity for proving to a troubled world that she is capable of acting more important parts than ingénues and roguish girls. She established her proof. And, being it is hoped, a reasonable as well as a very attractive young actress she will not take it amiss a remark to the effect that while her acting was very good, her understanding of the character in which she appeared was superficial to an exasperating degree."[78]

Written by Owen Davis, the play sounds like a hoot. Lola dies in an accident and is brought back to life but without her soul. As a result, the formerly kind, gentle Lola is transformed into a dangerous lunatic. Laurette played the part to the hilt — and to the last person sitting in the upper balcony. Whenever the word *soul* was mentioned in the play, Laurette emitted a shriek. "Miss Taylor knows all there is to know about the gentle art of shrieking. Cold shivers ran from orchestra to gallery when Lola shrieked."

According to the critic, Laurette's instincts were all wrong. "[If] you lose your soul you become vulgar, bad tempered, ugly, look like a fright, do up your hair with one of those first-aid-to-the-injured bandages now affected by the youthful fair, and take heartily to lying, thieving, drink and all the lusts of the flesh.... Miss Taylor does these things extremely well. But why does she do them at all?... Miss Taylor was performing a psychological study without any study of psychology."

The critic concluded, "Miss Taylor wastes her energy in this soulless piece. Nevertheless, she expressed her conception of the character with remarkable skill and power. If her object was to convince anybody that she can act 'emotional' parts, she achieved her purpose. Whether or not such a purpose is worth achieving, who shall say?... Laurette Taylor is an actress with a much

Laurette Taylor and Lewis Stone in *Bird of Paradise* (1912).

appreciated present and perhaps an illustrious future. But she needs to think further and deeper before she experiments again with tragedy. And in whatever she plays she should carefully avoid certain growing mannerisms — a carelessness of speech, a carelessness of movements, an excess of zeal for 'natural' effects."[79]

When *Seven Sisters* opened in Washington, D.C., at the Columbia, Laurette again received good notices. "Laurette Taylor has improved her art so much since her last visit to this city that there is every reason to believe she is reaching stardom by hard work as well as natural ability. Her performance was thoroughly pleasing from beginning to end."[80] The *Washington Post* also lauded the play. "Now and then, when swallows come in winter and sleighbells ring in summer, it is possible to give unreserved praise.... This is one of the occasions.... [I]t is one of the most delightfully whimsical and wholly entertaining comedies seen here this season."

The play moved on to Chicago in April 1911 where it became so successful that Sunday night performances were added "for the first time in years.... A more delightful play, more perfectly acted, has not been seen in Chicago for many years."[81] Percy Hammond thought she stole the show. As a man and a theatergoer, he finds "her charm irresistible, her tricks absolvable, her whirlwind impudence and irresponsibility wholly entrancing — in fact, everything she does [is] an unanswerable justification of the tired commercial person's [wish] to be diverted in the theater. At once, after her first entrance, she takes charge of the entire affair." Still, he chided her for hamming it up. "God has been good to Miss Taylor in bestowing upon her beauty, magnetism, and the knack in knowing in her heart how things should be done on the stage. Granting that the play is a farce, still she has not the right to be the farcical anarch that she was last evening — absolutely conscienceless, making her appeal almost altogether to the immature.... The most definite complaint to be offered in the matter is that her audience would have been just as worshipful had she eliminated some of the semi-buffonery which she seems determined to make her trademark in the theater."[82] This wasn't the first and wouldn't be the last time Laurette was cautioned to rein in her inner ham.

Laurette left the cast in June to vacation with Hartley. He was working on the play that would change their lives, *Peg o' My Heart*.

# Chapter 4

# Peg o' My Heart

*"I think Laurette Taylor did* Peg o' My Heart *4,000 times or something. I thought, 'No wonder she was an alcoholic.'"*[1]—Cherry Jones

Producer Oliver Morosco became closely tied to Laurette and Hartley. He first worked with Laurette on *The Bird of Paradise* in 1911, and they continued their business relationship with *Peg o' My Heart*. Unfortunately, the colossal hit play, a moneymaker if there ever was one, bitterly ended their relationship.

Morosco's biography is an interesting one. He started his show business career as an acrobat, made and lost several fortunes, and ended up broke and forgotten. A newspaper article reported the sad details of his life circa 1936. "A doddering man, well past middle age, stumbled and fell 25 steps from the dingy, second floor office of a Japanese rooming house today in what may be the final chapter in the life of Oliver Morosco."[2] It wasn't. He didn't die until 1945, but the heyday of Morosco was long over.

Still he had quite a run. Laurette and Hartley played a huge role in his success — and he in theirs. Ironically, Hartley tried to veto Laurette's appearance in Morosco's *The Bird of Paradise* because he thought it tawdry. Like *Yosemite*, it required her to appear half-naked to titillate the audience.

Oliver Morosco opened *The Bird of Paradise* in Chicago in 1911 with Bessie Barriscale as the lead actress. He was advised that Barriscale wasn't well known on the east coast, and Laurette Taylor would be a better choice. In fact, Annie Morosco, Morosco's wife at the time, was strongly in favor of Laurette for the role. Laurette later told a writer that the author [Richard Walton Tully] didn't want her in the role, but she wanted it desperately. "I think if he hadn't given in I'd have been willing to murder the author in order to get that role."[3]

The show opened on Thanksgiving in Rochester. According to Morosco, "Although the play looked good to me, it did a poor business. On our opening day ... the matinee performance drew only three hundred dollars. I was greatly disappointed. But that day something happened which was to make mine a name in dramatic history! Miss Taylor did not take off her make-up between the matinee and the evening performance but ordered dinner sent to her dressing room. After dinner she sent a messenger to me at the hotel requesting a conference before the evening performance. My hotel adjoined the theater so I went down immediately to see what she wanted, and there I was introduced to a charming young man from London, J. Hartley Manners."[4]

Laurette told Morosco she was engaged to Manners and said he'd "written a marvelous play for her. She said she had read it to manager after manager without exciting any enthusiasm; [George M.] Cohan and [Sam] Harris had not even let her finish the script, saying it was too much of a monologue. But she still insisted it was one of the greatest plays ever written and if I would produce it on Broadway, it would be the making of me."[5]

Morosco declined to read it, insisting he had has hands full with *The Bird of Paradise*, and secretly thinking that Laurette was blinded by love. Hartley tried a different approach. He asked Morosco if he could accompany him on a train ride that night to New York. Morosco agreed with one condition. "'[D]on't talk to me about your play. There is a volcano scene in *The Bird* with which I am not satisfied. I want to give it a good thinking over on the train tonight.'" Manners agreed, and Morosco couldn't help telling him, "'I'm predicting that *The Bird of Paradise* will be running long after your play has been forgotten.'"[6] Morosco would never have made it as a psychic.

Morosco was indeed obsessed with *The Bird of Paradise* at the time. Despite the slow start, Morosco still figured he had a hit. "My production was unsurpassed. The play opened with a magnificent cave scene in Honolulu. The accouterments of the stage had been imported directly from Hawaii and chosen carefully to be in keeping with the background. Many of the grass huts, bamboo, *leis*, and gourds were from Tully's personal collection. One of the most spectacular scenes I have ever witnessed closed the play — a smoking volcano which was so real that when Luana in her white feather robe plunged into its seething, gaping mouth, the awed exclamations of the audience were audible backstage."[7]

Still, Morosco knew he needed to do something to make the play more popular. He first convinced Tully to shorten the play. He also intentionally oversold the house to create lines and a fierce demand for tickets. It worked. "It was a veritable sensation.... Ours was a peerless play, interpreted by one of the finest aggregation of artists ever assembled on the American stage, and the difficulty and excitement the people had undergone in getting seats made them exceptionally responsive. They applauded scene after scene."[8]

*The Bird of Paradise* opened on January 8, 1912, at Daly's and ran for six months. The *New York Times* critic liked the play's sets and wrote as though

Laurette was a sex symbol. "Scenically the play is full of beauty.... Laurette Taylor made an enticing Hawaiian girl in the character of Luana and her work was most favorably received."[9] A later review by Adolph Klauber, however, suggested the play was a mess. "The fact that one comes away from Mr. Richard Walton Tully's play *The Bird of Paradise* without any definite resident impression of what the author regarded as of most importance in his scheme expresses in one phrase both a regret and a criticism."[10] He also pointed out Laurette's early strengths and weaknesses on stage. "Miss Taylor ... catches up into her personation [sic] innumerable little wiles and graces that serve not only to make the figure Luana fascinating in itself, but give it those qualities of something new and strange which are so desirable. This actress's worst fault is a careless enunciation, which makes her speech difficult to understand in hurried passages. But her general method is pliant, graceful, appealing."

*Life* agreed that Laurette made the play. "With all that has been done for *The Bird of Paradise* by the author and his aides, it would have failed in a large part of its message without the peculiar and potent abilities of Miss Laurette Taylor. To the part of the native Hawaiian princess, the last of her line, she brings a personality which has always seemed somewhat exotic.... Miss Taylor is naturally a comedienne and this, too, is not amiss in a portrayal which has its mirth-provoking as well as emotional and pathetic sides."[11]

Luana was a star-making role, though the play was, as Hartley suggested, cheap. The main theme seemed to be that a white man should never marry out of his race, but the spectacle was what sold it. "The Bird is a young and beautiful Hawaiian princess, literally young and beautiful because acted by Miss Laurette Taylor.... This play of Mr. Tully's, crude, rhetorical, and badly constructed as it is, is throughout alternately diverting and moving.... [I]t would be worth while to attend it if [for] no other attractions than those of the lithe and comely Miss Taylor, and the native music of Hawaii."[12]

Laurette was interviewed during the run of the play in her 56th Street apartment. She explained how she came up with her unique vocal style. "I hate to disabuse the public, but I don't know anything at all about Hawaii. I have never been there; I never met any Hawaiians until I began to study the role of Luana, and I'm sure I don't know whether the dialect I use in the play is real or not. Mr. Tully seems to think it is, and as he taught me, I suppose he knows. When I accepted the role he told me that the Hawaiian women were soft-spoken, that they fondled the vowels like all warm-climate people, and that they dropped the t's and d's. And another friend said that Hawaiian women always seemed to be apologizing when they spoke in English. So I took all of the suggestions, and that's why Luana speaks as she does."[13]

Once again, Laurette admitted to mimicking. "I spent hours with Hawaiian singers and stole their accent. But accent is only the trimmings. It was Mr. Tully, the playwright, who made me see the part. He showed me Luana's humble, dog-like devotion to her lover."[14]

Laurette admitted that the part of Luana was difficult. Not only did she have problems with the accent, but she was required to dance and sing, too. Singing was never her strength. "I didn't know how to sing. I went to a teacher who lived downstairs and told her I had to have a voice within three weeks. She said I had the possibility of a good contralto, but it would take years to develop it. But I took a lesson every morning before rehearsal time and I think I am 'getting away' with the song."[15]

Laurette had an unusual stage walk in *The Bird of Paradise*. Not all critics thought it was a good choice. Laurette admitted it was non-traditional. "I think actresses pay too much attention to the tradition of acting. That is a great mistake. It cramps creative instinct. I received a good deal of criticism for my walk in *The Bird of Paradise*. Some of the critics said I should be taught how to walk across the stage. Of course I paid no attention to that. My walk was the walk of the barefoot Italians who carry loads on their heads, and I had learned it from them. It certainly was not the traditional stage walk, but we are living in a time when simplicity and truth are the watchwords of the theatre. The traditional stage walk would not have fitted the character I played."[16]

Laurette explained that she wanted to stay positive about her career. "You know there is a considerable difference between a conceited person and a confident person. The one with conceit might rise to heights, but he cannot stand there. The one who is confident will keep rising unafraid. So I say to myself over and over and every day, 'success,' and I am confident that I shall achieve it."

Since this was one of Laurette's first major publicity pieces, it's interesting to hear her talk about her career. "My prayer ... my constant prayer is, Deliver me from personality. Let me be an actress. Give me the chance to play a part. Permit me to appear as something other than myself. You see, I want to be a female Mansfield. And yet managers have always seemed to think that I must be an ingénue, with a comedy role. If I have something of good looks now, I shan't have that always. I am bound to grow old. Someday I may become fat and have to wear stays. Then where shall I be if they do not let me show that I can do more than be a simple, 'lovable' girl?... So at last I have the chance to be something different.... The next thing I want to do is an Irish girl in a straight comedy." She and Hartley were already hoping that *Peg o' My Heart* would be her next role.

Guthrie McClintic met Laurette Taylor when she was appearing in *The*

*Bird of Paradise*. The meeting was arranged through his friend Linnie Love, who was one of several protégées Laurette would have throughout her career.[17] McClintic was then a young actor hoping for a role in Hartley's upcoming *The Harp of Life*. "In her dressing room Miss Taylor, looking wondrous in her Hawaiian grass skirt and dark makeup, welcomed me with a brilliant smile and warm handshake.... She was charming and direct, talking with simple eloquence while her searching, restless imagination reached out to find you. I came to know her very well in later years, and despite certain adversities that confronted her, as an artist in the theater she remained inviolate, untouched, always restless, always searching."[18]

On the basis of her success in *The Bird of Paradise*, Taylor signed a three-year contract with Morosco in February 1912, a deal that would come back to haunt her and Hartley. Still, there was no denying what one newspaper reported, "It is believed that she will be made a star."[19]

Fame is a double-edged sword, and Laurette quickly learned that celebrity came with a cost. In the summer she frantically requested that she be sent to California. According to Morosco, "Laurette Taylor was being threatened by a Black Hand organization in New York. She had received numerous letters threatening the lives of her two children. Panic-stricken, she wired me to bring her West that she might get her children out of danger. Articles in the New York papers showed me conclusively that Miss Taylor's fears were not groundless, so I had to arrange for some one to replace her at once."[20] One of the letters reportedly told Laurette she'd been targeted because she was too beautiful to live.

Another version of this story explained that Laurette had received a note at a performance. "[A] little while before the rise of the curtain, she received a note warning her that she had only five weeks to live. It was signed with a skull and crossbones. Miss Taylor was alarmed by the tone of the note and became hysterical."[21] Laurette steeled her nerves and went on stage. However, when called upon to read lines indicating how much she wanted to live, she became overly emotional. "She became terrified again and her speech emphasizing her wish to live became so hysterical that it was necessary for her to rush off the stage. The manager came out promptly, and, not knowing what explanation to give, said that Miss Taylor had been seized with an attack of ptomaine poisoning."

The audience must have wondered at her quick recovery because the show continued. In the last scene, however, when Laurette was supposed to throw herself into the volcano, she lost her nerve "and ran back in full view of the audience." Future performances were equally disastrous. "One evening during the play a man arose to take off his overcoat. Miss Taylor, thinking it

Laurette Taylor on the cover of *The Theatre* magazine (1912) (photograph courtesy of Mary Pearsall).

might be the writer of the mysterious note, screamed. On another occasion, a small ball rolling onto the stage from behind the wings set her in a panic."

A writer for *Life* suggested Laurette was the wrong target for such abuse. "If the Black Hand gentlemen will kindly make their identity known it will be easy to supply them with a list of persons now appearing on the stage to whom their efforts may be directed with greater advantage to the theatergoing public."[22]

Laurette left New York so abruptly that rumors were flying. A headline in the *Chicago Daily Tribune* stated "Laurette Taylor, Actress, Quits Job and Vanishes." The article went on to describe the threats and suggested that Laurette might have gone to a sanitarium. The article also mentioned the rumor that Laurette and Hartley were engaged. "Mr. Manners has been absent from his regular haunts for the last week."[23]

In any event, Blanche Hall replaced Laurette in *The Bird of Paradise*,[24] and Laurette, Hartley, Dwight, and Marguerite arrived in Los Angeles so she could appear in *The Seven Sisters* at the Burbank. Julian Johnson happily relayed the news that Laurette and Hartley had checked into the Alexandria Hotel under aliases. Laurette was Mrs. Tyler, and Hartley was Mr. Hartley.

Johnson wondered if Laurette was having a nervous breakdown — or if the couple was eloping. He also reported their sleeping arrangements. They were in separate rooms and on separate floors. "Miss Taylor has the 'Imperial suite' on the eighth floor of the Alexandria. Her entourage — if that's the word we should use — is certainly of royal proportions, with its big dining-room, its drawing and living rooms, its butler's pantry, its spacious hallway and its several bedrooms. Mr. Manners is more modestly ensconced, a floor lower down, in rooms of comfortable order, but of Uniroyal size."[25]

Laurette gave Johnson a quick interview and explained a few things. She was not yet willing to admit she'd been chased out of New York. "Miss Taylor, in a string of jade beads (and if I remember correctly there were some other dainty articles of apparel) lounged elegantly in her apartment late yesterday afternoon. 'It was this way,' smiled Miss Taylor in a patient and explanatory mood. 'I was very tired. The role of Luana had practically exhausted my nervous force, and I begged Mr. Morosco to let me have a few weeks' rest before coming to Los Angeles to work in my new plays. But you know how it is — if I had stopped work in New York I would simply have been showered with invitations for parties, week-ends, and days-by-the-shore, which I simply couldn't have refused. So I was at my wit's end.' Then Mr. Manners came to the rescue. 'Why can't we just get on the train and go quietly to Los Angeles without telling anybody?' 'My answer to that is shown in the fact that we came.'"[26] Laurette denied that they had eloped. Johnson asked if they had marriage plans. "Miss Taylor glanced demurely down at her red slipper. 'Well—I haven't been asked yet!'"

Rehearsals for *The Seven Sisters* didn't go well. According to Morosco, "After the first rehearsal things started happening. My leading man, Forrest Stanley, did not please Miss Taylor at all. She made fun of his clothes and said he had no transition in his voice. To her he was completely impossible. This made me furious, but I held my tongue, for I knew Mr. Stanley and his methods. I had never known him to exert himself at the first rehearsal."[27] Morosco attempted to run interference, first by pleading with Laurette to give the poor man a chance. He also bought new clothes for Stanley. Still, Laurette railed. "We opened one Sunday afternoon during the summer of 1912. The house was packed because Miss Taylor had been well publicized through New York notices on *The Bird of Paradise*, which had been picked up by our Los Angeles papers. Angelenos, proud of the fact that the play was a home product, turned out.... When the time came, Forrest Stanley marched on in his new tailor-made clothes looking like a modernized Apollo. His voice was never richer, and he put over his comedy as I had never seen him do it before. He walked away with the whole show. I looked on highly amused for I knew the boy was outdoing himself. The next morning the papers gave him the top credit over Miss Taylor and said he had scored by far the hit of the play."[28]

Meanwhile, Morosco had finally read Hartley's play, *Peg o' My Heart*. He had, in fact, read it on the train. "After the first page, I was so completely engrossed in that play that I knew nothing until I heard the conductor calling.... I was tingling with exhilaration, as if I had been drinking champagne. I hastily drew up a short contract, drew a check for five hundred dollars as advance royalties, shook Manners, and before he was fully awake had him sign the contract and accept the check.... When we alighted from the train I had under my arm a script entitled *Peg o' My Heart*, which, as is so often the case with theatrical producers, I had found quite by accident and which was ultimately to make me over five million dollars."[29]

While performing in *The Seven Sisters* in Los Angeles, Laurette began rehearsals for *Peg*. Morosco received assistance from his wife, Annie. According to Morosco, "She helped me with the scenery, furniture, and draperies.... We studied early English furniture and selected each piece with minute care, regardless of cost. In fact I paid two hundred and fifty dollars for one small chair which stood at the extreme right of the stage and was called in the play 'Jarvis' High Chair.' That was quite a price for a minor prop.... I had an all-oak set built and stained as English oak. The walls were canvassed with genuine tapestry above the six-foot wainscoting. The high windows were draped in blue velvet velour, and the English staircase and floor were carpeted deeply with a blue velvet carpet. The effect was not only decidedly English, but very elegant."[30]

While performing in Los Angeles, Laurette, as she often did in New York, visited with students and faculty at an acting school. In this case, it was Frank Egan's[31] school. She had studied with him in Seattle, and he'd started a school in Los Angeles.[32] Accompanying her were Hartley, Margaret Anglin, and others.[33] The *Los Angeles Times* reported on Laurette's speech. She got things off to a rollicking start by making a cute comment after Mr. Egan's speech. "I never heard an Irishman use so many big words in my life."[34] The reporter indicated that Laurette's speech was a hit. "Miss Taylor spoke longer than the others, and her remarks were tinctured with the subtly rich humor which is characteristic of the woman, as variety and resource are characteristic of the actress."

Her advice to drama students? "Cleanliness is a prime requisite. I mean not only cleanliness of body, hands and face, but cleanliness of life, cleanliness of motive and cleanliness of work. Slovenliness has ruined geniuses — many of them — whereas painstaking care has elevated many a creature of one talent to a position of pre-eminence."

Laurette also praised stock company experience — to a point. "Stock experience is a wonderful thing for an actor or actress, if not indulged in too long. Pushed to the limit, I think it ruins players. In judicious amounts — and invariably for beginners — I think it creates habits of study, upbuilds the faculty of concentration, makes energy a personal custom and gives the player courage to take up tasks on short notice, which the 'production' actor, devoid of this experience, never possesses."

Though Laurette suffered from stage fright, she was an excellent public speaker and was often called upon to speak long before the success of *Peg o' My Heart*. Marguerite Courtney believed Laurette further developed her skills in England when she was performing in *Peg*. "It was in England that Laurette first gained an enviable reputation as an after-dinner speaker. She spoke extemporaneously, asking only the one consideration that she be called upon last. Her wonderful sense of mimicry, her ability to give spontaneous expression to feelings and impressions which most people smother or lose altogether under stiff and formal verbiage, delighted her listeners. It was a style as evanescent as her acting but no less magical. Those who heard her might not remember long what she said, but they went home chuckling and feeling warm and full of good fellowship, even the bad speakers whom she sometimes parodied. She brought an artful originality to what is so often a deadly occupation, and many an after-dinner speaker, assiduously rehearsing before a mirror with carefully prepared notes, envied her achievement."[35]

Laurette visited the school on several other occasions, and a plan was hatched to have her return to act in productions with the students. Possible shows included *Cinderella*, *The Piper*, and, oh boy, *Peter Pan*. The *LA Times*, apparently with a straight face, commented on Laurette's ability to play Pan. "Miss Taylor as Peter would be a stellar attraction upon her own account, and no doubt she would actually rival Maude Adams in local interest, for local audiences have placed a very considerable valuation upon Laurette Taylor's work."[36] Yes, but *Peter Pan*? Laurette thought it a good idea too. "'No one in the world ... possesses the ... uncommercialized enthusiasm of a child. I love nothing better than to mingle with childish enthusiasms, and when they are rightly directed, artistic enthusiasms are perhaps the most ennobling of all.... Understand, I'm not making this venture to exploit my personality, or advertise any one else, or to make any money. I'm just going to put my hair in a braid — as it were — and go out in the big lot behind the barn, and swing, and play tag, and skip the rope with the liveliest and littlest of them. I want to get a children's play, and play it with them."

For now, Laurette had to be content with playing childlike Peg. *Peg o' My Heart* changed Laurette's life. It made her an international star and a millionaire. Still, she grew to have reservations about the play. "Must I talk about her?" she asked in a 1922 article. "When you'd done the same part 1,120 times, there are more thrilling topics of conversation, like the telephone directory."[37]

Ten years earlier the play was fresh and, if not original, at least it was something new to audiences. Hartley's timing couldn't have been better. For one thing, although there had been plays written about Irish boys, there were none about young Irish women. According to a 1914 *Los Angeles Times* critic, "*Peg o' My Heart* made its appearance at the very moment when public dramatic taste had completed a cycle. With all due respect to those producing them, the public was sick of mediocre musical comedies, revivals of good ones failed to satisfy, and the problem play had reached the limit of decency in the flood of white slave plays that spread their subtle stench over the country. And into the midst of all this came Peg, innocent, unsophisticated Irish girl, who finds the ways of rich relatives all too stilted for her care-free, wholesome abandon."[38]

Hartley, who'd always liked the title, had used it for an earlier play he'd written for Constance Collier. It was before he met Laurette, and the play was never produced. He asked Collier if he could have the title back, and she agreed.[39]

*Peg o' My Heart* was first produced in Los Angeles on May 26, 1912, at the Burbank Theater at 6th and Main. In 1925 Laurette told an interviewer that Peg opened in Los Angeles because New York managers "hooted at the thing when it was offered to them." She said she and her husband finally put it on at the old Burbank Theater in Los Angeles, because they just had to have something to fill in a week. No one was so astonished as she when it made one of the great triumphs of theater history. "And," she added ruefully, "I still hate the damn thing."[40] Taylor loved to tell people that the play was horrible. "Laurette Taylor says *Peg o' My Heart* was the worst play her husband, J. Hartley Manners, ever wrote."[41] Years later, after her success in *The Glass Menagerie*, Laurette said, "It's a much better play than *Peg o' My Heart*, which, as a matter of fact, was the worst play Hartley ever wrote. It was written too much for me — I had everything — all the laughs — the rest of the characters were preposterous caricatures. Not one-tenth — not one-hundredth — of the people who say, 'Oh, I saw you as Peg,' ever saw me in it at all.... Once in England as I was following my bags onto the boat to come home, I discovered my passport was wrong. I was never good at passports anyway, so I rushed to the American consulate and found everybody gone but one little man who was putting on his hat. He said it was too late, but all at once he saw my name and said, 'My goodness, Laurette Taylor! Why I saw you play *Peg o' My Heart* in San Francisco,' and fixed up my papers. For once in my life I didn't pop out with the truth, and caught the boat."[42]

**Laurette and Michael in *Peg o' My Heart* (1921).**

The *Los Angeles Times* heralded the play's opening. "*Peg o' My Heart*, a new comedy by J. Hartley Manners, will have its first production on any stage at the Burbank this afternoon. The part of Peg will be in the hands of Laurette Taylor, while the chief male role will be enacted by Henry Stanford.... The premiere of *Peg o' My Heart* is a theatrical event of more than ordinary importance, not only because it is the last work of a dramatist with a string of notable successes to his credit, but also from the fact that if it comes up to managerial expectations, it will be made use of as a vehicle for Miss Taylor's starring tour in the fall."[43]

Morosco immediately knew it was special. "The company gave an excellent performance, and Miss Taylor excelled herself in the role of a little Irish waif. She became, for the time, Peg, body and soul. When the curtain had gone down on the last act, and the audience had cheered and chattered happily as they gathered up their wraps and programs and gone laughing from the theater, I sat for a long time in my quiet, empty box, spellbound. I could picture the opening of *Peg o' My Heart* in New York City. The play had had but one performance, the first on any stage in the world, yet I knew it was a complete and overwhelming success. I did not need New York's approval. I knew. How it thrilled me to think that the play mine. 100 per cent mine."[44]

Critics agreed with Morosco. Otheman Stevens wrote, "It was Peg of everyone's heart at the Burbank yesterday when Mr. Manners' new play was produced. The brightness of the lines, the luring personality of Miss Taylor, the really perceptive playing to the point made the production memorably enjoyable. Miss Taylor's study of Peg resulted in an altogether charming portrait. It was marked by apparent spontaneity; certainly by ease and a gracious resourcefulness of sincerity. Her face would be her fortune if there was no intellect back of it; but there is a very discernable and direct reasoning process; this, with her personal lure, makes Miss Taylor's drawing of Peg entirely winsome."[45]

Julian Johnson had no inkling that the play would become an institution, but he knew it was another star-making role for Laurette. "*Peg* is a quaint, pug-nosed, diverting little play. It is not a big play, it is far from being a great play, but it is withal very human, is cleverly written, and has a great many touches of nature both smileful [sic] and dewy. The feature of the whole thing is Laurette Taylor as Peg. Peg à la Taylor is bigger than the play surrounding her. Miss Taylor has gone Manners one better, and shows herself not only a capable and intelligent impersonator of histrionic character, but one of the subtlest comediennes on our stage today. In fact, among our comediennes — purely as interpreters of comedy, not farce, mind you — who surpasses her? I know of none.... Peg as Laurette Taylor creates her is a bit of comedy fine art such as is seldom seen on any stage. If you love art in comedy you can't afford to miss this specimen."[46]

Johnson hit on a theme that would be repeated with future Laurette/Hartley productions — Laurette was better than the play. "As given yesterday afternoon, there was far too much talk in the piece. The pruning-knife must be well-wielded through the pages of this script." When it was announced that the play would play for a fourth week, Johnson gave credit where it was due. "In the role of the little Irish Girl Peg Miss Taylor has scored one of the most pronounced successes of her career, and her brilliant portrayal of the part has carried the Manners comedy of no small proportions."[47]

Johnson also commented on the set — Annie and Oliver Morosco's hard work had paid off. "The single setting, with its solid oak, its tapestries, its bronze lamps, and its massive and magnificent furniture, is, with the sole exception of *The Fox* surrounding, the finest ever seen in a local production."

Laurette gave partial credit for her performance to co-star Emilie Melville, who played the chilly Mrs. Chichester. "Miss Melville actually helps me with my part, for when I come on the stage I feel the chill of that cold, formal old heart setting against itself against my young American blood — and instinctively my Irish is up — I'm playing the part as Hartley wants me to, because I can't help it."[48]

Morosco was so excited by *Peg*'s success, he signed Hartley to a six-year deal that gave the producer first option on any play Hartley wrote.[49] This made sense because Morosco knew Laurette would be part of any future plays Hartley might write.

Animal lovers rejoice in the tale of Michael, the female dog who ended up playing Peg's beloved dog more than a thousand times. She was bought from the pound for a dollar only a day before she was scheduled to be put down. A replacement for a dog that had suddenly, unexpectedly died, Michael proved to be a born actor. According to Marguerite Courtney, "From the beginning Michael exhibited a captivating *sang-froid* toward the audience, combined with a burning devotion for his mistress which made his performance unforgettable.... From the opening in Los Angeles in 1912, through the New York and London runs, and again in the 1921 revival, Michael played every performance of *Peg*."[50] He made his own curtain calls. "Entering downstage left, he made a circuit of the stage at a brisk canter, exiting through the garden door upstage right. Invariably as he came flush with the footlights he rolled a laughing, roguish eye in the direction of the audience which won him a crescendo of applause."[51] Michael not only became an important member of the cast but was part of the Manners household for 17 years.

Because of *Peg*, Laurette Taylor became a phenomenon in Los Angeles. "We aren't tailored anymore. We are Taylored! Taylor is, of course, quite a general term, like Smith and Jones. Being qualified with a 'Laurette' makes all the difference. Laurette Taylor is the girl whose name is in our hearts and on our chewing gum! We are naming our sailboats and babies and soft drinks and new systems of philosophy after the charming little actress, and there is now a Laurette Taylor waltz, a Laurette Taylor cigar, and a Laurette Taylor sundae."[52]

If Laurette Taylor was a phenomenon, *Peg o' My Heart* was a fad. People had *Peg o' My Heart* parties, bought dogs and named them Michael, women affected Peg's stooped walk and even copied her dress. "'Everyone's doin' it — Peg and her charming little slouchy gait, and her dear little slovenly accent. What has become of the svelte figure that used to trip down Broadway? Gone. And in its place patters down-street, a quaint little shape, slouching along with daintily drooping shoulders and softly shuffling slippers.... When you go to a party nowadays, do you sit up nice and straight, and speak in a clear, ringing tone? Not by a long ways. You droop and wilt like a top-heavy lily, and talk in a soft little monotone with a thick tongue. And as for manners, why a little modest violet, beside a mossy stone is a great, rude, coarse creature compared to your gentleness — save that you occasionally allow yourself a saucy little bon-mot. And do you slick back your hair and roach it up neatly? No, sir, you scramble it.... [Y]ou wear a floppy hat so low that it looks like the cover to a dish. The more dejected and left-out-all-night you can make your hat look, nowadays, the more fashionable you are."[53]

In 1913 the song *Peg o' My Heart* became a hit. It had nothing to do with the play but was simply an attempt by Fred Fisher and Alfred Bryan to capitalize on its popularity.[54]

Publicity agents did what they could to keep Laurette's name in the newspaper. One of the oddest articles claimed she could run a nine-minute mile. "When it comes to running, Laurette Taylor is just about as good as she is at acting, and she's some actress. Recently, while in Los Angeles, she declared that every woman, no matter what her vocation or profession, should devote a few minutes each day to outdoor exercise. 'She would take far more interest in her work if she did,' declared Miss Taylor. Then just to prove that she is some athlete herself and that she knows what she is talking about, the actress made a trial sprint. Paced by an automobile making 20 miles an hour, her progress impeded by skirts, she covered a mile in nine minutes."[55] Laurette added that her "fighting weight" was 128 pounds.

Morosco wanted to open *Peg* in New York at John Cort's new theatre. However, Cort, despite attending *Peg* perhaps a half dozen times in Los Angeles, "smiled and said the play was a nice little bit, all right for Los Angeles, but that New York demanded something bigger."[56] Even after Morosco offered him 25 percent interest for an investment of $2,500, Cort turned him down. His investment, if he'd taken it, would have earned him more than a million dollars.

Before she opened *Peg* in New York, Laurette appeared in a new Manners play, *Barbaraza* on September 22, 1912, in Los Angeles. "Laurette Taylor, who is greatly smitten with the role of Barbaraza, in Hartley Manners' ferocious play of that name, is possessed with a deep fear that *Peg o' My Heart* will run the full length of her stay in Los Angeles."[57] In fact, *Peg o' My Heart* set attendance records and delayed *Barbaraza's* opening. By the time it finished its run *Peg* had run for ten record-breaking weeks.

*Los Angeles Times* critic Julian Johnson had a fit when they finally closed it. "*Peg o' My Heart*, the most successful play, as far as local popularity is concerned, which has ever been produced on a Los Angeles stage, will be assassinated tonight in the height of its dollarsign glory. This is its tenth week at the Burbank theater and its biggest."[58] Johnson estimated the grosses at $60,000 and Hartley's royalty at $4,000.[59]

Upon the play's close in Los Angeles, Johnson became one of the first, though surely not the last, to give almost all the credit to Laurette for its success. "While the charm of Mr. Manners' play cannot be denied — it is charming indeed, if not great — its overwhelming triumph is directly and solely due to the interpretative genius of Laurette Taylor, in the title role. I regard Laurette Taylor as the foremost young American actress. In her adaptability to widely differing parts she surpasses every woman on our stage, barring none. As an interpreter of serious roles we know her only as a comedienne. I am sure that she will make a great name, and she will be one of the foremost players of our time." Johnson concluded that, though Laurette sometimes came off as churlish off stage, she was one of a kind on stage. "Miss Taylor, who has a high disdain for a good many things out here, probably considers either praise or blame, in the West, idle and inconsequential.... Off stage I find her antagonistic; on stage she is that wonder of wonders, that rare bird — the genius. Miss Taylor has thrown about Manners' work an atmosphere of greatness. Miss Taylor is far bigger than her author."[60]

Julian Johnson had a strange relationship with Laurette that appeared to go beyond critic/actor. He wrote a second column where he again referred to Laurette as a genius and criticized her off-stage personality. "Like many another genius — for she is a genius — Laurette Taylor the woman is self-centered, withdrawn, coolly calculating. I told her the other day that I thought her perfectly selfish. She replied that she was not selfish, and that further, she vigorously objected to personalities in the paper."[61] Laurette let him have it. "Print what you think of me on the stage — and thank you, but please keep your off-stage opinion out of print. If you don't like me, tell me so to my face, but don't conceal it from me and tell a hundred thousand people. I may not like you, but I'm not stopping one of Mr. Morosco's productions to denounce you before an audience, am I? So what business have you to stop your reading audience in the middle of what we'll suppose is a story to tell them that you think Laurette Taylor is stuck-up, opinionated, and that you don't agree with her?" Johnson had the last public word. "Miss Taylor forgets that she is so much in the public eye that her private as well as public life belongs to the circulated prints — if the circulated prints choose to have it. That's the penalty of footlight fame, for an actor or an actress, as far as reading matter is concerned, is always regarded as a curious freak and never as a human being."[62]

*Barbaraza* bettered *Peg* in attendance for the first week, and offered Laurette a different kind of role. "*Barbaraza* is totally unlike anything in which Miss Taylor has ever before been seen, but it gives fresh evidence of her wonderful versatility and allows her to demonstrate her ability as an emotional actress to the fullest degree."[63] It was a tale of revenge, and Laurette was required to play an old woman in the prologue and a youth throughout the rest of the play. Johnson was impressed. "Laurette Taylor has proved herself a virtuoso of the emotions. No one especially desired to see her play tragedy; I doubt if she had any especial desire to play tragedy. But she was very curious to discover whether or no [sic] she had that Racinian talent; most of us who bark up successes and try to yelp down failure were also curious. She tried. She succeeded. And there you are. Succeeded in spite of herself, for essentially Laurette Taylor is a comedienne. She is far from overwhelming physically. Her voice is never opulent. She has no tremendous power at her call. But one thing she does possess which is greater than any one of all three of these classic necessities — a brain. We have had so many actresses running around with large, loose emotions and loose, large voices backed up by loose, empty heads that it is indeed an experience and a relief to find, as a sporadic variation from type, a calculating, cold-voiced comedienne who is clever enough, possessed of mentality enough, to stimulate anything which she coolly elects to be and by all means is not."[64] The play closed on October 12 after 101 performances, and Laurette went to New York to prepare for *Peg*'s opening.

Rehearsals didn't start off well. "There came the time for the first New York rehearsal, called for the stage of the old Weber & Fields Music Hall on a morning in the late fall of 1912. H. Reeves-Smith, Hassard Short, Christine Norman, Reginald Mason, and others of the company arrived at 11 A.M. and waited until one-thirty, but Miss Taylor did not appear. The stage manager suggested that everybody leave and return at two-thirty. The players were back at that time and waited until five-thirty. No Miss Taylor, no Mr. Manners. The same thing happened on the following day and again on the third day. On the fourth day the company, quite out of patience and ready to drop the play, was prepared for a walk-out when star and author appeared. They had an excuse: they had been married after the successful coast tryout of *Peg o' My Heart* and just did not want to interrupt their honeymoon."⁶⁵ In fact, Laurette and Hartley had quickly married in Philadelphia before returning to New York.

Hartley tried to make amends to the cast, but Laurette remained aloof. Her colleagues had already decided they hated her, but once the reading began their anger melted away. According to Hassard Short, "That alluring smile and those hazel blue eyes and that brogue ... were just too much for all of us and we suddenly found ourselves adoring Laurette as much as her audiences did for years."⁶⁶

Frances Marion, who later become a successful Hollywood writer, wasn't a fan of *Peg o' My Heart*, considering it a slight play at best. Marion was working as an artist and met Laurette when she was assigned to work on a publicity poster. "To me, a talent like hers was wasted on this sentimental little play⁶⁷ which I referred to, only in my diary, as 'Cinderella in the Doghouse.'"⁶⁸ Marion feared that Laurette had been miscast. After all, Peg was a teenager, and Laurette was far from that.

While *Peg* was in Rochester for a tryout, Morosco noticed a problem with a third scene act. However, Manners refused to change it. "The objectionable scene was between two solicitors — dragged into the play solely to give Miss Taylor a chance to change her dress. It retarded the action and hurt the play. In an earlier scene, Peg, much to her discomfort, had saved Ethel, proud daughter of a vain family, from disgrace. I felt that in place of the long and pointless speeches of the two solicitors Ethel, who was an important character in the English family, having snobbed Peg up to that point, could redeem herself by coming to the little Irish girl's assistance in the third act. It would improve the play and create a good role for Ethel. Manners objected to the change on the ground that it would detract from Peg's role; in other words, it would give someone other than Miss Taylor — Manners' sweetheart and the one for whom he had written the play — a major part, a thing he couldn't countenance."⁶⁹

Insistent that the act mucked up the entire play, Morosco played dirty pool with Manners. "In New Haven, after the show one night, I managed to get him [Manners] happily drunk, then maneuvered a master stroke. I took him up to his hotel room and, giving him a pencil and paper, cajoled him to write what I dictated, that is the scene I wanted to [put] into his play."⁷⁰ A sober Manners became enraged when he realized what had happened, but it was done. Morosco happily hired Violet Kemble-Cooper to play the part of Ethel.

Meanwhile, Cort told Morosco his new theater was now available, but it barely made the deadline for the New York premiere of *Peg*. "The day of the opening arrived and the carpets were not down. Neither were the lights turned on. I [Morosco] called a rehearsal and had to go through the play by candlelight. I dismissed the company at six o'clock, and still there were neither carpets nor lights in the house."[71] Fortunately, when the curtain rose that night, everything was in place. *Town and Country* described the opening of Cort's theatre. "On the opening night very elaborate programs were distributed descriptive of the new Cort Theatre, a delightful little Marie Antoinette playhouse with the ushers in pannier gowns and effective white kerchiefs and mob caps."

According to Morosco, he'd warned Laurette about overacting. "I had pled with Miss Taylor to underact Peg on the opening night in New York. Many times on the road she had done atrocious things. She bubbled with comedy, and I had seen her skate all over Mrs. Chickester's [sic] floors and clown ignominiously. She had solemnly promised me she would follow my instructions."[72]

Morosco claimed to have slept through most of opening night due to sheer exhaustion (he also claimed that Manners had gone off on a drunk). However, when he awoke he realized the play was a hit. "The next night there was a line at the box office a block long. *Peg o' My Heart*, December 20, 1912, was the biggest hit on Broadway."[73]

New York critics agreed that the play was so-so, but Laurette was wonderful. One critic spoke for many when he said, "*Peg o' My Heart* has come to stay. Not that the play itself amounts to much. But Laurette Taylor does. Of all the actresses in America, I could not name a half dozen who could have carried the new comedy to such success."[74] He compared Taylor to the legendary Ada Rehan. "[A]s was so often the case with that great comedienne, she has been called upon to carry a play that is no more than a monologue." For good measure, he pointed out Hartley's shortcomings. "Indeed, *Peg o' My Heart* might have been written by the late Augustin Daly in his early youth. What a mid–Victorian young man J. Hartley Manners seems to be."

The *New York Times* knew immediately that Laurette and Peg would become inseparable. "[I]t will be impossible to imagine *Peg* without Miss Taylor, or, for a long time to come, Miss Taylor without *Peg*." The critic added, "It would be difficult to ... think of another actress ... who could provide such a succession of fresh, exhilarating, spontaneous laughs as punctuated the play last night.... [W]hen Miss Taylor is off the stage the curtain might as well be down. Which is one reason, perhaps, why she is never off long."[75]

A.E. Matthews and Laurette Taylor in *Peg o' My Heart* (1921) (photograph courtesy of Mary Pearsall).

*Life Magazine* declared, "Miss Taylor has rapidly grown in popular and critical estimation, and this performance makes her right to the title of star a sure one."[76] Critic Sheldon Cheney summed up what many thought when he wrote that the play "is compounded of artificiality and sentimentality, owing its effectiveness to the charm of Laurette Taylor."[77]

The *Town and Country* critic wrote, "In the days of *Alias Jimmy Valentine* it was Laurette Taylor's plaint that her managers, in developing her as an emotional actress, were wasting a very good comedienne; and in *Peg o' My Heart* ... she fully justifies her faith in herself.... [S]he achieves an instant and gratifying success."[78]

By 1912, on the basis of her success in *Peg*, Laurette was described as one of the stage's greatest stars. According to Julian Johnson, "Miss Taylor is probably the foremost of the younger actresses in New York City today. In the parlance, she 'sneaked in on rubbers,' when she first came into the metropolis, appearing, I believe in the spring of 1909, in some unimportant production, in a very unimportant role.... Her talent was soon acclaimed extraordinary. She went from production to production, by the strength of her own personality, nearly saving several, and at length appeared in the principal feminine role in *Alias Jimmy Valentine*, which she created.... Miss Taylor has been compared to Duse, by several critics, for the intense and poignant characterization she has given the ill-starred Hawaiian princess."[79] A month later he again wrote of her fame: "The foremost position of Laurette Taylor may be attested by the fact that at the present time it is practically impossible to find any periodical of size which does not contain some one or more of her photographs, some article about her, or even some story from her pen."[80]

In December 1912 Laurette was interviewed by the *New York Times* and admitted she was tired of being interviewed. "It seems to me there is nothing I can say! I have given the history of my life from the cradle to the melodrama — from stock and to stardom.... I am sure there is nothing I can say unless you pump it out with sheer force."[81]

The interviewer didn't give up. She was asked about the kinds of parts she preferred. "I must have character parts. And then I don't care whether they are Chinese, Indian, or Irish. Of course, I love *Peg*, but still I liked *The Bird of Paradise*, too. I like to imagine I am different beings, and I must have a chance to show something that is different.... I am not like everybody else.... I mean that my talent — if I have any — shows itself to better advantage in parts that are a little out of the ordinary. I hate the ingénue sort of thing — for me, I mean."[82]

After several months Morosco decided it was time to send Peg out on tour. He stopped in at the Cort to see how the play was going and was horrified. "To my utter disappointment, Miss Taylor, whom I had often warned against so doing, was overacting her part sufficiently to make of it a low comedy performance. She had interpolated lines of her own which were out of keeping with the simplicity of Manners' comedy and was buffooning the entire show."[83] Morosco can't always be trusted, but in this case there might be some truth. Even Laurette admitted she could be a ham at times. She radiated oodles of charm, but at this point in her career no one was applauding her for her subtlety. That would come later, but for now she was a "busy" performer, doing just about anything to keep the audience's attention.

Morosco met Laurette and Hartley for drinks and suggested taking *Peg* on the road. As a producer, he wanted to wring every cent out of the play. "I knew that, unless the play was sent on the road while it was still in demand, we were going to lose a golden opportunity. I asked Manners if he did not think it advisable to put out four or five companies, reserving the big cities such as Chicago, Boston, Philadelphia, Baltimore, and the like for the original cast. Miss Taylor interrupted at this point to say she wished to go to England with *Peg* immediately following her Cort Theatre engagement. I told her that would be the mistake of her life, insisting that she should establish her popularity throughout the United States first and then go to Europe. She was unconvinced, and we agreed to reach a decision regarding her European production after closing at the Cort. I then turned back to Manners and pointed out the fact that, by releasing other companies of *Peg*, he would receive much greater royalties on his play. He, with a wry little smile, asked if I thought another actress could be found who could play Peg. I replied that it would be easy. Miss Taylor and he exchanged quick glances which I pretended not to notice. They were still laboring under the opinion, that, since it was written especially for her, Miss Taylor was the only woman alive who could play the role of Peg. Manners eventually agreed to the additional companies. I believe he did it expecting and willing to see them fail, despite the fact that it would count against his reputation, just to show me I was wrong."[84]

Morosco went ahead and sent road companies out while Taylor was still playing *Peg* in New York.[85] The actresses who took over the role were Peggy O'Neill, Elsa (also known as Elsie) Ryan, Marion Dentler, and Dorothy Mackaye. "I then did something which I kept a secret from both Hartley Manners and Laurette Taylor. I instructed those girls to report nightly to my manager, George Mooser, at the Cort Theatre, and watch every performance given by Miss Taylor, studying every intonation and move she made. After a month or so of this study, I put them all into rehearsals, directing them myself, and then turned them over to [director T. Daniel Frawley] to be drilled. Four girls were never put through a more intensive training than were those young actresses."[86] Morosco essentially encouraged the actors to mimic Laurette's portrayal.

While there's no question that Laurette's performance in *Peg o' My Heart* was masterful, there are many who believe that the role is one that can be played by any charming young actor with the right look. According to Morosco, "To my mind, there was never a more starring part written than that of Peg. I maintained then, and subsequent events have borne out, that any actress of any talent and the proper build could not fail in that role. Peg's, in the common terminology of the theater, is a foolproof part."[87]

Morosco wasn't the only one who thought the part was actor-proof. Critic Gardner Bradford wrote, "At first many were of the opinion that Peg and Laurette Taylor were synonymous, but subsequent developments have proved differently, as every one of the six Peg shows has been a triumph. Peg is what is known in the vernacular as a 'fat' part, one which, when well cast, will always get over, a fact which is greatly to the credit of Mr. Manners, by the way."[88]

Years later, Laurette gave credit to the actresses who followed her in *Peg*. "You know I always objected to the way Hartley never gave any of the other actresses billing in the road companies of *Peg*. It was always just *Peg o' My Heart* as created by Laurette Taylor when Peggy O'Neill played it in Chicago, or Elsie Ryan in other Middle Western cities, or Florence Martin in Boston and Philadelphia, or Blanche Hall in the South, or Rhea Martin in the Mountain and Pacific States, or Marion Dentler in Canada. It wasn't fair to them. My, but Hartley was certainly uxorious!"[89] In fact, the billing resulted in confusion, with some swearing they'd seen Laurette when in fact they'd seen an actress impersonating Laurette.

Believe it or not, *Peg o' My Heart* might be successfully revived today. The key to the play has always been Peg. In 1951 *Peg o' My Heart* was revived in Los Angeles at the Ivar Theater. Joan Evans played Peg. She admitted to studying recordings of Laurette as well as the film version of *Peg o' My Heart*. Her performance, too, was essentially a mimic of Laurette Taylor, and Edwin Schallert thought she did a good job. "Miss Evans manages with a peculiar self-possession to bring to life quite a unique stage personage."[90]

In 1974 it was revived with Duchess Dale playing the role for the Staircase Company. The *Los Angeles Times* critic wrote, "J. Hartley Manners' *Peg o' My Heart* was an extremely popular post–Victorian comedy which fondly suggested that goodness of heart, especially when possessed by a poor but honest young girl, is a far better thing than the brittle and myopic pretensions of a languid upper class.... The part is overwritten — her tedious idolatry for her absent father is reminiscent of an impassioned biography of Christ — but the play is charming anyway as it points its moral, dispenses with blackguards and misunderstanding, and demonstrates the triumph of goodness over all."[91] Critic Dan Sullivan also found himself liking the play despite his misgivings. "Peg's sweetness ... is incidental to her spunk, her humor, and her ability to take the bull by the horns. You like her on the stage as much as you would in real life."[92]

In 1977 New York's Lion Theater Company put on a straight-faced revival. After looking at the script, the director and actors concluded that Laurette's stardom was a cinch. "'No wonder she became a star,' said [director] Mr. [Gene] Nye. 'She was allowed to do anything in the world she wanted to.'" Nye and the actors attributed Laurette's success to the script's flexibility. "There are many stage directions ... and some of them are baffling ... but they indicate that it was Miss Taylor's vehicle. For instance, the stage direction at one juncture merely says, 'The dog business.' Another one notes, 'The business with Jarvis.' There are even variables permitted in the lines: 'He's not going' (or 'He doesn't know where to go'). The options are all in Peg's role."[93]

During the time she was playing in *Peg o' My Heart* Laurette received an opportunity to appear on stage with idol Sarah Bernhardt in a misguided vaudeville act at the Palace with Jane Cowl and Marguerite Clarke. Although on paper this sounds like a can't-miss, it was a disaster. "At her first matinee, when she entered as Phedre, Laurette Taylor, Jane Cowl, and Marguerite Clarke were her honorary handmaidens. At that time each of these lovely young women were stars in their own right, and as a gesture to Bernhardt, who was making her debut in vaudeville, chose to do this. Whatever one expected of these oncoming pillars of the American theater, they turned out to be as wooden a threesome of supers as ever hovered around a great star. Sarah ... wore a dress of what appeared to be chiffon. It was form-clinging and weighted with embroidery of rhinestones, turquoise, brilliants of all kinds — in fact everything was on it but cowbells. Her sleeves were skin-tight over her thin arms, and made of the same material as her dress with panels of material fastened from shoulder to wrists; and when she raised her arms in an emotional gesture these winglike sleeves swept the floor with the aid of their weights, also of brilliants and rhinestones. At the end of her great speeches she opened her arms wide with passionate fury, and as the audience acclaimed her in an ovation she kept her pose; it was fascinating to watch our young American beauties trying to disentangle themselves from the suffocation of her costume as it was tangled around them."[94]

Years later, Laurette talked about the experience with Bernhardt in her own inimitable way. "Sarah Bernhardt came over here during the run of *Peg o' My Heart*. It was arranged that she should be supported at her first performance by three American actresses, Marguerite Clarke and myself and another, a very beautiful woman [Cowl]. We were simply to let Sarah lean on us and carry her train. I had always admired her for her art and for the amazing vitality and superb confidence which carried her through everything. I was glad of the chance to meet, under any conditions. When the beautiful actress found that we must wear the old costumes furnished by the French company she rebelled. 'I want to have a new gown made for it,' she said. 'If I can't use my own costume, I won't appear.' I tried to make her see that this was no time for clothes to outdress a grand, brave woman. It was an honor just to be near Sarah Bernhardt. That was how I felt. But she wouldn't go on, so we took a stenographer for the third. I was awed and nervous, but the stenographer seemed to feel toward me as I did toward Bernhardt and that set me up a bit. As we entered, Sarah made a mighty effort, fairly lifting herself out of her physical weakness by the power of her will. She rose majestically to meet the people's applause. Then she bent her whole weight upon me, almost crushing me to the floor. It was well it wasn't little Marguerite Clarke. The stenographer was so frightened she couldn't get herself off the stage. Bernhardt was angry and waited till I took the poor girl away. I thought that was the end of the affair. But Bernhardt had seen that I was trying to help and she asked questions. She found that I come from a successful play of my own to honor a foreign artist; that I had accepted the costume offered and had urged the others to do likewise. She was always equally intense in her anger and in her enthusiasm. I had won her favor and she insisted on seeing me act."[95]

Laurette later explained how it came to be. "A special performance was arranged for Bernhardt alone. The doctor forbade her to go but she defied him and after two hours' effort she reached the theater. Not a newspaperman had been admitted to that performance. It was for Sarah alone. People told me it was a great waste of publicity. But my reward came when she wrote about me herself."[96]

Sarah Bernhardt indeed praised Taylor after seeing the play. "One young artist in New York has not allowed herself to be blinded. She has worked hard and is still working, although she is already a very agreeable comedienne, possessing humor, emotion and a rare thing for her age, power. I speak of Laurette Taylor, who will become within five years the foremost actress of this country."[97]

According to Hedda Hopper, Bernhardt acted every inch the diva during the performance. In her version, however, Bernhardt wasn't the only audience member. "When her [Taylor] idol, Sarah Bernhardt, was making a farewell appearance at the Empire Theatre, Laurette was playing at the Globe. She invited the great one to be her guest at a special matinee and moved her entire production to the Empire to make it more convenient for Bernhardt. The affair was strictly invitational; the house was packed with celebrities. Bernhardt swept in to occupy the second box, stage left. The view was better from there, but Madame Bernhardt didn't tolerate a second anything and demanded Box Number 1, already occupied by the aging and revered actress, Maggie Mitchell, who was brought in from the Actors' Home to see the performance. The switch was made, but I don't believe any player left the theater feeling the same respect for the French star as when they had entered."[98]

At the same performance Hopper sat next to playwright Winchell Smith. He mused to Hopper, "What a crime that she [Laurette] was born in America.... That's her real tragedy. If she'd been born in any other country, she'd be hailed as the greatest actress in the world, and we'd be spared all this drool about Bernhardt and Duse."[99]

Meanwhile, *Peg* was still going strong at the Cort. At the end of 1913, Emory B. Calvert wrote an article about its success. "If ever a young married couple has cause for self-congratulation, it is Mr. and Mrs. J. Hartley Manners.... [*Peg*] has filled the pockets of Mr. Manners. He and the leading lady have brought their romance to a happy marriage and should 'hubby' never write another success, which I consider an impossible condition, Mr. and Mrs. Manners would still have enough to carry their family expenses quite well from the profits of *Peg*."[100]

Calvert also provided some insight into how *Peg* was written. After explaining that Hartley wrote it in the summer of 1911 before marrying Laurette, Calvert reported that the couple squabbled over some of the play's details. Laurette, for example, who was unhappy that the entire play was set in England, wanted an act to take place in New York. She also wanted Peg's father in the play, perhaps as the butler.

Finally, Laurette simply wanted to hear Manners read the play. He did, but not without warning her first. "Mr. Manners warned me against himself, so to speak, but at length I told him that I positively refused to appear in it unless he read it to me at once. [H]e warned me again, most solemnly — and then proceeded. As he went on he became quite interested, and at length he looked up and interrogated smilingly: 'Well, how do you like it?' And I answered from the depths of my being: 'Hartley, it's awful!' That was the end of the author's reading and he vowed that it should be the end of my dallying with the play."

In fact, Manners had a deliberate method of writing plays. "His scripts were completely rewritten four times. The first version was formal and didactic. In the initial stages the story was pushed along, the scenes laid out more or less mechanically. Gradually with each rewriting the script became more supple and alive. Work on the dialogue came last."[101]

Hartley wrote *Peg o' My Heart* specifically for Laurette. She told an interviewer she thought the character might have been based on her grandmother. She often told him stories about her childhood which included anecdotes about her relatives. "'I had a difficult time with Dwight, and my grandmother, an Irish lady who had had 12 children of her own, was very impatient about it. 'By the time she's takin' to have the child,' she said, 'he might be the president of the United States.' She was always making such remarks, but I was the only member of the family who had courage enough to laugh at them. I think she was the real model for *Peg o' My Heart*.'"[102]

Laurette mentioned more than once that her portrayal was an homage to a grandmother who still thought Laurette's career was a ticket straight to hell. "I got the brogue from my grandmother.... She's the dearest old lady you ever saw. And so devout! And prays so much for me! If only her prayers were half heard I must be very good indeed! But she cannot reconcile herself to the stage. She'll never go to see me act. She lives in Jersey.... Once in a while I go to see her and I have a lovely time, and we talk about everything in the world except acting. We pretend that the theater doesn't exist."[103]

Laurette once told a story about inviting an elderly relative to see her in *Peg o' My Heart*. According to Taylor, "She had lived practically all her life in Ireland, [was] of a very religious turn of mind, and had never been inside a theatre till she was persuaded to come and see me play in *Peg o' My Heart*. At the end of the play I asked her what she thought of my acting. 'Is that all you get your money for?' she exclaimed. 'Sure, and I wouldn't call that acting at all. Why I've seen hundreds of young colleens behave just like that over in Ireland.'"[104]

If Laurette and Hartley were feeling it a bit, it's little wonder. The play made them millionaires, and because of *Peg*, one writer concluded that Laurette was "the most widely discussed actress in America."[105] It was a heady time, and Laurette's confidence was high. She finally tired of the play and decided to close it on May 30, 1914. Morosco disagreed with her decision. "Although I believed her very foolish for closing *Peg*'s run at the Cort when it was still doing a phenomenal business, I was ready to give Miss Taylor all due credit for her loyalty to her beloved part. She had given six hundred and four performances without intermission, save for Good Fridays; it was our custom to lay off that one day out of the year."[106]

The *New York Times* broke down what this really meant. "The total receipts of *Peg o' My Heart* for the 76 weeks it played at the Cort Theatre were $788,340. This means that the average weekly receipts were $10,373. The absolute capacity of the theatre is approximately $12,000 a week. The seating capacity of the Cort is 1,042. By comparing the receipts with the utmost capacity of the house it is seen that the audiences represented in the aggregate just five-sixths of the total seating space of the theatre. By these same methods of calculation the figures reveal that in the seventy-six weeks of the run Miss Taylor played Peg before 524,272 people. Making liberal allowance for the patrons who have seen the play two or more times, it is a safe estimate to say that over half a million theatergoers have witnessed the star's work in this one role. The most astonishing achievement is the individual effort of the star.... The part of Peg is quite a long one. The manuscript covers 83 pages known technically as 'sides.' There are ten lines to the page and an average of twelve words to the line. Multiplying the two divisions develops the startling fact that during the run of the play Miss Taylor has read 6,015,840 words to tell the story of Peg and her little visit to England.... She has never missed a performance."[107]

*Peg* made Laurette so famous it wasn't surprising when entertainers began including impersonations of her in their acts. Her friend Elsie Janis was one.[108] When she as appearing in *The Lady of the Slipper* at the Globe in 1913, she added Laurette to her repertoire. While in England in 1915, Janis also included Laurette in her revue at the Palace.[109]

In the summer of 1914 Laurette vacationed. One writer described her summer house as modest for the area but still quite comfortable and featuring a great view of the ocean. According to the writer, Laurette swam, boated, and played tennis. "[S]he believes tennis to be the best all-around exercise for women. 'It trains the eye and develops resourcefulness and judgment,' declares Miss Taylor, speaking of this, her favorite sport."[110] Although she found golf "tiresome," Laurette admitted to being a bit of a daredevil in the water and "dearly loves to do back-flips, double somersaults and jack-knives that are beyond the ability of the average masculine swimmer."[111] She claimed to be a pretty good cook as well and particularly enjoyed cooking for friends at her Sunday night dinners. The food included roasted corn, chicken, hotdogs, clams, and, of course, Irish potatoes.

Laurette said she didn't care for magazines or most novels, though she did read for research purposes. "For instance the year before I began to play Peg I read everything I could lay my hands on about Irish people and places and customs and characteristics — to put myself into the spirit of it: to be a little Irish girl as well as to seem one."[112]

Despite her vacation, the business of Peg never stopped. Morosco wanted eight Peg companies on tour, since the previous four had been tremendously successful. In fact, Morosco again warned Laurette about going to England.

The souvenir program cover from the London production of *Peg o' My Heart* (1915).

"Peggy O'Neill was fast becoming the *Peg o' My Heart* of the West. I was aware of this and knew if Miss Taylor insisted on going to England following her Broadway run, she would sacrifice her American popularity to Peggy O'Neill. All this I told to Manners in the lobby of the theater that day. He wavered, torn between what he must have seen to be the sensible thing, and the desire to show his bride the country of his birth. In the end he would not agree to give up the European trip, but he did, although with apparent reluctance, consent to the sending out of the four additional companies."[113]

Unfortunately, according to Morosco, Hartley went rogue and tried to break his contract with Morosco. Of course, lawyers were called in, and eventually Morosco prevailed, though the two remained bitterly estranged. "After his employing such tactics to rob me of my share in his play, I refused to have any further personal dealings with Manners."[114]

While Hartley and Laurette headed off to England, Morosco opened *Peg* in Chicago with Peggy O'Neill. According to Morosco, "Chicago had been originally reserved for Miss Taylor, but I had tried for over a year to get her to play it, and she had refused. I knew, and had told them, that by the time Miss Taylor finished her European tour, *Peg* would be too dated for Chicago, which demanded the first returns from New York. Then when Manners tried to steal my rights to the play, the rank ingratitude so angered me, I was determined not to jeopardize one of the best paying cities in America simply because he wanted to make a splurge in London."[115]

Laurette seemed particularly upset that Morosco waited till she'd boarded the ship before playing his hand. She wrote a letter expressing her concerns. "Morosco puts *Peg o' My Heart* in Chicago after I am on the ship. Don't you think it a shabby trick to a woman who worked continuously for him for two years?"[116]

It was again *on* between the producer and playwright. Manners rushed back to the United States, and the two faced a standoff in Chicago. According to Morosco, his Chicago attorney Levy Mayer ably defused Manners' demands. Morosco quoted Mayer as saying, "'Since Manners is the aggressor and a very offensive one at that, I'm going to make him pay for the English production and take all the chances. If there are any profits, you will get half of them; but if, on the contrary there are any losses due to London's refusal to accept *Peg*, you will bear no part of them.'"[117] One can certainly understand Hartley's view. He had, after all, created the play. However, the contracts favored producer Morosco, who'd taken the financial risk.

Content to let Hartley fight the legal battles, Laurette opened in *Peg o' My Heart* at the Comedy Theatre in London on October 10, 1914. It moved to the Globe Theatre, where it finally ended its run on October 18, 1915. The

Laurette Taylor in the garden of her London home (1915) (photograph courtesy of Jon Mirsalis).

London run was a huge hit, and critics applauded her effort. "The *London Times* speaks of Miss Taylor as 'genuinely and audaciously, and overwhelmingly new, with a marked individuality, a way of her own, a bundle of those personal qualities that are only to be felt in the presence of the person and can by no means be rendered in print.' 'Never did any new actress meet with a more unequivocal or more instantaneous success than Miss Taylor,' says the *Mail*. 'She has a way with her, Miss Laurette Taylor,' says the *Telegraph*. 'Whatever she does, she is a joy. Her laugh won't be denied. It makes you suddenly glad that you are there to laugh too.'"[118]

Actors, too, thought she was among the greatest. "According to Sir Charles Wyndham, England's oldest and most revered actor, the reception accorded Laurette Taylor ... has not been equaled since the night, half a century ago, Ellen Terry won her first triumph."[119]

Laurette was the toast of the town. "A society magazine reported: 'She is the first American actress to make a complete social conquest of London society. There is no function of importance now given at which she is not one of the most prominent guests.'"[120]

It was at one of these functions that Laurette first met Lynn Fontanne. Painfully shy, Fontanne was afraid to approach Laurette, "who was perched on a divan at the opposite end of the long room. She was not tall or graceful and she was got up in a garish flowered pink satin dress and an enormous black hat with ostrich plumes."[121] Hanging back, Lynn carefully observed Laurette and found her discontented. She sat next to Laurette, introduced herself, and promptly discovered that Laurette was familiar with her work. "She took Lynn's hand, and asked her: 'I've decided to form my own permanent acting company in America. Would you like to come to America and play with me?'"[122]

Thus began a long, complicated friendship between the two women. According to Maurice Zolotow, who wrote a biography on Alfred Lunt and Fontanne, "She [Fontanne] fell at once into the relationship of protégée and master, as she had with Ellen Terry; but Ellen Terry had been soft and considerate, and Laurette Taylor, during the decade of her relationship with Lynn Fontanne, was often to be selfish and cruel and tyrannical, these moods alternating with moods of warmth and kindness."[123]

Maurice Zolotow learned from Marguerite Courtney that Fontanne was the spitting image of Laurette's mother. "In Laurette's bedroom hung a full-length portrait of her mother, Mrs. Elizabeth Cooney. Marguerite Taylor Courtney, Laurette's daughter and biographer, once told me that Mrs. Cooney looked exactly like Lynn. She mentioned the resemblance to her mother. Laurette said, 'Yes, it might be Lynn — except the lips. Lynn's lips welcome the imprint of pleasure and never cry 'woe is me.'"[124]

For the time being, Laurette enjoyed Fontanne's company and vice versa. "Lynn became Miss Taylor's constant companion, the satellite to the planet, the confidante of Miss Taylor's problems and pleasures, the eternal protégée. She was backstage at the Globe every matinee and evening. She lived in Laurette's dressing room and dined regularly at Laurette's house in Regent Park. She joined Laurette's ménage (or menagerie), the hurricane of people and excitement in which Laurette moved — the husband and the two children and all the servants and guests and eccentric friends. There were suppers and teas and weekends at Laurette's country place in Maidenhead, up the Thames. Lynn often wondered about the strange, quiet, thoughtful gentleman who was Laurette's husband, the playwright J. Hartley Manners."[125]

A publicity photograph of Laurette Taylor and Violet Kemble-Cooper for the London production of *Peg o' My Heart*.

Laurette was still going strong in London in the spring of 1915, along with another American, her good friend Elsie Janis. "One thing is certain — these brilliant American actresses — Miss Elsie Janis and Miss Laurette Taylor, have stormed and seized the affections of London's theater-going public. There was no resistance. Miss Janis is installed at the Palace, while Miss Taylor has the Globe at her feet. They are better than medicine — these two. They pierce the thick war gloom with shafts of wit and make mirth dance and sing where worry sulked."[126]

Actress Blanche Sweet once asked Taylor how she could stand doing the same play so many times. "I asked her, 'Don't you get tired of doing the same thing over and over and over again?' She said, 'No, because it's always a new audience.' Other people have said that, and I think they probably meant it.

I know Laurette meant it."[127] She may have meant it, but anyone would be sick to death of playing the same part in the same play more than a thousand times. Remember, Laurette also said, "[S]uccess in the theater really amounts to a sentence."[128]

While Laurette was in London, the *New York Herald* reported that she begged the audience to stay away from *Peg*. "I'm very much obliged to you for coming to see me so often, but I don't mind tellin' you I do wish you'd stay away. If you want to know how bored I am with this part go home and try to smile at yourselves in the mirror a thousand times in succession. I've played it so long I've lost all me social style. I slide into a drawin' room and I slide out again, and for the life of me, I can't speak without an accent. I told a lady that I was tired of sayin' the same things night after night and she said to me 'Sure, Peg, there are lots women that say the same things night after night and day after day — and they don't get paid for it.' That made me a little more contented. I'm glad you like the play, but don't do like the others and come again."[129]

It's difficult to understand just how pervasive *Peg o' My Heart* was during this era. An ad for the motion picture tried to put the success of the stage play in context. "To get a picture of what popularity 15,000 performances of a play denotes, suppose that '*Peg o' My Heart*' had been given not in many theatres, but in only one. Had this been so and the play just winding up its run, the premiere would have been back in 1882, the year of the great white blizzard, the year President Garfield was shot — before the Brooklyn Bridge was opened or King Alfonso of Spain had had his turn at being born. 15,000 performances, given consecutively, means a run of 41 years."[130]

By summer it seemed a good idea to return to America, especially since London was facing ferocious bombing attacks. "Laurette Taylor, now the idol of London, may have to return to this country hastened. She is to appear under the directions of Klaw & Erlanger and George C. Tyler in a repertoire of plays next season. In a letter just received by Mr. Tyler she writes: 'The latest news is that in the near future the theatres in London will all be closed. The authorities wish every one to be home these nights and presently owing to the likelihood of Zeppelin raids, it is the intention to close all places of amusement.' Miss Taylor also thanked Mr. Tyler in her letter for his cabled congratulations on her one thousandth appearance as Peg ... which took place recently at the Globe Theatre in London."[131]

Laurette hung on a little while longer, but, finally, in November came word that she was returning home. "Laurette Taylor has decided suddenly that she cannot remain in London and endure the shock of Zeppelin raids any longer. She will sail for New York on November 29, and after a brief rest, will begin an American tour in Chicago under the direction of George Tyler and Klaw & Erlanger. Her play will be *Happiness*."¹³²

In fact, Laurette found the Zeppelin raids terrifying. Of course, anyone in her right mind would be rattled by bombing raids. She wrote a letter to George C. Tyler describing one incident: "The night the Zeppelins came I was just finishing the last act. It seemed difficult for a few moments to realize (after a year of darkened streets and threatening talk) that they were really over the housetops. I went down in the cellar and, like a good Catholic, said my prayers. The company followed me into the cellar, but I was the only one that said my prayers. 'A lot of heathens,' I calls 'em. For three days afterward I was really fearfully ill. I had fully determined never to act again in London until the war had finished, but, as everybody else went on, 'business as usual,' you know, I didn't feel as though I could afford to prove that I am not afraid, but I don't mind telling you I am scared to death. I will say the English are the most remarkable race I have ever met with, and, if I were a German, I should hate their insides. Even Hartley, whom I have never considered a particularly brave man, went up on the roof of the Green Room Club to look at the Zeppelins, and walked all the way over here to the Globe, and finding me in the cellar, quoted one of the lines from *Peg*: 'Come out and look at it; they're beautiful in this part of the country.' I was furious with him."¹³³

A publicity photograph of Laurette Taylor from the souvenir program of the London production of *Peg o' My Heart* (1915).

After she returned to the United States, Laurette further discussed her adventures in wartime London. "All season they had been saying they were coming till we had become hardened to it.... The one night along in the last act, where there is a thunderstorm, you may remember, there was an extra roar and I thought to myself, 'The man with the drum has dropped it.' When the booming kept up I thought I should have to get after him for being careless, and then the noise of the guns, answering the bombs, broke out. I ran to the cellar and stayed till it was all over, but Hartley, being an Englishman, went out to watch it. We were living in the country, and when we went back to the station to go home we had to come back because no trains were running. The order had gone out for no trains to leave the station because of the light they throw up from their smokestacks. I returned to town Monday, and the following Wednesday the Zeppelins came again. This time they arrived at the beginning of the second act. We went right on with the performance. My legs were shaking and my knees knocking together, but the audience didn't give a sign. There was no laughter nor applause during the bombardment, which lasted about a half hour, but no one left the theatre. That finished me, and I gave it up."[134] She promised, however, to return. "Of course, I shall go back, but not until this war is over."[135] For now, too, Laurette could leave *Peg* behind.

## Chapter 5

# AFTER *PEG*

*"All my plays ... are working up to one big play—after awhile. Some day you will see what I mean."*[1]

It was major news when Laurette returned home. According to the *Washington Post*, "Laurette Taylor ... who has within the last year achieved the greatest success ever enjoyed in a foreign country by an American actress, arrives in New York today from London ready to begin preparations for a renewal of acquaintance with the American public.... After a brief sojourn at Palm Beach she is to return to New York to begin rehearsals in *Happiness*.... Regardless of whatever success it may achieve, it will be followed by *The Wooing of Eve*, and from the two will be chosen the play in which she will be seen in New York when she reappears in that city at the beginning of next season. Both plays are comedies."[2]

Unfortunately, Laurette suffered a major loss on December 17, 1915, when her beloved mother, Elizabeth Cooney, died at the age of 51. In addition, Laurette, who'd been suffering from abdominal pain, underwent surgery for a hernia.

In January, just back from London, Laurette appeared in a scene from *Peg* at a benefit for the Actors' Fund. Despite this, Laurette made it clear that she was through with *Peg*. "I am going to get well as quick as I can ... and then watch me. You will see a bright streak up Fifth Avenue and Broadway. That will be me buying clothes and seeing the new plays. I am going to spend some of the money we have been making on *Peg*.... Hartley and I have been getting rich.... And then I'm going to try to become a fine actress. I'm going to try to forget I ever was Peg and to act something that every young actress with a pretty face can't follow me in. I have all the money I need now and I am ambitious to be a really great artiste if I can. When one is poor, money is apt to be the goal. Then after one gets a certain amount of money all that more money can do is to make one fatter and more comfortable. Then it is one begins to want to do something for the sake of doing it well, and that is where I am now.... Gradually I hope to build up a repertoire of contrasted roles."[3]

Despite her boredom with the role, the years of playing Peg resulted in a further honing of Laurette's stage instinct. "The development of a play becomes a more and more instinctive thing. One learns to think quickly, even before an audience.... In *Peg* I acquired freedom enough to improvise. One could play more directly to the audience, as in a vaudeville turn. If somebody whispered or rustled a program, I'd remark, 'There's a lot of noise in that next room!' The people got it, too."[4]

The first play Laurette performed in following her return was Hartley's *The Wooing of Eve*, which opened in March 1916 in Rochester, New York. In April the production moved to Philadelphia, but poor reviews closed it. Hartley decided it needed to be rewritten, and it would not reopen until November 26 at the Liberty.

Problems began before it opened when Laurette insisted that George Tyler pay for Lynn Fontanne to come to the United States. Tyler refused, believing that Fontanne wasn't crucial to the play's success. According to Maurice Zolotow, "Laurette ... insisted that her husband had written the part just for Miss Fontanne, and that they had to have her, as she was 'a very rare bird.' Tyler still wouldn't put up the passage money; so J. Hartley Manners cabled her the 50 pounds out of his own pocket."[5] Tyler made no mention of this in his autobiography and praised Fontanne. According to him, Laurette didn't return to the United States alone. She brought back "a startlingly capable beginner named Lynn Fontanne — shy and awkward enough — always turned her toes in, and a time she had breaking herself of the habit — but through all her shyness you could see she was blessed with the grand manner even then."[6]

Rehearsals had already started before Fontanne made her passage to America. She had been delayed because it was near impossible to get a wartime visa and passport. "I got it finally ... by falling to my knees and crying and putting on a marvelous scene before a nice old gentleman in some office in Whitehall. Oh, it was the best piece of acting I'd done since *Milestones*. I pleaded and cajoled and Ellen-Terryed him to the limit of my ability, and to get rid of me he gave me the passport. I got the visa by doing another hysterical scene. Hysteria is so easy to act. A week later I was on a boat to New York."[7]

Tyler never warmed up to her, and Fontanne quickly realized the play was a dud. "She had traveled 3,000 miles through submarine-infested waters to play a stupid role, lacking body and cleverness, in a confused play, a mélange of sentimental light comedy and melodramatic intrigue (though the dialogue was good).... In her first scene, the stage directions called for her to burst into tears no less than 19 times! To Lynn it seemed impossible to play this idiotic character straight, but Manners was directing her to play her seriously and she would have to do it."[8] Fortunately, when *The Wooing of Eve* was later revived, Fontanne convinced Hartley to let her do it her way. She reduced the waterworks considerably and created a more compelling character.

*The Wooing of Eve* was the story of an American woman visiting London, Eve Alverstone, who plots to help her cousin avoid marriage to an older man. In fact, Eve had a previous relationship with the man and ends up reconciling with him. According to the *New York Times*, "It became immediately evident that the piece was a bad failure." In fact, the *Times* stage critic raved about Laurette, who played Eve, suggesting she handled a difficult role "with consummate ... subtlety and charm, the consummate feeling for true comedy, and the no less consummate sense of histrionic effect, which mark her as potentially by far the most interesting actress on our stage."[9]

*Life* slammed Manners' play. "It is to be feared that Laurette Taylor, as an American girl fixing things in England, won't be quite so successful on that job in *The Wooing of Eve* as she was in the Peg o' many hearts. Mr. Manners has not given her by any means as good a medium in the way of a play.... Despite this, the efforts of a well chosen company and the ability and irresistible charm of the star, one comes away from *The Wooing of Eve* with the feeling that there was a lack of something. Analysis shows that it was a lack of something to redeem the admitted artificiality of the play."[10] According to one writer, Laurette's role "came across as an unsympathetic bitch. Manners could do what he liked with the other roles, but it wouldn't do for Laurette to look like a bitch."[11] In reading the play today, there are similarities between Eve and Peg in that both are amusing, cheeky young girls who seem to have more sense than anyone else around them. Although critics damned the play, *The Wooing of Eve* does have its comical moments, and Eve comes across not so much as a bitch but rather a clever, experienced woman who's vulnerable when she's in love.

*The Harp of Life* was Laurette's next play. It opened November 27, 1916, at the Globe Theatre in New York. Cast members include Philip Merivale, Frank Kemble-Cooper, Dion Titheradge, Ffolliet Paget, and Lynn Fontanne.

Laurette played a mother who schemes to keep her son from the clutches of a notorious woman. It was, at least, far away from Peg, and Laurette was thrilled. "The temptation, of course, when one has made a success in a part, is to follow it up with another like it and die playing Pegs. But I would rather die playing other types and failing in them all than going on stunting my artistic growth."[12]

According to Laurette, she contributed dialogue to the piece. "You would be surprised how many speeches in the play were taken from life, things Mr. Manners has heard me say, speeches of his I have remembered, or lines we have put down that others have coined. So there must be something of real life in the play."[13]

Upon its opening, the *New York Times* applauded Hartley and Laurette. "His new play, a finer, more delicate, and more lofty work, is a tender and penetrating comedy of motherhood.... The mother is played by Miss Taylor — a role deliberately chosen for its divergence from the adorable Peg. But Sylvia is no less adorable, and in this new character she gives a true and heartwarming performance that lifts perceptibly her already enviable standing as an actress in this community. Here is acting that has back of it a fine precision of expression.... It is warm with humanity. It strengthens her position in that little group in that little group at the forefront of the English-speaking stage. Laurette Taylor is one of the great ladies of our time."[14]

Not everyone was so fond of the play. Guthrie McClintic blamed Hartley for its failure — and was relieved he didn't end up with a role in the production. Still, he praised Laurette. "Her performance was beguiling and fresh but her radiance could not conceal the shoddiness of her material. As I watched her I didn't grieve that another [Dion Titheradge] was playing her son and not I myself."[15]

The drama critic for *Life* agreed. "Mr. Manners embodies his ideas ... in a long and didactic speech which, delivered by anyone else and with less charm than Laurette Taylor gave to it, would probably have driven his first audience from the theatre and kept others away.... *The Harp of Life* interests and is well done throughout, but it may show Mr. Manners that education from the stage should be indirect instead of so frankly didactic. And please, Laurette Taylor, don't become a stage mother just yet. Lovable as you are in the role, we like you better as a girl. And please take notice that in urging this request not once in this notice has appeared a comparison with or mention of a certain other play with which your name has been connected."[16]

According to another writer, "The new play is unusual not only in respect to the age of the star, however. It is not even a star-built vehicle. There are three other parts as striking as Miss Taylor's, and she dominates the others only by sheer force of merit and personality."[17] *The Independent* wrote that the play was "[u]nusual, purposeful and inspiring."[18] *McClure's* snippily wrote that *The Harp of Life* was worth seeing "because it proves that Laurette Taylor is a charming actress, even when she has little or nothing to do."[19] Alan Dale echoed that sentiment. "You may have the message contained in *The Harp of Life*— you may have it all — but please leave me Laurette Taylor, and please let me gloat over the fact that many years ago — not too many of course — when a very awful play called *Mrs. Dakon* was reluctantly matineed in New York, I apparently discovered Miss Taylor, and asserted that she was so natural, so unaffected, and so simple, that she should be immediately derricked from her gloomy surroundings. Oh, let me gloat!"[20]

In fact, Mr. Dale was head over heels about Laurette. "Laurette Taylor herself is exquisite.... She is universal. There is no actress before the public to-day who is so affably appealing. The art of pause, the strange quality of drawl, and the peculiar effect of intonation were luminously displayed. Occasionally I thought of Sarah Bernhardt ... as I listened to Miss Taylor's speech. The English language, as she delivered it, was as joy."

Much was made about the costumes Laurette wore for *The Harp of Life*. "There is a three-piece afternoon costume ... of tan-bark brown velour, with long silk fringe for trimming. The entire upper section of the gown is of self-toned chiffon cloth, which joins the velour at the middle of the blouse, where Egyptian embroidery in shades of brown and orange appears. The embroidery extends around the bodice, and there is an oval medallion at the corsage. The sleeve of the chiffon cloth is loose bell shape to the elbow, with an undersleeve of the same material fitted tightly over the wrist. The skirt has a pointed tunic reaching to the knees, but only in the back, the front disappearing under the front panel. The hips are swathed with two front ends of the velour, tied in front, a little to the left side, and finished with an oval medallion, and the deep silk fringe. There is a straight little jacket to this suit which, when buttoned up the front with cloth-covered buttons, gives it the effect of a one-piece dress. The collar has a square tab-like section at the back, from which the fringe hangs nearly to the waistline, the jacket ending at that point so that the clever arrangement of the sash, which forms a yoke effect, is still visible."[21]

Despite this, Laurette didn't obsess over costumes. "Too much importance is laid on clothes. In the main, I think that all clothes hamper unless they express the character. Personally, I detest 'straight' parts for that reason. They necessitate the clothes that make me self-conscious — or, rather, 'clothes conscious.' I want to get right inside the character and act from the heart as well as from the head. That is impossible unless one is free from outside interference."[22]

Before the play closed in March 1917 the *New York Times* offered one last review. While acknowledging the fine performances of Laurette, Lynn Fontanne, Philip Merivale, and Dion Titheradge, Alexander Woollcott called Manners' play a "penetrating and pathetic but somewhat oversaturated comedy." He insisted the first two acts were fine, but the last act "disappointing."[23]

After reading the play I disagree. The last act features the confrontation between Sylvia, Leonard's mother, and Zeila, Leonard's lover, and it packs quite a punch until it dissolves into a sappy, sentimental ending that's cringeworthy. Zeila is a much more interesting character than Sylvia. Of course, the "bad woman" is usually more complicated and dimensional. In this case, Laurette's character is a flat stereotype, and I felt sorry for her when I read her lines about the pure love of a mother and wife. She must have been enormously talented if she could sincerely deliver these lines. Zeila would have been a much more interesting role for Laurette to play, but it's unlikely Hartley would have even considered such a departure for her. The part of Zeila was played by Gail Kane, who was already a well known silent film actress.

Although *The Harp of Life* was unsuccessful, it helped make Lynn Fontanne a star. During this time Laurette and Fontanne became closer, though the relationship was dominated by Laurette. "That summer of 1916, Lynn was rehearsing in *The Harp of Life* and becoming more closely intertwined with Laurette in the relationship of disciple and master. She was in complete subjection to Laurette. On weekends she would go up to the summer home of Laurette and Hartley in Tokeneke, Connecticut, on Long Island Sound. Laurette thought that Lynn's constancy to her war lover [Edmund Byrne, who was later killed in action], fighting in France, was idiotic. Laurette was a compulsive flirt, and had open liaisons with lovers under the eyes of her husband. Laurette criticized Lynn for her 'shyness' and her 'fidelity' and said that one could not blossom into a great actress without periodic bouts of great passion to vitalize one's erotic energies, which were the source of the vitality one emanated on the stage. She shared with Ellen Terry the theory that one converted — or, in Stanislavsky jargon, one *used*— the emotions stirred up by a new love affair into the artificial situations of the theatre."[24]

Laurette had made Fontanne her special project, insisting, among other things, that she gain weight. "Laurette Taylor picked on Lynn constantly, calling her a 'bag of bones' with 'arms as thin as rails.' One of her favorite jibes was: 'In me, dressmakers lose the pins — on Lynn they bend them.' Laurette believed Lynn could become beautiful only by becoming plumper. Years later, in 1942, she remarked: 'Lynn is the only woman I ever knew that twenty pounds turned into a real beauty.'"[25]

In the summer of 1917 Laurette was considering plans for her future and leaning toward doing a Christmas fantasy. "I think it is about time I wore a little gauze and acted a fairy."[26] Still, Laurette insisted she would appear only in Hartley's plays. "Whenever people ask me why I act a season in my husband's plays exclusively I reply that others do the same with Shakespeare's and then they feel uncomfortable. We may be wrong but we have a feeling tinged with hope that some day we may do something big together."[27]

That fall Laurette was one of many actors who appeared in a film short for the Liberty Loan committee. The film, titled *Three Billion Dollars in Four Weeks*, was composed of episodes featuring American history and wars. Among the personalities in the film were Thomas Edison, President Wilson, De Wolf Hopper, Raymond Hitchcock, Douglas Fairbanks, Will Rogers, Mary Pickford, Pauline Frederick, Ethel Barrymore, Nance O'Neil, Elsie Janis, and many others.[28] This was Laurette's second appearance in a motion picture. She had also appeared in 1914 in *Our Mutual Girl*, a kind of serial that featured Norma Phillips hobnobbing with New York celebrities while solving crimes.

An interesting profile on Laurette came out at the end of 1917. It went into detail about her two homes. "Laurette Taylor is one of the fortunate beings who have two homes: one for work time and one for play time. The winter home is a charming apartment, taking up almost a whole floor, high up in a New York apartment house; an apartment furnished for utmost comfort and not for show, and with wide windows that command a view of the city, spread out like a panorama far below. There are some wonderful Italian and Spanish furnishings in this apartment, things picked up during travels abroad. Miss Taylor admits an admiration for the dignified and impressive Italian and Spanish pieces and has a specially fine collection of Italian wall panels, ancient carvings dark and rich in tone. She has some fine tapestries also, and some rare old Spanish mission furniture. 'It has always seemed to me such a pity,' she declares, 'that the Italians did not use rugs. Their rugs would have been so beautiful — if there had been any.'"[29]

The article explained that during the winter, when Laurette was on stage, she kept a rigid schedule. She breakfasted at ten, then exercised, followed by lunch, and then a matinee. On days when she had no matinee she met with dressmakers, photographers, and spoke to her manager. She usually ate dinner at the theater in her dressing room before she went on stage. Her dressing room was described in some detail. "A delightful room is the dressing room of Laurette Taylor: a room furnished in rose chintz and more artistically lighted than the usual theatre dressing rooms. The walls are hung with many signed photographs of well known folks in the literary and dramatic world and on table and dresser, in addition to lovely flowers, are many little knick-knacks which speak of the affection and admiration of hosts of friends."[30]

After the performance, according to the article, Laurette returned home. "Miss Taylor goes straight home and after a bite of supper, reads in bed until the wee small hours, reads her tense, wrought-up nerves — high-keyed by the performance into which she has put all her physical energy and all her soul — into a quiet that admits a possibility of sleep. When asked what books she reads to make herself sleepy in those dead-of-night hours when most people who have been enthralled by her acting are snoozing peacefully on their pil-

Laurette Taylor in *Out There* (1917) (photograph courtesy of Mary Pearsall).

lows, she replied: 'Oh, sometimes serious books, and sometimes novels — anything not too exciting.'"[31]

Summer reading was a different story. "Character study absorbs her most. She is deeply interested in biographies and even in story books that bring out development of character, and, of course, some delving into psychology accompanies the analysis of character."[32]

Laurette acknowledged she was focused on her career. "She ... is a woman of one idea — success in the thing that she has undertaken to do; and declares that she has no time for small pursuits — for fads, in short."[33] Still, she acknowledged that she could sew, cook, and garden — if only there was enough time.

The writer, like many, was overwhelmed by Laurette's charisma. "Her personality impresses you restfully. You feel sub-consciously a tremendous reserve of energy, of vitality, of capability, all concentrated to one supreme end: her outward impression on you is one of gentle courtesy, of exquisite poise, of a fine restraint in manner and gesture that results obviously from an inward serenity and balance unharassed by 'nerves' or self-consciousness. It is this natural restraint, contrasted with moments of great emotional feeling that make Laurette Taylor's acting so fascinating and so compelling. She admires particularly the Spanish school of acting: its dignity, its restraint of gesture, with a perfect expressiveness conveyed by more subtle art. 'All my plays,' she says, 'are working up to one big play — after awhile. Some day you will see what I mean.'"[34]

When Laurette returned to Broadway in 1917, she was rich and famous. At the time, *Puck* claimed, "It is safe to say that, with the possible exception of Maude Adams, Miss Taylor is the best loved actress now appearing before the public."[35]

In fact, Laurette, too, was a huge fan of Adams.' According to Laurette, "Recall her work in *Chantecler*. Without her tremendous imagination to gild her impersonation, this frail little woman would have been hopeless in the part. Yet through her marvelous richness of imagination she produced the illusion of bigness that many women better fitted physically could not have done. One would never say that Maude Adams is beautiful, in the sense that she is pretty or has a beautiful physique; but she has charm, magnetism and imagination. These three make a beauty that transcends mere beauty."[36]

*Out There* opened on March 27, 1917, at the Globe. It closed in the summer and then briefly reopened in September. The total run was 80 performances. As usual, Manners wrote *Out There* as a showcase for Laurette. She was so excited about the role of a Cockney nurse that she claimed it was "better than Peg or any other she ever had."[37]

Hartley bragged to George Tyler that he'd written the play in four weeks.

He also came to believe it was his best work. "If anything I have written lives for — well, shall I say twenty years? — it will be *Out There*."[38] He'd originally conceived it as a one-act play but quickly saw that it could be further developed. A *New York Times* writer claimed that Hartley used experiences he and Laurette had in England for the characters and details. "*Out There* has been pretty generally accepted as Mr. Manners' best play and the best war drama the conflict has produced to date. Its excellence consists primarily in the fidelity in which it mirrors life. Mr. Manners, who has shown skill before in delineating character, has utilized this skill in conjunction with unusual opportunities for observation. He and Miss Taylor were in England for the first year of the war and they did their bits in helping care for and amuse convalescing Tommies. They were richly rewarded, as it turned out, for several of the characters in *Out There* had their prototypes among the invalided soldiers who came under their observation."[39]

Laurette improvised an amusing bit while she was making up the hospital beds. "When I began playing *Out There*, I used to make up the hospital beds in a hurry. A friend who had been a nurse at the front showed me that it could not be done so quickly and done right. So I got her to teach me every detail. But that took more time and the audience might lose interest in the process. So I began to sing absurd little songs to amuse them, such as 'Please Don't Steal My Prayer Book, Mr. Burglar' and 'They're Afraid He'll Set the Water Works On Fire.' The songs made a hit, besides giving me time to make up those beds as they ought to be made."[40]

The *New York Times* thought the play was quite good — until the third act, calling it "grievously disappointing ... awkward, uninspired, truly calamitous." In fact, the critic even faulted Laurette. "With this last act everything went wrong last night. During the first half the actors seemed to be making it up as they went along; during the second half Miss Taylor had no grip on her material or her audience. To make matters worse, an unseen minion of the theatre, probably convinced that it had gone far enough, lowered the curtain before Miss Taylor was done." Other than the cursed third act, Laurette was praised. "You can imagine how completely winning an 'Aunted Annie' Miss Taylor is, and in the enthusiasm of this account there would be no reservations if it were not for the ... third act."[41]

Alan Dale, writing for *Puck*, also thought the third act was terrible, but Laurette was sublime. "Miss Taylor was simply entrancing. In spite of the cockney dialect that she misunderstood and maltreated, she was perpetually charming. She was so 'natural'— and only the most experienced actress knows the perfectly theatrical art of being 'natural'— that she disarmed us all. Her voice is so soft and appealing; her manner so unconstrained and gentle."[42]

Alexander Woollcott called the play "the latest and best of the war plays, a simple, uncomplicated, unperplexed study of patriotism that is quite glorified by the eloquent and infinitely touching performance of Laurette Taylor."[43] He also complained about the third act, which was revised after the disastrous first night.

According to *Current Opinion*, "it is immensely successful as a wartime play for wartime audiences.... Laurette Taylor has succeeded in creating an illusion of pathetic reality in her interpretation of this pathetic little daughter of the slums."[44]

*Life* saw it for the propaganda piece it was. "It would not be difficult to point out flaws in the dramatic construction of Mr. Manners' play, nor to show where at the first performance Miss Taylor failed to reach the possibilities of her role, but coming just at the moment when it does, when American needs an incentive to the putting aside of individual gain and individual comfort for the country's good, *Out There* and its performance seem to have a special mission and to accomplish it well."[45]

Maurice Zolotow described *Out There* as "a militaristic play written in

The program from Laurette's ill-fated attempt at Shakespeare (1918) (photograph courtesy of Mary Pearsall).

white hate."[46] Still, upon Manners' death, at least one newspaper columnist indicated that this might have been his best, especially compared to *Peg o' My Heart*. "[T]he war play *Out There* ... seemed an example of higher thought and better craftsmanship."[47]

In the fall of 1917 Lew Fields was seen at several *Out There* performances. His purpose was to study the play, and in particular Laurette, so he could perfect a skit lampooning her in a new revue. "Mr. Fields, whose genius for travesty is probably the greatest in the land, will undertake to play Laurette Taylor's part in the burlesque.... Incidentally, the value of being burlesqued at the Century will be considerable to any show which is so fortunate as to achieve that honor, as the Century revue will be seen by twenty-five or thirty thousand people a week. In the old Weberfield days the managers were quick to realize the value of having their attractions travestied, and frequently called the attention of Weber and Fields to points in their shows which they opined could be seized upon."[48]

Eventually Laurette decided she'd "do" Shakespeare and felt comfortable enough to put her own spin on the bard in March 1918. She was at the height of her confidence, though in this case there was a thin line between confidence and arrogance. "Laurette Taylor, inspired by her own, as opposed to any traditional or orthodox, interpretation of the characters, is to come before New York as Portia, Juliet, and Katherine."[49] To make it even more fun, many of her coplayers also had no experience playing Shakespeare. Laurette did her best to spin this to her advantage. "All of us ... will bring fresh minds to our task, unfettered and unhampered by the traditions of another day. We are going about our rehearsals just as if the plays had come to us fresh from the author. I positively refused to have the scenes put on under the direction of any one who had devoted many years to soaking up all the traditional ideas in connection with them, though the services of several 'thoroughly experienced' directors were offered to me. We are working out all our own 'business' and detail. I know that I will be considered supremely presumptuous in attempting so much all at once, but I am hopeful that my public may like me in at least one of the three parts, and if it does I hope that I may be able to make an elaborate revival of the particular play in which this character plays."[50] We're still left wondering, Laurette, what were you thinking?

While admirably ambitious, it was ill-conceived and incredibly naïve of Laurette to think she could pull it off. In fact, Hartley wisely tried to talk her out of it. Laurette disregarded his warning. He finally agreed to direct the production, but she proved to be a horror show during rehearsals. "Taylor continually contradicted or ignored his instructions, not only with regard to her own performance but in respect of the other actors as well. She made it

**Laurette Taylor does Shakespeare (1918) (photograph courtesy of Mary Pearsall).**

clear that this was to be *her* production, in every sense. But her ignorance of Shakespeare, so proudly flaunted, was woeful, and the choices she made, as actress and as *de facto* director, were invariably foolish ones."[51]

It opened on April 5, 1918. The *New York Times* gave her a bad review but one laced with kindness and respect. "It cannot be said that Miss Taylor is already a Shakespearean actress — far from it. Yet beneath the surface of her many shortcomings it is already evident that she has powers which, with experience and study, will carry her to the heights. In her modest little curtain speech, she spoke of her performances as a crucifixion. It was — both to her and Shakespeare."[52] Laurette never hit the right note. "[C]rude as the performance was, it revealed powers that are, potentially, of the highest order. The error was one, not of poverty, but of superabundance of energy." A critic for *Life* also thought the endeavor was a failure. "Miss Laurette Taylor attempted the impossible.... The experiment was interesting, although not even her most ardent admirers could claim that it was successful."[53]

According to Guthrie McClintic, "She knew the plots but not the lines, and that makes a difference when you are playing Shakespeare. Julia Marlowe attended that first matinee and it was rumored her hair turned white before

The cast of *Out There* included Laurette, Helen Ware, Beryl Mercer, H.B. Warner, James T. Powers, George Arliss, Chauncey Olcott, O.P. Heggie, James K. Hackett, George MacFarlane, George M. Cohan, Julia Arthur. Here the cast assembles for a reading of the play with Hartley in 1917.

the performance ended. Miss Taylor herself put her own evaluation on the exhibit when the matinee was over by stepping before the curtain and saying 'Shakespeare has been crucified — so have I — long live Hartley Manners!'"[54]

There were times when the audience inappropriately laughed. Helen Hayes said that the scene from *Romeo and Juliet* was "absolutely unforgettable. When she did the balcony scene ... and Romeo revealed himself beneath the balcony, our Laurette actually met his eye and whispered, 'Hello, Romeo.' It was goodbye, Juliet, from that moment on.'"[55]

Courtenay Savage wrote, "Her conception of the three widely different characters is interesting, but almost too heroic an attempt for one afternoon. Frankly, Miss Taylor was not at her best. She did not reach the high quality she has reached so continuously in modern comedies."[56]

Years later, a newspaper writer concurred that Taylor's Shakespeare was a disaster. "Laurette Taylor was at the height of her career when the bug bit her and audiences had to suffer through *Peg o' My Heart* in six of Katherine's scenes in *Taming of the Shrew*, not to speak of Juliet's balcony scene and Portia's courtroom scene in *The Merchant of Venice*."[57]

Laurette defended herself in the *New York Times* on April 14, 1918. She sounded defensive and bitter, implying that she would be justified in the end. "Time's whirliwig works strange miracles. Mayhaps the opinions of certain gentlemen concerning mine own poor self will change in time. Of course, I know I suffer from a terrible handicap. I wasn't born with a deep chest, a heaving bosom and a heavy voice. These, I have been told, are the fundamental requirements for a Shakespearean actress, and nature vouchsafed me none of them. It is regrettable, but true. However, if my public doesn't like me in these roles, I can only say, with wifely devotion: 'Shakespeare is dead, long live Manners!'"[58]

Laurette responded to her critics with a point-by-point analysis of each criticism. It is almost always a mistake to do this. You end up looking defensive and bitter. She explained why she took the strategy she did. "I confess that I approached the plays in a modern spirit and endeavored to give them a modern interpretation. I rendered myself liable to criticism for that, perhaps, but because I have tried to be modern is no justification for the use of a prehistoric ax by the critics. That is the weapon that a few of them used. It is my humble opinion that any American actress who attempts to put Shakespeare on the stage should be encouraged and not vilified. Her faults, and I have them, should be pointed out to her in a kindly spirit."[59] In truth, Laurette wasn't used to criticism or failure. She truly believed she could pull this off. This experience hurt, and her confidence took a blow.

About a month after Laurette's foray into Shakespeare, *Out There* was used as a fundraiser for the Red Cross. The story goes that Laurette told George Tyler, "I want to do something for the Red Cross ... something really big. Can't you think of something that I can do?"[60]

According to Tyler, when the United States entered World War I, "there wasn't a department of life that it didn't touch. It was miraculous how quickly things happened one night after I discovered that Laurette Taylor was figuring on doing something to raise funds for the Red Cross. Out of that bee in her bonnet

**Mrs. Minnie Maddern Fiske. This was the publicity still used in 1918 in Laurette Taylor's book *The Greatest of These—*.**

came the great all-star tour of *Out There*, which raised $683,248 in twenty-three performances. Tackle that with cube root or calculus or trigonometry and it's still an all-time world's box-office record. In the best days of the late lamented bull-market, the theatre never dreamed of anything like it."[61]

Once the idea of a benefit was mentioned, other stars wanted to join in. According to Tyler, "[T]he minute I broached the idea to the biggest names on the stage, they dropped everything — some of them right in the middle of important productions too — and said sure, we'll be right along, no matter how small the part.... Just Laurette Taylor, George M. Cohan, Mrs. Fiske, Chauncey Olcott, George Arliss, James T. Powers, H.B. Warner, Julia Arthur, James K. Hackett, O.P. Heggie, George MacFarlane, Beryl Mercer, with Lynn Fontanne and Catherine Proctor for understudies, Burr McIntosh and DeWolf Hopper for auctioneers and Madame Eleanor de Cisneros to sing. In the lump they'd have cost 'round forty thousand dollars a week. But they asked no salary, paid their own expenses, the theatres asked no rent, royalties were waived on the play — every cent taken in was to go right where it would do the most good."[62]

The auctions were big moneymakers. Before the actors arrived in town, seats were auctioned by Hopper. McIntosh then auctioned signed programs to the highest bidder. The biggest problem the organizers had was with local Red Cross committees who horned in. "That sort of monkey-business started right away in Washington, our first stand. The curtain was to rise at eight to allow time for the auction. But the great American theatre-goer naturally wouldn't take that lying down — when the curtain rose, about the only spectators down-stairs were President and Mrs. Wilson in the stage-box. And the local committee wouldn't let McIntosh auctioneer — they wanted some local light — so the program went for a measly thousand dollars and that was bid by Nora Bayes, an actress herself, which was a scandal."[63]

**Laurette Taylor in 1918, when her book *The Greatest of These* — was published.**

By the time, the production ended in Pittsburgh, they'd gotten their act together. "Our final performance in Pittsburgh netted a cool one hundred and twenty-nine thousand dollars. That was one of the towns where the citizenry really got behind us. Alex Moore, Lillian Russell's husband, worked himself and his paper, the Pittsburgh *Leader,* blue in the face — we sent to New York for David Warfield and installed him and Miss Russell as supplementary auctioneers — and when they got all the millionaires in Pittsburgh bidding against one another, the sky was the limit. The total take from the whole tour would undoubtedly have been millions if we'd had the same cooperation everywhere."[64]

As you can imagine, the collection of star power resulted in unusual interactions and shenanigans. "Harassing George Arliss was the favorite sport throughout. Arliss was always meticulously careful to check up his props on the set before going on, making sure that the paper and the book and the matches, say, were in the proper places — and then the others would sneak on and switch them on him, which drove his orderly soul close to lunacy."[65] Another time the sets failed to arrive by show time so the performers improvised a variety show that proved to be at least as entertaining as *Out There.*

There were lots of hams in the production, and sometimes the acts would go on and on. George M. Cohan quipped that he was going to write a book titled *My Fours Years in the Second Act.*[66]

Mrs. Fiske was one of the biggest stars at the time, though a recluse and a bit of a nut. In her book, Laurette explained that although they traveled together for *Out There,* she had never actually met her or spent any time with her. Columnist Hedda Hopper later wrote about the tour. "In the last war, when the greatest stars of Broadway made a tour of the country for the Red Cross, they not only gave free performances, but paid their living expenses and traveling expenses. One of the amusing incidents of that tour was Laurette Taylor trying to get to know Minnie Maddern Fiske. And once in Pittsburgh, I believe it was, Mrs. Fiske moved her makeup kit to the roof so as not to be disturbed. Not that she didn't want to meet Miss Taylor. She had a job to do and wanted no interference from anyone."[67] Laurette was intrigued. "I keep wondering what Mrs. Fiske is like. At a distance I adore her but one feels one must go carefully with her. Some friends you achieve, and some you thrust yourself upon."[68]

Laurette quickly realized she and Mrs. Fiske were of quite different temperament. One night Mrs. Fiske didn't go on until well after midnight. "During all those hours she sat patiently waiting, curiously quiet yet most vibrantly alive, nothing moving except her foot, which kept up an incessant tapping. Isn't it interesting when a placid, still personality sort of *chugs underneath* like a Pierce-Arrow? Being a Ford myself— all noise and rattle — I admire tremendously the other thing. We both have our places in the world."[69]

Laurette continued to try to approach Mrs. Fiske. "Why are people afraid of others? I want most frightfully to talk to Mrs. Fiske, but one rarely sees her, and the only opening speech I can think of is, 'Do you play bridge?' If she should say 'No,' where do I go from there?"[70]

Chicago critic Percy Hammond noted that these kinds of extravaganzas often didn't come off well. In this case, however, he found it exceeded his expectations. "It was a great show, no matter what it cost." Laurette, in his opinion, was the star of the show. "Miss Taylor is a vast reservoir of all the human tricks of histrionism; the moods and emotions perform for her with no reluctance. Her engaging humor alternates with her irresistible gifts of pathos, and she bestows them all upon you."[71]

At the end of 1918 Laurette became an author when Doran published a sort of diary of the tour. Titled *The Greatest of These —*, the book was described by one newspaper writer as "an unusual document, filled with the most amazingly personal details concerning her fellow players and containing flashes of the peculiar wit which distinguishes her conversation."[72] The *Los Angeles Times* described it as "very pleasing."[73] The *New York Times* wrote that it included "interesting, unusual, and chatty accounts."[74] *The Independent* suggested that it gave readers a glimpse of Laurette's charm. "If you have ever had the opportunity to talk with Miss Taylor informally off stage you will not need to be told that the book is full of the piquancy of Laurette Taylor conversation. She writes just as she talks.... Even if you're not interested in stage folk you'll enjoy reading about these."[75]

Laurette dedicated the book to Hartley: "Dedicated to J. Hartley Manners and all other fine writers with apologies for stepping heavily into their country that they have made so beautiful." The book is funny and cheerful. For example, Laurette discusses the train leaving Pennsylvania Station on May 13, 1918: "We all have cute, little, uncomfortable rooms, so we have to look each other in the face only when the impulse moves us. For the

Laurette as a Red Cross worker in *Out There* (1917).

married ones there is no escape. You sit opposite each other and gaze and gaze until the sight becomes blurred with the eternal nearness of 'the beloved face.' However, I drew a nice one, and I like to look!"[76]

Laurette claimed she couldn't write. "Hartley does the family writing. I'd hate to have him go on the stage and get famous as an actor, now wouldn't I? So I ought to keep out of his game.... Now I don't know the first thing about punctuation. When in the course of human events the time seems to have arrived for a mark of some kind, I put in a dash and go dashing on to the end. I'd hate to have somebody else forcing commas and semicolons on me. They might change the whole color scheme!"[77]

Laurette liked to tell the story about how she found a pile of *The Greatest of These*—sitting around a bookstore. She feigned outrage to the clerk. "'Why will these actresses write books?' I asked the girl. 'Haven't they enough to do on the stage?' Evidently, she thought so, for she answered: 'Yes, and it's only ninety pages.'"[78]

Hartley's play *Out There* was also published as a book in 1918. The *New York Times* reviewer, however, did not like it. "The play is rhetoric and characterization pure and simple, with no development or plot. It may go fairly on Broadway — in fact, it did — but as a book it lacks all the qualities that make for interest and permanence."[79] Walter Prichard Eaton also slammed it as a literary work. "[I]t is formless and unprogressive, a combination of amusing character sketches, interesting little individual scenes, and a rather crude appeal to 'patriotism,' about which it really says nothing. It belongs to the large mass of 'war books' which have come in on the tide, and will go out on the ebb."[80] *The Independent's* critic disagreed. "Those who have seen Miss Taylor will doubly enjoy reading the play; others, less fortunate, will find it one of the worth while war stories."[81] Read today, it comes across as a strident message play that relies heavily on dialect, which doesn't make for smooth reading. Laurette's character is yet again good-hearted if simple. Her goal is to help in the war effort and make everyone else see the importance of volunteering. The character on the page is one-dimensional and uninteresting.

For her next play, Laurette shrewdly decided to go with the tried and true. Though she was now 33, she would again play a teenager in *Happiness*. "In a season in which it is necessary to produce a big hit to get even a fair success it seemed wise to play the piece that appeared to have the greatest popular appeal'.... Briefly and bluntly, the reason why Laurette Taylor is now acting in *Happiness* is because she and her husband figured that *Happiness* was the kind of play that people would like. Miss Taylor, as is now more or less generally known, is ambitious."[82]

At the same time, Laurette didn't want her new role in *Happiness* to be too successful. "[T]he bugaboo of Laurette Taylor's life is the fear that she will have another play so successful that she will have to play in it three or four seasons."[83]

*Happiness* had originally been a one-act play. During *Peg's* long run, Laurette appeared in several matinees in March 1914 that featured the one-act version of *Happiness*, along with two other one-act plays from Manners—*Just as Well* and *The Day of Dupes*.[84] *Just as Well* featured Laurette as Doleen Sweetmarch, an immature, childlike young woman on the verge of marriage to Captain Trawbridge. It's a cute play that features clever lines tossed back and forth with the equally immature Trawbridge. The couple, who are on the verge of calling off their marriage when the play begins, ultimately realize that they might just as well get married when their new sweethearts turn out not to be what they'd thought. *The Day of Dupes*, described as an allegory, featured characters named The Artist, The Politician, The Financier, The Litterateur, and The Attendant. Laurette played The Dupe. I'm being kind when I say it never comes together.

Burns Mantle suggested that Laurette did the three one-act plays to get away from Peg. "Clara Morris used to say that there came [a time] during the run of every popular success when, no matter how much money it was drawing or how much was being written in praise of it, the star loathed the thought of going night after night to the same theater, standing in the same spot, listening for the same cues, and repeating after the author the same old lines." In any event, Mantle heaped praise on Laurette while slighting Hartley. "To any one who has not seen Miss Taylor in one of her middle class studies it is quite impossible to describe the art with which she plays them. There is no suggestion of maudlin sentimentality, even though one is inclined to believe Mr. Manners intended there should be when he wrote the lines. In fact, the suggestion is very strong that Miss Taylor writes her own speeches in this family arrangement of playwright and star."[85]

*Life* magazine got a bit cynical about the whole thing. "Miss Laurette Taylor and Mr. Hartley Manners got tired of the monotony of success connected with the clever combination of their powers as author and interpreter shown in *Peg o' My Heart*."[86] While agreeing that the three short playlets "certainly show the versatility of both writer and artist," the critic concluded the matinee provided uneven entertainment. Not surprisingly, the *New York Times* critic preferred Laurette in *Happiness*, which was the most like Peg. Indeed, the character was a naïve, simple, and kind-hearted young woman who knew happiness was simply "looking forward." The critic wrote, "[W]hile there is in the bill of plays arranged for her sufficient contrast to display a considerable range of ability, it must be chronicled that she is most conspicuously successful and captivating in the part most reminiscent of Peg. This is the role of Shabby Jenny in *Happiness*, the staunch, tired little girl from the dressmaker's shop."[87]

*Happiness* had the best potential to become a full-length play — *Just As Well* had nowhere to go once it ended, and *The Day of Dupes* was simply awful — so Hartley set to work developing the first of these. *Happiness*, now a full-length play, opened on December 31, 1917, at the Criterion. Expectations were high. The *New York Times* critic, of course, found it reminiscent of *Peg*. "The qualities of heart and humor which shrined our red-headed Peg of old in the hearts of so many were in evidence again. And [we] once more marveled at Miss Taylor's skill, her supple and searching virtuosity. As far as all that went — and, really, that is very far — the occasion was one of exquisite perfection."[88]

Percy Hammond liked Laurette and the play. "It has been the fashion in some quarters, among which this has been one, to decry Miss Taylor's lack of conscience in her playing. But in *Happiness* her honesty is seldom to be impugned, and the quaint, lovable, humorous attributes of the heroine are set forth with a minimum of tricks and a maximum of charm....*Happiness* is more than a good show; it is intelligent and adult as well."[89]

Not every critic loved *Happiness*. Hartley, who was apparently a tad thin-skinned, decided to answer his critics in a long — and long-winded — essay published in the *New York Times*. Titled "The Freedom of the Dramatist: A Defense and a Plea," it explained, among other things, why he'd chosen to divide *Happiness* into what he called "phases," rather than acts. He does go on, but his conclusion is the most interesting part of the piece. "In conclusion, I would be more than churlish if I did not pay a wholehearted tribute to the creator of both Annie and Jenny, the artiste who put blood and spirit and imagination into both, who made of one the soul of patriotism, of the other the inspirer to effort — Laurette Taylor."[90]

Lynn Fontanne was also in *Happiness*. Her association with Laurette had resulted in a booming career. As she had with Hartley, Laurette and Fontanne became, in a sense, collaborators. "Laurette wasn't at all jealous of her protégée's success. She enjoyed it. She made her take every curtain call she could get. Laurette could be cruel and malicious in her personal relations with Lynn, but artistically she was sure of herself. Lynn found her amusing and lovable, sometimes, even in their private lives, but usually she was 'maddening.' On stage, however, Laurette was a dedicated artist. She showed Lynn how to relax on a stage, how never to be afraid if one forgot one's lines — one could simply improvise dialogue as long as one felt the character and was relaxed. 'We would often ad lib whole scenes during rehearsal,' Lynn says, 'and sometimes our lines were so good that Hartley Manners would make notes on what we said and put the speeches, word for word, in the script. This is true especially of *Out There* and *Happiness*.' Laurette wrote: 'While acting with Lynn I forgot we were actresses. We lost our identities completely and became the people of the play.'"[91]

According to Jared Brown, "The two of them spent as much time together outside the theatre as they spent within it. They shopped together, ate together, joked together, shared secrets, spoke to one another in Cockney accents and flirted with the same men, later to compare notes on them. In many ways they behaved like adolescents, giggling and gossiping."[92] Brown admitted that Fontanne imitated Laurette, at least at the beginning of her career. "Taylor's acting style ... influenced Lynn enormously. Her timing and the unique way she paced her words within a speech were picked up by Fontanne; for several years the similarity in approach was obvious to anyone familiar with their performances." Ultimately, of course, Fontanne came to realize that she needed to develop her own style and she stopped imitating Taylor's mannerisms and speech.[93]

Alcohol was already creating problems for Laurette and Hartley. According to Maurice Zolotow, Laurette told Fontanne that Hartley was drinking too much. "She [Laurette] didn't, at first, drink seriously. She hated alcohol, the more so because her husband was drinking heavily now. She confided to Lynn that whisky was his 'liquid bride.' During the tour of *Happiness*, Lynn and Laurette were at a Philadelphia country club. Lynn was dancing with one of the local gentry. Laurette imagined Lynn was flirting with 'her man,' although Lynn did not know Laurette had a crush on the gentleman. Laurette turned on Lynn. She accused her of making a play for him."[94]

Despite personal and professional problems, by 1918, Laurette was an internationally known star. The *New York Times* recapped her career in an interesting article. "The present eminence of Laurette Taylor in the theatre has thrown so far into the perspective the days of her early struggles that the circumstances which attended her rise from obscurity rarely are inquired into. Thus it is known only in the most hazy way, if at all, that Miss Taylor is the proprietor of a melodramatic past which included tours of Joseph Santley in that actor's ten-twenty-thirty days in a Seattle stock company as Topsy in *Uncle Tom's Cabin*, and as the heroines of *Camille*, *Tosca*, *Ten Nights in a Bar Room*, and *East Lynne*."[95]

Laurette was more than an established Broadway star. She was an institution. "With the closing of her second consecutive season in New York last night, Laurette Taylor completed a record which is probably without precedent in the history of the theatre. Within the last five years she has played nearly four entire seasons in New York City and one solid year in London.... Within the five years and a half she has appeared in this city in five long plays by J. Hartley Manners, in scenes from three Shakespearean plays, and in upward of a dozen one-act pieces, the last named being primarily given principally at special benefit performances. As a volunteer at benefits she probably holds all the known championships at all weights. A rough computation which she made the other night resulted in the announcement that she had appeared at eighty-seven since she first opened in *Peg o' My Heart*."[96]

By the end of 1918 Laurette was in Chicago appearing in Hartley's *Happiness*. Critics were thrilled with Laurette's performance. Percy Hammond wrote "More than a good show ... it is good beyond belief." Ashton Stevens described it as "a ravishing entertainment — the best actress in the best play of the season."[97]

By 1919 it was acknowledged that Laurette was at the top of her game. Her failures, including the Shakespeare experiment, hadn't hurt her. "Not since Maude Adams came into public view has an actress won such universal acclaim. She has succeeded in interesting the New York public in her work and her plays so successfully that she has been able to remain in the metropolis continuously for the last six years, at the head of her own company, save for one year when she played in London. In private life the wife of J. Hartley Manners, whose plays she presents exclusively, and through past achievements made financially independent, she is able to play only those characters in which she feels in sympathy."[98]

In December 1919 Taylor was performing in New York in *One Night in Rome*. Alexander Woollcott suspected the play had been written because Laurette, tiring of Peg-like parts, had asked for something more exotic, resulting in "this poor, uncertain little comedy, so anemic and so troubled at its joints." He also called it "clumsy" but pointed out, "It is apparent that Miss Taylor can act plays faster than Mr. Manners can turn them out. It must be said that her performance ... is a delight from beginning to end.... Every moment that she is before the audience, the interest is kept keen."[99] He later wrote that the play was "a scant and awkward comedy" and that Manners "has outfitted the lady this time with a garment that won't wear and which any one can see through."[100]

Another critic wrote, "The whole play is very charmingly put on. Miss Taylor keeps the foreign-born accent so perfectly that one almost thinks that she is Nazimova and not Laurette Taylor."[101] Another opined, "*One Night in Rome* ... lacks the element of plot. The characterization is clever, the lines interesting, but the missing action often makes the play talky.... Miss Taylor is, of course, excellent, her picture of an Italian woman of culture being the result of careful study."[102] *Motion Picture Classic* agreed that Laurette was

Alfred Lunt and Lynn Fontanne in *The Guardsman*. Fontanne was Laurette's protégée until they became estranged.

excellent but found the play weak. "The play itself is but a pallid melodramatic background for the big role. This, however, is so vividly written that it lifts *One Night in Rome* into the ultra-interesting class."[103]

Laurette admitted she wanted a change of pace and put in an order to Hartley. "I had played almost every other character.... Irish, Jewish, English and French. So I thought it was high time Hartley wrote a play that would give me an Italian characterization. Italians are red-blooded, they feel deeply, and their hearts as well as their brains control their thoughts and actions. So Hartley obliged me. He had had the idea for the play in mind since his first visit to Rome years ago."[104]

Laurette always did extensive preparation for her roles. "I must admit I do go through a thorough preparation for my plays, because my husband writes them for me, and I know exactly what I am going to do. I studied Italian before I played this role on the stage. Also I visited about twenty fortune tellers just to see how they handled the hands of their patrons. No, I don't believe in it at all. I think the lines in the hand are made by the things you hold in your hands and the way you use the members. Everything in my hand contradicted everything else, anyway. One fortune teller told me I was going to be shot before I was 45. Maybe she meant by the camera!"[105]

Once again, costumes were an important part of Laurette's role. "Laurette Taylor wears [a] modern variation of a Spanish cape in *One Night in Rome*— and wears it charmingly, which is a point to be thought of, for not all women can wear a cape gracefully." The article continued by saying that the cape in the play was "an emerald green with gold embroidery.... The cape is three yards long, fringed its entire length, and again across its slanted ends. Miss Taylor throws one end ... over the shoulder, the weight of the fringe holding it in place, then winds the rest of it diagonally across the back and around the waist when the other end is flung over the arm."[106]

During this time Laurette was perhaps overly involved in the romantic adventures of protégée Lynn Fontanne, now dating Alfred Lunt. Lunt and Fontanne often fought over the same issue — Lunt's overprotective mother. "After these quarrels, Lynn would seek out Laurette Taylor. Laurette understood the agonies of unrequited love. She and Lynn would talk until the middle of the night — and many times Lynn slept in a guest room of the bizarre Gothic building on Riverside Drive in which Laurette and Hartley Manners lived.... Laurette heard her out. She counseled her. She comforted her."[107] Maurice Zolotow, however, thought Laurette had an ulterior reason. "Laurette ... was jealous of Alfred's hold over Lynn, for she wanted Lynn all to herself."[108]

When Lunt and Fontanne patched up their differences, a rift occurred between Laurette and Fontanne. Jared Brown thought it was because Laurette was jealous of Fontanne's beauty and talent. In addition, Fontanne was worn out by Laurette's often manic behavior. She also tired of Laurette's sharp tongue. It wasn't unusual for Laurette to snap at her former protégée and hurl insults. Much of it, as you might suspect, was alcohol-related, but it didn't matter. It was abusive, and Fontanne wanted no part of it.

There's no question Laurette had a complex, intense relationship with Fontanne. Fontanne eventually married Lunt, though many suspected that the marriage was a cover for two homosexuals. In any event, Laurette and Fontanne drifted further apart when Fontanne's career became enmeshed with Lunt's. One of Fontanne's last performances with Laurette was in London in *One Night in Rome*. To everyone's great surprise and consternation, the opening performance turned into a riot. It was such a sensation, one newspaperman wrote, "It is difficult to see how her press agent could have possibly managed to get Laurette Taylor any more publicity than she has received for her new play."[109]

*One Night in Rome* ran until April 1920 in New York, and then Laurette and Hartley boarded the S.S. Lapland. During a performance at the Garrick Theater on Thursday, April 29, 1920, a riot was started by some hooligans. "The opening performance ... was suddenly halted in the second act after rowdies in the gallery had hooted and yelled during the first act and then had thrown articles on the stage at the opening of the second act. They claimed that the curtain had not been raised high enough to permit them to see the show."[110]

James Douglas was a critic for London's *Daily Express*. He had a slightly different version. "When I am old, bald and toothless I shall be able to sit in the cozy corner of the club lounge and tell the next generation all about the celebrated Garrick Theater riot. Be sure I shall lay on the colors thick and slab. But today I must be a drab and dreadful realist. I must tell you precisely what I saw, what I heard, and what I felt."[111] According to him, there had been hard feelings when Laurette left London during World War I while on her *Peg o' My Heart* tour. Some felt she deserted them at their time of need, though Douglas hastened to mention that Taylor had small children at home and a dying mother. He then went on to describe what happened that night. "The thing was pure Balzac and [Arnold] Bennett ready made. An orgy of thrills and hysteria! A feast of tears and comedy! The Garrick is one of those old theaters that ought to have been rebuilt 20 years ago. It was not built for the modern gods. The seats at the sides of the gallery are abominable. The upper boxes are no better, for from them you peer down at the heads of the players. Probably at least 40 gods cannot see any play. As for the gods who stand at the back, Heaven help them! They see nothing at all. But—and it is a big but—some of the gods came armed with glass stink bombs and boxes of electric snuff.... Here let me say the sale of stink bombs and electric snuff ought to be prohibited. Who were the gods that threw these missiles? There are many hypotheses—all equally absurd.... I think I know the true secret of the mystery, but I refuse to reveal it. Probably it will never be revealed. But what an orgy of thrills! Laurette ... was certainly full of pluck and fight when she faced gods. 'It's not awfully English,' she cried, and we all cheered her like mad. And it was not 'awfully English.' The whole house proved that by its thunderous acclaim."

Douglas made his way to Taylor's dressing room. "I found her lying in an armchair in the last stage of hysteria. She was pale as death under her make-up. She was shivering like an ague-stricken invalid, surrounded by Job's comforters, who were all valiantly proving that black was white. Laurette bore their loving lies as long as possible. Then her Irish blood exploded. 'Yes,' she cried. 'I understand. It is the immaculate conception of an evil deed!' One of Job's comforters was ejected, and Laurette cried, 'If they let her in again I'll go mad!' I think the climax of the tragic-comic scene was reached when the white-haired patriarch, Belasco, knelt at Laurette's feet, held her hands and soothed her. He did more good than all the rest of us. Presently Laurette ... got up and walked stoutly to the stage door, thrust her head out of the window and talked to the gallery first nighters, who were eager to pour balm upon her wounds. These were the real gods, and they put fresh life into the distraught lady." Finally, according to Douglas, they all talked the incident to death and ended up back at Laurette's rooms at the Berkeley Hotel.

Londoners were outraged by Laurette's treatment. "The British press and public joined today in severely condemning the organized hoodlumism which broke up Laurette Taylor's show *One Night in Rome* at the Garrick Theater last night. Several newspapers [took] particular pains to point out that the demonstration was not to be interpreted as 'anti–American feeling.'... Regular first night galleryites and the bulk of the people in the theater were indignant at the demonstration, which provided one of the most sensational evenings London theater goers have ever seen. It was generally agreed that the opposition did not come from regular patrons."[112]

Laurette admitted she was demoralized. "'My first thought was to take the next boat home. But I am sure the British public are still my friends. So many of them have been around to tell me so.'"

Several theories were suggested for the riot. According to one theory, Germans were to blame because they were upset with what they perceived as anti–German sentiment from stage manager C.B. Cochran. Cochran was also blamed for making a comment that praised American actresses over British ones.[113] Another theory was that individuals were trying to stoke negative feelings between the English and America. Another blamed Laurette for apparently telling a newspaper that she was glad to leave "that dreadful England" when she departed in 1917.[114]

Marguerite Courtney subscribed to the theory that Peggy O'Neill's boyfriend had started it. She'd heard this from William Brady, and the reason was petty resentment over the whole Chicago thing. "O'Neill's tough boyfriend decided to avenge the wrong and organized a gang to break up Laurette's first night."[115]

Americans were appalled at her treatment. The *Fort Wayne Journal-Gazette* wrote a scathing editorial on the incident. "Nothing more disgraceful has shamed the English stage in almost a century as the demonstration against Laurette Taylor ... by a gang of London hoodlums.... It was not only an insult to an American woman but to the American ambassador and the American people.... George Haven Putman should get these London hoodlums under better control."[116]

Despite her fears, Taylor went back on stage.[117] The *London Times* warned patrons to be on their best behavior. "[F]or the sake of the good name of the British playgoing public it is to be hoped that there will be no repetition of the disgraceful scenes of Thursday evening.... Miss Laurette Taylor is assured of an enthusiastic welcome this evening, and the temper of the regular gallery 'first-nighters' is such that anyone who creates a disturbance a second time will do so at his peril."[118] Fortunately, the reaction to her was much different. "An enthusiastic audience packed every corner of the Garrick Theater Monday night for the postponed performance of *One Night in Rome*.... At the end of the first act, when each member of the cast took a separate curtain call.... Laurette Taylor ... was greeted enthusiastically. The performance went with the utmost smoothness and there was no sign of anything but good will.... A long line of people had waited outside the theater from 1 o'clock yesterday afternoon to obtain seats."[119]

According to the *London Times*, the play's most dramatic moment came during Laurette's curtain call. "There had been a great welcome for Miss Laurette Taylor when she made her first appearance — one of those scenes which will long be remembered by those who saw it — and there had been tremendous enthusiasm throughout. But when the curtain fell, Miss Taylor came to the front of the stage by herself and, sitting on a couch, proceeded to chat to the audience for at least five minutes. It was a speech which sparkled with good points. She told us of her fears, her aspirations, her amazement at the discovery that after all there was somebody in the world who did not love her and her haunting dread over the week-end that she might develop into an 'international incident.' She thanked us for our great anxiety that the performance should not be disturbed by a single sound, so that, to use her own words, if anybody laughed he was immediately silenced and if anybody applauded the rest of the audience looked round to see if he had a bomb. In a few serious sentences she expressed her regret that anybody should have ever doubted her great loyalty to England and to America, and declared that a country which had produced such charming actresses as the Terrys, the Vanbrughs, and Miss Marie Lohr need never fear the competition of another nation. She told of a madman who apparently wanted nothing from her, but had sent her a threatening letter, remarking that she would rather receive such communications from a sane man who wanted something than a madman who wanted nothing. She explained why she had discarded *Peg o' My Heart* and how she wished when she was 50 to play the part of a woman of 50. When she was 60 her roles should be those of women of 60, and when she was a hundred—but at this point someone lowered the curtain."[120] Once again, Laurette charmed everyone.

The *London Times* critic, however, was not so enamored of the play. Convinced that the playwright intentionally wrote a character who was the opposite of Peg, the critic blamed Hartley for the play's failure. "It is not Miss

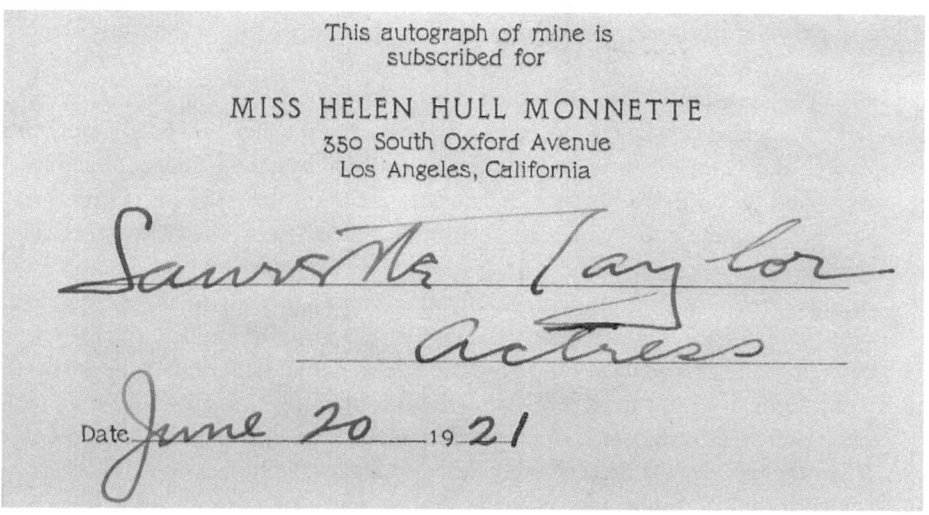

Orra Eugene Monnette wanted to build an autograph collection for his three-year-old daughter Helen Hull Monnette. He wrote to various celebrities and asked them to sign the card, indicate their profession, date it, and mail it back. This is what his daughter received from Laurette in June 1921.

Laurette Taylor's fault if the part is not unduly convincing. A more complete contrast to *Peg* until the last few moments, it would be impossible to imagine. Miss Taylor played some very difficult scenes, particularly that in which she carried on an animated conversation in Italian, with considerable skill, but so much of the play is pitched in one key that the effect is monotonous."[121]

The play did moderately well for the rest of the tour and ran for 104 performances. "[T]hat new play that was 'boo-ed' when Miss Laurette Taylor appeared first before a British audience a few weeks ago, much to her discomfiture, was only a temporary frost. Later in the same week it was received with enthusiasm and has ever since been playing to capacity houses."[122]

Later that summer Laurette appeared in a charity performance of *Peg o' My Heart*. Unfortunately, it didn't sell out, and the *London Times* scolded its readers. "It is to be hoped that the theatre-going public, who, after all, owe a great deal to actors and actors for their untiring efforts for charity during the war, will rally to Miss Laurette Taylor's support better than they did at the Garrick Theatre yesterday afternoon. Miss Taylor, anxious to show her appreciation of the kindness which she had received at the hands of the public after a certain regrettable incident, decided to give three special performances of *Peg o' My Heart* and to devote the proceeds to three highly deserving causes — the Actors' Benevolent Fund, the Rehearsal Club, and the Actors' Orphanage. One expected to find the Garrick packed to the doors for the first performance. There was a large audience, but it was not large enough."[123]

The newspaper also explained Laurette's charm and the popularity of *Peg*. "Mr. Hartley Manners may continue to write comedies, and Miss Laurette Taylor may continue to appear in them, but it will be a long time before 'Peg' is robbed of her pride of place. It is nearly six years since she burst upon us for the first time and was hailed with unbounded joy by the critics because she was something entirely and utterly new. The part itself, the child of nature dumped down in an impossible family amid impossible surroundings, was as old as the hills; it was Miss Laurette Taylor who was new and full of that *joie de vivre* which a real artist can communicate to her audiences. Peg did something to relieve the anxieties of the first winter of war, and it is interesting to see how she fares in the new surroundings of peace. One of the charms of Miss Taylor's performance was the little tricks and mannerisms with which she endowed it. A few have been forgotten, but most of them are still here, to the great joy of the audience. *Peg o' My Heart* was described ... as a 'comedy of youth.' All of us have aged a little since those days, even 'Peg' herself, but it is really remarkable how kindly time has treated her. She is a little more austere, and she does not romp quite so much, but she is still the same delightful Irish-American girl who has already charmed London on more than a thousand occasions."[124]

In January 1921, after Laurette and Hartley returned, Laurette was in Chicago, where she was appearing in *Smiling Through*. Rumors were swirling that she'd revisit *Peg* on stage. Eight years had passed since she'd last played the Irish lass in America.[125] In that time, she and Hartley hadn't had a play come close to *Peg's* success. Sure enough, the following month Laurette appeared in a successful revival at the Cort. She was now almost 37. "Just as Joe Jefferson never could play anything but Rip, and just as Frank Bacon will always have to play Lightnin,' so Laurette Taylor has been sentenced for life to Peg.... During the previous run it created a fad for Irish terriers, gave birth to a jazzy popular number and resulted in 9,000,000 innocent babies getting named Peg. Heavens knows what it may do this time!"[126]

Alexander Woollcott reviewed the revival and claimed Laurette hadn't missed a beat. He urged playgoers to see the play in order to experience "one of the finest characterizations in comedy which has graced the American stage in our time." Although he took an unfortunate whack at Michael, "who has become sadly bloated since that night in 1912 when, slim and frisky, she made her first appearance on any stage," he found age hadn't touched Laurette. "To one seeing the play again after seven years it seems as though that role had somehow mellowed and sweetened with the years, and as though a hundred and one new touches of warmth and laughter had been added to it. One fancies Miss Taylor forever and forever recreating it, but perhaps this is just an illusion wrought by her skillful suggestion of always seeming to be playing the part for the first time in her wide-eyed and gratified existence."[127] *The Independent* also made an unkind comment about Michael while praising Laurette. "Laurette Taylor is as refreshing as ever as the saucy Peg, but Michael has changed from a thin, eager dog to a fat, dignified one."[128]

Robert Benchley made the point that revivals often fail because they seem stale after numerous imitations spring up. This was not the case with this revival. "The difference is, of course, that none of the imitating playwrights have had Laurette Taylor to play their Pegs for them. And that is all the difference in the world."[129] Later he again congratulated Laurette on a part well played but ripped the play a bit. "It is [a part] she has played more than a thousand times but she possesses the secret of never letting a part grow stale, the art of making every night a premiere. It is quite true that the buoyant Peg seems particularly fascinating because the rest of the stage is peopled with little wooden figures, which the author probably filched from a Noah's Ark in some unguarded nursery."[130]

Despite Peg's success, Laurette's well-earned temper got a workout during a Boys' Club benefit that March. The idea had been a good one. Gather together Broadway's biggest stars and have them perform a skit. It was a disaster. "Since last Sunday night, a large number of the [notables] of art and such have 'had a mad.'.... Everything went wrong and everybody went home not speaking to anybody else." The actors included Charles Coburn, Frank Bacon, Holbrook Blinn, Laurette, and others. "It was certainly a whale of a piece when they rehearsed it, but when it came to the house performance they forgot their 'pieces.' Like the Friday afternoon speaking at a district school they stood in a row and glared at each other.... Laurette Taylor gave them a glance of terrible disdain and went back stage and sat down. The act dribbled to a miserable close and they all went home mad."[131]

The next play Hartley wrote for Laurette was *The National Anthem*. This play didn't hit the right note with audiences or critics. It opened on January 23, 1922, at the Henry Miller Theater and was lucky to run for three months. "[T]he customers did not care for it and it languished pitiably and died of its mysterious anemia."[132] According to one writer, "[T]he title misled everyone who had failed to read the advance notices, because they expected flags and sentiment and patriotism, and instead they found themselves and their generation assailed for its dominating spirit of jazz." The critic complained that Hartley "scold[ed] us a bit" but found Laurette "charming and splendid."[133]

According to Laurette, the inspiration for the play came one night when she and Hartley were at a restaurant and observed a young girl having a telephone conversation. The news the girl shared with her friend was sad. She was broke and would soon be homeless. However, while telling her story, "the girl's feet were in motion, keeping time to the music. The contrast between her words and the gay rhythm produced the effect of intense drama." Laurette added, "Hartley wrote that play because the drink-and-dance madness all around us got on his nerves."[134]

For Laurette's role in *The National Anthem*, Hartley suggested that she become more subtle. "From the moment I came on, I became Marian, a girl carefully brought up — though without severity. No matter how strong my feeling I could not let myself go as I did in *Peg*. When I first played the drunken scene in *The National Anthem*, Hartley said, 'You reel too much.' 'That's the way I feel it.' 'Yes, but you must never lose control of your feelings.' So I forced myself to play it more quietly, to suggest the effect of drink by subtlety. And the scene really gained in depth and power."[135]

Helen Hayes was at the opening, thrilled that Ethel Frankau of Bergdorf Goodman had been put in charge of Laurette's wardrobe. "'Thank goodness, Ethel, she's in good hands at last,' I said. The designer leaned forward discreetly. 'What a time we had with her. But it all worked out just fine. Just wait,' she cooed. When Laurette walked out on the stage in a strange dress of gold cloth, Ethel's voice cut thru the loud applause. 'My God,' she moaned, 'she's got the damned thing on backwards!'"[136]

Alexander Woollcott found the play a diatribe but also thought it "a good play, vigorous, direct, dramatic and interesting all the way through."[137] As for Laurette, he wrote that hers was "a superb performance by a great actress." He singled out several scenes in which she particularly excelled. "You see her at last on a night in Paris when her eyes won't see for her and her lips won't talk for her, and when her nerves seem strung on a thousand little hot wires ... while her mind looks on in sober panic upon the dismal, dreary wreckage of her health and her happiness. That whole scene of tipsy despondency and the terror that follows her swallowing of the poison is brilliantly played by Miss Taylor. And yet there are quieter moments in the play, such as the radiant little interlude between her and Mr. Thomas in the second act, when she reaches out still nearer to perfection."

Robert Benchley wrote that it was "all right for a tract ... but it makes a pretty artificial play.... Needless to say, Miss Laurette Taylor helps a great deal by her vivid acting to take her husband's play out of the church-vestry and place it in the theatre."[138]

A couple weeks later Woollcott again sang Laurette's praises. "To miss it is to miss ... a chance to see a superb actress at the height of her powers. Laurette Taylor's present performance is that of a woman of perfected art, true insight and genuine creative genius. We surrendered to her long ago, so this is a mere re-capitulation."[139]

*The National Anthem* was anti-modern, anti-jazz, and anti-alcohol. It was a 'these darn kids today' play. "Mr. Manners believes that jazz is ruining the race; and writes his play to prove it.... What the play really establishes is that a woman should not marry a man to reform him. Even the most casual theatregoer has had that proved to him; but *The National Anthem* does it in a different way, a most adroit and novel way."[140]

Laurette admitted she too was anti-jazz and came off sounding a bit like a fuddy-duddy. "You may remember ... my line in *The National Anthem*. I say, 'I'm sick of seeing young people dance around as though they can't help it. It's not dancing but a series of collisions.' Now, I do really think this jazz is a menace to the country. From the point of view of health, it is poisonous, nerve-wracking, shattering, the din and clatter, the tomtom music—no rhythm, no melody—just sex and bedlam! And the young men! My word! As one of them is made to say in the play, 'If you don't drink, I don't see what you do with yourself.'... Please don't think I am taking a high moral tone about this thing.... I love to dance ... in fact, if it were not for my job I think I should

**King Vidor and Laurette Taylor (1924) (photograph courtesy of Mary Pearsall).**

abandon myself to pleasure.... I suspect that Hartley wrote this play to get even with me. He doesn't dance, you see, and last summer I left him stranded and solitary so often at parties that he revenged himself in true husband fashion by writing this counterblast against jazz. And it worked! I'm cured!"[141]

Hartley also defended his play's theme. "I merely tried to represent life....

Prohibition has done much to create the idea among persons between 15 and 30 that to carry a flask in the hip pocket is heroic. The intellectual life of the young people is at a temporary standstill."[142]

He wasn't alone in blaming jazz for the ills of America. In fact, Irving Berlin was one of the few who insisted it had value. "Jazz, he said, is the music of America, still imperfect but going through a refining process."[143]

Perhaps the most interesting thing about the play was its hypocrisy. Laurette and Hartley were both alcoholics. Ellen Margolis claimed that the character Madeline, an actress who doesn't drink, may have been based on Lynn Fontanne. "Statements like Madeline's on the importance of rest and the damaging effects of drinking for actors have been attributed to Fontanne, and descriptions of Fontanne's maintaining her cool self-possession while those around her grew frenzied and faded are remarkably similar to other characters' observations of Madeline."[144]

Upon reading the play today, it offers a harrowing look at how alcoholism can ruin lives. Marian Hale marries her boyfriend, Arthur, despite protests from Arthur's own father. He tells Marian his son is an alcoholic loser who'll never amount to anything and ruin her life. He's right, and Marian's descent into an alcoholic hell with Arthur is compelling, dramatic, and realistic.

Laurette found the role taxing. On the verge of a nervous breakdown, and now under a doctor's care, she asked that the play be closed. *The National Anthem* was later adapted into a silent movie. Hartley explained with a touch of bitterness in late 1924 why he allowed the film to be made without Laurette. "We could not possibly have made *The National Anthem* as a picture until next spring, and as the number of anti-jazz films seems endless (*The National Anthem* was the first play on the subject and no pictures had been made then on my theme), we decided to accept a very generous offer from the First National to make it with Corinne Griffith. They have agreed to use the title, keep the spirit of the play, and to do everything possible to reproduce the effect I aimed at in writing it. Their attitude is in marked contrast to some producers, who destroy every semblance to an original play, change the title and story and give the public a botch. The First National people seem inspired by a feeling of courtesy to the creator and his play."[145]

As you can see, Hartley became bitter about his Hollywood experience. Following the failure of *The National Anthem*, though, he and Laurette were looking forward to this new opportunity. Laurette was supposed to report to Hollywood in July 1922 to begin work on the film version of *Peg o' My Heart*, but doctor's orders required a rest for her after *The National Anthem* closed.

## Chapter 6

# LAURETTE IN HOLLYWOOD

*"To his great credit, King Vidor was not willing to be directed by Laurette Taylor."*[1]

Laurette knew. She shrewdly viewed motion pictures as the surest road to immortality. "'I make pictures because they give me a perpetual record of my plays. *'Peg o' My Heart,' 'Happiness'* ... they will not fade away in the *potpourri* of the memoried mind ... not now. They will live on. They have the splendid chance of immortality. *And so have I* [italics in the original]. It is one thing, and a great thing, to have one's name immortalized. But it is even greater, is it not, to have one's visual self, all one's gestures, all of one's actual dramatic achievements there before one's eyes when one grows very old and also before the eyes of succeeding generations, assuming that they will care to look."[2]

She echoed this in a different interview. "The films appeal to me because they are permanent. What would the world give today to see Duse in her youth or Bernhardt at the height of her power on the screen? The picture I made of *Peg* will be treasured as long as I live, and by my children's children long after I'm gone, I hope. That's vanity, but I'm human, and I believe that the same feeling may inspire the preference of many actresses for the screen."[3]

Laurette correctly pointed out that Enrico Caruso's fame was partially due to the phonograph. "It is an indubitable fact that Caruso's name would never die. But thanks to the phonograph, Caruso's voice will never die either. And the screen does for dramatic work much what the recording machines do for the human voice."[4]

Laurette hadn't always felt this way. Screenwriter Frances Marion recalled the disdain stage performers had for those who worked in flickers. According to her, Laurette once said, "'I shall never be lured into it, though they have trapped Madame [Sarah] Bernhardt, Lillie Langtry, and Minnie Maddern Fiske.'"[5]

Early on, Laurette viewed movies unfavorably, mainly because they were silent. As a stage actress, she viewed this as a disastrous disadvantage. In 1916 she said, "Well, you may be able to give realism on the screen ... but thank goodness you can't give us our voices."[6]

It wasn't surprising that Hollywood would come calling after Laurette's phenomenal stage success. However, by the time they called, Laurette was in her 30s — while the character of Peg eternally remained 18. Still, Hollywood wanted Peg and Laurette. Early on, Laurette was asked what it would take to get her to Hollywood. "One million dollars" was her flippant reply. When Goldwyn assistant Roi Cooper Megrue called back a few days later to start negotiations, she backed off.

In 1918 it looked like Hollywood might finally get Laurette to sign. According to the *New York Times*, Laurette "admitted ... that the prospect of earning a huge sum of money easily was not entirely unalluring."[7] She was probably worried about competitors too. Mary Pickford[8] was interested in the role and had, reportedly, "made an offer considerably in excess of the highest amount ever paid for the picture rights to a play or a story." In fact, some producers tried to persuade Laurette that it'd be a mistake to appear in the film version. "The head of one prominent company, who is particularly desirous of securing Miss Taylor's services, has pointed out to the actress that it would be commercially unwise for her to appear in *Peg*, inasmuch as Miss Taylor alone would be certain of a great following, and *Peg o' My Heart*, with almost anyone in the leading role, also would be popular." Laurette likely made a face when told this. "Her own idea is to make one picture and one only — *Peg o' My Heart*— and then eschew the celluloid forever."[9]

An earlier film had been produced in 1919. Famous Players–Lasky hired William de Mille to direct, and Wanda Hawley and Thomas Meighan were the leads.[10] However, the picture was never released. This was one legal battle with Morosco that Hartley won. According to Laurette, "It was claimed that I was jealous because I was not asked to play Peg. As a matter of fact, I was asked. But that wasn't the point at all. Whatever rights the Lasky company may have thought they had, they did not have picture rights for the play given them or sold them by Mr. Manners. It was his play, and he held the picture rights. They went ahead without dealing with him, paying no attention to his protests. Then his fighting spirit was up, and he got an injunction against the picture ever being shown. He had to take it to the Supreme Court — but he did, and we won out."[11]

In June 1922 a newspaper explained more about the controversy. "The securing of the picture rights by Metro from J. Hartley Manners ends a bitter battle by motion picture producers for the famous play. Several years ago Famous Players produced *Peg o' My Heart* with Wanda Hawley[12] in the title role. It was never released, however, because of litigation between Oliver

Morosco and Manners over the screen rights in which Mr. Manners was victorious in court."[13] Hartley was reportedly offered $125,000 if he allowed the Hawley film to be released, but he refused.[14] Certainly it made no sense to have the picture released when Laurette would star in her own version.

In 1922 it was finally announced that Laurette would make a film. "Laurette Taylor is ... to become a film actress, long enough at least to appear in *Peg o' My Heart*. For a number of years the various film companies have been offering her huge sums, and last summer she almost went abroad to do Peg for an English company, but the scheme fell to pieces. But now the play has been purchased and Miss Taylor will go to the coast to begin work in July. It is said the actress films even better than she stages."[15]

Probably due to her advancing age as well as insecurities about a new medium, Laurette had a push-pull relationship with Hollywood. She played a teasing kind of game with producers. "Please believe me, it was not at my suggestion that I came out here to do Peg. And if the character was just that of a sweet pretty little girl, I would say, 'No, let some sweet, pretty little ingénue do it. But Peg isn't that sort. She's a little gamin, who doesn't depend on her looks to get by. That's why I knew I could her — just this once more."[16]

When Laurette went west to make her first film there was a big debate about whether stage actresses should do film work. For example, Jane Cowl was dead-set against it for several reasons. "Players who pursue art through the films never catch up with it. The screen shows only their shadows, while the stage retains their substance. The screen is to stage what the stage is to life. If the stage is a reflection of life, the screen is merely the photograph of that reflection. The screen is silent, colorless, with two dimensions, length and breadth. Depth, which the screen lacks is perhaps the most important dimension of all. This incompleteness pervades the whole film field. The human voice is half of acting and the photoplay silences it.... Then too, a finished photoplay is permanently fixed. Every presentation is an exact duplicate of every other. A motion picture cannot be developed to its highest artistry under the strong light of public opinion, as stage drama is developed to perfection.... Screen technique is largely expressive emotionalism, and easy for an actress of experience to acquire. Do screen actresses succeed as readily on the stage? No. Four-fifths of a motion picture is contributed by the director. Screen stars have been developed frequently from nothing by directors, a condition almost impossible on the stage."[17]

Still, Laurette and Hartley made the decision to make a film version of *Peg*. In part, Laurette hoped it'd be the end of Peg for her. She told at least one interviewer that she was sick to death of Peg. "*I'll kill her....* I've got to kill her — or she'll kill me!"[18] She added that the film was meant "to be Peg's epitaph!" Adding a note of insecurity, she concluded, "All I hope is that you won't be disappointed in her epitaph."[19]

When Laurette finally traveled to California in early August 1922, Hartley accompanied her. His role, according to newspapers, was to help with Mary O'Hara's adaptation. "'No one will ever know of the thrilling sensation I had when we stepped from the train yesterday,' declared Miss Taylor soon after her arrival. 'This is our home, and it has been ten years since I have been back. How wonderful it will be to see all my friends and visit all our familiar haunts again.'"[20] The plan was for Laurette to stay in California at least two months, "and possibly longer, in case she decides to do another picture." Still, Laurette was expected back in New York in the fall for a stage version of *Humoresque*.

Much was made of Laurette's trip to Hollywood. Newspapers reported on her progress as Metro announced that "*Peg o' My Heart* as a motion picture will equal and in many cases surpass the long run records the stage play has set in the great cities of the world."[21] Reportedly, by this time, Laurette had appeared as Peg on stage a total of 1,127 times (the play had been produced an astounding 14,925 times).

Laurette announced she was disappointed in Hollywood upon her arrival. "It isn't a bit as I expected it would be,' she confessed one day soon after her arrival. I suppose it was silly of me, but I actually visualized a community where the streets would be filled with famous stars. I was terribly disappointed when I drove from the railroad station the first day and never even caught a glimpse of Rudolph Valentino, Bert Lytell or any of the other famous motion picture stars. I felt like criticizing the driver for not taking us over the proper street. Then on the first evening after my arrival I dressed up and after dinner drove from Beverly Hills all through Hollywood expecting to see throngs of people and plenty of excitement. However, I was disappointed again for all I could see was a sleeping looking city street."[22] Despite her "disappointment," she quickly became friendly with Hollywood's king and queens — Mary Pickford, Douglas Fairbanks, Charlie Chaplin, and others. In fact, Laurette was such a huge star she found Hollywood stars courting *her*. "There was a great ovation for this well known actress when she arrived in Hollywood and every star has helped entertain her and introduce her into the sacred circle of cameras."[23]

Laurette often got her name in local newspapers. She and Hartley stayed at the Beverly Hills Hotel, where she was rudely awakened most mornings by an untalented young musician. "'That girl must be taking singing lessons,' J. Hartley Manners ... declared one morning. 'She must be taking poison,' said Miss Taylor."[24]

Hiram Abrams, president of United Artists, assigned Marshall Neilan to adapt the play. However, Neilan, who at one time had been Oliver Morosco's chauffeur, reportedly turned down the assignment. King Vidor, then a young director for Metro Pictures, was given the job. The studio suspected that Laurette was going to be a problem. "They picked out King Vidor to direct her. He was a Christian Science student and they thought he would have the patience. He did."[25]

Of course, Vidor had heard of the legendary stage actress. According to him, "Although I had never seen Miss Taylor, her name carried with it a certain magic to my young ears.... Her undeniable success in the theater had caused her to refuse persistently to succumb to the new medium of movies, yet I had been chosen to launch her new career when she did accept."[26]

Vidor, who also had his own small studio at the time, accepted the job because he needed the money — and also because he was looking forward to the challenge of adapting a stage play into a film. He was only 28. "This was a new adventure for me, to take an established star and a well-known play and see what I could do with it. I wanted to see if I could make it faithful to the theatre, or whether I should transform it into a motion picture. In the theatre, remember, it was all talk. In movies it was deadly if you had too many titles. Films would just not be released if they had too many titles."[27]

When Vidor read the play, he became worried. "I was shocked to find that all the action took place in a single set. I wondered how so much stage talk could be transformed into motion-picture action."[28] Vidor's worries increased when he read the adaptation. "I was next given a script which had already been prepared and it seemed terribly static and non-filmic. I finally determined to ignore this script and wait until I could meet the actress and her husband."[29]

Even then, there were concerns about adapting well-known novels or plays to the screen. *Los Angeles Times* critic Edwin Schallert wrote about *Peg*'s specific problem. "It is one of my pet contentions that a literal adaptation of a play or a novel to the screen is neither good sense nor good art. We've had many pictures, to be sure, that have attempted this, and we've had a number that have failed utterly to get over any semblance of the author's purpose. *Peg o' My Heart*, I understand, is to be among those pictures that follow closely the method of strict adaptation. It is to adhere to the form of the play, substituting, of course, action for the dialogue via the titles, when this is possible. In the instance of *Peg o' My Heart*, with Laurette Taylor playing the star role, I can see some merit in this method. The play is so well known that if the producer did not stick by the original there would be no end of criticism."[30]

Vidor's next concern was Laurette's screen test. "[W]e received a screen test of Miss Taylor made in New York by ace cameraman Billy Bitzer, head cameraman for D.W. Griffith, who had photographed *The Birth of a Nation* and *Intolerance*. I followed the studio executives into the projection room for a look. To our astonishment, the test made Miss Taylor look seventy years old. I could only think of one of Peg's opening lines in the play. 'My father says I am old enough to start thinking about my education. He wants me to go to school.' In most of the story, she was supposed to be no more than eighteen or twenty. What to do? 'Have no part of it,' was my first impulse."[31]

One of the problems with the screen test was a wig Laurette had made for the film. According to Laurette, "I wasn't intending to use my own hair.... I had a lovely wig all made to order, with blond curly hair that I thought was simply immense. But Mr. Vidor very tactfully let me have a screen test with it — and it was terrible. I had thought that red hair would photograph black. But mine doesn't; it suggests redness somehow, even on the screen. So my beautiful wig [was] discarded."[32]

Vidor was nervous about meeting Laurette. Her reputation preceded her, and he assumed the worst. "I was without experience either in directing a temperamental stage star or in transforming a well-known play to the medium of the movies. However, I had a surprise in store for me. I was met at the hotel by a charming, vivacious woman with sparkling eyes who simply oozed personality from her entire being. Her husband was equally charming, and I noticed that my nervousness and uncertainty seemed transferred to them in their cautious and fearful approach to the new medium. Laurette Taylor was then around forty-two [oops, she was 38], but I saw occasional flashes of youth and gaiety that completely overshadowed all else. I wondered if these moments, by some magic, could be sustained for the duration of a scene and thereby for the length of a whole picture. I had never seen *Peg* performed, and I wanted to hear about it from the two who had created it."[33]

Despite these diplomatic words written in Vidor's autobiography, years later he told interviewer Nancy Dowd a different story. "When I saw her ... my hopes fell. She had done quite a bit of drinking in her time, and I didn't know how she could do it."[34]

Fortunately, all three hit it off very well. "Hartley and Laurette (we were soon calling each other by our first names) alternatively read the play, and occasionally interrupted themselves to discuss laugh-provoking moments and high points. This was fun. The bugaboo of adapting a stage play to the silent screen soon began to disappear. Wherever they talked about 'outside' action, I planned to transpose this into a photographic scene. Also I discovered that for much of the dialogue, pantomime could be substituted. The better the technique of the director, the fewer the subtitles. A few silent films were to be produced without the aid of a single subtitle, but I knew this would not be one."[35]

In his autobiography, Vidor explained that he was particularly worried about Laurette's age. "In the theater her age might not be noticeable, but on the screen every line, wrinkle, and slight defect would present a major problem in lighting and photography. Fortunately, I recalled that during one of my recent pictures, no matter how dreadful the leading woman looked in any one day's rushes, the still photographs of the same day would be beautiful. Yet these photos were made with the same lighting as the motion-picture scenes. I surmised that it must be some peculiarity of the still-camera lens, a distortion that photographed the face with more flattering results."[36]

Vidor conferred with cameraman George Barnes. Cinematographer Barnes, once married to Joan Blondell, eventually won an Oscar for his work on *Rebecca* in 1940. He also received nominations for a number of other films including *Sadie Thompson, Our Dancing Daughters, Spellbound,* and *Samson and Delilah.* According to Vidor, "I had the lucky remembrance that in *Love*

Percy Ames, Laurette, Helen Ferrers, and Violet Kemble-Cooper in *Peg o' My Heart* (1915).

*Never Dies* the stills had looked excellent. I thought, Why couldn't we use the lens on the eight-by-ten still camera? George Barnes, the cameraman on *Peg o' My Heart*, said we could. We had to set up the still camera lenses in front of the motion picture cameras, but there was such a long telephoto lens on the still camera that for a big close-up, Laurette Taylor was all the way across the stage. However, Barnes worked out a type of rifle lighting. He used a key light that he put sights on, just like a gun. Wherever she went, the electrician followed her with those sights."[37]

Vidor further explained how the movie magic worked. "It was at such a height that it threw a false shadow around her chin. This eliminated the wrinkles around her throat. It made her face into a round, pear-faced face. In this trick lens it was distorted just enough to make her face more round than long. The distortion wasn't supposed to be apparent, it just happened. The result was that after several days of tests, we finally accomplished a test where she looked very young and very lovely. We took the wig off, and she had beautiful hair of her own. In running the film today I noticed that her long blonde hair was just beautiful, and made all the difference in the world."[38]

Laurette never considered herself a beauty and was insecure about appearing on film. "To be called upon to live upon my face entirely when I only used my cunning before.... Never at any time having had a face that could launch even a hundred ships or lure an Anthony, the summons was a bit disconcerting. Having been on the speaking stage since childhood, I had naturally come to regard my voice as my best asset. Yet here I was offered the fabled treasure of the Indies to take my face West and leave my voice behind in New York. Learning early in life the shortcomings of my face, I had focused on my voice entirely. Imagine my dismay."[39]

In truth, Laurette wasn't conventionally attractive. "She is a pretty woman, but the top part of her eyes is sunken deeply beneath the frontal bone of her forehead, which makes a tough problem for a photographer even in the youngest and roundest of faces."[40] Playwright George Oppenheimer believed Laurette's charm made her beautiful. "'Delightful' was the word for Laurette. She was wistful, quaint, beguiling, not a beauty but so full of charm and spirit that she seemed beautiful."[41] Vincent Price described Tallulah Bankhead, Judith Anderson, and Laurette Taylor as having a "magnificent beauty that is ugly in a funny way.... They came off as being the most beautiful women in the world through an illumination of their own personality."[42]

Hartley took it upon himself to rewrite the scenario and also became "supervisor" on the film. His intense interest in the picture may have come about when he noticed the growing attraction between director and star.

According to Vidor, Laurette fell in love with him. He attributed it to her gratitude for his ability to make her look youthful. He further indicated that their affair lasted until they worked together on *Happiness*. Vidor, too, was married. He'd married Florence Arto in 1915.

Metro was then located on Romaine Street, but much of the picture was filmed outside the studio, especially around Sherwood Lake. "When we started the picture, our location was the San Fernando Valley in August with a burning California sun. On a hilltop high above a mountain-enclosed lake, we had built an Irish cottage, Peg's home before she went to live with her English cousins."[43]

In fact, the whole setup was a significant change from Laurette's stage experience, whose usual working schedule included late nights and few mornings. She had to make a major adjustment. "On the first day, I called for Laurette at her hotel to transport her to the location. I was there at 6:45 A.M. so we could start shooting at eight. In order to make up, eat, and try to relax from her nervousness and excitement, she had awakened at five. Never in her life in the theater had she been up so early."[44]

The first day of filming didn't go well. According to Vidor, "We arrived at the location a little before eight. Hartley was dressed in white buck shoes, white flannel trousers, tweed sport coat, cane, and Panama hat. An obese colored maid carried Laurette's pregnant bitch, Michael, who was to recreate the *male* role she had in the play! Our cars had to stop at the bottom of the dusty trail leading a mile up a steep mountainside to the Irish cottage. Today we would use jeeps for such ascents; in those days we simply hiked. About halfway, Hartley sat down, his white shoes and clothes darkened with dust. 'Go ahead,' he said. 'I'll join you later.' Before reaching the summit, Laurette, the maid, and Michael had also fallen by the wayside in exhaustion. With the aid of some of the huskier members of the crew, Laurette was helped to the location site. After a complete re-do of her make-up, she was ready for her inaugural scene."

Laurette immediately balked when she learned the actors had no intention of saying their actual lines out loud. "The action started at the gate before the little cottage. Peg's father was to speak the line, 'old enough to think about your education.' Instead he came forth with some gobbledygook double talk that, as far as the camera was concerned, was supposed to mean the same thing. Laurette stopped cold and said, 'The actors must speak the proper lines or I can't go on.'"

"'All right,' I said, 'speak what it says in the script, Russ. Now, Miss Taylor, start the scene but don't get out of those chalk marks by your feet. Action! Camera!'"

"'If you think I'm going to turn on my emotions whenever you say so, like a hot and cold water faucet while standing on a space allotted to me no bigger than a dollar bill, you are mad — stark, staring mad!'"

"'All right, Miss Taylor, but if you step over these chalk marks, you won't be in the camera.' I was enough of a lip reader to understand the vile epithets she snarled to herself as she began to do the scene again."[45]

In the meantime, the heat on the soundstage began to take its toll. "Barnes, to help his age-eradicating lighting, had concentrated a battery of shining tin reflectors on the small area in which Laurette was required to perform. These had the effect of increasing the summer sun a dozenfold. Now the intensified heat and the suppressed anger welled up inside our star until in desperation she shook her fists, started to cry, then conveniently fainted. We picked her up and carried her into the cottage. The property men, unaware that this lone interior would suddenly be used as a first-aid station, had been storing ducks, geese, pigs, and goats safely out of the range of the camera until called for by the director. The place, badly ventilated, stunk to high heaven. Miss Laurette Taylor, the great stage star, was deposited on the floor within inches of a crate of frightened geese. At once she opened her eyes, jumped to her feet in sudden and full recovery, and stormed out of the cottage and down the steep hill, crying, 'What an insult! Such frightful beasts! How dare they?' She was followed by J. Hartley, a disgusted maid, and Michael in all her pregnancy. After making certain that Miss Taylor was not fooling, I ordered the crew to load up and return to the studio. As yet, the first scene of *Peg o' My Heart* was not in the camera."[46]

After the first day, Vidor, to no one's surprise, began having second thoughts about this production. "On the way back to the studio, I contemplated our star's temperament, the difficulties of photography, [and] the questionable success of transferring an art form based principally on spoken lines to the plastic silence of the screen. In addition, I thought of the little problem of concealing Michael's bulging abdomen from the camera — and decided it wasn't worth it. If Laurette didn't change her mind and come back, I determined not to change mine. I'd had enough."[47]

The studio, however, had other ideas, probably because so much money had already been spent on the project. "[L]ate that afternoon, the studio bosses wisely brought us all together again over cocktails; Laurette kissed me affectionately and asked forgiveness. I apologized for the pigs, the geese, the chalk marks, and the weather and we went on to one of the happiest and most satisfying experiences of my career."[48]

Despite having never worked on a feature film, Laurette arrived in Hollywood with fixed and stubborn ideas. By the time she'd decided to make a film, she was sick to death of hearing about the mystique of motion picture acting. "What is there about the movie acting that is so sacred and so mysterious? You would think that you had to inherit or learn it in a Tibetan monastery or get it by some strange necromancy. It makes me sick."[49]

In fact, there *were* huge difference between stage and film acting. Vidor, who apparently understood the psychology of actors and women, calmly let Laurette be Laurette. And then he showed her the rushes. Laurette later explained the episode in colorful terms. "King Vidor ... was very quiet the first day. He just went ahead and made scenes. I didn't work the next day but I was at the studio in the evening to sit in the projection room with Mr. Vidor and the cameraman when the first day's film was projected on the screen. I was horrified, then sick. I was sure that creature that seemed to be throwing her arms and making faces all over the place couldn't be me. Her face was made up like a circus clown's, too. Then Mr. Vidor gently explained that there was a slight difference between presenting a story on the stage and on the screen. I learned that screen tempo wasn't as nonsensical as I had suspected. Oh, I learned a great many things."[50]

Like many who come from the stage, Laurette found it difficult to adjust to the stopping and starting on a movie set. "Where the work was most exacting was in the constant interruptions. Acting here in New York on the stage I go on for a thirty-minute stretch. I am allowed to progress step by step to a climax through logical shades and nuances of feeling. But for pictures one does three minutes of acting and then there is a wait of half an hour while cameras are brought in closer and lights are adjusted. Then the actor must begin where he left off a half hour before, striking the exact shade he was employing. I had such difficulty in adjusting myself to these interruptions that frequently I went back to the beginning of a scene and worked through the lines up to the place where the cameras started taking me, in order to make the action uniformly smooth. And the limits of space in making pictures are awkward for a speaking actor. If told to sweep queenly by the camera, I did not have the room there is upon the stage. It was like trying to dance upon a dollar bill, at first."[51]

Laurette, who had a natural curiosity about things, was intrigued by the differences between stage and screen acting. She remarked that "When an actress on the speaking stage is shouting or acting disagreement or violence, the audience hardly looks at her face. Her voice is everything. She strikes terror by the chill of her tones. She doesn't play upon the eyes, but upon the spine. But in the pictures there is only one way to impress an emotion deeply, and that is by the muscles of the face. One cannot become as violent in pictures as on the stage. To glower in rage or weep in maudlin fashion kills the picture — the face simply becomes a fixed mask. I first had to realize that restraint is the cardinal virtue of acting for the screen."[52] Truer words were never spoken.

One of the key differences between film and the stage, in Laurette's opinion, was the screen's size. "One's face is enlarged, say, six times in a close-up. Proportionately one's gestures must be graduated inversely as the picture grows larger. There isn't a tremendous lot of difference in acting by the two mediums — one might say there is just the slightest bit of difference — facial restraint. But in the process of making the picture there are many things to surprise one accustomed to speaking to gain emphasis."[53]

Laurette was diplomatic when she was asked which she considered the most important art. "Laurette ... gave the Irish answer: 'Both!'"[54] She explained that acting was acting whether it was on stage or film. "I believe a thorough actress should be effective on screen or stage. If the screen is incomplete, the stage is not yet perfect, but the art of acting might be made complete by the actress at her best in spoken and silent drama too. While I have had far more experience on the stage, I cannot agree that the stage requires greater physical effort. The waits and the rests necessitated in screen work convince me that patience is indeed a virtue.... On the stage, we can see our audience, it's true, but never ourselves. On the screen, we can see ourselves and be part of our own audience as well. An important advantage that the screen possesses is the ability of the camera to reveal one's soul. The lens strikes below the surface and reveals nuances of emotion that cannot be shown on the stage. Those who scoff that motion pictures lack depth should beware the camera or they'll find their souls exposed when [they] may least desire it! The variety of the screen appeals strongly to me, and the thrill of seeing the rushes is something like that of a first night."[55]

Laurette envisioned a career that would include both stage and film work. "Oh, yes, of course, I'm doing more pictures, but I'll never really desert the stage. I do think that a stage star can 'put across' a play while a screen star rarely can. The director must assume the great responsibility out there, and he should to obtain the harmony of effort and effect necessary on the screen, and often nearly impossible on the stage. The ideal condition would be for a stage player to be able to appear at one time in many places. That is impossible, but we may go forth in films or travel with the stage or utilize the two forms of art. The voice is the glorious thing that the stage retains, of course, making the appeal of the screen indirect and mute. Yet there is an attraction in the films that is irresistible to me when I am on the stage toward the end of a run — just as, when I am near the finish of a film, the call of the stage commands me. Is it the conflict between the personal pull of the stage and the permanent promise of the screen? Someone else will have to answer that question. How can I choose between them when my nature won't let me? My choice is: BOTH!"⁵⁶

Laurette, who enjoyed late-night activities, was forced to curtail such things in Hollywood. "One cannot dance until late at night, or sit up to talk until after midnight, when making pictures. On the stage I can go on tired and force myself through a performance. If it is not up to the standard, I can better it the next night. But the film is fixed like death itself. Once made, it stands for your work, in America, England, Japan — everywhere."⁵⁷

Laurette quickly caught on to the fact that Vidor knew much more than she did about moviemaking, "which ... was very fortunate for us all. In New York a star has pretty much her own way in the matter of direction, but out there the director is an absolute monarch. The sooner we of the speaking stage learn that the pictures are entirely different from our first method of expression the better it will be."⁵⁸ Laurette also told an interviewer, "'[T]he screen is different. There is no audience for you. You ... feel your way along but as to whether you are right or wrong is only between you and the director. You trust solely that future audiences will watch for your interpretation as you've seen it in your heart.'"⁵⁹

She explained that there was a learning curve. "'They say such funny things!' she confided. 'Hit her with the spot! Kill the baby! And 'Bring over a nigger!' Why at first I couldn't make out what they were talking about. Still, it isn't so different as I expected it would be. It's just stage acting with your belt tightened. I was scared at first, but Mr. Vidor soon put me at ease. He'd tell me what action was wanted, then he'd say, 'Show me how you would do it on the stage.' Then he'd give me suggestions as to condensing the action, and that was about all. I've lost my fear of the camera now. But at first I was conscious of it every minute. It was like a big unblinking eye, staring at me continually, and I'd catch myself looking over at it, right in the middle of a scene."⁶⁰

Vidor did everything possible to keep Laurette in a good mood on the set. "When she was in a good mood, when she was laughing or smiling, her face was up and right and round, and when she was sunk, her whole face and expression would go down. Each scene was shot by kidding and laughing and making jokes and doing all kinds of things to keep her amused."⁶¹ Vidor sometimes had to trick Laurette in order to get the look he wanted. "Another trick I employed with great effectiveness in all medium and long shots where we could not use the still-camera lens was to play some joke or prank just before each 'take' to get Laurette in a laughing mood. Then without warning we would start the camera. When she would hear the grinding of the camera, she would start acting the already rehearsed scene, but the playful and youthful expression would remain until the scene had ended."[62]

Laurette reportedly wore the same costumes in the movie version of *Peg* that she wore on stage, including shoes, hats, and dresses.[63] "Upon her arrival in New York to present *Peg* to Broadway, Miss Taylor had a complete new wardrobe made and put away for keepsakes the dresses, hats and shoes that she had worn when she made her initial bow in the famous role. When she decided to appear in the screen version of her greatest success, Miss Taylor took this wardrobe from its storage place and decided to wear it before the camera. Being her initial screen appearance, she felt more like Peg in the quaint old clothes that she had worn in the first presentation in Los Angeles. One of the dresses Miss Taylor wears in the early episodes of *Peg o' My Heart* is a blue serge which, in keeping with the character, is shabby and a very poor fit. The hat is a plain old-fashioned straw with a broad brim trimmed with a few flowers. It is kept bright by polishing with ordinary shoe polish. The other dress she wears in the early episodes of the picture is a very plain blouse and skirt of brown cotton material. The hat is a straw with a narrow tattered brim. Several of her toes protrude from the shoes. In the later episodes of *Peg o' My Heart*, Miss Taylor wears dresses of a more opulent style. She had several beautiful gowns designed in New York, which she wears for the first time in the picture. One of these is a yellow georgette made in bouffant style and trimmed with a design of the same material. It has a round neck, outlined with a lace collar and puff sleeves edged with ruffles of lace. With this [are] worn salmon slippers and stockings."[64]

Hartley announced that the motion picture would be different from the stage play — but not worse. "Both Miss Taylor and I feel that complete justice has been done *Peg* in the photo-play ... and we know that the character and the play will win even more friends wherever it is shown. We have tried to preserve the flavor of the spoken story in its new version, although it was no simple matter to accomplish the transition into a new medium.... I, for one, think that she is more completely developed in the photoplay than she was on the stage. One can see the character grow more vividly."[65]

Filming continued until mid-October. Some of the last scenes, shot in Lankershim, were used for exterior shots.

The film's premiere was at Loew's State in Los Angeles on December 18, 1922. Publicity proclaimed it the "true and painstaking reproduction in celluloid of the best-loved story of the century."[66] In general, critics were kind to the film, though the *New York Times* pointed to the flaw of film versus the stage. "It's a Peg without her voice ... and something is lost, too, in the absence of her physical presence, but it's a true Peg, nevertheless, for Miss Taylor has

A scene from the silent film *Peg o' My Heart* (1922) (photograph courtesy of Kathy Starr).

taken naturally to the studio, and by her pantomime, her vitality and variety of manner she has made Peg an actively present person despite the fact that she is silent and only a shadow."[67]

Poet Charles Hanson Towne also pointed out that something of Taylor's magic was lost on the screen. "Her lovely voice was lost to us on the screen, more's the pity — that voice so full of pathos and plaintiveness, nuances that no one may imitate."[68]

Another reviewer proclaimed her one of the great film comediennes. After noting that only Mabel Normand was in the same league with Chaplin, Harold Lloyd, and Buster Keaton, the reviewer noted, "Miss Normand ... *was* the only one. For Laurette Taylor has entered the silent drama, and good old *Peg o' My Heart* is the sturdy vehicle which has carried her through the pearly portals of that shadowy realm which is technically known as 'filmdom.'"[69]

Acknowledging that Vidor and Manners were competent in the role they played in bringing the stage play to the screen, *Life's* reviewer made it clear that Laurette was something special. "The original flavor of the piece is there, with some of the original hokum. But Laurette Taylor is the whole story. Without her *Peg o' My Heart* would be a good, average film. With her, it is a thing of beauty. By her presence, she has transformed a strip of celluloid into a fairylike ribbon of spun gold."[70]

Another reviewer proclaimed her a new star and compared her to Pola Negri, who was about as far away from Laurette's style as could be imagined. "Laurette Taylor and *Peg o' My Heart* are a combination which should prove mightily potent in any motion picture house lucky enough to secure them. To begin with, it may be asserted that the screen lost a great star when Miss Taylor decided to stick to the legitimate stage. Although with her debut as Peg her motion picture offers ought certainly to be renewed, for there are few, if any artists of the cinema, who can compare with her, with the possible exception of Pola Negri. Miss Taylor leads in intelligence, in pantomiming ability, in human understanding, in caprice and pathos, and one is driven to use again that word so much overworked by critics in just praise of this actress — magnetism. Certainly no one else in the films could have encompassed Peg.... In short, no praise is too high for this Peg o' the screen. She is an artist par excellence.... In conclusion, if any fault might be found with this picture, it would be the addenda — not used in the play, which shows the presentation of Peg at the Court of England. The elimination of this episode, which is superfluous and not as good photographically as what precedes it, will enhance the film appreciably, and it seems certain that Peg will live as long on the screen as she did on the stage. More power to her! To the field of motion picture artists many are called, but few are chosen, and to mix the literary metaphor, Miss Taylor seems likely to join the small and select group whose names ... lead all the rest."[71]

Critic Billy Leyser wrote that "Laurette Taylor scores convincingly. She possesses personality, plus ability and an abundance of talent.... There seems to be a combination of Mary Pickford and Mabel Normand in the 'make-up' of this player."[72]

*Los Angeles Times* critic Harry Carr took a swipe at Laurette's age and personality while praising her acting. "All things considered, *Peg o' My Heart* was an extraordinary performance. There were moments when Peg looked a little weary and worn: but there were other moments when she didn't look more than 15 years old. Of course, to get this effect they simply burned her up with lights until sometimes her face was like a white sheet. She was wonderful to me because she was the first comedienne I ever saw who didn't imitate either Dorothy Gish, Mabel Normand, Louise Fazenda or Mary Pickford. Her methods were absolutely individual and as much her own as her Irish eyes. As a matter of technique, Peg was delightful. She scored her effects with a touch as sure and as deft as a great painter laying in colors on a canvas. She didn't make one unnecessary or futile movement.... Personally, Laurette Taylor is not a likeable woman; but this picture shows her to be a great artiste of the most subtle and unusual power."[73]

Helen Klumph reported that she heard an audience member praise cameraman George Barnes "because he succeeded in making Laurette Taylor look so young and unwrinkled. 'If he can do that for her,' said an unidentified voice in the audience, 'just think what he could probably do for Elsie Ferguson.'" Klumph added her own review. "Personally I am as tired of Peg as though I'd played her every one of the thousand — or is it a million? — times that Miss Taylor has. And yet I rather enjoyed the film."[74]

Many reviewers hit the same theme — they fervently hoped that Miss Taylor would return to films. "*Peg o' My Heart*, Laurette Taylor's first venture into pictures, is a beautiful photoplay. More than that, the impression it gives is so pleasant one leaves the Capital Theatre with the hope that the star will not stop with this, but go right on devoting at least part of her time to the screen.... She has proved that she is as much at ease in the studio as she is before the footlights."[75]

Another reviewer noted, "It is too bad Miss Taylor did not enter the ranks of the movie stars long ago, but now that she has appeared once we feel sure that there will be a decided demand for more of her interesting performances. It only takes the one production to prove that Miss Taylor might prove a dangerous rival for Mary Pickford. At times some of her outrageous antics as the incorrigible little Peg strongly resemble some of the winning mannerisms of Miss Pickford. We can think of none but Miss Pickford who could play Peg as well as Miss Taylor. The latter by no means seems a novice in pictures. Indeed, she appears particularly at home before the camera."[76]

*Variety* gave Laurette a glowing review: "Peg on the screen isn't the full, rich racy character she was on the stage ... but still stands head and shoulders over almost any comedienne the screen has. Laurette Taylor does a unique piece of work here. New to the camera, she masters that pitiless instrument by sheer naturalness and abandon."[77]

Some reviewers were mystified how a mature woman could look so youthful. "If Laurette Taylor will pass on to the women of this day and generation the secret of how she makes herself look 16 years old.... To be in your thirties and to look 16 is no easy matter; it is either a gift or a trick; if a trick, Miss Taylor owes it to womankind to divulge it.... *Peg o' My Heart* makes a very entertaining screen play largely because of Miss Taylor's excellent acting."[78]

*Film Daily* also praised Laurette. "Both Miss Taylor, and King Vidor, who directed, have fulfilled the hopes of those who have been waiting to see

Laurette Taylor (left) and Ethel Barrymore. She told Laurette she'd be glad to come to dinner as long as she didn't have to watch *Peg o' My Heart* again (photograph courtesy of Mary Pearsall).

*Peg o' My Heart* in pictures. The star, to begin with, photographs surprisingly well and proves that she knows the art of pantomime. Her facial expressions are delightful and she can say a lot with her eyes. They are going to love that frolicking left eye wink and the pensive expression when she finds herself in love with Jerry. Miss Taylor is a real trouper and her charming characterization of Peg, her first film role, will certainly gain many admirers for her."[79]

The *Los Angeles Examiner* attributed the realistic feel to the film to the fact that both Laurette and Hartley had some familiarity with England. Furthermore, many of the actors, including Mahlon Hamilton,[80] Nigel Barrie, Lionel Belmore, D.R.O. Hatswell, and Fred Huntly, were either born in England or lived there for some time.[81] Interestingly, Hamilton was said to be chosen "because the character requires a visible English accent."[82] What does an English accent look like?

According to film historian and curator James Card, Vidor's skill was "his ability to use professional players, strip them of their standard theatrical-behavior specialties and allow them to perform with the naturalism that Vittorio De Sica achieved from his auto-worker star of *The Bicycle Thief*."[83] Not everyone agreed, however, that Laurette had been stripped of her stage 'business.' John Baxter, who wrote a book on Vidor, wasn't a fan of Laurette's film acting style. "He [Vidor] could eradicate some signs of age but not the habits of a lifetime, which made her performance a riot of scene-stealing mannerisms. Friends of the star dropped in periodically to suggest new scenes; one in which Peg looks for a flea on her dog was created by Douglas Fairbanks. Her movements are exaggerated, her performance spotted with bits of business — blowing her nose becomes a production, with the handkerchief being folded and re-folded, tucked under her belt, and fastened with a safety pin; she even picks something from her teeth before proceeding with the next scene."[84]

When Laurette was asked, after *Peg*, if she planned to appear in more pictures, she replied, "Not more than one a season ... I like to hear the sound of my own voice too well to leave the stage long. But I do like pictures. More so now that I understand the effort and the work behind them.... The stage controls the people, however, like the picture play never can. But the money there is in pictures! When I start acting here in Fannie Hurst's *Humoresque* this winter I shall feel like giving my weekly salary check to the call boy and saying: 'Here, go get yourself a glass of beer.'"[85]

*Peg o' My Heart* was always Laurette's favorite film, and she watched it dozens of times in her New York home. According to Vidor, "When the picture was finished Laurette was so delighted with her appearance and her performance that she obtained her own print of the film for frequent showings in her New York home."[86] Laurette admitted that she pulled out that film "on the slightest provocation. I have a projection room in my house in New York.... A lot of my friends are invited to dinner, and then I plunge the room in darkness and show *Peg*. They simply cannot get away.... Narcissus had nothing on me when it comes to *Peg*."[87]

Ethel Barrymore once accepted an invitation with this caveat: "Miss Barrymore accepts with pleasure if she is assured she will not have to sit through *Peg o' my Heart* again."[88] Barrymore and Laurette were friends and shared many luncheons and dinners. "Another of the happy memories is of going to Sunday night dinners with that magical Laurette Taylor and her husband, Hartley Manners, in their big house on Riverside Drive. She had made a silent picture of *Peg o' My Heart* and always after dinner they would show it to us. Some years afterward she said to me, 'Ethel, did you ever see my picture *Peg o' My Heart*?' I said, 'All one winter.' I hadn't meant to be funny, but Laurette loved it and kept repeating it."[89]

Laurette went to Hollywood partly because of restlessness. "'Beware of the rut,' cautions Laurette Taylor.' A person may imagine he's sitting on the world, as the colloquialism goes, and in reality he's moving in a groove which has nothing but futility ahead.... It is not enough to be successful. One must keep growing. I have played in 1,186 performances of *Peg o' My Heart* on the stage. But I realized in time that while this play by J. Hartley Manners could go on indefinitely and keep the public favor, I must do other things or find myself in a rut. So I appeared in other plays by Mr. Manners. I played in *Romeo and Juliet* and studied other modes of expression. This year, under the direction of King Vidor, I have portrayed Peg on the screen for the Metro company. It was a wonderfully refreshing experience. I can't remember when I had more fun."[90] Still, she was ready to return to New York and get back on stage.

Laurette and Hartley returned to New York in mid–November 1922 accompanied on the train by Laurette's friend Alla Nazimova. Rehearsals for *Humoresque* started in early December. Hartley directed his wife, but weeks of rehearsals didn't go smoothly. Cast members came and went, and though the play was supposed to open around the holidays, it didn't have its New York premiere until February 27, 1923.[91]

*Humoresque* is important because it was her first stage play since her film work. In addition, the play wasn't based on an original work by Hartley, though he did direct the Fannie Hurst adaptation. This time Laurette was playing a mother, not a teenager. In fact, her character begins the play at age 30 and then progresses to 60. Laurette had wowed *Humoresque* writer Fannie Hurst during a reading. Laurette defied conventional casting by playing a Jewish mother. She also told a reporter, "The fact of the matter is ... that I have a wonderful Jewish accent. I don't know where I got it, but I have it."[92]

In February 1923 the Lotos Club hosted a dinner for Laurette. Hartley used the occasion to blast New York theatre managers who refused to book *Humoresque*. "We have been trying out with varying success ... a new play in a number of towns. Not one of the glorified janitors calling themselves managers have offered Laurette Taylor a New York home for this play. They all insist on comfortable guarantees running several months. We are barred from New York." An equally fired up Laurette said, "No one can keep us out of New York."[93] Unfortunately, Hartley's remarks would come back to haunt him.

E.M. Kelley gave us a hint of Laurette's charisma in a story he told about a New York dinner he attended. "We attended a dinner where a great many notables did short turns. A line of well-known actors and literary people stood before us and innocent of make-up or stage craft, spoke their little pieces. It was a nice folksy sort of program, and Helen Hayes, Irene Castle, Anita Loos and Alice Duer Miller among others all contributed to the entertainment, but when Laurette Taylor spoke her first syllable, she stood among the others like a star in the poem, only she was shining as in the sky. We shall never forget how solemnly we said to ourselves 'now that is personality.'" As for *Humoresque,* Kelley liked Laurette more than the play. "[W]e find ourselves growing cold to everything excepting Miss Taylor's performance."[94]

Another reviewer remarked, "Miss Taylor holds a place unique on the American stage. Her role in *Humoresque* is not like those in which we are accustomed to see her, but she gives as usual a distinctive portrayal."[95]

The *New York Times* began its review like this: "In the first act of *Humoresque,* Laurette Taylor gave a performance of character acting, indeed of emotional acting of the finer sort, that was incomparably subtle and beautiful.... Here was a creation of great external virtuosity and of far greater spirit within. Her walk and gestures were racial in the extreme, yet always with an indefinable dignity. How it was done escaped analysis, but she positively dropped in the nose, slanted in the eyes and bowed orientally at the lips. It was a face of surpassing beauty, alight with the fires of deep maternal passion." Alas, the critic decided Laurette was the only reason to see the play. "When a production has so much to offer, what does it matter that there is no play—or, worse, a bad one?"[96]

Robert Benchley began his review of *Humoresque* with these words: "One of the best indications of Laurette Taylor's acting ability is the manner in which she emerges unscathed from bad plays." Uh-oh. "Aside from its first act, *Humoresque* is pretty nearly all paste.... And yet, out of all this mass of imitation jewelry, Miss Taylor shines forth as genuine. Not a genuine Jewess perhaps, for there is always the sparkling Irish eye of the ever-young Peg to belie the assumed dialect and the wig. But certainly a genuine actress, crying out for a genuine play."[97]

*Time* also slammed the play but raved about Laurette. "[T]he play never does get much of anywhere after the first excellent act. What saves it is that no one cares about anything but the astonishing excellence of Miss Laurette Taylor as the infinitely pathetic mother."[98]

Burns Mantle acknowledged that she would likely anger the Irish and the Jews with her portrayal. Nevertheless, he dubbed it a "fine performance."[99]

The play closed in March after only three weeks. According to the *New York Times,* "Theatrical traditions were violently shaken yesterday with the appearance of an advertisement in all New York papers announcing that 'despite the unanimous and enthusiastic praise bestowed by the press upon Laurette Taylor for her remarkable performance ... her engagement at the

Vanderbilt Theatre will end next Saturday night (March 24) owing to lack of public support.' This is the first time the failure of a popular star in a Broadway production has been openly admitted to be due to lack of box-office patronage."[100] Truly, the announcement made news because no one ever admitted that a show closed due to poor box office. According to another newspaper, "A new era of honesty in making theatrical announcements would be welcome indeed, but it is to be feared that this does not mean a permanent reform in press agent methods. It only means that Laurette Taylor is so big and successful that she can afford to tell the truth."[101]

The *New York Times* mocked Hartley for his outburst at the Lotos Club. "Despite the competition of the resounding volume of gasps that came from the theatergoing public at this unheard-of frankness, a hearty, rumbling chuckle was audible around Times Square all week. It has since been analyzed as coming from the commercial managers whom Mr. Hartley termed 'glorified janitors.'"[102]

Even if *Humoresque* was a failure, critics found Laurette's performance subtle and original. She'd learned something important when performing on film and was able to transfer it to the stage. It's quite possible that Laurette, in watching, studying, and analyzing the footage over and over in the comfort of her home, had decided to tone it down a bit. Something had changed, because critics united on the theme of her subtlety. Indeed, while Laurette was charming, funny, and delightful in *Peg o' My Heart*, no one accused her of being subtle.

Famed acting teacher Stanislavsky saw Laurette in *Humoresque* and was wowed. "The Russians of the Moscow Art Theatre did not like either *Hamlet* or *The Hairy Ape*. But after seeing Laurette Taylor in *Humoresque*, Constantin Stanislavsky, one of the two founders and directors, remarked: 'It is a marvelous adventure in realism!' So saying, he climbed up on the stage and congratulated Miss Taylor."[103]

Stanislavsky and Taylor collaborated on a benefit performance of *La Locandiera*. The plan was that she would speak English, and his Moscow Art Theatre actors would use Russian. The idea of Stanislavsky "directing" Taylor seems like the basis for a *Saturday Night Live* skit, but it actually happened. An interpreter explained to Taylor that the director wanted her to pick up a bracelet and count to five before setting it down. Later Laurette explained to Hartley that she couldn't do it. He advised her to ignore Stanislavsky's instructions and do it her way. She later told Betsy Blair what happened at the next rehearsal. "'[H]e stopped the rehearsal again at the same spot, walked down toward me, lifting his arm —'*Odin—dva—tre—cheteri—piat*.' He lowered his arm and said 'That was exactly right, Miss Taylor — one — two — three —

four—five.' I just smiled.'"[104] Unfortunately, the benefit was cancelled, and no audience ever saw Laurette Taylor "directed" by Stanislavsky. Still, Stanislavsky later told people that "in America he had seen only two actresses who knew instinctively everything he had discovered himself about acting: Pauline Lord and Laurette Taylor."[105]

A strange clipping from April 1923 suggests that not everyone was a fan of Laurette. "Among our pet aversions, and we'll wager among yours, is the Pollyanna pest, Laurette Taylor. She is another Janet Beecher, with mayonnaise dressing. Her husband, Hartley Manners, who has gained himself, currently, the undying vendetta of the Theatrical Trust, is our 1923 male Mrs. Malaprop. Hartley is the Pickwick's Fat Boy of our generation. Laurette is ... nearing the dangerous and grateful age, and should be willing to acknowledge the days when, but for the 'glorified janitors,' both she and her amiable collaborator would have taken annual reservations of a table at the Automat. Altogether, two of the most bumptious and inconsequential entities now functioning in the theatrical terrain, doomed to an all but imminent limbo reserved for parasites and renegades."[106] This was from a publication titled *Broadway Brevities*, a New York tabloid that was so mean and vicious it landed the publisher in prison. The magazine, started by Canadian Stephen G. Clow in 1916, was known for its mean-spiritedness as well as its willingness to name gay and lesbian performers. Clow was convicted in 1925 of using the tabloid as a blackmailing racket and served two years in an Atlanta prison.

Despite her foray into film and the failure of *Humoresque*, Laurette's stage reputation remained intact. Heywood Broun named four women "as the ... leading women of the American theatre"[107] in 1923. They were Mrs. Fiske, Jane Cowl, Laurette Taylor, and Ethel Barrymore.

After *Humoresque* closed, Laurette next appeared with Alfred Lunt and Lynn Fontanne in *Sweet Nell of Old Drury*. It was a benefit for the Equity Players, and all the actors worked at a reduced rate. According to Jared Brown, Laurette was allowed to choose the play. "*Sweet Nell of Old Drury*, the prototype of early-twentieth-century comic melodrama, was hardly an adventurous selection. It was full of ridiculous situations and improbable dialogue, but Taylor selected it because of its history of success and its old-fashioned hokum.... The purpose of the benefit was to make money, and in that aim the production was successful."[108]

Laurette explained in a curtain call why she chose the play. "This old play, fantastic and unreal as it may seem to present-day audiences, appealed to me as just the thing to do in the spring, because there's no doubt to which character is the hero, which the heroine, and which the villain. There's no mental strain about it; you just come and have a good time."[109]

One critic described Taylor as "twinkling and alluring."[110] *Time* found the play "sentimental, pleasant claptrap" and praised Laurette as "charming and well assisted."[111] The *New York Times* wrote, "The performance will not, of course, rank with Miss Taylor's best. She is an artist of the finer shadings of reality, a humorist of subtler strokes than are to be imposed upon [playwright] Mr. Kester's preposterous situations and slap-stick repartee.... But there can be no doubt of her success with her audience."[112]

By 1924, *Peg* was still going strong. The play had been performed, sometimes thousands of times, in the United States, Canada, Great Britain, India, Holland, Spain, Italy, Australia, New Zealand, South Africa, the Orient, South America, and Mexico. Hartley Manners' novelization had sold more than 200,000 copies, making it a best-seller. It sold more than 70,000 copies in England alone.[113]

In fact, all kinds of ideas were tossed to Laurette and Hartley on how to further exploit *Peg*. Tony Sarg wanted to do a puppet version, but this idea was turned down. One of the spin-offs that came to fruition was *Peg o' My Dreams*, a musical version of *Peg*, which opened in 1924. David Carb complained it didn't equal in any way the original *Peg*. "[T]his arrangement of the story of the red haired Irish girl cast into a group of English snobs is in no way exceptional," though he did like the dancers Lovey Lee and Albertina Vitak, "the latter the most rhythmical and graceful dancer I have ever seen in musical comedy."[114] *Time* suggested that the new version paled considerably next to Laurette's *Peg*. "[T]he whole production, coming after Miss Taylor's sunny California radiance, seems bathed in a quiet, phosphorescent glow."[115] Robert Benchley, who you'd expect not to like it, found it wasn't too bad. "On the face of it, a musical comedy made out of *Peg o' My Heart* with someone other than Laurette Taylor playing *Peg* sounds pretty dismal. As a matter of fact, *Peg o' My Dreams* ... is very satisfying indeed."[116]

The film version of *Peg o' My* Heart[117] was a box office and critical success, and Metro decided to team Laurette again with Vidor on another of Hartley's adaptations. It was announced in August 1924 that Laurette and Hartley would return to Los Angeles to work on *Happiness*. Before Laurette left, exterior scenes for *Happiness* were filmed on the East coast.

A newspaper blurb reported that Laurette felt experienced enough now to offer suggestions to her director. "At the start of the filming of *Happiness*, Miss Taylor suggested that instead of following the usual procedure of rehearsing each scene and photographing it, a whole sequence of scenes be rehearsed and then the individual scenes photographed in order without rehearsing. The plan was put into effect by King Vidor ... and it proved immediately successful."[118]

In fact, Laurette and Vidor were often at odds during the filming of *Happiness*. Still, she was a shrewd woman and had learned whom to fight and with whom to make friends. "She found out that a star can quarrel with reasonable safety with anybody in the studio except the electricians and stagehands — especially the electricians. Consequently the 'juice squad' found her a merry pal. But this time she fought it out to a finish with the director. One thing she absolutely insisted upon; that is acting a scene clear thru — just as she would on the stage. The cameras were at liberty to begin shooting any time in the proceedings that they saw fit, but Laurette began at A and ended at Izzard in every scene. She found that only so could she get the 'feel' of the scene. Having learned a lot about pictures in the meantime, she insisted this time upon having her own way in regard to the photography and the cutting. The result has been a good deal of grief and woe; but also the result has been that Laurette has made good where the other stage comedians have failed. She is herself on the screen. Nearly every other girl in pictures copies either Mabel Normand, Mary Pickford, or Dorothy Gish. Laurette Taylor has come thru with some stuff that is as individual and as much her own as her hair."[119]

Vidor was certainly diplomatic when he observed, "Not a thing occurring on the set escapes Miss Taylor.... She asks questions occasionally but not often. She has an intuition about the work that is amazing."

According to one writer who'd known Laurette years before, she looked younger. She'd changed in other ways, too. "I found her changed from what she had been when last I talked with her some three or four years ago. That time, four years ago, I had a sense of constraint with her. She bordered perilously on the verge of being what is commonly referred to as 'up-stage.' At that time, while admitting her indubitable charm, I thought: She knows that she is great and is proud of it. She has a superiority complex and hasn't learned to hide it. But now, her horizon has widened and stretched away. Limitless. And one is lonely when one stands on the edge of a far horizon. Lonely. Humble. And a little bit afraid."[120]

Not surprisingly, Taylor earned a reputation for being difficult. "They say at the studios that the fair Laurette is difficult; yes, to be frank about it, they say she is belligerent and full of fight."[121] Another writer stated "She has many warm friends in the studio and she has some who would like nothing better than to meet her with an ax in a dark alley out of hearing of the police. Which is another way of saying that she is a witty, charming, belligerent, lovable, bad-tempered artiste of the highest genius. Of her high standing on the legitimate stage there can be no possible doubt whatever; and now it seems that her screen rating will be second only to that older art."[122]

Another writer defended her. "She knows her own stuff. She has the brains to realize that if she were handled in the same way the little flappers on the screen are handled she would get nowhere. She made up her mind what she ought to do and stood up for her rights." The writer concluded, "To my mind, one of the most remarkable women of the screen is Laurette Taylor.... There isn't a flapper on the screen so exuberant with the pulse and thrill of girlhood as she was in *Peg o' My Heart*.... She is one of the greatest of all artists — a fact which has never been wholly and completely recognized."[123]

King Vidor recreated Fifth Avenue for *Happiness* when the original wouldn't do. "We are re-creating a more real Fifth Avenue and a traffic jam.... We took a few atmospheric scenes in the East, but could not work the traffic jam, through which Jennie [sometimes written as Jenny] makes her way, in her haste and impetuously climbing over the tops of the motors to the other side of the street. A mere traffic jam is no hindrance to our energetic Jennie, but in New York we could not get just the dense effect of motors that we wanted."[124]

Laurette again wore some of her own clothing for *Happiness*, just as she had in her first film. "Laurette Taylor's wardrobe in the early scenes ... consists chiefly of a cheap cotton dress and stockings and a pair of tan shoes that have done yeoman service for Miss Taylor on the stage for many years."[125]

Laurette was again cast as a teenager, which created challenges for her new cameraman, Chester Lyons. "Probably one of the most monumental film struggles in history was the creating of a 16-year-old Laurette Taylor for *Happiness*. Miss Taylor has all the poise of a woman of— well, not 16, at any rate. She has womanly curves, and womanly curves are the bane of the cameraman. Chester Lyons, who did the filming of *Happiness*, spent one-half of the time in despair of obtaining any sort of results and the rest in a state of ecstasy over the beauty of Miss Taylor's acting. As a result the picture, although not a success financially, was certainly a triumph for its cameraman."[126]

While in Hollywood to make *Happiness* for Metro Pictures in 1924, Laurette was spotted dancing at the Montmartre. She also attended Cecil B. DeMille's *Ten Commandments* with husband Manners and Charlie Chaplin. Laurette and Hartley were staying in a Beverly Hills Hotel bungalow.

During this point in her career Taylor was generating lots of publicity. Not surprisingly she offered beauty tips. "In these modern times, when women adopt every ridiculous method to preserve their beauty and youth, it is refreshing to hear the simple solution that Laurette Taylor, Metro star, has found to this problem. The charming star of *Happiness*...believes that the easiest way to 'do the trick' is to keep happy. 'If you are discontented or worrying,' says Miss Taylor, 'you will grow thin and haggard looking. If you are idle and have no ambitions you'll become fat and expressionless. But looking ahead to some

Laurette Taylor and John Gilbert (1924) (photograph courtesy of Mary Pearsall).

goal, the achievement of which is going to make you happy, will keep you alive, young and interesting to others. It's really surprising how lenient Father Time is with the happy."[127]

While making *Happiness*, Laurette enjoyed perhaps her most passionate romance. At least it was her most public affair. The romance with Vidor had faded. While *Happiness* was in production, Vidor became involved with Eleanor Boardman, who became his second wife. Through Vidor, Laurette, now 40, met 27 year old John Gilbert and began a whirlwind romance with him.

The romance's biggest complication wasn't Hartley, who was apparently content to let Laurette go from fling to fling, but Gilbert's pregnant wife. Gilbert, known to his friends as Jack, was married to the beautiful actress Leatrice Joy,[128] who was quite pregnant with their first child, Leatrice Joy II. Gilbert's daughter would grow up to write a wonderful biography about her mercurial father. According to her, Laurette met Gilbert at Pickfair where Vidor was staying. "Laurette Taylor was a woman of inexhaustible vitality. Upon meeting Jack one Sunday at Vidor's house and getting to know him over the next two or three weekends, she declared that she had finally met someone who could play as hard as she did. She found him not only handsome and witty, but, rarest of all, kind. She fell wildly, besottedly, and publicly in love with him."[129]

Leatrice Joy later blamed Laurette for her divorce. "Laurette Taylor may have encouraged him.... In fact, she is the straw that broke the camel's back because when I left Jack, she said she was going to marry him. It was all a very, very unhappy thing."[130]

Gilbert had endured a Dickensian childhood with a struggling, often unstable, stage actress mother who died when he was 13. He was a film extra before making his fortune as a matinee idol. A romantic, he impulsively married Olivia Burwell, whom he barely knew. Unfortunately, he was unable to provide for her, and she returned to her family.

His next romance and marriage was with Leatrice Joy, who in 1922 was a bigger star than he. Leatrice was a protégée of Cecil B. DeMille, who didn't like Jack and tried to break them apart. While the marriage between the Gilberts was passionate, they were experiencing marital troubles by the time Laurette arrived in Hollywood to make the ironically named *Happiness*.

While Laurette and Jack cavorted in public, a depressed and self-conscious Leatrice often stayed home, lamenting her weight gain, public humiliation, and the loss of her career and husband. Laurette and Jack — both had a bit of the ham in them — delighted in making home movies. "They made reel after reel of silly home movies, some with Jack doing John Barrymore imitations and Laurette playing a simpering Mary Pickford. Soon Sunday afternoons were not enough for Laurette. She began showing up at Jack's dressing room, on the set, and even calling him at home. She would talk about the marvelous John Gilbert to anyone who would listen, and before long their romance, whether real or presumed, became the talk of Hollywood."[131]

The first time Leatrice saw Laurette and Jack together at Pickfair she realized the marriage was in trouble. "Laurette would say, 'Come on, Jack darling. Remember you sit here, sweetheart, come on, Jack.' I didn't need an elephant to knock me down to know that something was going on. He came home with "On the Sunny Side of Life," a record she had made and given him. Boy, he played it and played it and played it till I got so nervous that I took my toothbrush, left the house and walked for about two miles. There was no house I could stop to sit and rest, and it was just four months before my daughter, Leatrice, was born. I walked until I finally reached a drugstore that was open all night, and I called Mother. She came over, picked me up and I never went back.... I was in his life wanting to bear his child, and this Laurette Taylor who was old enough to be his grandmother — I don't mean that. Why do I say that? She wasn't that old. I didn't see him for quite some time after the baby was born."[132]

The affair ruined the Gilberts' marriage. Leatrice thought Jack should have been strong enough to resist Laurette. During the affair she visited Pickfair with friends Alice and Barney Glazer. "Whatever she suspected, all she walked in on was another of the group's home movies. But there was Laurette, playing both star and director, blocking out scenes and ordering people about, 'No, *no*, Jack darling. You were over here with me. Don't you remember?' And then she would smile sweetly at Leatrice, who sat alone under a beach umbrella knitting furiously. Later, when the movie was shown, it was full of Jack and Laurette mugging and kissing and being silly, with frequent cuts back to Leatrice, very pregnant and scowling over her knitting needles."[133]

Laurette was proud of her "movie" and showed it when they entertained. "Laurette Taylor and Hartley Manners gave a party at their bungalow adjoining the Beverly Hills hotel. The party began in the afternoon with swimming up at the Fairbanks' home and tennis at the hotel, and ended late. Laurette Taylor is one of those perfectly painless hostesses. She provides entertainment, but you don't feel that it is compulsory. So this party was easy and informal and charming. There was a buffet supper served partially by the brilliant Laurette when the waiters lagged, and she didn't mind telling you, either, that you had to take a dish so long as she had brought it in to you with her own fair hands. There was a Hawaiian orchestra and dancing. Then there was the picture! No, nothing serious. Just a couple of reels showing the guests who frequent Miss Taylor's popular parties at tennis, swimming, dancing and flirting."¹³⁴

The *Los Angeles Times* reported further on the unusual mini-movie. "If Miss Taylor ever wants to turn screen producer, she can probably do so. A little picture shown at her bungalow the other evening showed her talent in that direction. In it was a great cast, but she starred no one. Though she was in it herself, she showed how modest a truly great person can be by keeping much in the background. The fact of the matter is, she was in a bathing suit most of the time — not one of those thirstless suits, but a practical bathing suit — but even thus, without make-up, well, you know how a woman usually looks in a bathing suit — she stood the acid test. Her activities were confined to swimming and tennis. It was Jack Gilbert who was starred most of the time, though he didn't appear as much of a hero at that, particularly when Lionel Belmore ducked him.... Leatrice Joy sat knitting mysteriously and Thelma Morgan Converse looked lovely. King Vidor never got a chance at starring, but as a tennis player proved he was a good director. Elinor Glyn was afraid she couldn't keep her tiara on straight, so she didn't go into the water. The subtitles were a howl. Although Miss Taylor was modest about them, we found out. Indeed, in the announcement, the foreword ran, 'Director: Why mention the name?' 'Subtitles: Why mention her?' The swimming was done at the Fairbanks swimming pool, so that one subtitle gave them credit — 'Overhead — by Doug and Mary.' 'Climate,' said another subtitle, 'by California.' And still another, 'Scenery by God.'"¹³⁵

Leatrice's daughter offered a different version of how her parents' marriage ended. According to her, the final straw occurred when Leatrice intercepted a telegram Laurette sent Jack. It was the end of the summer of 1924, and Laurette and Hartley had taken a train back to New

Hartley Manners stayed with Laurette despiter her affair with John Gilbert in 1924.

York. Laurette sent the following telegram from the train station: "DARLING, THANKS FOR THE ROSES. IT WAS EQUALLY HARD TO LEAVE YOU. ALWAYS, LAURETTE."[136] Upon reading the telegram, Leatrice packed up and left. When Jack returned to the empty house, he found the telegram and made a wild chase to locate his wife. Once he learned that she was living with her mother in a Long Beach apartment, he made a grand, if misguided, effort to win her back. "Uncertain of what to do next, he sent her an enormous basket of roses, together with a note that apologized for everything he could think of that might possibly have led to her leaving. The roses were an unfortunate choice. Leatrice telegraphed her response, which brutally mimicked Laurette's: DARLING, THANKS FOR THE ROSES. IT WAS EQUALLY HARD TO LEAVE YOU. ALWAYS, LEATRICE."[137]

Jack didn't give up. He continued to pester her to return, and finally Leatrice agreed to stay with him at least until the baby arrived. However, she surprised him at their home one August afternoon and walked in on a drunken binge. The house was a mess, and Jack was nowhere to be seen. She left and contacted a lawyer the next day. Interestingly, when she filed for divorce she didn't charge him with infidelity. "She charged intemperance, cruelty, and ill temper.... She'd first pleaded with him, her complaint read, to give up the use of excessive intoxicants, but she left when 'Gilbert and a number of his men friends were enjoying a wild carousal, wearing dressing gowns and pajamas. In the last year Gilbert continued to bring large quantities of liquor into their home. As a result her nerves became affected and on account of her delicate condition she is unable to work at present."[138]

On September 6, 1924, Leatrice Joy II was born. Gilbert made further attempts to reconcile with his estranged wife, but she'd made up her mind. She requested that he move out of their house, which he did. "When he moved out of the Sweetzer Avenue house and into the Athletic Club, he left a quotation from Luke 6:38 on Leatrice's desk in a silver frame. It read: 'For the same measure that ye mete withal it shall be measured to you again to full and overflowing.'"[139]

Yes, the end of this marriage was quite bitter, though Leatrice and Jack would eventually set aside their anger and remain friends until his death. They were even talking about remarriage around the time Gilbert met Swedish actor Greta Garbo in 1926. After the affair with Garbo ended, he met Broadway star Ina Claire, dated her for six weeks, and impulsively married her in 1929. Their bliss didn't last long. Ina was asked how it felt to be married to one of America's biggest stars. "'I don't' know,' the new bride replied sweetly. 'Why don't you ask Mr. Gilbert?'"[140] Ina was brilliant, funny, and good-hearted. Jack shared these traits. However, the two were a mismatch and almost immediately began getting on each other's nerves. They divorced in 1931.

Apparently unable to be alone, Gilbert remarried the next year. This time the lucky bride was 21-year-old Virginia Bruce. A former Goldwyn Girl, Virginia was an ethereal-looking blond with beautiful eyes. They fell in love while on the set of *Downstairs* (1932). Unfortunately, Gilbert was drinking heavily, partly because he correctly feared that his career was ending. The Hollywood myth is that his career failed because his voice was too high-pitched. His voice was fine. However, his long feud with MGM head honcho Louis B. Mayer eventually did him in. The feud, coupled with Gilbert's streak of self-destructiveness, made the marriage with Virginia Bruce impossible. Their daughter, Susan Ann Gilbert, was born in 1933. Bruce divorced Gilbert in 1934.

Gilbert then had a brief fling with Mexican actress Lupe Velez. His last romantic attachment was with German film star Marlene Dietrich. She vainly tried to get him to stop drinking. On January 9, 1936, Gilbert, an insomniac for years, was given medication to help him sleep. The medication resulted in a severe reaction, and Gilbert swallowed his tongue. The official cause of death was a heart attack. Gilbert was alone when he died. Colleen Moore once asked him his true love. Gilbert didn't name Greta, Marlene, or Laurette. He said it was Leatrice. When asked why it hadn't worked out, Gilbert took the blame. "'It's me. I can't seem to hang on to anything I love.'"[141]

Hedda Hopper wrote about the affair between Laurette and Gilbert in her autobiography. "Laurette was an incurable romantic. While she was making a picture at Metro, she came in contact with Jack Gilbert. She responded to his youth and he bowed low to her talent. They would stand in the center of the lot and gas away to each other for hours."[142]

Laurette and Hartley hosted a party at their Beverly Hills Hotel bungalow before they returned to New York. Guests included Hopper, King Vidor, Lady Thelma Furness, Monta Bell, Eleanor Boardman, and others. Hopper had this to say: "Jack Gilbert turned up with a complete Hawaiian band to serenade Laurette as a farewell gesture. He instructed them what songs to sing, and we sat on the porch while the Hawaiians played ad infinitum, not to say ad nauseum. Finally, I couldn't take any more and jumped up to tell Jack off, but Hartley laid a hand on mine. 'Please don't,' he said quietly. En route to the train next morning Hartley stopped at a florist's to send me flowers with this note: 'We understand. They will in time. Until then, God bless you.'"[143]

Hartley, for his part, mostly suffered in silence. He wasn't a man of grand dramatic gestures. In late January 1924 it was reported that Laurette and Hartley were returning east with a print of *Happiness*. "The first showing of *Happiness* will take place at the Riverside Drive home of the star. To this screening a few friends of the couple and Metro officials will be invited."[144] It's likely that the attendees sensed tension between the couple. Laurette supposedly asked Hartley for a divorce, but he refused, telling her in no uncertain terms that she'd ruin her career.

In *Happiness* Laurette played Jenny, a poor New York girl who supports her mother. Jenny delivers a hat to a rich but bored socialite, who is charmed by her. Jenny is next introduced to the socialite's mother and becomes a member of the household. She realizes, however, that the life of the idle rich doesn't make her happy, and after brightening the lives of everyone she meets, she leaves to open a dressmaking shop.

Publicity materials for *Happiness* suggested that it was a better film than *Peg*. "According to all advance reports, *Happiness* even outdoes *Peg* in its sure appeal, its delightful comedy and variety of entertainment, which is saying a great deal. Take a joy ride with Laurette Taylor in *Happiness*. Happiness is something that we all seek — but few find. You will surely find it in this delightful picture bubbling over with Irish wit and Irish love."[145] Another ad laid it on a bit thick: "Speedy as the rushing wind, light as spring atmosphere, fresh as morning dew, bright as the sunlight's beams, as delightful as an old Irish folk song. It means happiness for all who see it."[146] Still another asked a question. "Are you dissatisfied with life? See what Jennie, the little shop girl, thinks about persons who want air castles. Laurette Taylor is simply delightful as the little shop girl who brings joy to everyone she meets."[147]

Hartley Manners described the story as "just a sweet, simple story, with character development as the main consideration. We do not try for big, dramatic clashes, for sweeping passions or for panopiled [sic] background. Character, to my mind, in its realism is the pivotal point of drama. Illusion creates a momentary beauty but is quickly forgotten. Real folks — or imaginary characters so faithfully interpreted that they seem real — linger in the memory.... Not great drama, we admit ... but human, with a spirited characterization."[148]

Hartley admitted that he wrote the part specifically for Laurette's talents. "The picture's appeal will depend primarily upon Miss Taylor's personality, as did her first film.... Indeed, Mr. Manners told me [interviewer Myrtle Gebhart] that *Happiness* will carry even more strongly the mannerisms, the little lovable ways and fiery impetuosities of Miss Taylor. Being her husband as well as the author of her most successful plays, naturally he has studied her and understands how to bring out her individualisms."[149]

Vidor later admitted he was distracted by his romance with Eleanor

Boardman and didn't put as much energy into this film as he had with *Peg o' My Heart*. Still, he thought the end result was a success. "I didn't feel at the time that I had concentrated enough and dedicated myself enough to get everything there was to get out of this picture, but I was wrong. Looking at it today, maybe it was a good idea that I didn't take it too seriously. I sort of light-heartedly went through it. Well, there was a love affair going on between Laurette Taylor and me, and there was a wonderful rapport and spirit between us. It seemed to show up in the film, because there was a sort of delighted expression on her face all of the time, and she moved with the freedom I like to see actresses and actors move with, a certain unexpected freedom.... There was a wonderful spirit we had going."[150]

Cameraman Chester Lyons continued to use the spotlight camera on Laurette in *Happiness*. However, the still lens was no longer needed because there were fewer close-ups. "We didn't have so many big close-ups in *Happiness* because the age thing was not so apparent. In that film there was no age stated, except that she was going to be married to a young guy. We did use the spot, though."[151]

The film opens with a street scene where Laurette enters wearing a mask. King Vidor commented on this in a later interview. "That scene was not in the play, but she may have come in with the mask on, I don't really know. It did remind me of *Street Scene*, but it was not done on New York streets. It was done on the studio lot in Hollywood, because I recognized the organ grinder. He was a Hollywood figure at the time, and that's how I can place it in Hollywood."[152]

Overall, reviews for *Happiness* weren't as ecstatic as they'd been for *Peg o' My Heart*. Interest had waned a bit in the novelty of seeing Laurette on the screen. The *New York Times* wrote, "Through her presence, and not always her acting, Miss Laurette Taylor ... saves the film from being a most ordinary picture.... Judging from the handling of some scenes in this picture, one surmises that Miss Taylor did part of her own directing." Indeed the reviewer blames Laurette's hammy performance on ... Laurette. "In many of the scenes she overdoes the part of the mischievous errand girl in a Fifth Avenue dressmaking establishment. Miss Taylor is too sophisticated to be kittenish, and therefore she does not always elicit sympathy for Jenny, especially when her antics reach riotous heights."[153]

Some reviewers weren't looking for subtlety from Laurette — and they didn't get it. "Miss Taylor gives a beautiful performance. She has a whimsical way, clapping her hands together, slapping people on the back, jumping up and down and then in more somber moments she lends a wistfulness and pathos that is delightful. There are few artists on the screen who are her equals.

The picture is long, too long for the simple story, but every moment that Laurette Taylor is on the screen is a joy."[154]

A slightly sour note was heard from reviewer Chester J. Smith. "The one fault with the picture seems to be that it is overacted. Miss Taylor is splendid for the most part but she seems inclined to rather overdo the little flippancies that are bound to win favor until too often repeated.... Save for the early sequence where the Brooklyn youngsters display some local color, the picture is inclined to drag a bit through the first reel or two."[155]

In truth, some reviewers were sick to death of the trite message that the poor are happy and the rich unhappy. One particularly irritated reviewer blasted the film and Laurette. "We are poor and we know two or three millionaires. Our poverty has never brought us contentment, self-satisfaction or the one thing essential to happiness, the much despised leisure.... In the films, fortunately, life works out in better ways, and Miss Taylor goes blithely through a badly told story to the crystal coach and the golden palace. The direction is unspeakable, Miss Taylor being consistently before the camera, exhibiting her hair. She is much too old to play the part of an errand girl and her scenes, scheduled for humor, such as nose-blowing and carving a chicken all over the table are gross."[156]

In another particularly brutal review, the critic was miffed and disillusioned because he had once thought Vidor a director to be compared with Ernst Lubitsch, Charles Chaplin, and Rex Ingram. "Vidor directed *Happiness* and *Happiness* runs *Thy Name Is Woman*, a close second for worst-picture-of-the-year honors. It is an adaptation of the J. Hartley Manners play of the same name in which Laurette Taylor played the leading role. Miss Taylor has the same role in the picturization [sic], but for what she has done to it any self-respecting motion picture director would have been entirely justified had he taken her across his knee and give her a right smart spanking. (Friend husband Hartley Manners willing, of course.) But ... the fact remains — and very obviously — that King Vidor's was very, very mediocre direction. Characters were introduced and they went stumbling through their 10-reel lives much the way characters made their bow and stumbled off away back in the earliest days of the cinema. There wasn't a realistic situation in the entire production, though good direction could have provided some. The settings were cheap and artificial."[157]

Another unflattering review pointed out that Laurette's second film paled considerably to her first. "The artful lighting effects which made Laurette Taylor look so attractively youthful in *Peg o' My Heart* are sadly absent in *Happiness*, which is to be regretted. Also, the well-knit story of *Peg o' My Heart* is incomparably superior to what passes for story in *Happiness*. This latest picture of Miss Taylor's is not really a drama; it is merely a series of more or less amusing incidents, which serve to give the star an opportunity of displaying her talents for comedy. There is no construction to the story; it just goes on and on and then it ends. No working up to a climax, no climax; everything just meanders along in one tone."

One reviewer suggested the film needed editing: "*Happiness* is a sad name in this case. Shears aplenty may help make it 'happier,' but in its present conglomerate mass of by-play, it fails to measure up to good entertainment."[158]

Another film critic panned Laurette and the film. "It's a pity, but true, that charm on the stage is not always charm on the screen. Take Laurette Taylor, for instance. Now Laurette is to my liking in the speakies. She has something which gets across — a note in her voice perhaps, a subtle appeal I can't put my finger on, but which I recognize nonetheless. Then take Laurette in the movies, *Happiness*, for example. Terrible! Painful to look at! Full of inescapable boorishness and tiresome to a serious degree! She seems always to be hitting someone on the back or flicking water in someone's face, or splashing soup about, or tweaking the nose of Pat O' Malley. Custard-pie comedies have been more refined, in spots, than *Happiness*.... I am convinced that Laurette's place is near footlights, not Klieg lights."[159]

Not everyone agreed, of course. Rose Pelswick wrote that "Miss Taylor is amusingly vivacious."[160] Another pointed out that Laurette is the main reason to see the film. "The story is slender — too much so for an extensive film — but when Miss Taylor is to the fore, story does not count so much. It is her personality then that 'gets you.' She has a whole-hearted good nature — a humor that is infectious — and she is so optimistic."[161]

Mae Tinnee believed Laurette made the picture. "[T]he picture would have proved rather unnecessary if not carried along, chucked under the chin and crooned over by the star with her big eyes, wild hair, and infectious smile."[162]

Writer Harry Carr concluded, "*Happiness* may not be a world-rocking comedy — but it has the flavor of the real Laurette Taylor. It is as Irish as a shamrock. It has quaintness and mockery and charm. It is all wrong according to most movie standards; but it is wonderful, in so far as Laurette Taylor is concerned. She looks and acts like a gay-hearted little impudent girl and makes you believe it."[163]

*Life* favorably, if inexplicably, compared Laurette to child star Jackie Coogan. Critic Robert Sherwood also found similarities to the plot of *Cinderella*. Still, the reviewer concluded, "Miss Taylor ... needs little to work with. She carries her own equipment, and she uses it with the practiced skill of a genuine artist. Her own infinite variety is still immune from the withering effects of time."[164]

**Laurette Taylor with Alan Hale in the film *One Night in Rome* (1924).**

Grace Kingsley raved about Laurette when *Happiness* was released in Los Angeles in early June 1924. "Laurette ... has done it again, has established herself firmly as one of the greatest personalities of the screen in *Happiness*, which charmed and delighted us through and through yesterday.... Laurette Taylor is as great a pantomimist as Charlie Chaplin, and that is saying about all there is to say on the subject. Then there is that endlessly expressive face of hers, and her bubbling brilliant personality that holds you, no matter what she may be doing."[165]

According to film scholar Kevin Brownlow, "I was enormously impressed by her performance in *Happiness*. She is one of those comediennes, like Mabel Normand and Marion Davies, who comes across with their personality as effervescent as it was in the 20s."[166]

John Baxter, hardly a fan of Taylor's, wrote that "Her mannerisms are subdued in the story of a New York shop girl charming everyone with her optimism."[167] According to James Card, *Happiness* "was an achievement of major proportions for both star and director. Once again King Vidor showed that his special forte was keeping his shadow players magically human — even when some of them, by long movie habit, fought hard against it. *Happiness* is an irresistible film. In almost the same way that Cher shed years and a long-established mystique in *Moonstruck*, Laurette Taylor was able to charm film fans devoted to the likes of Norma Talmadge and Gloria Swanson, even Mary Pickford, to accept the live theatre's Laurette Taylor as an exception — a non-movie queen worthy of their warm response."[168]

In January 1924 it was reported that Hartley and Laurette had returned to New York, but would stay for only a month because they needed to return to Los Angeles to make *One Night in Rome*. This obviously left no time for stage work.

For this film Laurette would work with a different director. King Vidor was out of her life, personally and professionally. According to Vidor, he later visited her in New York. They'd remained friendly, though he hadn't seen her in years. "Years later on a New Year's Day she was at her daughter's home, and her daughter called me and said, 'Be prepared for a shock.' When I went through the door I saw how old she had gotten to be. It was a shock, but I stayed with her and we talked for a long time. It was the last time I saw her."[169]

When a newspaper proclaimed, "LAURETTE QUITS POLLYANNA ROLES,"[170] it wasn't kidding. Indeed, her role in *One Night in Rome* was no Pollyanna, and, thank God, she was no longer playing a teenager. In the fall of 1924 Laurette warned against being typecast. "'I think that a player loses very much by playing the same type of part all the time. I have always held to that theory on the stage and I am going to follow it now that I have ventured into motion pictures. It is true that I played whimsical comedy roles in [the] first two productions for the screen — *Peg o' My Heart* and *Happiness*— but it's also true that I'm now doing *One Night in Rome*, which gives me a straight romantic role to depict. If a player never is the same, has various roles and moods, the public will learn to expect and to count upon the player's unexpectedness. In that way the public never will grow weary of a player, and as he or she grows older he always will be able to count upon not only an admiring but a loving audience.'"[171]

Clarence Badger was announced as the director in March 1924. He'd begun his film career in 1914 for Mack Sennett. Originally hired as a writer, he was finally given the opportunity to direct and ended up helming several comedies starring Bobby (sometimes spelled Bobbie) Vernon and Gloria Swanson, including *The Nick of Time Baby* (1916), *Teddy at the Throttle* (1917), and *The Sultan's Wife* (1917). Before working on *One Night in Rome*, he'd directed *The Shooting of Dan McGrew*, which starred the tempestuous Barbara La Marr.

He'd also directed such well-known stars as Marie Prevost, Colleen Moore, Anna Q. Nilsson, and Will Rogers.

Badger was impressed with Laurette. "She is almost psychic.... She anticipates almost every word from her director during the filming of a scene. Indeed, so great is her power of visualization that she goes through whole sequences without a word being spoken to her. It is a joy beyond words to work with such an artist."[172]

Promotional materials continued to proclaim her a stage legend. "The drama of a woman's soul bared beneath the pitiless lash of Fate, the great stage success in which Laurette Taylor's magnificent artistry was acclaimed by packed houses has now become a tremendous motion picture. Laurette Taylor repeats in the films her sensational portrait of a wife unjustly besmirched by the accusations of infidelity, battling against a hostile world for the right to live a clean, happy life. With Clarence Badger's sure knowledge of audience values in direction; enacted by Laurette Taylor and a splendid supporting cast of star names, it has become an attraction which its producers take sincere pride in offering to exhibitors."[173] Another ad proclaimed: "America's Favorite Actress in a Thrilling Mystery-Romance of Eternal Love in the Eternal City."[174]

One newspaper provided the movie's synopsis. "Laurette Taylor, forsaking the rags of 'Peg' and 'Jenny,' appears as a beautiful young Italian Duchess. Following the mysterious death of her worthless husband, she is forced to flee Italy and she takes the guise of a fortune teller in London. The excitement of *One Night in Rome*, tense tho it is, fades into insignificance when the story carries the characters to one night in a castle near London."[175]

Compared to Peg and Jenny, the main character in *One Night in Rome* was truly a departure for Laurette. "In *One Night in Rome*, Miss Taylor has done up her hair, left off the trade-mark hanky fastened with a safety pin and is all grown up — dignity, marcel wave, sex appeal and everything." It was not an easy shoot, though, and even Laurette admitted, "I had an awful time keeping away from Peg and Jenny.... You see, as the heroine, I'm disguised as an Italian fortune teller.... It was a funny effect when I took my wig off in the later scenes, my hair looked just like Jenny's.... So I curled it up after that, because it would never do to remind anybody of that wild little Jenny when I was emoting my prettiest! I use my hands so much when I'm acting that I always have a lot of pockets to stuff them into when I want to be quiet. In the Italian part of the picture, I use them a great deal, of course. I thought I looked so dignified and grand in those scenes — and then when we came to look at the rushes, I found that I looked exactly like Peg! I never knew I had mannerisms until then. Of course we had to take some of those scenes over."[176]

This was the first serious film role of Laurette's career, though it did have some comedic scenes. Make-up was an important ingredient in *One Night in Rome*. According to Laurette, "[A]s to my Italian make-up, a man was engaged especially to make my nose look thin! We used up a lot of red paint turning my nose from an Irish pug into an Italian classic."[177]

While making the film, Laurette explained that she struggled to remain slim. "In *One Night in Rome*, I must have an especially sylph-like figure. Rosie, my maid, is my conscience. She keeps me at my swimming, tennis playing and dieting. But one scene in the picture ... calls for me to eat three or four chocolates, and when that scene came around, to Rosie's horror, I ate the biggest creams in the box. The scene was filmed again and yet again with Rosie approaching closer to the brink of hysteria with the disappearance of each chocolate. But I think she will recover. I am reduced to a marshmallow in the way that I am dressed, because they ordered me to do it — and I am all but drowned in a marcel wave." Laurette was not happy with the hairstyle. "It wasn't my idea, and I put up a battle. Clarence Badger, my director, stood by me, and I won out to a certain extent. But Mr. Rapf, I believe, has put a sign on his door that I am not to be allowed in! Well, maybe the public will think I look 'elegant.'"[178]

The film opened to mixed reviews. According to one critic, *One Night in Rome* "earned many critical plaudits though it revealed none of the elements which made Peg almost a national institution."[179] Edwin Schallert, critic for the *Los Angeles Times*, wrote, "The director really deserves a good majority of credit for a well-told story, in which the suspense is held creditable. The only blame that might attach is that he seemed to allow the star a chance occasionally to break into stage technique with customarily jumpy results.... *A* [sic] *Night in Rome* is in no sense an exciting picture [but] will have an appeal to a large majority because of its star and technical excellence."[180]

*Motion Picture World* offered a positive review. "This is a thoroughly entertaining picture, possessing a plot of real dramatic power. It is a picture filled with incident and action, which fact made it a success as a play on Broadway. The star of the stage production is also the star of the screen adaptation. That personage is Laurette Taylor and be it said right here that this is the best thing Miss Taylor has contributed to screen literature to date. Her characterization ... is one of the most enjoyable portraits we've seen in many months.... We can't imagine anyone but Laurette Taylor in the stellar role of this production. It is her work that makes the picture interesting. Her colorful and convincing characterization is the outstanding feature of the production. It is a delight to view."

The *Chicago Daily Tribune* critic thought Laurette carried the picture.

"Laurette Taylor ... is the chief reason for seeing the picture. She has a wistful charm and she knows the trick of talking with her eyes, her shoulders and her hands."[181]

Reviewer Herbert Crooker liked Laurette but not the film: "*One Night in Rome* owed what success it enjoyed on the stage because of the personal charm of Laurette Taylor. In the screen version much of this is lost. The story becomes a silly, unconvincing affair. The sets are good, but the direction and lighting are below the standard for such a pretentious production.... Laurette Taylor will please many in the interpretation of her role. It is unfortunate that she has been given such poor lighting, as her beauty is almost a negative quality.... As a whole, *One Night in Rome* is not worth the effort."[182]

C. S. Sewell found the movie implausible and suggested Laurette was miscast. "While the action starts off well, the interest lessens later and never regains its original force. This is due not only to the nature of the story, but to the fact that Miss Taylor has a role that does not altogether suit her. Her acting and mannerisms which were so delightful in her portrayal of the little Irish girl in *Peg o' My Heart* do not seem to fit into the role of the Italian duchess."[183]

By the time *One Night in Rome* was released, Laurette's short career in film was over. She showed *One Night in Rome* at home as she had with *Peg*, but this time it was to poke fun at her performance. "Watching this exhibition in the dark of her living room, Laurette would rock with laughter and call out, 'My God! I never saw a fan do so much acting!' or hurl insulting advice at her shadowy image, 'Ere now, my gal, not so busy with the fan! 'Ow abaht a bit of 'acting?' But if her friends laughed with quite the same heartiness she would be cross, and say, 'I'm not going to show this picture if you laugh. It's all right for me to laugh, but you can't.'"[184]

Though she made only three pictures, Laurette's film career made her a better stage actress. Likely, it was through watching her performances over and over in the darkness of her home that she learned subtlety. She also learned that less is more when it comes to acting. The result was that after Hollywood she became a more natural, nuanced actor.

Laurette continued her stage career, but Hartley's was no longer thriving. He explained that he felt out of place. "[H]e could not compete with sex dramas that flooded the New York stage and he advocated a return to what he termed a clean theater."[185] Hartley turned his attention to the stock market. He became obsessed with his new hobby, and it, rather than writing, took up his waking hours.

Hartley was remarkably bitter about the Hollywood experience. In October 1924 he wrote to the *Los Angeles Times* and told of his plans for Laurette.

"We propose ... to open about Christmas with a new play, with a wonderful part for Laurette. It is entirely unlike anything she has ever played, and we have great hopes of it appealing to New York audiences. In addition it should make a fine picture. In view of our unhappy experience in making the last picture we shall make them in the East in the future. We would like to begin the picture before the end of the run of the play, using such members of the company as will photograph well. By having the picture ready to release at the end of the run we would forestall the numberless imitators of original work."[186] There would be no pictures, however, in the future of either Laurette or Hartley.

# Chapter 7

# AFTER HOLLYWOOD

*"Just when you're learning to act, you're too tired to do it."*[1]

Alexander Woollcott organized a benefit in the spring of 1925 and enlisted Laurette to make an appearance along with other entertainers. His stipulation was that the artist could perform nothing already in his or her repertoire. Laurette, who apparently had not learned her lesson from the Shakespeare disaster, decided to perform in pantomime as Pierrot.

This time Laurette took a crash course in the art form and enlisted the aid of pantomime expert Ottokar Bartik. Still, much of it made little sense to Laurette, and, frankly, tested her patience. "Miss Taylor has learned many things that must have surprised her. Thus, a turn to the right indicates beauty and a turn to the left a lack thereof, or maybe vice versa.... And what will come out of her insistence that a real handkerchief be used for the business of picking up a handkerchief is impossible of prophecy — perhaps it will be a revolution. Wars have been started over less.... Whatever happens pantomime will certainly never again be what it was when Laurette Taylor has finished with it."[2]

In March 1925 Taylor appeared in *Pierrot the Prodigal* at the Actors Theater on 48th Street. Galina Kopernak was also in the cast, along with Ivan Lazareff, Michellette Burani, Jack Thornton, and Clarence Derwent. Alexander Woollcott couldn't help himself and wrote, "Yesterday the Actors' Theatre revived the famous pantomime *L'Enfant prodigue* without benefit of Clerget."[3]

Stark Young was enthusiastic about George Copeland's piano but less so about Laurette. "When the curtain rose ... you saw Laurette Taylor's wistful face, touching, boyish, something in it of the eternal, elusive, baffled Pierrot out of all time. It was an extraordinary mask for the part. After this there were signs from time to time of Miss Taylor's great natural talent and of her feeling for the dramatic meaning of the scene. There was a hint of good pantomime when she caught the fly from the sleeping beauty and scolded it before she let it buzz away. Otherwise of the art of pantomime there was none."[4] According to Young, Laurette was out of her league.

Helen Hayes thought Laurette failed in her portrayal. "Like most geniuses, she could be as dreadful as she could be great. Her taste could be appalling, her stage deportment reprehensible. When she did a performance of *Pierrot* all in mime, which she had never bothered to study, she made no sense whatsoever. She was all stammering hands and adorable bewilderment."[5]

*Time* was kinder in their appraisal. "Miss Taylor's face is a painted mask of eternal, baffled laughter, of moon-blanched sorrow; her gestures are eloquent, her insight unfailing."[6]

Laurette was asked by agent Max Bentham to perform the piece in vaudeville. The venues included the Palace Theatre in New York and Keith's in Washington. In April 1925, with Kopernak replaced by Edith King, the experiment was tried out. According to Clarence Derwent, "The vaudeville audience was puzzled and undemonstrative but adopted an attitude of respect toward Laurette's eminence in the theatrical world. In Washington, however, they were stonily silent and quite obviously disliked the whole thing. As the week progressed the evening audiences became almost hostile. This did not disturb me but Laurette took it greatly to heart and after the Saturday matinee went to dinner with some friends who apparently forgot about the evening performance. Dashing into the theatre at the last moment she had no time for her elaborate Pierrot makeup and went on with a somewhat disheveled appearance."[7]

The performance was a disaster. "Being very tired she dragged behind the music and generally gave a careless and disappointing performance. The curtain fell in silence and in response to the handful who applauded on the call Laurette thumbed her nose at the audience and rushed to the dressing room."[8]

Later that night Laurette and Hartley hosted a party at the Washington Hotel. Many of the guests had attended the ill-fated performance, and the mood was not joyous. Laurette decided to drown her sorrows. Clarence Derwint said, "Laurette, tired and dispirited, was acutely conscious of the party hanging fire and several times handed me her glass with the request that I replenish it. Hartley begged me to see that nothing stronger than ginger ale went into it but on this admonition I compromised feeling that both the party and Laurette were in need of some simulation."[9] If you're guessing that Laurette once again outdid herself, you're right. "Like many members of our profession great and small, Laurette was extremely fond of talking about herself. This was always done with a childish naïveté which disarmed criticism, but on this occasion, at a later hour when the party seemed to have completely bogged down, there occurred one of those silences in the midst of which Laurette was heard to say in a loud voice, 'You people may not know it but I am a combination of Bernhardt and Duse!' An uneasy pause followed this surprising announcement during which a small figure, tucked up in a large armchair, who had remained silent all evening, suddenly rose and advancing towards Laurette, remarked in a tone audible to the entire room, 'Miss Taylor, there is just one thing I would like to tell you that apparently you do not know. There is only one guy who gets away with dumb pantomime in Washington and that is Calvin Coolidge.'"[10] The man was Woodrow Wilson's secretary, Joseph Tumulty, and he effectively cleared the room and sent Laurette and Hartley back to New York.

Derwent still considered Laurette "one of the greatest actresses and wittiest personalities to adorn the American theatre during my time."[11] He recalled a time when Grace George was acting with a performer who couldn't remember his lines. To make matters worse he'd neglected to button his fly during a costume change. "After the interminable scene had reached its end and the curtain finally descended, we had all taken our last bows when Laurette came tearing through the pass door, rushed up to Grace George and said: 'My dear, I don't mind his not knowing his part but need he show it?'"[12]

In June 1925 Taylor appeared in Pinero's *Trelawny of the "Wells."* It was produced by the Players Club as part of their annual event. Pinero's play had previously been produced with Mary Mannering and Edward J. Morgan, and then later with Ethel Barrymore and Eugene O'Brien. "It tells a story of actors and their love of acting, even of their love for one another, their loyalty, their vanities, their humiliations and their successes."[13]

Burns Mantle found Laurette's performance the highlight. "Laurette Taylor ... is playing Rose Trelawny, and by the sheer sincerity with which she accepted that actress person's passion for her somewhat sappy young Harold she gave the story a cohesiveness the stage director and, I suspect, the author, missed. She was hauntingly wistful and honestly charming."[14]

Another critic thought Taylor was fine but the production so-so. "Miss Laurette Taylor was by far the finest Rose Trelawny I have ever seen. Of all the players ... it was Miss Taylor who had not only learned Pinero's lines but who evidently had read between them.... [I]t was only Miss Taylor who seemed to understand just what Pinero meant. For the most part, the actors, every one of them established successes in their profession, were apparently trying to turn character into caricature and to be groping their way through an uncharted land. It seems to me that in Miss Taylor they should have found a guide to lead them out of their wilderness."[15]

Brett Page wrote of Laurette, "Miss Taylor, needless to say, brings to the role of Rose precisely those qualities of dewy charm and unstaled [sic] innocence of the heart which one would expect."[16] Stark Young found the production and cast uneven but raved about Laurette: "The part of Rose Trelawney at [sic] Laurette Taylor's hands seemed to have been waiting these many year for her, so great was her pathetic and shy nuance, so subtle her transitions, so touchingly developed her change from the Gypsy player to the young lady who has seen gentle living and fallen in love with the grandson of the formidable aristocratic grandfather. Miss Taylor's beautiful, appealing rhythm of movement and mind was everywhere in her playing, her extraordinary talent ran quietly and completely throughout her portrayal of character. What a voice, what a dramatic mask and what shy precision she has."[17] *Time* also praised Laurette. "Laurette Taylor's startling genius gave the breath and brilliancy of life to the name role."[18]

It was during this time that daughter Marguerite noticed Laurette's drinking increasing. She'd also become less reliable about attending rehearsals and learning lines. Marital troubles, an ill-fated affair, and career uncertainty were sending Laurette on a bad path. She became argumentative, destroyed friendships, and made life at home a hell for her children and husband.

Why do so many creative people end up abusing alcohol? Does it make their talent better? Talented people are notoriously insecure. Alcohol helps. However, it's never helped someone become a better actor, writer, or artist, though it does give one momentary confidence. It takes the edge off of doubts. Alcohol didn't make Laurette a better performer, but it did give her the confidence to step on the stage. According to Helen Hayes, Laurette didn't understand her own talent. "There is no way of describing the light, the glow of her. When I first became addicted to Laurette, she was winsome and joyous, but unlike Mrs. Fiske, she didn't know (I believe) what wonders she was working and how she worked them. Laurette was tuned in. She transcended technique and even triumphed over her lack of propriety."[19] Unfortunately, without the alcohol, Laurette would have been at least as good, and she wouldn't have ruined relationships and, ultimately, her career.

In 1925 Taylor announced that she and Manners were going their separate ways ... professionally. "'[W]e have agreed on a professional divorce this season.... We have been too close a corporation. We have been limiting each other. This year I am in a play by Phillip Barry, *In a Garden*, and he is writing a play in which there will be no part for me. I love to act in his plays, and consider him one of the finest of playwrights, but I don't want to cramp his style. We both will be better off, and have more to talk about at home, if we widen our circles.'"[20]

Phillip Barry's play, once titled *The Happy Man*, was about marital discord. Specifically, a playwright sets up an opportunity for his wife to cheat on him to see if she will. Laurette played the playwright's wife, Lissa Terry.

Rehearsals didn't go well. In fact, Laurette finally barred Barry after he complained once too often about her departures from his script.

George Cukor had fond memories of her performance. "[He] vividly recalled a romantic scene with [Louis] Calhern in the foreground and Taylor half-obscured in shadow, yet Taylor riveting the audience with only her voice."[21]

The *New York Times* critic wrote, "Mr. Barry has not thought out his material clearly.... [T]he result bewilders where it might incite." As for Laurette, however, "Miss Taylor gives a splendid performance.... Her movements on the stage have a certain deliberation and her delivery of the lines has an artlessness that make for perfect illusion."[22]

Alexander Woollcott raved about Taylor. "Laurette Taylor touches the high peak of her career, and justifies, I think, an old suspicion that here is a truly great actress."[23] He described the play as "singularly beautiful" but added, "I doubt if *In a Garden* has a wide public."

*Time* agreed with Woollcott that most people wouldn't "get" the play. "To many the play will be an adventure in the worried field of the inexplicable. Most minds will not understand and will therefore condemn it. Almost any fine forward-looking endeavor in the arts runs this maddening risk." As for Laurette, the critic simply wrote: "There is an ever growing impression that Laurette Taylor is the greatest U.S. actress."[24]

Another critic didn't like the play — or Laurette. "It is such a play as only the brave Arthur Hopkins would have produced. It is not likely to be seen by any of you who read this review. Not even the popularity of Laurette Taylor will keep it alive for more than a limited period.... Laurette Taylor was never more charming. But there is something in the lassitude in her acting that has ever seemed stagey to this writer."[25]

Percy Hammond was kinder. "Miss Taylor's acting is quite the truest and most fascinating representation to be seen in New York.... The play is probably too elusive for the matter-of-fact Broadway. As Ashton Stevens would say, Mr. Barry has cast pearls."[26]

Burns Mantle believed it wasn't a good role for Laurette. "She plays earnestly, but without much variety of mood, and her fine humor is buried for the time."[27]

Gilbert Seldes wrote that "Miss Taylor's grave lightness is matchless; there was only a touch too much of the plaintive."[28] R. Dana Skinner slammed the play. "One always hopes, when Laurette Taylor is announced in a new play, for something of real distinction. How long this hope will spring eternal is a serious question if she adopts many more such vehicles as Philip Barry's new play, *In a Garden*.... The wife alone has signs of life apart from the general tenor of the play, and this is where Miss Taylor might have swung into a fine attack. But instead of approaching her character simply, she has made the wife heavy, almost melodramatic, and at other times needlessly complex."[29]

Larry Barretto thought the play was unjustly criticized. "Laurette Taylor appeared in *In a Garden* and we were delighted that this brilliant actress had at last obtained a part worthy of her.... We hope ... that Miss Taylor is not going to register another artistic triumph and commercial failure. She has not had one really popular play since *Peg o' My Heart*, but perhaps that is enough for one actress in one lifetime."[30]

Louis Calhern played the young lover. He also played a dastardly trick on her. There's a scene in the play where Laurette lists the ten things she likes best. "'She was afraid she might not remember all ... and I would spread my fingers on the grass and tick them off as she named them. Once, for the devil of it, after she had finished, I said, 'And ten more?' She threw her head back, gazed up at the fake moonlight, and went on with scarcely a break naming ten more simple, heart-warming things just as lovely as the ones she had already said. As soon as we came off she turned and gave me a furious slap on the cheek, 'Don't you ever play a trick on me like that again!' she said, and was truly, utterly furious. But the wonderful thing to me was that she was so completely at home in the play, the part, the set, with the man she loved sitting beside her, that it was perfectly simple for her to sustain that beautiful speech. This triumph meant nothing to her, however; she took it as a matter of course, and it in no way lessened her rage at my treachery.'"[31]

Taylor was probably never a good fit for *In a Garden*. After her final performance she addressed the audience. "She agreed that the comedy had been a semi-failure; yet she found merit in it, obscured though it was by the faults of the playwright. She then recited these shortcomings — quite oblivious to the fact that Barry was sitting in the theater ready to hand her his gratitude in roses."[32]

In 1925 a play written by Laurette was published in a book. Oddly, it wasn't mentioned in Marguerite Courtney's biography. Credit goes to Ellen Marie Margolis, who uncovered *The Dying Wife* when writing her dissertation. Laurette's one-act play, along with one by Hartley, appeared in *One Act Plays for Stage and Study*.[33] It's not a very good play and, in fact, seems quite "first playish," but it's fascinating for its subject matter. The play has two characters, a married couple. The husband, middle-aged Maurice Fitz-Maurice, informs his "perhaps twenty-four or possibly twenty-five" year-old wife, Arabella, that she has only eight minutes to live. She uses the time to admit to an affair and ask his forgiveness. Maurice then tells her he knew of the affair and has given her poison. When she dies "he breaks into fiendish laughter."[34] Little is known about the play's genesis, though it does seem to reflect Laurette's disastrous affair with John Gilbert. There's also an interesting note that appears at the bottom of the first page: "The author wishes to express her indebtedness to the Jug-Slav homily 'Knowledge is death when the wronged are instructed thereof.'"

Around this time Hartley went to Laurette and told her he'd done quite well in the stock market. He could cash out his holdings, and they could start the theatre company they'd once dreamed of. She told him she had no interest. According to Marguerite Courtney, "In retrospect it was from that moment that Hartley dated the disintegration of the family and the life they had shared. Months later, when suffering, physical and mental, had broken down his vast inner reserve, he confided to Dwight and Marguerite, 'Something died inside of me when Laurie said that. I didn't care any more, because she didn't. Everything we had planned for was dust.'"[35] Hartley gave up his hobby of playing the market. The couple drifted further apart.

Around April there were rumors that Laurette would appear in *Her Cardboard Lover*. Laurette and Hartley had seen the French production of Jacques Deval's play. Though they returned together, the fact that they'd traveled abroad separately led to speculation about their marriage. Indeed, Laurette and Hartley were at odds. Hartley advised Laurette against doing *Her Cardboard Lover*, suggesting it would disappoint her fans. In July 1926, fresh off the Mauretania, Hartley and Laurette gave interviews that hinted at a rift in their professional relationship. Hartley complained about the lack of moral plays. "'[O]ne good, sound, normal play would end the period of lasciviousness'.... He said that he had neither written nor produced any plays for the past two years because he would not compete with sex plays." Laurette countered, "It's hardly fair, Hartley, when I am to appear in one."[36]

*Her Cardboard Lover* has been described as "the Americanization of a modish French play that posited the wholesome heroine of *Peg o' My Heart* as a liberated Parisian lady who engages a penniless young fellow to masquerade as her lover."[37] According to Cukor's biographer Patrick McGilligan, Cukor adored Laurette and thought her a great talent. However, Laurette wasn't a good fit for the role. "[S]she was uncomfortable in a chic bedroom farce. Added to Taylor's discomfort was the antagonism between her and producer Gilbert Miller, and the wrangling between French author Jacques Deval and adapter Valerie Wyngate, both on the spot for rehearsals and tryouts."[38]

Cukor did his best to make Laurette feel comfortable. "On the road with *Her Cardboard Lover*, a sympathetic Cukor was attentive to Taylor's vulnerabilities, and took pains with the lighting to protect her vanity in scenes where she had to disrobe. The long preview tour in the fall of 1926 was an ordeal, however. Although Cukor thought Taylor's performance was 'comic, distraught, light as a feather, and heartbreaking all at the same time,' the out-of-town critics disagreed — they thought the play licentious, and Taylor woefully miscast."[39] Of course, not everyone agreed. The *New York Times* claimed in October 1926 that "A sophisticated observer ... reports that it is Miss Taylor's best play in many years."[40]

Leslie Howard, who had once played in a *Peg o' My Heart* road company and was a frequent dinner party guest at Laurette's, told friends and family that Laurette and producer Gilbert Miller didn't get along. He reported the conflict in a letter home. "I am off to Easthampton to-day [to stay with Laurette Taylor and Hartley Manners]. We are supposed to rehearse on Monday. Laurette and Gilbert are not hitting it off at all well. He said to me: 'All I want is for you to walk away with the show.' He has got the French author here and the woman who adapted it and Laurette is holding up rehearsals because of her contract. To-day I shall hear Laurette's version. As usual I am the confidant of both sides — my mission in life."[41]

By the time rehearsals started everyone was in a bad mood. In a biography written by Howard's daughter, she explained that Laurette was peeved at the producers and didn't trust them. According to her, Howard described the conflict as "the extreme of dreariness [with] 'Laurette looking more acid than vitriol.'"[42]

Howard rehearsed with Laurette on weekends at her country house. "He felt the play might be all right because Laurette Taylor was very good, though he found the intimate scenes with her a little difficult."[43]

In fact, when the first tryout opened on September 27, Howard foresaw disaster. "Laurette Taylor was still unhappy with her part and had been thoroughly unnerved by the hostile attitude of the author. During the first act ... she felt very sick, and he [Howard] was afraid she was going to be so at any moment. In the second act, everything got rather muddled, and few lines seemed to come out as rehearsed, which terrified Leslie."[44]

The play traveled to other cities but didn't appear destined to play New York. "Laurette Taylor seemed miscast and still unhappy and unsure of her part. Leslie, although he continued to look upon her as a great and remarkable actress, found performances painful and difficult."[45] George Cukor, however, recalled Laurette's performance as brilliant. "Laurette Taylor gave an absolutely memorable performance, a brilliant comedy performance."[46]

Finally, Laurette was out of the play, replaced by Jeanne Eagels. In essence, however, the producers merely replaced one difficult actress with one even more temperamental. "Jeanne Eagels ... was a frightened young woman when the curtain finally went up. She had been difficult to manage during rehearsals. Actors and actresses were removed from the company because Miss Eagels

Postcards promoting *Happiness* (1917) (photographs courtesy of Mary Pearsall).

wanted just the right inflection. Never was a play more fraught with friction and dogged by difficulties."[47]

Laurette didn't go away quietly. According to Alexander Woollcott, "[Laurette's] hold on the part was a matter of contract and from the ensuing arbitration she emerged minus the part but appeased with a good round sum — not so good, I'll wager, as she must have been in certain scenes of the play, but not so round, the management swears, as was Miss Taylor herself when she showed up at rehearsals."[48] On January 16, 1927, the *New York Times* reported that A.H. Woods had breached the contract with Laurette and awarded her $4,000 in damages.[49]

In any event, with Eagles as the star, the play didn't do well, despite a critically acclaimed performance by Howard. One critic wrote that it was not a "great, original, or perfect piece."[50]

In the midst of the difficulties off *Her Cardboard Lover*, Laurette asked Hartley to write her a short sketch. Within one day he completed *The Comedienne*, based on an idea Laurette had given him. The play, referred to as a play-let, first played as a sketch at the Palace in New York in December 1926. According to the *New York Times*, "[I]n her [Laurette's] hands, *The Comedienne* becomes a diverting interlude, enlisting, though naturally in smaller measures, several of her undoubted talents."[51]

Hartley struggled to make it into a full-length play. It first opened in Louisville before going to Chicago in February 1927. The play was about a comedienne who wants to play tragedy. One newspaper summarized it as "a romance of the American theatre. In the course of three acts of the comedy the glamour of the theatre is shown, its triumphs, its defeats, its gayety, its depression, its keen ambition, its great handicaps."[52]

The *Chicago Daily Tribune* critic was disappointed in the play. "Mr. Manners has written nothing to tax Miss Taylor, who can do so much and can do most of it better than any other actress speaking English. Whatever she is called upon to do in *The Comedienne* she does; and there is so little of this all that matters that one thinks wistfully of her as Peg or as the forlorn little errand-girl in *Happiness* and wishes that Mr. Manners ... had written for her another role so meaty and so rewardful."[53]

"It is reported as good, but not great."[54] In fact, the brief tour was a failure. "The show closed in Cincinnati, and after the fiasco she [Taylor] announced that in the future she would spend every other year on tour. Meaning, of course, that the 'road' has sort of forgotten *Peg o' My Heart* and begun to pray before other shrines."[55]

Laurette's daughter Marguerite Courtney remembered this time as one of the worst. Her mother's drinking had gotten so bad, and her behavior so erratic, that Marguerite moved out. No one, especially Hartley, wanted to confront Laurette. Typical of families of alcoholics, he chose denial. "Laurette grew progressively worse. The nights in the frame house [they were at their summer home at Easthampton] were unspeakable. Each conspirator lay in bed frozen with misery and horror listening to the sounds emanating from the third floor, sounds which seemed to come from hell and under."[56]

In the fall of 1927 it was announced that Taylor would appear in a new play by Hartley, tentatively titled *Delicate Justice*. George C. Tyler would produce.[57] Laurette's role was a spiritual healer named The Visitor. It didn't work out. "After a brief try-out on the road, *Delicate Justice* was found to be not worth much in its present form. Laurette Taylor withdrew it and J. Hartley Manners is trying to doctor it."[58]

Marguerite Courtney suggested that Hartley wrote it partly as a way to discourage Laurette's drinking. Upon preparing for a new play, she often cut back on alcohol and attempted greater discipline in her personal life. Hartley hoped a new play would give her the structure she needed. Jessie Royce Landis was a cast member. "After a three-day try-out in Allentown, Pa., we opened in Philadelphia. The play was panned to high heaven. Laurette received a rave press and my notices were excellent. I was dreading the rehearsal call the next morning. Laurette was furious because the critics had pulled Hartley and the play to bits. He took it very well and set about trying to alter it."

Landis, a cast member, grew to love Laurette — but not at first. In fact, the first rehearsal was a nightmare. "Laurette, James Dale, Frederick Warlock and I had the leading parts. We were given 'sides' which consist of your part only, and the last few words of the previous speech, called a 'cue.' I had not been able to read the script, as Mr. Tyler kept putting me off, saying that Hartley was still re-writing. So on the day of the first rehearsal, with the cast assembled to read, I was so nervous I could barely see the words. I have always been, and still am, a bad sight reader. I'd listen intently for those last few words and then, like a horse taking a hurdle, blurt out my line, with the result that I sounded like a very bad amateur. Laurette would say: 'No, no, Miss Landis.' And then she would read it beautifully. Finally I became desperate and blurted out: 'Oh, please, Miss Taylor!' I implored her. 'If you think I sound bad to you, you've no idea how awful I sound to *me*! But I've never seen the script, and I'm terribly nervous.'"[59]

Hartley implored Laurette to give Landis an opportunity to prove herself. Feeling lucky she hadn't been fired, Landis arrived at the next rehearsal better prepared. Still, Laurette picked on her. "I remember one evening rehearsal when Laurette was sitting out front with some people who had dropped in to see how we were progressing. During a scene, Laurette called up to me,

'Miss Landis, you are gabbling. You've a very bad habit of running your words together.'"

"I walked down to the footlights, to her utter surprise and mine, and said, 'I beg your pardon, Miss Taylor. I have no such habit. You don't know me; you've never seen me before. How can you know my habits? I may be doing it now, but I assure you I won't when I know the part.'"

"She said, 'All right, all right, go on.'"

"I said, 'No, I'll go back and do the speech again.'"

"She yelled, 'No, go on!'"

"I deliberately went back and carefully enunciated the speech. That was the last time she was ever rude to me."[60]

Laurette had a thing about poor enunciation, probably because she'd been criticized for it early in her career. "We Americans enunciate so carelessly, slur our syllables, leave out letters. In fact I never learned how to speak the English language until my British husband taught me. I used to pronounce the word 'months' as if it were spelled m-u-n-s-e!"[61]

Hartley asked Landis to sing "I Love You Truly" in the play. According to Landis, "When I finished singing, Laurette came up to me and said: 'My God, girl, you have a voice like that, and you don't use it! You're mad, child, you're simply mad!' Laurette didn't make her entrance until the end of the first act every night. She'd interrupt her make-up and would come to the wings to listen to me sing. Thereafter her whole attitude towards me changed. She couldn't do enough for me. The play closed after a week, but back in New York, I was invited to every dinner party she gave where I could meet people who might be of help to me. I was invariably introduced as 'the girl with the beautiful voice'—who wouldn't sing!"[62]

While appearing in *Delicate Justice* Laurette was often rude to other cast members. She hadn't stopped drinking, though she'd gotten better at hiding it. She was also unprofessional, missing rehearsals and not learning her lines. Laurette barely made it to the Allentown opening on time. Hartley wondered if she'd arrive at all. On occasion, Laurette took a few positive steps toward controlling her drinking, including seeing a doctor and psychologist. However, like most alcoholics, her decision to control rather than stop drinking doomed her.

In November 1927 Taylor made a radio appearance on *The Eveready Hour*, in which she did readings from *Peg o' My Heart*, *Bird of Paradise*, and *Happiness*. This was Taylor's second appearance on the show. "Radio critics have attributed to Miss Taylor the faculty rare among actresses of being able to project her personality over the air. This Tuesday's program will mark her second appearance on *The Eveready Hour*. Her engagement last year, which marked her radio debut, was quite generally acclaimed as an emphatic success."[63]

Interestingly, in 1925, Laurette had appeared with Louis Wolheim at a Drama Guild luncheon where Wolheim ripped radio, calling it "soulless" and no competition to theatre. Sounding like a kook, Wolheim said things like, "[T]heater is a part of the spiritual development of mankind and there is nothing that will be able to banish it. True, the radio may attract a certain number of people away from the theatre, but the kind of people who could be attracted away do not belong to the theatre anyway, and we don't need them." Laurette followed Wolheim and was demure, saying "she somewhat shared his views as to radio's inefficacy as a competitor with the stage, but did not feel his 'jealousy of science' and thought the radio question would work out all right in the end."[64]

In fact, Laurette would have been a natural for radio. Her voice was perfect for the new medium, but she never took full advantage of the opportunity, though she made occasional appearances.

By 1928, on the eve of talkies, most assumed that Laurette's movie career was over. Harry Carr put it bluntly when he wrote, "Doris Keane, Laurette Taylor, Nazimova were flops in the movies on account of the ruthless and cruel demand for the blush o' youth. With words, they would have made great screen hits with *Romance*, *Peg o' My Heart*, and *A Doll's House*."[65]

Laurette decided to do a modern play and appeared in *The Furies*, a Zoe Akins play, in 1928. Akins described the play as "a jazz nocturne, presenting a definite musical theory."[66] Oh boy. A critic described it as a "somewhat unfortunate drama."[67]

According to Patrick McGilligan, "Zoe Akins wrote *The Furies* expressly to boost Laurette Taylor's sagging career, and in the spring of 1928 Cukor directed the actress in this stage whodunit about a wife accused of killing her millionaire husband."[68] This is an interesting statement, because at one point, before Laurette was chosen, Billie Burke was being considered for the role. Laurette's drinking was by now well known, so the producers approached the remarkably candid Alice Brady to take over the role. "Well, I drink too....I'd like to do the play—you bet I would—but I drink too, and Laurette would be simply wonderful in the part."[69] The producers kept Laurette, even when she missed rehearsals.

George Cukor was the director. Two years later, he signed a Hollywood contract to become a film director. He was already known as a "woman's director," having directed Laurette, Ethel Barrymore in *The Constant Wife*, Jeanne Eagels in *Her Cardboard Lover*, and Dorothy Gish in *Young Love*.

Jessie Royce Landis was asked to join the cast when Estelle Winwood left. Landis received a desperate telegram from Laurette. Unfortunately, Landis was grieving over her child, who had recently died. "I wired back that I couldn't. Then Laurette phoned and said work was the best thing for me and also that she was stuck as they couldn't find anyone right for the part who would do it, since the play was only going to run for a few more weeks."[70]

Landis, who had only four days to prepare, reluctantly agreed to the "strange play." Laurette's advice to her was to play her role "*for comedy* [italics in original]."[71] Laurette reemphasized this when she showed up for rehearsal. "Remember, this part *must* get the laughs or the play is cooked." However, playwright Zoe Akins pulled her aside and gave Landis *her* words of advice. "'My dear,' cooed Zoe, 'this part is most important to the play. It is like a violin obbligato — it's the overtone, the Greek chorus. She's poignant. Yes, she's my violin obbligato.'"[72] A confused Landis played the role serious. "Despite my obligation to Laurette, I felt I had an even greater one to the author to portray Fern as she had conceived her. All I could do was to pray that Laurette's wrath could be borne." Feeling "like a Judas,"[73] Landis went on and said her lines as serious as a cup of coffee. Still, the audience howled. "From that time until the final curtain, every time I opened my mouth I got a laugh. The audience had decided Fern was comedy relief. Laurette threw her arms around me and said: 'What a little comedienne! Darling, you're marvelous!' But I was truly distressed. I had, with the best intentions in the world, let Zoe down. If only I could get out of the theatre without her seeing me. But I'd hardly reached the dressing-room when Zoe burst in, even more enthusiastic than Laurette, saying: 'You *are* my Fern!'"[74] Regardless, the play lasted only 45 performances.[75] The film version came out in 1930 and featured Lois Wilson as Fifi.

Brooks Atkinson thought the acting was quite good but the play wasn't. "In spite of excellent acting and a splendid production in general, Zoe Akins' new play, *The Furies*, put on at the Shubert last night, turns out to be excessively maudlin. As the chief character in this disorderly play, Laurette Taylor plays with a soft, beguiling beauty worthy of the very best of dramas.... As Fifi ... Laurette Taylor makes a breath-catching entrance — all excitement, all aglow. All through the drama she plays with depth of perception and precision of means. What marvelous range Miss Taylor has at her command!"[76]

*Time* called Laurette's performance "magnificent" and pointed out that she was only getting better, noting that *Peg o' My Heart* had been produced 15 years before. "Now Laurette Taylor is a better actress than ever."[77]

Albert Carroll was one of the best-known impersonators of the time. He appeared in *Slants on Famous Personalities* in April 1928 at the Booth Theatre. He also appeared with other impersonators in *The Grand Street Follies* in June of that same year. The impressions at this revue ranged from Laurette, Pavlova, Mrs. Fiske, Alexander Moissi, Ruth St. Denis, Ethel and John Barrymore, Haidee Wright, and others.[78] According to *Time*, "The Grand Street Follies are built upon the eminently sound principle of burlesquing all recent attractions at Manhattan theatres. A sophisticate must loudly giggle, when Albert Carroll comes on the stage impersonating Laurette Taylor or when Dorothy Sands pretends she is Ina Claire, lest neighbors in the audience suffer from the illusion that he has not viewed the original from which the parody derives. Yokels, too, are compelled by their anxious timidity to give deceitful titters."[79]

According to the *New York Times*, Carroll's Laurette impression was particularly good. "Three of his delineations stood out last night—those of Laurette Taylor in a zany bit called 'Furious Interlude,' Haidee Wright as she appears in *The Royal Family*, and a 'stunt' impersonation of Mrs. Fiske and Ethel Barrymore."[80] By the way, the "stunt" impression involved using one side of his face as Fiske, while the other side was made up to look like Barrymore. In any event, critic Ernest Boyd thought Carroll did a fine job zeroing in on "some of the idiosyncrasies of Miss Laurette Taylor, with deadly precision."[81] Robert Benchley found Carroll's impersonation of Laurette "a startling reproduction."[82]

According to Carroll, perfecting his impression of Laurette was a hard nut to crack. "[I]t is impossible for him to transmute his own personality into that of another unless the other person strikes a responsive chord in himself. After several vain attempts to catch the qualities which he so admired in Laurette Taylor, they were vouchsafed him this Winter in the fortuitous combination of play, role and dialogue—to say nothing of the costume—which *The Furies* provided."[83] In December 1929 Carroll performed in a show with Fred Keating. This time his Laurette bit was "as Ophelia in the mad scene."[84]

Laurette asked Hartley to

Laurette was devastated when her husband, Hartley Manners, died in 1928 (photograph courtesy of Mary Pearsall).

write her a new comedy. The poor man spent night after night staring at a blank piece of paper in the typewriter, utterly unable to write. He told Marguerite, "Everything has gone from this house.... This is what alcohol does. When it comes into a home everything goes, love, affection, loyalty, all decent human feeling — it leaves nothing. That is its terrible curse."[85] In the spring Laurette went to a sanitarium. When she came out in the summer, she was looking forward to staying in the vacation house. Meanwhile, Hartley finished the comedy, but it wasn't for Laurette. He offered it to Billie Burke, who turned it down. Unfortunately, after a persistent cough, Hartley, a heavy smoker for many years, was told he had cancer of the esophagus. When Laurette was told, she began drinking again.

In September 1928 Laurette and Hartley participated in — believe it or not — a television show at the Radio World's Fair. It was a hugely popular event. One elderly woman in a New York subway was heard to tell her son, "All I want to see is that television machine at the radio show." More than 40,000 people visited the television exhibits. According to the *New York Times* on September 21, 1928, "Among those who appeared yesterday before the 'eye' of the television camera were J. Hartley Manners and his wife, Laurette Taylor."[86] It was, sadly, one of Hartley's last public appearances.

By this point, he was a very sick man. Jessie Royce Landis described how she'd play bridge with Laurette "while her husband Hartley Manners was dying of cancer upstairs. Laurette was drinking very heavily then, but who could blame her? Hartley had always been there as a buffer between Laurette and all the unpleasant things of life; situations caused by Laurette's quick temper and sharp undisciplined tongue were always smoothed over by him; and now he was upstairs dying, and Laurette was lost in that mausoleum of a house on Riverside Drive, with its huge sunken living-room that looked like an old monastery. The only thing she wanted to do was to play bridge and drink — anything but be alone."[87]

## Chapter 8

# THE LONGEST WAKE

*"I could never understand why Hartley was taken away from me. I mean to speak to God about it when I see Him."*[1]

Hartley had surgery and returned home on December 6, 1928, but his health quickly deteriorated. According to Landis, "One by one the hangers-on slipped away until only Dr. Devol, Sybil Ames, old Allen McCreary, and I remained. Towards the end, when I'd go up to see Hartley, he could just manage to whisper, 'Girl, sing,' and I'd sing softly until he dozed off, with Laurette standing at the window, staring out at nothing, her large brown [sic] eyes like those of a haunted deer."[2]

J. Hartley Manners died of cancer on December 19, 1928, at 7:30 P.M. in their Riverside Drive home. According to an obituary, "He was 58 years old. Mr. Manners had been ill since last summer and a month ago underwent an operation. His health failed steadily since then."[3]

The obituary added that *Peg* had been his greatest success. "It has been estimated that *Peg o' My Heart* has been played more than 500,000 times on various stages and has been translated into almost every known language. It is estimated to have earned its author more royalties than any play in the history of the theater with the exception of *Abie's Irish Rose*."[4] In fact, the statistics were astounding. "In all, the part of Peg was played by Miss Taylor in the United States and England for 1,099 performances. The comedy has been performed in the United States and Canada 5,987 times, eight companies at one time touring it during the season of 1914–1915; 1,001 times in London, during which run it was played at the Comedy, Globe, Apollo, and St. James's Theatres; 2,475 times in the English provinces; 457 times in Australia and New Zealand; and 191 times in South Africa.... It has also been played in India and the Far East, and in Holland, and arrangements have been made for its translation and adaptation into French, Italian, and Spanish. The total number of performances recorded to date in all parts of the world is 10,233."[5] It had played just about everywhere except Germany because Hartley wouldn't allow it. He never got over his bitterness over Germany's actions during World War I.

After the funeral, Laurette had Hartley's belongings removed. She also destroyed all memorabilia related to her career with Hartley. She regretted it. "Someone should have stopped me ... but who was to know I was quite off my head."[6]

Laurette ultimately decided she could no longer live at Riverside Drive. According to Landis, "After his death, I stayed many nights in that house which was like a ghost house, until we found an apartment and Laurette moved."[7]

Following Manners' death, many blamed Laurette's drinking and inactivity on the loss of her husband. Genevieve Parkhurst summed it up in a 1945 newspaper article. "Theirs had been more than a marriage of the heart. It was well a communion of talents and of interests.... They had everything that life can give — fame, wealth, and a perfect love. When Manners died in 1928, all interest in life seemed to die for his grief-stricken wife."[8]

Taylor also gave interviews where she perpetuated this myth. "'In losing Hartley I lost my anchor and was desolated. I gave up my work, refusing to see anyone. I rattled around in my apartment until it became unbearable. I did the same in the luxury hotels in England, France, and Italy. My blind, blundering efforts to forget the loss of my husband made me a nuisance to my friends, and a burden to myself.'"[9]

While she was, of course, grieving the loss of her husband, in truth, she'd already been working erratically and drinking heavily. There was some truth, however, to the claim that Hartley seemed to be the only person who could get through to her. Helen Hayes believed he kept her in line. "Manners had been able to keep her under control by tapping her on the shoulder after the second drink, but he was gone."[10] Indeed, there was something about Hartley's presence that kept Laurette from going too far, at least most of the time. "When Hartley was alive ... I was kept like a very fine racehorse."[11]

Upon Laurette's comeback in 1939 in *Outward Bound*, another article repeated the myth. "Their fifteen years of married life had been so close and wonderful that his death was such a shock to the actress that she retired from the stage."[12] Laurette echoed this in an interview. "Sometimes the difficulty with a part is that you can't forget your own troubles. That happened to me when I came back to the stage after Hartley died.... I tried to act, but the magic was gone. It was Laurette who got in the way. That was the greatest lesson in acting I ever had: you've got to leave yourself behind."[13]

Hedda Hopper blamed guilt for Laurette's inactivity. "Hartley died ... before Laurette could say, 'I'm sorry,' or pour out her gratitude toward him. Remorse drove her into hiding, and for years no one saw her. She put on a mountain of flesh. Not until she got the play *The Glass Menagerie* and became interested in its author, Tennessee Williams, did she slim down and return to the stage."[14]

Laurette, who always championed Hartley's plays, later described her loss in this way. "The person who had the greatest influence on my life was Hartley Manners, to whom I was married for fifteen years. I'd always imagined our growing old together and when he died it completely threw me. I lost my religion and went in for the longest wake in history. If such a man as Hartley could be taken away from me, what did anything matter?... I began drinking harder and harder, and it was only my success in *Outward Bound* that finally pulled me out of it. Then along came this blessed *Glass Menagerie* and I knew I was all right — and that I would be forever. Hartley Manners was a graceful man, a gentle man, a wonderful man. He wrote *Peg o' My Heart* for me. I still get royalties from *Peg*— from churches and little theater groups and summer stock and all that sort of thing. My! How old that girl is! She goes right back to 1912 and T.R. [Theodore Roosevelt] and William Jennings Bryan and Woodrow Wilson and the Red Sox beating the New York Giants in the World Series. I loved *Peg* and still do, but it's always made me furious that amateurs haven't wanted to do Hartley's better plays, such as *The National Anthem* and *The Harp of Life*."[15]

A pensive Laurette Taylor following her success in *Peg o' My Heart* (photograph courtesy of Meg Courtney).

In the spring of 1929 details of Manners' will were released. As expected, Taylor inherited the bulk of his estate, including royalties to his literary works. "An unusual provision of the will was a bequest that 100 pounds sterling be paid annually for six years to the Royal General Theatrical Guild of England, provided that organization stages two of Manners' plays, *All Clear* and *God of My Fathers*, at its annual benefit, usually given at the Drury Lane Theater, London. The plays are to be staged alternately during the six years, each play to be given three times.... [T]he playwright's reason for the unusual bequest was his 'desire that these plays be performed during these years so that the remembrance of the atrocities committed against the English people by the Germans might be kept alive.'"[16] The Guild renounced the gift.

Manners also bequeathed sets of his works to Harvard, Princeton, Yale, Oxford, and Cambridge. He willed a portrait of himself by Ben Ali Haggin, valued at $50, to the Lotos Club, but for some unknown reason they renounced the bequest.

Dwight and Marguerite, who were fond of Hartley and vice versa, were left small bequests, and it was stipulated that they would receive royalties upon Laurette's death or when they reached the age of 30. Unfortunately, Laurette quickly ran through Hartley's estate. Hartley had suffered huge losses after he quit playing the stock market. In addition, the Depression significantly reduced his estate. Laurette ended up dipping into her children's trust funds, and they ended up with nothing from Hartley's estate.

In the fall of 1929 a small newspaper blurb announced that Taylor was back in New York after a two-month trip to Italy. She was, the newspaper said, looking for a play. Noting that son Dwight had recently sold three plays to New York producers, columnist Wood Soanes cynically suggested, "Perhaps he can help her."[17] In truth, Dwight ended up doing quite well. No doubt he had connections, being the son of Laurette Taylor, but there is no question that he, like Marguerite, was a talented writer. His play *Jailbreak* was sold to the movies around 1929 and adapted into *Numbered Men*, starring Conrad Nagel. In the early 1930s MGM hired him, and he worked on scripts for *The Gay Divorcee* (1934), *Top Hat* (1935), *Barbary Coast* (1935), *The Awful Truth* (1937), and many others. Interestingly, he may have used some of Hartley's plays to pave his way to success in Hollywood. When interviewed by Carl A. Rossi, Eloise Sheldon remembered Laurette giving Dwight some of Hartley's plays from their library with the idea that he'd adapt them for the movies.[18] Screenwriter Allan Scott claimed that Dwight's screenplay for *The Gay Divorcee* "was a revised version of one of Hartley Manners' plays."[19]

By 1930 Laurette was on the verge of fading into obscurity. Percy Hammond, however, still remembered her. He was asked by Hiram Motherwell, *Theater Guild Magazine*'s editor, to compile a list of the best actors. His eclectic list included Laurette, Ethel Barrymore, Helen Hayes, Alfred Lunt, Lee Tracy, Lynn Fontanne, Guy Kibbee, Louis Calhern, Joseph Sweeney, Helen Westley, Dudley Digges, Y.Y. Ysu, Walter Connolly, Osgood Perkins, Joe Cook, Eva Le Gallienne, Anna May Wong, Sigfried Rumann, and Sam Jaffe.[20]

In February 1930 Laurette, along with several other actors, testified before Albany, New York, legislators concerning a bill that would prohibit the arrests of actors when a play was closed because of a morals charge. "It's hard to tell what a dirty play is because it all depends upon what kind of a mind you have," said Miss Taylor, while members of the codes committee chuckled. "The present law is frightfully unfair because we never can tell ahead of time what lines we will have, and for that reason we have no opportunity to decide whether or not the play is immoral."[21]

In September 1931 theater columnist Wood Soanes included a blurb that stated, "Laurette Taylor is ready to make a reappearance if some writer who knows his or her trade will oblige her with a manuscript."[22] In that same year she also received the welcome news that she had $1,000 she was unaware of. Her brother Edward had deposited $590 in a bank account in both their names in 1916 before he went off to war. He died shortly after the war, and the deposit was forgotten until a list of names was published in the newspaper. The savings account had grown with interest. A reporter found her name on a list of found money and contacted her.[23] Laurette happily retrieved it. "Lots of people call me up, but no one has ever done it before in order to tell me that I own money.... Isn't that a dreadful thing to do, forgetting money like that?"[24]

Laurette had been out of the news for so long that many wrote her off. Richard Massock mused in 1931, "Haven't seen her in moons. Will be remembered for only one performance, I suspect—*Peg o' My Heart*."[25] He added that she would also be remembered for bringing Lynn Fontanne to America.

At the time Taylor was still traveling abroad and not thinking about the stage. "For two years and more I had been traveling in Europe and visiting friends.... I was trying to get interested in social affairs, but I realized more and more that it was useless."[26] This was about to change.

Laurette announced in February 1932 that she was returning to Broadway to appear in two James M. Barrie plays, *Alice-Sit-by-the-Fire* and *The Old Lady Shows Her Medals*. Producer Bill Brady convinced her to do the plays when she ran into him on a trip to Washington to campaign against theater ticket taxes. "'After it was over and we were on the train coming back, Mr. Brady began mentioning plays.... I told him I didn't think much of the modern crop of playwrights. Most of them are confused and think they are depicting life with drawing-room scenes in which everybody drinks and dashes about madly, and our older playwrights have lost their bearings in a changing world. Then he suggested Barrie.'"[27]

Laurette wondered if he meant the Philip Barrie. "I will make an exception in the case of Philip. He is one young playwright who has found himself and has something to say. Anyway, when Bill Brady said Barrie my first reaction was against it. Now, don't ask me to do *Peter Pan*, Bill,"[28] she joked.

Critics were thrilled with her return. Percy Hammond celebrated by reminding readers she'd last appeared "five years or thereabouts [when] Miss Taylor discouraged herself and her onlookers in *The Furies*, a garish tantrum by Miss Zoe Akins." According to Hammond, "[S]he was more magical than ever, and ... caused us to regret that she had been so long away." [29]

According to another critic, "Appearing in two Barrie plays, Miss Taylor has shocked the critics into relieved and tumultuous applause. They wanted to clap hands for her for old time's sake, but they didn't expect to be able to do it so wholeheartedly. In the revival of *Alice-Sit-by-the-Fire*, Miss Taylor took them all off-guard. Forty-five if she is a day [she was almost 48], she gave them a thrill with her luminous eyes and her perky mask of a face. After a great absence, broken only by a brief appearance four years ago in a play by Zoe Akins, Laurette Taylor has reestablished herself as a reigning figure of the theater."[30]

Another columnist noted how four years in theater can seem much longer and noted Taylor's apparent nervousness. "Four years in Broadway time frequently brings a complete change in tastes and types. It's a brave actress who ventures back, after having reached the peaks; particularly when she brings as her vehicles such vintage pieces as *Alice-Sit-by-the-Fire* and *The Old Lady Shows Her Medals*.... During the first seven to ten minutes on the eve of her appearance, the nervousness of Miss Taylor was almost embarrassingly apparent. Then she took herself in hand for a personal triumph. It is not likely in the light of this comeback that Miss Taylor will disappear again for a while."[31]

Another reporter echoed the sentiment. "The re-appearance of Laurette Taylor upon the Broadway stage was hailed with almost as much sentimental enthusiasm as was the return of Maude Adams. The darling of *Peg o' My Heart* has long been not one of the stage's most competent actresses, but also one of its most beloved."[32]

One critic noted that Barrie's *Alice-Sit-by-the-Fire* was "one of Barrie's weakest moments." However, "Miss Taylor's acting lends it such charm and glamour that one is almost persuaded that, after all *Alice* may be a great play." The critic suggested that *The Old Lady Shows Her Medals* wasn't a good choice for Taylor as "Miss Taylor's sophisticated charm is not suited for the motherly qualities of part best done by Beryl Mercer." The article concludes, though, that "Nevertheless Broadway is being exceptionally sincere in welcoming Miss Taylor back."[33]

Brooks Atkinson found Laurette's return triumphant. "[P]lease God, may she never be absent again! As the artful wife in *Alice-Sit-by-the-Fire* ... she does not tamely remind us of what a superb actress she is. It as though we had never seen her before. In every scene of this trivial playlet she appears to be creating something fine and rapturous that has never been on the stage before. To have Miss Taylor back is a wondrous thing, for she is an actress by inspiration.... The word 'magnificent' is often recklessly used in the rush of play reviewing. Let it be used here scrupulously. Miss Taylor is magnificent."[34]

According to *Time*, "*A Night of Barrie* is really a night with Laurette Taylor. Actress Taylor is very definitely qualified for Barrie work. Her heavy eyelids, fluttering hands and a manner of speaking as though she were slightly awed by the possibility of vocal communication, create about her an atmosphere of wistfulness and unreality. These qualities she puts to good advance in *Alice*.... *The Old Lady* ... is cut a bit too rough to suit Actress Taylor's style. But many a Taylor and Barrie fan who goes to see this bill will come away well satisfied."[35]

Unfortunately, Laurette, who was by now a full-blown alcoholic, called in sick once too often. "The second indisposition within recent weeks of Laurette Taylor, noted actress, led William A. Brady, Broadway producer, today to close abruptly the revival of two plays by Sir James M. Barrie in which Miss Taylor starred."[36]

The same month Laurette was canned she almost got the opportunity to play herself on stage. During an appearance in *Hay Fever*, Constance Collier suffered an eye injury. It proved serious enough that there was talk of Laurette replacing her.[37] Now that would have been odd. Laurette playing Judith Bliss, who was based on, well, Laurette. The *New York Times* announced on April 19, 1932, that Collier would resume her role on May 2, and Laurette was no longer needed.[38]

In an effort to continue her wavering career, Laurette appeared in *Finale* at the Berkshire Playhouse in August. Written by S.K. Lauren, the play was about an opera diva. Leo G. Carroll, Geoffrey Wardwell, Marcella Swanson, and George Coulouris also appeared in the production.[39] The following month the play opened at the Country Playhouse in Westport, Connecticut. Kathleen Comegys was added to the cast, and it was hoped the play would go on to Broadway. It never happened.

It must have been bittersweet when the new screen version of *Peg o' My Heart* was released in 1933. The decision was made in late 1931 when movie studios decided "the death knell has sounded for the cycle of gangster and sophisticated sex dramas, and the motion picture public is showing a decided preference for the simpler but more wholesome form of entertainment."[40] Laurette was thrilled with the money she received for the film rights, but it must have been a cruel reminder of her less than successful film career.

Obviously in sound now, the picture starred Marion Davies, who claimed playing the role was a "childhood dream [come] true.... It was in a New York attic that Miss Davies first played Peg, then the hit of the stage, with Laurette Taylor in the original cast. Togged out in some of her older sisters' hand-me-downs, a neighbor's dog tucked under her arm and a dilapidated carpet bag to complete the characterization, she played the part before an appreciative audience of other children."[41]

When MGM bought sound rights in 1931, columnist Muriel Babcock suggested actresses Helen Hayes, Joan Crawford, Norma Shearer, and, tongue in cheek, Greta Garbo.[42] Davies, however, was a good choice. An excellent mimic, Davies used an Irish accent and added the song "Sweetheart Darlin.'" The supporting cast included Onslow Stevens as Sir Gerald, with the wonderful Juliette Compton playing cousin Ethel, Tyrell Davis as Alaric, and Irene Browne as the aunt.

Davies admitted being intimidated at the thought of following in Laurette's huge steps. "'I admit I was frightened to death at the very thought of playing Peg, as much as I have longed for years to make the picture.... It is hard enough to create a new character, but to play a part that has become a theatre tradition through the brilliant performance of an actress like Laurette Taylor is still more difficult. Like millions of others, I had seen Miss Taylor on the stage in *Peg o' My Heart* and also in the silent picture version of the play about ten years ago. I could not very well start out without having her portrayal somewhere in mind.... I realized, after studying Peg, that Miss Taylor had submerged her own individuality into Peg's personality, one of the greatest accomplishments of a gifted actress. It remained for me, then, to play the character as faithfully as I could, leaving myself completely out of it.'"[43] Davies graciously invited Taylor to Hollywood. "She was the week-end guest of Marion Davies.... She is not here to go into the movies, although she was asked to play the part of the mother in *Little Women*. She is writing her own play, *Enchantment*, and hopes to star in it on the stage in the fall."[44]

Yes, Laurette decided she needed a new direction and career. She wanted to be a writer. Newspaper astrologer Stella examined Laurette's birth chart in 1926. "A glance at the ... chart ... will be sufficient to show why this popular actress has been so successful. A strong feeling for romance is shown by the positions of Neptune and Mercury, and it is highly probable that she could succeed as a novelist if she decided to devote more of her time to writing."[45]

Of course, Laurette had written *The Greatest of These*—, and she'd also written the short play along with some newspaper columns in 1922. The columns allowed Laurette the opportunity to turn the tables and become a critic when several newspaper writers put on a skit for a benefit. Her columns on "No Sirree" were laugh-out-loud funny. One of them, a take-off on friend Alexander Woollcott's "Second Thoughts on First Nights" column, was titled "Sickened Thoughts."[46]

One of the least explored areas of Laurette's life has been her writing career. She was proud of it, as well she should have been. In addition to *The Greatest of These—*, she wrote several unpublished book-length manuscripts, both fiction and nonfiction. She later had numerous articles published in magazines and newspapers and also added several plays to her resume. Doctoral student Ellen Margolis was impressed with the plays. "I was not prepared for her plays. They were, first of all, disciplined, fun, and thoroughly developed. Their theatricality, timing, and implicit trust of subtext were tributes to a great understanding of the life of the stage."[47] She added, "[A]rtistically, Taylor's 'wake' for Hartley Manners coincided with her own artistic awakening and self-determination. Thus, the protagonists of the plays she wrote during this time, self-possessed if self-destructive women of approximately her own age and general profile, are much more than merely intriguing footnotes to her biography."[48]

Laurette's play *Enchantment* was about a mermaid. She enlisted friend Jose Ruben to revise it, and it was announced that the play would open on April 18, 1933, at the Plymouth Theatre with Laurette playing the mermaid, Crystal. Cast members included Julia Hoyt, Ruth Vonnegut, and Elsa Gray,[49] and Robert Edmond Jones was asked to direct and design sets and costumes. It never came together. The play was postponed once before finally being cancelled.[50]

That same year there was talk about Laurette appearing in a film version of *The Harp of Life*. George Cukor championed Laurette for the role, but this too never came about, mainly because there wasn't enough excitement about Hartley's play. There was also the issue of Laurette's notorious unreliability.

It became commonplace for Laurette to be announced for film and stage roles that were never realized. In early 1933 she was mentioned for a part in the film *The Silver Cord*. The role of the mother had been created on stage by Laura Hope Crews, and she was also being considered for the role. According to Louella O. Parsons, "The mother is the most important role, even more important than the role of the man's wife." According to Parsons, David O. Selznick, who was on the verge of moving from RKO to MGM, "has been in communication with Miss Taylor."[51] Crews, an outstanding actress in her own right, though largely forgotten but for her role as Miss Pittypat in *Gone with the Wind*, ended up making the 1933 RKO picture with Irene Dunne and Joel McCrea.

In March it was announced that Laurette would appear in *I'm Over 39*, a new play by S.K. Lauren that she'd tried out the previous fall in Stockbridge, Massachusetts, The opening was set for the Geary Theater in San Francisco on May 15, and it was hoped the play would eventually end up on Broadway.[52] This was yet another project that didn't materialize.

In November it was reported that Taylor had agreed to appear in MGM's *It Happened One Day* with John Barrymore. "Laurette Taylor has said a great big 'yes' to M.G.M's offer ... W.K. Howard, the director, and John Considine Jr., the producer of this unit, put in a bid for Miss Taylor's services days ago but it was not until Saturday that she agreed to sign the contract."[53] The film was apparently never made, though another newspaper also reported it was a done deal. "[S]he will leave for the coast immediately. The studio considers this a real break for she has refused many film offers."[54]

Columnist Lloyd Pantages questioned Laurette's future film career in February 1935. "Just what will happen to the film career, if any, of Laurette Taylor still remains a mystery. Practically every producer in Hollywood have [sic] offered her at one time or another, something mighty tasty."[55]

That same month an intriguing blurb appeared in the *New York Times*. Laurette was considering a play written by Mercedes de Acosta. It was titled *Mother of Christ*, and Laurette called it a "simple, reverential play."[56] Plans were for an Easter production with sets by Norman Bel Geddes, but it never happened.

On August 15, 1934, Taylor appeared on the radio from Ogunquit, Maine (WAAB), performing a scene from her play *At Marian's*. Laurette hoped the play would be on Broadway by Thanksgiving. The previous night she'd opened the play in Ogunquit. According to the *New York Times*, the play "is concerned with the struggle of an authoress to escape from a morbid fear of the dissipation which, during her first marriage, had led to an attempt at suicide. She seeks a new life in the love of national tennis star whose clean, orderly way of living offers the escape which she desires."[57] According to Ellen Margolis, "*At Marian's* can be read as not only autobiographical, but as a kind of sequel to *The National Anthem*."[58] Marguerite Courtney didn't think it was a good play. "Many aspects of it were Laurette's story thinly disguised. It was not a very good play and parts were extremely muddled in thought. Produced as a comedy, the audience had found it heavy and depressing.... What was vastly important was that Laurette had written direct, hard-punching lines about an alcoholic, and spoken them herself; that while still denying such a problem existed in her own life, she was telling of the weaknesses and fears that destroy an alcoholic, of the ugliness and utter degradation that comes with drink."[59]

Later that month Laurette was scheduled to appear in *Behind the Verdict* at the Newport Casino.[60] However, she withdrew and was replaced by Muriel

Starr. Once again, Laurette was drinking. She was in poor health but refused treatment.

George Cukor offered her a screen test for *The Distaff Side*. Laurette was in such bad health that a rehearsal was scheduled for her apartment. This was yet another role that slipped through the cracks.

She was now living at 14 East 60th Street on the top floor of an apartment-hotel. Finally, Laurette, who feared she had cancer, agreed to an operation on April 10, 1935. No cancer was found, and Laurette again tried to get well. Soon, however, she had a setback and became reclusive, wouldn't return phone calls, and so on.

Family and friends feared the worst, but she pulled herself together and in August 1935 appeared in *At Marian's* in Newport, Rhode Island, at the Casino Theatre. It was a full house. "Miss Taylor was warmly greeted when she made her first appearance, and the applause at the end, requiring several curtain calls, indicated that many in the audience had an enjoyable evening."[61] Although Laurette had rewritten the play, the local paper noted it had its rough spots. "It is a performance that provokes thought on the philosophy expressed, and will gain in smoothness as the week progresses.... It required some time for the plot to gain the momentum desired, but this point was apparently reached in the final act, and from there on the play moved swiftly to a novel ending. Despite the fact that Miss Taylor had the responsibility that goes with an author in watching the progress of the plot, she showed flashes of the brilliance that has made her nationally known."[62]

Though revised, the plot was still the same, and most guessed that it was autobiographical. A newspaper article described it as "a psychological study of the effect of a habit, this particular one being drink. Miss Taylor was the central figure around whom the entire plot progressed, and for that reason it was best when she was on the stage."[63]

It appeared in the fall of 1935 that Laurette might once again choose a movie role. "If Laurette Taylor likes the script, she will return to pictures in *A Son Comes Home*. Said script has been air-mailed to the stage star in New York, and so her decision is likely to be made — any moment. *A Son Comes Home* was mentioned at one time for Pauline Lord. Tom Brown is in the picture in the title part.... Start of *A Son Comes Home* is scheduled for November 11."[64] The picture was released without Laurette — or Tom Brown — in 1936. The stars were Mary Boland, Julie Haydon, Donald Woods, and Wallace Ford.

An intriguing rumor circulated in December 1935 that Laurette would appear with Maude Adams in *Twelfth Night*. Unfortunately, it appears that though Laurette was eager to do it, Adams was not.[65]

By this point in her career, Laurette was scrambling to find jobs to pay the bills. Still, there were some who considered her a legend. "Vincent Price remembered that, when he first appeared on Broadway [in 1936] as Prince Albert in *Victoria Regina*, 'there were three separate factions as to who was the greatest stage actress of the time — Laurette Taylor, Nazimova, or [Eva] Le Gallienne.'"[66]

On January 6, 1936, *At Marian's* opened at the Miami Playhouse. Staged by the Manhattan Repertory Theatre Company, it represented an attempt by producer Walter Hartwig to bring theater to Florida's winter colony.[67] The attempt failed, and the show closed on January 25. According to the *New York Times*, Laurette returned to New York in early February and set about rewriting the play, "putting more comedy into it."[68]

She spent the summer of 1936 in Ogunquit, where she mingled with student actors, telling stories and offering advice. This is where she met Eloise Sheldon, a young actress who became her newest protégée. According to Marguerite Courtney, "Generally there was a promising young actress to whom Laurette gave special attention, working extra hours at home on scenes, personally supervising clothes and fittings, seeing to it that she 'ate properly.' The pattern of the relationship first established with Lynn Fontanne, although never again as close, was repeated many times."[69]

Sheldon, hoping to start a theatre career, returned with Laurette to New York. She became Laurette's friend and eventually moved into her apartment to help with expenses. Years later she also became friend/confidante to Eva Le Gallienne. "Although she was eighteen years younger than Le Gallienne, Eloise possessed an old-world grace, quiet intelligence, and unflappable common sense that the older woman appreciated. 'Laurette was lucky to find her,' Le Gallienne observed."[70]

Meanwhile, Laurette was working on a new play, *Of the Theatre*, which was again autobiographical. It was, according to Marguerite, "the story of an old actress who sits in the audience and exchanges views with young drama students rehearsing on the stage."[71]

In late September a Los Angeles columnist included a short blurb that suggested Taylor wanted to work again. "Max Gordon is looking around for a play for Laurette Taylor, and it might just be one of that pair he is expecting from Sidney Howard. It has been a long time since Miss Taylor found a Broadway vehicle to her liking."[72]

In November it was announced that Laurette had finally found a play. "After an absence of more than four years from the Broadway stage, Laurette Taylor is expected to return next month in Gilbert Miller's production of *Promise*, for which Sir Cedric Hardwicke and Frank Lawton already have been announced."[73] However, in December it was announced that the play would be delayed, and Laurette had been replaced. "Wednesday, December 30, is the new date for *Promise*, whose postponement had already been announced. The name of Laurette Taylor is omitted in the latest bulletin from the Gilbert Miller office, and that of Irene Browne added, indicating a replacement."[74]

In August 1937 Taylor premiered her play *Of the Theater* in summer theatre at the Colony in Ogunquit, Maine. "With Lillian Foster in the second feminine role, it tells the story of two actresses, one of whom clings to the days of romantic performances and the other moves forward with modern ideas of acting."[75]

Other than the companionship of Eloise, one of the few things Laurette enjoyed during this period was working with students. In March 1938 the *New York Times* reported that Laurette was making a special appearance at the Plymouth Theatre. "Supported by a group of eleven actors, Laurette Taylor will appear as guest artist this afternoon at the Plymouth Theatre in the sixth audition conducted by the Apprentice Theatre of the American Theatre Council. They will be seen in the first half of the first act of Miss Taylor's play, *Of the Theatre*.... The author-actress has staged the performance and also has directed another number on the bill, *One Word Sketch*, by Frank Egan. It is a ten-minute play with a cast of only two players, each of whom has only one word of dialogue to speak."[76] A follow-up article the next day added, "Six years absent from the New York stage, Laurette Taylor returned for a few moments yesterday afternoon.... There was an ovation."[77]

That same year Laurette turned down a role in *The Young in Heart*. Producer David Selznick also tried to get Mary Pickford, Maude Adams, Grace George, Doro-

Laurette Taylor in *Outward Bound* (1939).

thy Gish, and Lillian Gish.[78] Stage actress Minnie Dupree eventually ended up with the role.

Desperate for parts, Laurette agreed to play in Shaw's *Candida* in August at Mt. Kisco.[79] *New York Times* critic Brooks Atkinson found her performance lacking. "It is a little difficult to discover just what her ideas about Shaw's second best heroine may be, for her performance is still in the tentative and submissive state until the last act, when she takes command and suffuses the stage with the warmth of womanly acting. During the first two acts she casually passes through the play." According to Atkinson, the audience didn't see "a great actress in one of her best parts or characterizations. But they had an opportunity to discover how liquid human speech can be when Miss Taylor pours her voice into it."[80]

Robert Lewis saw her in *Candida* ever day. "I started out in a rickety 'Flivver,' early every afternoon to allow for daily breakdowns along the way. I was in my seat for the opening curtain every night that unforgettable week."[81] Lewis never forgot Laurette's amazing performance. "Taylor's face, marked with lines honorably won in her fierce battle with a difficult life, was lit up from inside with the beauty of her thought and feeling."[82] Other critics described her performance as "incandescent," though at least two cast members were "perfectly dreadful."[83] When asked why their lack of talent didn't affect her performance, she had an interesting comment. "Oh, I believe they are great. They are just having problems showing it. And every night, I go on the stage to support them and give them the energy to be great." Larry Moss summed up her approach. "Instead of complaining about having to work with inferior actors, she just endowed them with great talent and love, and played that. That's why we still talk about Laurette Taylor to this very day."[84]

In the fall of 1938, Laurette was mentioned several times as a possible cast member for *The Merchant of Yonkers*, which was to be directed by Max Reinhardt. "Laurette Taylor is mentioned for a role that is practically enormous; also, she would speak with an Irish brogue, though the character is reported to be a 'Mrs. Levy.' Vincente Minnelli has been approached to design the settings."[85] The producer asked her to audition, plainly telling her that she now had a reputation for being unable to remember her lines. She flatly refused.

# Chapter 9

# OUTWARD BOUND

*"Yes, I am back in the theater, and, this time, I hope to stay."*[1]

Laurette made yet another comeback in *Outward Bound*. Sutton Vane's play was an oldie but goodie about a shipload of passengers who come to realize they're all dead and are now on their way to what they deserve.

Otto Preminger, working out of a rent-free office above Sardi's restaurant, had reached an agreement with Lee Shubert to use the office in exchange for first look at Preminger productions. Meanwhile, Jean Rodney, whom Preminger described as "the stage-struck daughter of a wealthy Wall Street broker"[2] had started Playhouse Company with the idea of presenting a season of plays. *Outward Bound* would be the first.

Cast member Bramwell Fletcher was the original director, but Rodney later asked Preminger to take over. "Otto accepted immediately, even knowing that he would be facing the same problem that had caused Fletcher to depart—Laurette Taylor, a beloved star making a comeback after ten years' absence from the stage, who was also a troublesome alcoholic.... Taylor had quarreled with every suggestion Fletcher had made, and when Otto took over she continued to be snappish, distant, and wary."[3]

In his autobiography, Preminger wrote, "I cast Laurette Taylor to play Mrs. Midgit, the key part. Laurette was then fifty-four years old. She had been an alcoholic for ten years, had started rehearsals on several plays but always dropped out, and this was to be yet another comeback attempt."[4]

Preminger had first met her when she was at a rehearsal for *L'Espoir* [*Promise*]. "Gilbert Miller had cast her in the production of *L'Espoir*. I visited one of the rehearsals. Afterward I met her in Gilbert's office. She kept up a stream of complaints about her leading man, Sir Cedric Hardwicke. 'I can't act with that ham,' she told Miller. 'He's already looking out at the audience and there isn't a soul there yet. What do you think he'll be like when there are people out front?' It was an obsession with her, that performers should look at one another. Eye contact was most important, she felt, and she was right. One day she didn't turn up for rehearsal. When she stayed away for a whole week,

Miller preferred charges to Actors Equity. The union suspended her for a year. She returned to the bottle."⁵

Miller warned Preminger that it would be disastrous to cast Laurette. "Laurette was a great actress — once.... Now she had a drinking problem. She was unsure of herself. Her memory was not as good as it used to be. She could be very awkward."⁶

Producer Bill Brady also tried to talk him out of casting her. "'Believe me, she's a hopeless drunk. She'll never be able to remember her lines and eventually she won't show up and we'll have to get someone else. To save time I will have my wife [Grace George] sit in the balcony and watch rehearsals. When Laurette drops out, she'll step in.'"⁷

Preminger wooed Laurette during lunches and was honest about the rumors surrounding her. Laurette confessed that Grace George's presence made her nervous. It should have, considering Brady's plan. "The actress expressed her fear that the producers had hired her only for the publicity value and that they were planning to replace her with George."⁸

According to Preminger, Laurette invited him to lunch and handed him her script. "'I saw that bitch in the balcony and I know what she's waiting for. Let's not delay things. Here's my script. She can have the part right now.'"⁹ Preminger soothed her bruised feelings. "'Look, Laurette ... I will give you a script with all the changes and cuts that I plan to make. You take it home and learn your part. If it takes two days, fine. If it takes ten days, fine. I promise you that Grace George will not rehearse in the meantime. Only your understudy will rehearse. You will play this part, and only you.' She was back in a few days, letter-perfect. The other members of the cast were still fighting to remember their lines and that made her feel secure. She stayed sober through the rehearsals and didn't waver during the critical days of stress before the opening."¹⁰

Preminger patted himself on the back for successfully controlling Laurette. "'It would have been quite hopeless to approach her with a 'promise-me-you'll-be-a-good-girl,' Preminger recalled. 'There was a demon in her that would not be boxed like that. It was in part what made her so weird on the stage — surprising you with unexpected phrasing and accent; the fluid, the unexpected, this was the nub of her inspiration. To approach her with a program of being good, of never touching another drop, was to try and box her demon. She would never allow it. I knew this at once.'"¹¹

The two temperamental artists bonded through humor, perfectionism, and abrasiveness. According to Willi Frischauer, Preminger and Laurette were similar. "They discussed every aspect of the play.... Though their backgrounds were so different, their views on acting were amazingly similar. She would not tolerate incompetent partners. 'She could be sharp about other actors' weaknesses,' Preminger said. That applied also to Preminger. 'She was not in any sense a mild woman!' Nor was Preminger a mild man. During rehearsals her voice rang out gaily: 'M'sieur Printemps'—her name for Preminger. He amused her. She imitated his heavy accent and the way he wiggled his fingers over his head when he was excited. He treated her thoughtfully."[12]

Of course, they didn't always get along. "It did not mean he was soft with her or the rest of the cast. He called them for rehearsal on opening day and kept them in the theatre in the late afternoon: 'Nobody has ever asked me to do that!' Laurette protested. Preminger, all sweetness: 'I think it is better if we do it this way.' Laurette never had a chance to become depressed and take to the bottle."[13]

Opening night was December 22, 1938, and Laurette received a long ovation when she made her first appearance. She also received 22 curtain calls. According to Preminger, "Many people wept."[14] Laurette gave much of the credit to Preminger who "approached her with deep patience and tact that earned him the respect of the cast."[15] Otto Preminger was grateful for the opportunity to direct her and said she was "the greatest actress ever born."[16]

Laurette had become friendly with fellow cast member Vincent Price, who was married to her good friend Edith Barrett. Laurette found him charming. She said Vincent had "eyes like a rolltop desk." According to Price's daughter, "After her spectacular reception that night, as she walked arm in arm with the Prices to dinner at their apartment, she said, 'It really wasn't a good performance.'" In Price's mind, however, "working with Laurette was a kind of culmination of his stage career to date."[17]

Taylor played Mrs. Midgit, an elderly woman who spends much the play knitting. "I love the role of the old scrubwoman. The part that carries the heart is the part that carries the piece."[18] For her role Laurette had to learn to knit. According to a newspaper writer, "It's just a long blob in dark green. The funny part is that when the action calls for her to show anger, she knits furiously and makes hopeless snarls at these points. Where it's quiet, she goes right along. I saw the knitting and it was like a graph, every snarl at regular intervals shows her places to emote. And on the first night, when she was nervous, the whole thing was a mess."[19]

Since Laurette played someone quite a bit older than herself, she was heavily made-up and wore a wig and unattractive shoes. "She hates them all, takes off the make-up and wig to take her final curtain bow, and unlaces the shoes in her dressing room. She had to tromp miles to find a pair—finally she located them in a bargain basement."[20]

When interviewed about the comeback, Taylor seemed excited about the opportunities coming her way. "There are radio things to do, and probably more revivals and, of course, all those plays I wrote myself which nobody would produce — *At Marian's, Of the Theater* and *Enchantment*. Also another one, written under a pomme de terre or nom de theater, or whatever you call it, which really is going to be — but that is still a secret."[21]

Florence Reed, of *Shanghai Gesture* fame, was also in the play. Laurette had little respect for Reed's talent. "When friends visited backstage she mentioned co-star Florence Reed. 'Poor Florence, she's so terrible in this part, you know.' The visitors tried to hush Laurette. Miss Reed occupied an adjoining dressing room and through paper-thin walls could hear everything. 'Oh, don't worry. Florence knows how awful she is. It doesn't bother her.'"[22]

Paul Shinkman wrote that the play was "[a] strikingly beautiful revival of one of the few plays ever to be an outstanding success in both England and America," and added that Taylor and Reed are "as unlike in their acting as two actresses could be."[23] Still, it worked. Walter Winchell wrote in his column that the play "offers some of the finest acting in town."[24] Richard Watts, Jr., singled out Laurette for praise. "There is no more brilliant actress in the world than Miss Taylor and her long absence from the theater is one of the tragedies of the American stage. In the Sutton Vane play she has the role of the little old charwoman, who is the work's most sympathetic character, and she plays with such glowing magnificence that we can all see once more what a superb player she really is."[25]

Preminger believed that one of the keys to Laurette's genius was her ability to focus. "Laurette had a rare gift of concentration. She always looked at the other actors even if it meant playing with her back to the audience. She never had to raise her voice. She was so much the character she acted that audiences were gathered in to her and could hear what she was saying even if she whispered. And she took direction beautifully. She put her faith in the director and followed his instructions without question."[26]

The play was so successful that it ran until November 1939. Tallulah Bankhead reportedly saw the play six times and called Laurette the "greatest actress in the world."[27]

Cast member Diana Barrymore was less impressed with Laurette and bitterly complained about her unprofessionalism. Barrymore met her when she read for the part. "I came on stage in the empty theater to find the cast there. I knew none of the actors, although I'd heard all my life of Laurette Taylor and Florence Reed. Miss Taylor was a small, mousy woman who seemed preoccupied."[28] Barrymore played Ann, one of the suicidal lovers, and toured with the play to Philadelphia and then on to Chicago.

Laurette was the star and received the last curtain call. According to Barrymore, "When we took our curtain calls, I was in the first group of four to appear; then, finally, Florence and Laurette; then Laurette alone. I watched from the wings as she came forward on the stage, all alone, and bowed humbly to the thunderous ovation, for her alone. I said to myself, if ever I take a call alone, if ever I become a star, as long as I live, I'll do it the way she does. She comes out, with little, hesitant steps, as if to say, 'Who me? Are you sure it's me you want?' As if to say, in astonishment, almost in bewilderment, 'What, you are applauding me? For what? For what ...?' It was a consummate piece of acting. The audience loved it. I loved it."[29]

Barrymore believed Laurette resented her because she'd wanted Eloise Sheldon to play Ann. She described Sheldon as "a girl my age who was her secretary and protégée."[30] Barrymore found Laurette a bit of a bully. "During the entire tour Laurette was distant. Now and then she criticized my delivery. Once she reduced me to tears." Perhaps another reason Barrymore didn't like Laurette was because of the trick she played on Bramwell Fletcher, who later became Diana's husband. Otto Preminger explained that Laurette "was impatient with other members of the cast when they looked at the audience while they were addressing her. Bramwell Fletcher had many scenes with her in *Outward Bound*. In rehearsal I compelled him to look at her but once the play began its long run of 255 performances he began to turn to the audience more and more. She warned him one day that if he did it one more time she would embarrass him so that he would never forget it. When he turned from her that night and spoke his lines out to the audience she began to stare at his fly. It is an actor's nightmare that he might be on stage with an unbuttoned or unzipped fly. Fletcher was aghast but didn't dare check it in front of the audience. He ad-libbed some excuse and went off stage. He found that there was nothing wrong but he was so shaken by the experience that he never let his attention drift again. When he was supposed to look at Laurette, he looked at her."[31]

Barrymore also complained about Laurette's drinking. Yes, a Barrymore criticizing someone else's drinking is hysterical. Still, in her autobiography, Barrymore chided Laurette for drinking on the tour. Barrymore later developed her own drinking problem, which led to a ruined career and personal life and ultimately to her suicide in 1960, when she was 38. Still, in her 1957 autobiography, Barrymore complained that Laurette was unprofessional. "On stage Laurette was a great actress. Backstage she was an unhappy woman fighting alcohol. She had made a sensational comeback in this play after years of absence. Her notices were eulogies. But she drank. Fortunately she could play Mrs. Midget drunk or sober. Mrs. Midget was self-effacing and fearful, unconsciously funny and unconsciously pathetic — always a little confused. The part called for a fluttering of hands, a slurring of words, nervous, uncertain mannerisms. The audience suspected; it never knew. But backstage there were doctors and vitamin B injections and pots of black coffee and distraught stage managers, and cast members angry and bitter because they never knew what cue Laurette might throw them — or fail to throw them.... Though I was humble before Laurette's superb acting, I thought it disgraceful for anyone, no matter how great, to take the theater so lightly as to drink before a performance."[32]

According to Barrymore, opening night in Chicago at the Harris was cancelled because Laurette was too drunk to go on. She'd also injured her head after falling on the radiator. Barrymore arrived shortly before eight o'clock and saw a commotion outside Laurette's open dressing room door. "I peeped in and gasped. There sat Laurette before her mirror, her clothes disheveled, blood trickling from an ugly gash in her forehead. One of the cast was carefully staunching the cut. Laurette was trying, unsteadily to make up. 'I will go on,' she said thickly. 'Nobody can tell me I'm drunk! I'm perfectly able —' Someone closed the door."[33]

The audience was told that Taylor had a stomach ailment. She was also unable to perform the following night. Her first performance, then, was a Wednesday matinee. Laurette told people she'd had a heart attack. In fact, the *Los Angeles* Times reported on November 30, 1939, that Laurette missed the opening night in Chicago because of a heart attack. She missed no other performances on the 12-week tour.

Acting teacher Uta Hagen often stressed to students the importance of making an entrance. One of her favorite examples was Laurette in *Outward Bound*. "I will never forget the magic created by Laurette Taylor's first entrance in *Outward Bound*. She came onto the stage *backwards*, stepping over the high sill from the deck to the salon of the boat, still nodding and bidding farewell to an imagined passenger on the outer deck. Once into the salon, she turned to the people on the stage, and recognized her son with a wailing, 'Owwww!' Did that entrance ever come from a past into the present with a future!"[34]

Director Robert Lewis also found Laurette's performance spell-binding. "I remember her arriving (she never 'made an entrance') in the bar of the ship in *Outward Bound*, looking like all the Hundred Neediest Cases, seeming not to know where she was, who all those people were, and what was going on. I sat forward in my seat and wanted to cry out, 'Don't worry, honey, it's only that you're dead.' Now, mind you, once she was in the scene she found out whatever she needed to know, but it all happened completely spontaneously and seemed to have no sense of anticipatory preparation."[35]

Laurette was also pretty good with exits. Helen Hayes studied Laurette after George Tyler assigned her to observe various actresses early in her career including Mrs. Fiske and Laurette. According to Hayes, "She was beyond technique and had the gift of intimacy on the stage. Whatever she was doing seemed utterly spontaneous, as if it had just occurred to her. She was so at home on the stage, so absorbed in the story, you hardly noticed her performance until you realized how effective it was. I always loved her exits. There's a temptation among actors to make an exit a momentous happening in order to bring a round of applause. Laurette simply walked out of the room."[36]

In *Time's* review of *Outward Bound*, the critic first pointed out that revivals rarely worked. "Seeing an attractive play again after 15 years is usually as disillusioning as re-encountering a once-attractive woman." But this revival was different. "*Outward Bound* comes off better than 'well-preserved,' still retains its humor, imaginativeness, suspense and its more elusive quality of theatre."[37]

Brooks Atkinson described her as "one of the theatre's great ladies." He also wrote that her performance was subtle. "Her buoyant, shy acting with its little steps forward or back to create emphasis in a scene makes the part she is playing come wholly alive and seem like improvisation.... From the theatrical point of view it may not be a fat part, but it is certainly actable, and in Miss Taylor's effulgent playing it is triumphant. She is all grace, undulation and breathlessness when she first hesitatingly appears in strange surroundings. By her keenness of imagination and innocence of spirit Miss Taylor can always convince you that the character she is playing has never been on the stage before; she is like Pauline Lord in that respect."[38]

Barnard Hughes saw the play and was impressed. "She fidgeted and twisted those first five minutes. I thought, 'Oh, my God, what does that poor woman think she's doing?' And all of a sudden my hair was standing up on my head."[39]

Playwright Horton Foote wrote that seeing Laurette in *Outward Bound* changed his life. "Suddenly, I began to realize that talent was abundant but genius and originality were quite rare."[40]

Lynn Fontanne came to see Laurette in *Outward Bound*, though they'd been estranged for years. When Hartley died, Laurette was bitter that Fontanne didn't visit her. "Lynn lived within five blocks of me ... and I had no desire to see anyone except Lynn. I expected some mental help from the friend I had helped when she was miserable." Fontanne had sent Laurette a leather bag and violets on the opening night of *Alice-Sit-by-the-Fire*, but Laurette groused that "they were six years too late." Finally, in 1938, they sat down and talked after Laurette's performance. "The women stayed up and talked all through the night. They reminisced about the events in their long friendship and all the plays they had done together and all the odd and beautiful and talented people they had known in London and New York and the men they had loved. When they separated, they had come to some sort of terms with their pasts and with each other."[41]

Taylor received the Barter Theater's Laymen's Committee Award for outstanding stage performance of the year for her role in *Outward Bound*. Eleanor Roosevelt presented the citation to Laurette at a luncheon. "One acre of land on the side of a mountain near Abingdon, Va.; two jobs at the Barter Theatre this summer for two young actors chosen by Miss Taylor; one sugar-cured Virginia ham and one statuette of Mrs. Midgit."[42] Laurette was referred to as "the first lady of the theater." When accepting the award, Laurette said, "In the theater, opportunity knocks almost every day, and I delayed opening the door. I've been in the shade a long time. It's nice being in the sun again.'"[43] After auditioning 68 participants for the summer internship gig, Laurette chose Larry Gates and Edith Sommer.[44]

There was talk about Taylor appearing in a film version of *Outward Bound*. "There seems a definite promise in the air of bringing Laurette Taylor ... to the coast for a local staging of the Sutton Vane drama. Miss Taylor, who has been acclaimed by critics for the brilliance of her performance, might possibly be in the film version Warner Bros. is planning."[45] Hedda Hopper also wanted Laurette to appear in the film. "If Warners does a remake of *Outward Bound* and casts Laurette Taylor in the same part she's been playing in New York, they'll have one of the greatest stars who ever hit the screen."[46] The film was not made until 1944. Titled *Between Two Worlds*, it starred John Garfield and Eleanor Parker. Sara Allgood played Mrs. Midget.

In January the cast of *Outward Bound* performed at the National Theatre in a command performance for President and Mrs. Roosevelt. The event was the President's birthday as well as a March of Dimes benefit. She was scared out of her wits upon being told that the president asked to sit next to her. Laurette was a big Roosevelt supporter but quite intimidated. "Laurette just stared at him, her face ashen and all the questions she had planned to ask forgotten. Roosevelt was aware of her petrified condition. To help her relax, he began to complain laughingly about a certain duty of his office that every year spoiled his birthday for him. 'It's that son of a bitch Hitler,' he explained, looking directly at Laurette. 'My birthday is also the anniversary of his coming to power. He makes one of his speeches at the occasion and I, on my birthday, must listen to that crap.'"[47]

Laurette reflected on her past and future when she was interviewed during *Outward Bound*'s run. "My best role? It was in *The National Anthem*, which was also Hartley's best play, but ahead of its time.... [M]y past still haunts me, you see. Apparently my grandmother does, too, for I've just completed

Marguerite Taylor and her father, Charles Taylor (photograph courtesy of Meg Courtney).

a novel called *An Irish Fable*. What's more, I've sold it."⁴⁸ The book was never published.

Fame is fleeting. Hedda Hopper reported in a 1939 column that Laurette was unknown to a new generation. "One of the noted glamour girls on returning from New York said: 'The best performance I saw was Laurette Taylor in *Outward Bound*. Wonder who she is?' Laurette happens to be Dwight's mother, and had she been born in any other country would have been hailed as the greatest living actress."⁴⁹

In 1940 Robert Lewis tried to talk Laurette into appearing with John Garfield in *Heavenly Express*. She declined,⁵⁰ but Lewis picked her brain about her acting technique. "She insisted she devised and 'set' every last move, gesture, look, and line-reading in rehearsal and then faithfully executed them all on stage. I could only surmise that if, indeed, that were so, she certainly seemed to forget them all once she came on. For no one had more of a sense of 'the first time' and less of a studied look than Laurette Taylor.... I surmised that, with performing artists, what they say they do, and what they actually do may be quite dissimilar."⁵¹

In the spring Hedda Hopper announced that Laurette might make another film. "Metro has brought Laurette Taylor from New York to test for one of the acting plums of the year, the part of Emma Ritter in *Escape*.... This will be Laurette's third [sic] fling at the movies. Years ago she did *Peg o' My Heart*.... Those were the days when anyone over 20 was a liability, not an asset. Now, I feel she'll come into her own."[52] Nazimova, Judith Anderson, and Jane Cowl were also up for the role. Nazimova ended up with it.

Again, in July 1940, there was talk that Laurette would return to Hollywood. "Real drive is on, I hear, to recruit Laurette Taylor for the movies again.... Paramount, it appears, is the studio which has designs and intentions of contracting her to delineate the title personage in *Miss Susie Slagle's*, the story of the boardinghouse keeper who caters to the young medical students of Johns Hopkins."[53] The picture wasn't released until 1946, and Lillian Gish ended up playing the role.

In late 1941 columnist Hedda Hopper wrote — again — that Laurette would soon be appearing in a motion picture. "Good news that Laurette Taylor is coming out for a picture. She's had many offers but didn't like parts Hollywood offered her. No doubt about it, Laurette's one of the greatest actresses in America."[54] Although Hopper didn't mention the film, it might have been a remake of *Anna Christie*. Director John Ford was toying with making the film with a cast that included Laurette (no doubt playing the Marie Dressler role), Ingrid Bergman, John Wayne, and Thomas Mitchell. If made, Gregg Toland would have been behind the camera, and Dudley Nichols would write the adaptation.[55] Alas, it never came to pass.

Charles Taylor, the "Master of Melodrama," died on March 20, 1942, at the age of 78. He was survived by the children he had with Laurette, Dwight and Marguerite, as well as a son, Charles E. Taylor, who was born from a marriage to Emma McKenna, who'd died in 1888.[56] Taylor had dropped out of their lives for the most part after the divorce. Occasionally Dwight spent time with him, especially soon after the break. Very quickly, Laurette's fortunes had improved while Charles' had not. He was forced to compete with a new medium, silent film, and never came up with another big hit.

The *New York Times* reported that Laurette had been reading scripts but "none [have] met her fancy." Instead, Laurette was focusing on her writing career. "A bit irked at this situation, Miss Taylor decided to desert the stage (momentarily) for the study, and her typewriter has been working overtime of late. For *Town and Country* she has been writing a series of portraits: Noël Coward, Lynn Fontanne, Mrs. Patrick Campbell. In between she has been laboring over a novel she calls, at this moment, *I'll Know My Love*, which is about an Irish immigrant family."[57] This manuscript, which was probably a revision of her earlier novel, was also never published.

Playbill for *The Glass Menagerie* (1945) (photograph courtesy of Mary Pearsall).

In December 1943 Laurette decided she would "play" grandmother. Marguerite had just had her first child, and Laurette felt a grandmotherly urge. Perhaps in the same way that she'd decided to "do" Shakespeare and pantomime, Laurette impulsively decided to "do" family. Laurette informed a friend she was going to California to visit relatives. During this trip she stayed with Dwight and his three young children. Unfortunately, granddaughter Audrey Wallace-Taylor's memory is a traumatic one. She recalled pleading with a drunken Laurette to keep the noise down because she was unable to sleep. Laurette lost her temper and threw a radio at the teenager's door. Whatever fantasy Laurette had in her head about bonding with family didn't materialize. She later told a friend, "[T]hey didn't like me very much, and I didn't like them."[58]

In the beginning of 1944 Hedda Hopper was pleading with Hollywood to hire Laurette to replace Marie Dressler, who'd died in 1934. Noting that Laurette was in Hollywood visiting son Dwight, Hopper wrote, "Since Marie Dressler's passing, we've been wanting some one to take her place. Might I humbly suggest to Metro that Laurette receive that honor? She is one of the great actresses of our time. Frances Marion, who wrote most of Marie's successes, is at Metro, so it would seem to me a set-up. How about it fellows?"[59] Someone must have been paying attention, because the following year Dorothy Kilgallen wrote, "L.B. Mayer would like Laurette Taylor to take over the celluloid roles originally purchased for the late Marie Dressler."[60]

Hopper continued campaigning for Laurette in March 1944. "How about Laurette Taylor in *The Old Lady Shows Her Medals* with Jimmy Stewart? I can dream, can't I?"[61] However, Laurette's next success would be in the play that made her a Broadway legend.

## Chapter 10

# THE GLASS MENAGERIE

*"That just goes to show that the postman can ring twice."*[1]

Taylor claimed that she accepted no parts between *Outward Bound* and *The Glass Menagerie* because the roles were mediocre. "'[E]ven a good actress cannot do much with a poor play,'"[2] she complained. According to the same article, Laurette focused on writing. "She ... tried her luck at a play, which was not accepted for New York, and later a novel which has been turned down after two writings. Even now, that she has returned to the stage, she still devotes so many hours a day to writing."[3]

Ultimately, however, Laurette Taylor chose to return to acting when offered a role in *The Glass Menagerie*. Her success in this play surpassed even *Peg o' My Heart*. According to theatre researcher Mary C. Henderson, "Although the role (Amanda Wingfield) has been played frequently by other actresses on stage, screen, and television, Laurette Taylor's performance has remained the touchstone."[4]

Nevertheless, the play had a troubled genesis. Tennessee Williams had originally written a screenplay about "an aging Southern belle."[5] He submitted it to MGM, who promptly turned it down. After MGM let him go, Williams worked on converting the screenplay to a play, tentatively titled *The Gentleman Caller*. By the time agent Audrey Wood showed it around, the title had been changed to *The Glass Menagerie*. Eddie Dowling optioned it. According to one of the first blurbs about it, the *New York Times* wrote, "It's a sentimental story about a worried mother's problems in marrying off her crippled daughter."[6]

Naysayers doubted it would succeed. "Despite advice from theatrical friends that *The Glass Menagerie* would never be a success because of its fragile plot and unhappy ending, Mr. Dowling went ahead trying to raise money."[7] Louis J. Singer was convinced to invest $75,000. Dowling told him, "You are going to lose all your money in this play, but it will be a lovely failure, Laurette Taylor will be glorious, and people will say nice things about you."[8]

According to Jessie Royce Landis, critic George Jean Nathan was responsible for Laurette being cast. The two had long feuded because Laurette thought Nathan had been unfair to Hartley. This was common knowledge to everyone but Landis, who made the mistake of inviting both to a Thanksgiving party. Once alerted to the acrimony, Landis set out to do everything she could to keep the two apart. "I knew George's rapier-like wit and Laurette's caustic tongue, and I could imagine the result." However, the two found each other — and behaved charmingly. "[T]here were George and Laurette sitting on the sofa like two love-birds. I think each was trying to prove how wrong the other had been: each was trying to out-fascinate the other! It was because of that meeting that Laurette had a chance to make a wonderful come-back in the theatre after several years of retirement. It was George Jean Nathan's idea that Eddie Dowling cast her in the part of Amanda in *The Glass Menagerie*, Tennessee Williams' first hit in New York."[9]

Ward Morehouse also wrote that it was Nathan who convinced Dowling to hire Laurette. "And the actress for the mother? Jane Cowl, perhaps. She could do it, Dowling decided, but he ... listened to George Jean Nathan and the role was offered to Laurette Taylor."[10]

Playwright George Oppenheimer, who wrote that Taylor gave "the finest female performance I have ever seen"[11] in *The Glass Menagerie*, explained that Eddie Dowling heard the rumors about Laurette's drinking. He wisely went to her bartender to find out the truth. The barkeep admitted that Laurette had two drinks but no more. "You have my word for it that she's never tight. And if you signed her," the bartender added, "that would give her such security that she wouldn't even need two drinks."[12]

Tennessee Williams' mother attended the Chicago rehearsals and noticed "the friction that seems part of the birth pangs of every play." Williams and Dowling feuded because Dowling wanted to add comedy. Dowling and Laurette feuded, too. "Mr. Dowling and Laurette engaged in a quarrel or two, usually under their breaths, and Laurette, who was trying to make a comeback in this part, would retire for a while to the nearest bar to recover."[13]

The necessary southern accent proved troublesome to Taylor. Williams' mother watched it evolve during rehearsals. "Laurette was a genius in the rapidity with which she acquired a southern accent. Describing herself as a 'southerner out of Ireland,' she said she had never been below Washington, D.C., except to Florida, but she had visited Southern Italy, if that helped. At first she kept charging up and down the stage, her head wrapped in a bandana, looking like a southern mammy and talking like one. I whispered to Tom, 'A southern lady doesn't sound like a southern mammy imitating a southern lady.' Laurette toned it down for the opening and thereafter. She tried at first, according to a newspaper interview, to learn a southern accent by imitating

Tom [Tennessee]. At one point, he interrupted her to say, 'Youah ayaccent's too thick, Miz' Tayluh.'"

"But I'm trying to imitate yours, Tennessee," she said.

"*Mah* accent?" Tom said in surprise. "Ah don't hayev any ayaccent."[14]

Irving Rapper described how Laurette conquered the accent. "[W]hat was wonderful about Laurette Taylor, aside from being a genius of an actress, she didn't play a southern accent. She suggested it.... She just touched it lightly. She got the inflections of it and it didn't make the whole part a stunt.... She didn't do it literally."[15]

During rehearsals of *The Glass Menagerie*, Williams was worried about more than Laurette's accent. In a letter to frequent correspondent Donald Wyndham, he expressed disappointment with Laurette. "Taylor was ad libbing practically every speech and the show sounded like the Aunt Jemima Pancake Hour. We all got drunk, and this A.M. Taylor was even *worse*. I finally lost my temper and when she made one of her little insertions, I screamed over the footlights, 'My God, what corn!' She screamed back that I was a fool and all playwrights made her sick — that she had not only been a star for 40 years but had made a living as a writer which was better than I had done — then came back after lunch and suddenly began giving a real acting performance — so good that Julie and I, the sentimental element in the company, wept. So I don't know what to think or expect."[16]

Claudia Cassidy, drama critic for *The Chicago Tribune*, had her doubts about Laurette before opening night. "I remember a day before the play opened. A woman crossed the stage, script in hand, mumbling. She wore pants and sweaters, scarf and big, muffling coat. Her hair was a scramble, her face what happens when a lovely one is puffed up, stretched out of shape, and then collapsed. That was Laurette."[17]

In fact, Laurette had gone on a drunk. Paul Bowles said that she hadn't been drinking, "but suddenly the dress rehearsal coming up was too much. The night of the dress rehearsal she was nowhere to be found. And finally she was found, unconscious, down behind the furnace in the basement, by the janitor. And there was gloom, I can tell you, all over the theatre because no one thought she would be able to go on the next night. She pulled herself together and gave, as you know, an historic performance the next night, and from then. It was marvelous."[18]

The play opened on December 26, 1944, one of the coldest nights of the year in Chicago. According to Mrs. Williams, "Everything seemed against the play, even the weather. The streets were so ice-laden we could not find a taxi to take us to the Civic Theatre and had to walk. The gale blowing off Lake Michigan literally hurled us through the theater door. Tom went backstage, unable to sit still, to find everyone gripped by a slight case of opening night d.t.'s. It had taken twenty-four hours to erect the single set because the man slated to supervise had gone off on a binge and could not be located. Laurette was discovered a few minutes before curtain time dyeing an old bathrobe she was supposed to wear in the second act, because she suddenly did not like its shade."[19]

Somehow, though, the troubled play came together. Mrs. Williams was one of many who used the word *magic* to describe opening night in Chicago. "After the curtain went up, I became lost in the magic of the words and the superb performance of its four players. You couldn't call Laurette or Julie pretty but they imbued their parts with a strong spiritual quality. This was the first of Tom's plays I had seen ... and I was thrilled to think he had created a play without a wasted word and one in which every moment added drama. I don't think there's been a play like it, before or since.... The audience, too, seemed spellbound."[20]

When Mrs. Williams went backstage, she was stunned when Laurette admitted that she was playing her. "I wanted to congratulate Laurette, who had brought down the house with her amazing performance as Amanda Wingfield, the faded, fretful, dominating mother lost in the dream world of her past, bullying her son into finding a gentleman caller for his abnormally shy sister. I entered Laurette's dressing room, not knowing what to expect, for she was sometimes quite eccentric. She was sitting with her feet propped up on the radiator, trying to keep warm. Before I had a chance to get out a word, she greeted me. 'Well, how did you like you'selff, Miz' Williams?' she asked. I was so shocked I didn't know what to say. It had not occurred to me as I watched Tom's play that *I* was Amanda."[21] Later, in her book, *Remember Me to Tom*, Mrs. Williams stated, "I think it is high time the ghost of Amanda was laid. I am *not* Amanda. I'm sure if Tom stops to think, he realizes I am not. The only resemblance I have to Amanda is that we both like jonquils."[22] Whatever you say, Mrs. Williams.

Speaking of jonquils, Laurette asked Tennessee to remove some of them from the script. "It sounds like too many jonquils to me," she said. "Can't you cut out a few jonquils, Tennessee?"

"Laurette," Tom said, "it's got rhythm. I need all those jonquils."

She practiced the lines at home, "sort of sang them to myself," she reported. She returned to admit, "Tennessee, you were right."[23]

Claudia Cassidy's review of *The Glass Menagerie* became legendary. She wrote, "This brand new play, which turned the Civic Theatre into a place of steadily increasing enchantment last night, is still fluid with change, but it is vividly written, and in the main superbly acted." She found minor faults with

Anthony Ross and Eddie Dowling and was particularly hard on Julie Haydon. However, she had only praise for Laurette. "[A]h, that Laurette Taylor! I never saw Miss Taylor as Peg, but if that was the role of her youth, this is the role of her maturity.... [S]he gives a magnificent performance."[24] Cassidy kept going back to see the play, mainly to watch Laurette. "At the beginning, this ... belle of the old south is sunk deep in frustration, pricked only by the nagging urge not to admit defeat. She looks like the scuffed, rundown slipper that outlived the ball. Yet when for a brief moment she knows hope, she leans on the tenement stoop and gazes at the moon that might have been that very slipper, brand new. And over her face flit all the lovely ghosts of girlhood when 17 gentlemen callers came riding to pay her tribute. You won't see a more radiant sight than Laurette Taylor at that magic moment."[25] Box office receipts got off to a slow start, but partly through the cajoling from Cassidy and other critics, audiences began streaming in.

Geraldine Page was an usher for the Chicago production. "'I stopped to watch Miss Taylor start and thought to myself, "Oh, the poor woman. She can't act. I've been to acting school for six months, and I know." And then, entranced, "the next thing I knew, the play was over."[26]

Shelley Winters, who saw *The Glass Menagerie* in Chicago, had never heard of Laurette Taylor. She went to see the play because she was Tony Ross' friend. "I thought she actually changed her clothes and make-up and became a young girl in one scene. I'll never forget the performance I saw!.... I couldn't believe this transformation happened before my eyes! Just with the words. Because I knew nothing about *any kind* of acting, much less method acting. She suddenly became a young girl! She had a filmy, raggedy chiffon dress. It was an incredible thing. She suddenly became a young girl. She blushed. Her face became flushed. And it was an incredible thing. I thought it was some kind of trick."[27] Winters, who was a budding starlet at the time, gave Laurette some advice. "Do you have an agent? You know, you really should be in Hollywood." Before she left that night, Winters got Laurette to autograph a photo for her.

Julie Haydon carried her hero worship of Laurette too far. On opening night in Chicago, "when they were taking curtain calls, Julie Haydon knelt down, grabbed Laurette's hand and kissed it. Later Laurette said, 'Don't do that any more, Julie, it's too embarrassing.' Julie did it again the second night — ditto the third. But never again. Fourth night Laurette slapped her right before the customers."[28] Marguerite Courtney claimed the story wasn't true. According to Laurette's explanation, it was more of love tap. "True, she kissed my hand and I told her not to, but what I did was pull my hand up as she held it, chucking her lightly under the jaw. It's ridiculous to say that I slapped her."[29]

In fact, Julie was a bit of a nut. Tennessee Williams told a friend that Laurette enjoyed "tormenting poor Julie unmercifully but I think Julie is getting back at her in her own sweet way. For instance, Laurette declared furiously that Julie had called her up at two o'clock last night to enquire sweetly if 'she could go out and buy me an apple.' I think that is the funniest Julie story I've heard yet, but they are unlimited. What *characters*! The company is more amusing than the show!"[30]

Williams also wrote about a prank Haydon played on Laurette. "Julie gave Laurette a nigger baby doll. I think it was a dig at Laurette's nigger accent. Anyway Laurette was furious and threw it out of her dressing-room, yelling 'Who put that horrible thing in here?' It was several days before Julie confessed."[31]

Years later, in 1980, Haydon played Amanda in *The Glass Menagerie* at the Lion Theatre.[32] "Miss Haydon doesn't want to imitate Miss Taylor, she says, but feels a responsibility to pass on 'a *bit*' of her characterization as a sort of homage." In fact, by 1980 Haydon had played Amanda many times and tried different approaches, but always had Laurette's performance in her mind.

Haydon recounted the first time she met Laurette. "Laurette Taylor, whom she remembered as having 'great big bewildered, beautiful eyes and the darlingness of a toddler,' told her when they first met, 'We are going to be very good friends and you can ask me anything you want.' So she asked Miss Taylor how she would limp if she were acting the crippled Laura. She said, 'Why, I'm ashamed of you,' Miss Haydon recounted. 'You should understand the heart and soul of this girl before you even *consider* the limp.' Two weeks later, midrehearsal, Miss Taylor called out, 'All right, Julie, you may limp now.'"[33]

Haydon explained that she had several uh-oh moments during rehearsals. "Although Laurette Taylor became 'one of my dearest, dearest friends' ... things were a bit difficult at first, partly due to a lack of rehearsal space in the Chicago theater where the play opened.... The actors had to practice ... in a ladies' lounge."[34]

It worried Dowling that during rehearsals Laurette didn't seem to know her lines. According to Haydon, Laurette provided little indication of how she was going to play her character. Dowling finally confronted her. "'Laurette, do you have any idea how you're going to play the character?' And Laurette said, 'I don't know, really. It depends on what the rest of you actors do and how the audience behaves.' And the next day we opened, and, oh, what a performance! She was *great*! I never could touch what she did."[35]

Betsy Blair was Julie Haydon's understudy. She explained that Laurette required a weekly understudy rehearsal. Blair, who described Laurette as "small and round" and "cozy," wasn't complaining. She was overwhelmed by Laurette. "Laurette Taylor! I saw her, I knew her, I watched her. I listened to her, and I tried to understand her style of acting.... [I]t was in these rehearsals that I started to learn my craft."[36] Blair always referred to her as "Miss Taylor," and Laurette never suggested she be called anything else. In Blair's opinion, there was no one like her. She'd seen Maureen Stapleton, Uta Hagen, Kim Stanley — but no one was Laurette Taylor. "She was a genius. Talent like hers can't really be explained; it just leaps out like a flame.... Every moment of her performance was filled with her grace. She was still but fluttering; she was real but intensely poetic; she was tragic and comic; dark and light — dark with sadness and light with gaiety. It was her ability to combine and glory in these contradictory elements that made her unique."[37]

Blair explained that Laurette often requested she sit with her in her dressing room while the older actress told stories about her life and career. She also recalled that Laurette was ill during the production. "Watching from the wings I saw her leave in the middle of a scene, come offstage and throw up, and float right back into the play. The enchantment she cast was so strong that I don't think the audience was even aware that it had happened."[38]

Everyone was worried about Laurette's drinking. Tennessee Williams wrote to a friend, "Taylor has been drinking but so far no signs of drunkenness. In fact everyone in the company except Julie and Eddie have been devoting all free hours to drink. Margo [Jones] is like the scoutmaster of some very jolly but wayward troop. Everybody makes drunken declarations of love to everybody."[39]

At the same time *The Glass Menagerie* was playing in Chicago, Helen Hayes was also in the city appearing in *Harriet*. Laurette was as concerned as anyone about her drinking. "'I'm going to break this witch's curse,' she kept saying over and over, like an incantation."[40] Laurette knew how easy it would be to totally fall off the wagon. "When we were strolling down State Street, or wherever, and she saw a liquor store, she would dash off like a thing possessed, with me trying to find her in the crowd. She was that terrified that the mere window display would lure her to her doom."[41]

Hayes described how Laurette usually drank one martini before dinner and then a double scotch after her performance. "Laurette and I would get together after work every night. Tennessee often joined us, and we'd got to a State Street bar where we could all relax. Laurette could handle one or two drinks at most, and she stayed within that limit." However, Hayes received a desperate call from Laurette one night. Her throat was bothering her. "If I don't go on, everyone will think I'm drunk. If they say I'm drunk, I *will* get drunk and stay drunk till I die." Fortunately, Hayes was resourceful. She always traveled with an electric steam kettle for her own throat problems. She took it with her to Laurette's room at the Sherman House and stayed up with Laurette administering the healing effects of the kettle. "The next evening she gave a magnificent performance."[42] After this, Laurette often didn't talk during the day, saving her voice for the nightly performance. Laurette asked Hayes to take over if she was unable to, though Hayes was reluctant, mainly because Laurette "owned" the part. Hayes also didn't like the character.

Hayes ended up doing the role in England in 1948 following Laurette's death. Hayes prepared for the role by sending for Laurette's understudy, Laura Walker, "to coach me on all the ad-lib lines and business Laurette had done. Laurette and Tennessee had fought over what he called her ad-libbing, but her improvisation clearly hadn't hurt his play's success. The understudy had stood in the wings and written down Laurette's every variation in the script. I tried to emulate her, though of course I couldn't be a carbon copy."[43] The play wasn't a huge success in England, partly, Hayes believed, because the play was too American. She later performed in a revival of *The Glass Menagerie* in 1955 at a benefit for the New York City Opera. Enough time had passed, and Hayes decided it was important to do the role her own way. "At City Center I played Amanda more my own way, trying to ignore Laurette's performance as much as possible."[44]

Laurette and Eddie Dowling, never the best of friends, had several blow-ups in Chicago. According to Williams, people were afraid of Laurette. "Five lines added at the end and the final tableau blacked out — which made Laurette furious. Nobody told her she was going to be blacked out — they were scared to. So they just blacked her — Julie came up to the candles — Laurette comes up right behind her! Last night Laurette got in a fight with Eddie backstage and missed her cue after the love scene — Julie gives Tony the broken glass and says 'a souvenir' which is Laurette's entrance cue. No Laurette. So Julie raises her voice and repeats it. Still no Laurette. Tony says — 'Thanks for the — *souvenir.*' Still no Laurette. Julie drifts over to the glass cabinet and ad-libs — 'Here is another just like it.' 'Aw, gee, thanks!' says Tony. Still no Laurette. Julie is just about to start back for a third souvenir when they get the old bag on — still frothing! But she is the whole show."[45]

With their success in Chicago, cast members were eager to take the production to New York. According to Tennessee Williams, "Everybody except Dowling is eager to get into New York — especially Laurette. She gets better all the time."[46] Still, there was lots of drama backstage. As for the antics of the cast and crew, Williams wrote in a letter to Windham: "'The menagerie' is no lie about this company — and neither is glass! I sometimes wonder if we'll really get to New York in one piece. The play back-stage is far more exciting than the one *on*."[47]

*The Glass Menagerie* closed in Chicago on March 24. Claudia Cassidy lamented Chicago's loss. "Whatever happens to *The Glass Menagerie* when it leaves us — how could so poignant a production have less than triumph in any town? — It struck our season's peak of playgoing."[48]

When *The Glass Menagerie* opened in New York on March 31, 1945, stars turned out in force. In the opening night audience were Greta Garbo, Katharine Hepburn, and Eva Le Gallienne.[49] Le Gallienne, who must have been difficult to please, was unimpressed with Laurette *and* Garbo, whom she'd long wanted to meet. "Either Laurette 'wasn't playing well or else I'm crazy,' she wrote. 'Cheryl [Crawford] felt as I did ... Hepburn & Garbo sat in the row in front of us. What a strange face G. has. Beautiful but so tortured & discontented — not a nice face I thought. I felt so horribly let down.'"[50]

Despite Le Gallienne's criticism, most thought that Laurette's performance was a success. George Jean Nathan sent a bottle of Scotch to her dressing room with congratulations. She wrote him back: "Thanks for the vote of confidence."[51]

Katharine Hepburn had first seen Laurette's performance in Chicago. Accompanied by Theatre Guild's Theresa Helburn, Hepburn found it "breathtaking. Laurette was so wonderful. It was the perfect marriage of part and actress. I still tingle after 30 years at the memory of that evening.... Laurette had a quality that's beyond measure. The same quality Spencer Tracy had. You didn't know how they did it."[52] Hepburn added, "Everything is a question of simplifying, simplifying, simplifying. Spencer Tracy and Laurette Taylor were simple, direct, transparent. Their technique disappeared as soon as they walked on stage."[53] Hepburn concluded, "I would love to have been as good an actress as Laurette Taylor.... She was brilliant."[54]

People couldn't stop talking about Laurette in *The Glass Menagerie*. "Not since she did *Peg o' My Heart*, exactly thirty years ago, has she been so talked and written about," Lloyd Lewis wrote in January 1945. "When Miss Taylor mumbles in magnificent realism she is still enough of a vocal wizard to be intelligible to her audiences, and when she pouts, nags or struts in pathetic bursts of romantic memory she is superb at pantomime. Her descents into hysteria are masterpieces of understatement, dramatic in that they force her audience to do the acting for her. She accomplishes her tour de force of acting without a single gesture which could be charged with showmanship. Some of her most telling lines are fumbling mutterings delivered over her shoulder. And in a scene wherein she prods her son into bringing home somebody, anybody, who might possibly marry his psychopathic sister before he himself wanders off, as his mother knows he will, into the big, blue and tipsy yonder, she gives a performance that could fit into the best of the Abbey Theatre's Irish plays. One moment she is a ridiculous pretender and the next only a poor old woman dreading so soon to be dead because her helpless daughter will then be alone. When a 'caller' is eventually dragooned and brought to the house for dinner, Miss Taylor's appearance in an ancient taffeta and high-toned manners is a delicate feat in the creation of that narrow line between the absurd and the sad."[55] As for the play, Lewis thought it a tenuous and moody tragedy ... so overlain with poetry as to overshadow the earthiness of its strong scenes." As for Dowling, "his great feat is that of having seen that young *Peg o' My Heart* could be a ridiculous, irritating, pathetic old woman."

Indeed, critics generally loved Laurette but weren't as impressed by the play. *Time* found the play flawed but Laurette flawless. "As a play, *The Glass Menagerie* has its faults and needless frills.... Laurette Taylor gives the most fascinating and memorable performance of the season.... Actress Taylor's devices are those of a superb performer: with mumbled words, fluttery gestures, unpredictable movements, small changes of pace and stress, she bit by bit reveals what she is, was, thinks she was, pretends to be, vaguely dreams of becoming."[56]

The *New York Times* critic wrote, "'Memorable' is an overworked word, but that is the only one to describe Laurette Taylor's performance.... Miss Taylor's picture of a blowsy, impoverished woman who is living on memories of a flower-scented southern past is completely perfect."[57]

Frank Morriss declared that the play "boasts the most wonderful acting performance I have ever seen in my life. The play is *The Glass Menagerie*, and the star is Laurette Taylor.... [S]he is giving a performance ... that has the stamp of authentic greatness." He explained that trying to describe what she did was impossible. Indeed, Marguerite Courtney wrote in *Laurette* that "This inability to describe what Laurette did, even by the most articulate, had plagued the critics from the outset of her career."[58] Still, many tried. "Trying to analyze the way she plays the role is impossible. There is no forcing to get effect. It is all done so simply, and so superbly that you feel that it comes, not merely from a shrewd performer, who has learned all the tricks of the acting game, but from a woman who senses the inner meaning of the part, and is able to make you see the poignancy and tragedy of the whole thing. A phrase I once read in a book describes it, and the phrase is 'the tears in things.'"[59]

Laurette's performance became legendary. Ward Morehouse was another who tried to explain the magic in Taylor's performance. "As a faded southern belle, living in fretful discontent with a son and daughter in a St. Louis tenement, she scaled the heights of acting and made it look as easy as a stroll down a country lane. She captured a southern accent magically and with her mumblings and pauses, her detached, half-completed sentences, she brought to life a woman both pathetic and monstrous, the character named Amanda Wingfield, unable to forget her white-columned girlhood. How can anyone forget this frowsy, run-down slipper of a woman sitting at the telephone patiently and cunningly corralling magazine subscriptions from indifferent friends in the D.A.R.? Or the sly, relentless way she prodded her son to bring home a Gentleman Caller, somebody, anybody, who might marry his crippled sister? Or the moment when she turned on her son to ask 'Why? Why? Why?' in a desperate outburst of pain and bewilderment? It was a portrait made up of many small strokes — subtle shifts of emphasis, sudden bursts of energy, vague little movements, and tired little pauses. It was unforgettable."[60]

According to Robert Lewis, "People always ask, 'What was so great about Laurette Taylor?' It's hard to explain because she was simple, so devoid of mannerisms.... In *The Glass Menagerie*, Amanda has a scene with Laura on the fire escape and she asks her daughter to wish on the moon for happiness and good fortune. Since their chances for either were doubtful, Laurette realized that that was a poignant, sad line. So she tried to make a game out of it. That only made it sadder. On the other hand, when she was on the telephone trying to sell subscriptions to a magazine containing some cliché serial, she played it with all the frantic praise of someone who really believed in the story.... Laurette knew the speech was funny: she didn't have to make it funny."[61]

Harold Clurman also attempted to explain what Laurette accomplished in *The Glass Menagerie*. "When Laurette Taylor was on the stage in *The Glass Menagerie*, we perceived not only Williams' chagrin over a certain kind of mother, we were moved by the pathos of a bewildered and pained searching within a simple woman's heart. As we watched, we did not think about the compliments we ought to pay the artisans of our emotions, what prizes they ought to win, what 'quotes' would honor them or how long the play would run — all this should come later, if at all. What we felt was a satisfaction in being with the people on the stage, feeling with them and knowing something in common with them which was related to something which had been brought to a glorious fulfillment by our having seen it."[62] In fact, Clurman thought Laurette transcended the script and direction. "It is often said that the director 'molds' the actors' interpretations. This is largely true — and most flattering to the director — but an actress like Laurette Taylor was herself a creator and every accomplished actor may be one."[63]

Norris Houghton wrote, "The student of acting sits before her performance and marvels at the series of constant surprises with which she rewards him. Her phrasing and accent of a line is so often unexpected, her movement so unanticipated. But each surprise is confirmed and is justified by its inevitability.... To traffic in the unexpected for its own sake is dangerous; when Miss Taylor offers the unexpected, you say 'Of course. That is the only way it should have been done.' There is not a single cliché in her performance from beginning to end. That is why you sit so breathless to see what this woman will do next."[64]

Audience members also struggled to explain Laurette's stage presence. Playwright Stephen Adly Guirgis[65] wrote about an upstairs neighbor who told him about "seeing Laurette Taylor in *The Glass Menagerie* five times in a row because she thought a crazy person had taken over the stage because she couldn't see any 'acting' going on."

Another theatergoer tried to explain Laurette's talent to David Hanna. "*Magic* is the only word. I never saw an actress who could project like Laurette Taylor, who could fill the theatre with her character—not her personality. She left that behind in the dressing room. Laurette's imagination made you a believer—that was it. Magic."[66]

Playwright William Inge described her work in *The Glass Menagerie* as "the finest piece of acting—I don't think to this day I have seen a piece of acting as fine as hers. She was thrilling and terribly exciting to watch."[67]

It became an event for actors to see Laurette in *The Glass Menagerie*. "The New York actors and actresses, whenever they had an afternoon off, would go to *The Glass Menagerie* and watch Laurette Taylor."[68] Shirley Booth, who later took on the role of Amanda despite misgivings, said of Laurette in *The Glass Menagerie*. "I remember that performance so vividly—she really contributed something important to theater with it."[69]

Zero Mostel believed Laurette Taylor was the greatest actress in history. "I saw her eleven times in *The Glass Menagerie* on Broadway. The great ones just do it, and it's never vulgar."[70]

Judy Holliday, who would later play Laurette on stage, told Carroll Baker that Laurette's performance "was something so personal you were embarrassed to be sitting there and to be seeing such intimate scenes in a woman's life."[71]

John Garfield was yet another actor blown away by Taylor. "One of the serious things about the education I got is that there are so many ways of doing things, that as you grow older your choice is supposed to get better.... I saw Laurette Taylor in New York, who was terrific in her choices."[72] In fact, the concept of choices is an important one when discussing Laurette's acting mastery. Sheena Iyengar discussed the idea of choices with jazz musician Wynton Marsalis. Although he was talking about jazz, what he says is also true of other arts, including acting. Iyengar reports as follows: "According to Marsalis,

'Jazz always has some restrictions. Otherwise, it might sound like noise.' The ability to improvise, he said, comes from fundamental knowledge, and this knowledge 'limits the choices you can make and will make. Knowledge is always important where there's a choice.' The resulting action is based on informed intuition, or as he calls it, 'superthought.' In jazz, super-thought goes beyond determining the 'right' answer: it allows one to see new possibilities where others see only more of the same, and to construct the rare 'useful combination.'"[73]

Uta Hagen decided to carefully analyze Laurette in order to determine how the magic was conjured. "[She] said she went to watch Laurette Taylor's performance [in *The Glass Menagerie*] four times to try to figure out her technique for being so believable in everything she said and did, but each time Uta Hagen became so completely absorbed in the play that she forgot she was watching an actress and believed she was watching a woman named Amanda Wingfield live. Uta Hagen complained that she never learned a damn thing from Laurette Taylor because she could never catch her acting!"[74]

Ben Gazzara bristled when the term *great* was overused. "I've seen greatness once, and that was when Laurette Taylor turned in a totally great performance in *The Glass Menagerie*. Since then, I've seen Marlon Brando and Kim Stanley attain moments of greatness and that's it."[75] He saw Laurette in *The Glass Menagerie* six times. "Her acting impressed me so deeply.... I had no way of knowing it then, but now I realize that I was watching a truly great performance."[76]

Kitty Carlisle Hart described Laurette in *The Glass Menagerie* as "magical. Yes, that's the only word I can think of."[77] Gregory Peck also thought Laurette's performance in *The Glass Menagerie* was "the greatest."[78]

Maureen Stapleton, who ended up playing Amanda in a revival, saw Laurette in *The Glass Menagerie*. "[W]hile I couldn't say why I knew she was *numero uno*, I sure as hell knew it.... [W]omen like Miss Cornell, Laurette Taylor, and Jane Cowl had a very special ingredient — presence."[79] Stapleton knew that following Laurette in the role was foolish unless enough time had passed. "After 20 years had passed, you just hoped that most of the people seeing it wouldn't have seen Laurette. It was devastating to see her. Even I, young as I was at the time, knew that that was the real McCoy. The best I could do was just try for some half-baked imitation. Any little thing I could remember that she did I tried to do, but I could never could figure out how she did it, and I don't even remember what any of those things were now.... You wouldn't have dared to do it if it had only been like ten years — it's too fresh, there are still too many people who would have remembered."[80] Like some said about *Peg o' My Heart*, Stapleton thought the part of Amanda was actor-proof. "Actually, Amanda is such a fabulously written role anyone could play her with the exception of Harpo Marx."[81]

Actor David Wayne also thought Laurette was great. He met her while appearing in the play *Escape the Night*. He described her as "the greatest actress in the world. I never knew what the theater was until I saw her."[82]

Tony Randall told everyone who'd listen that "the best actress he's ever seen in his life was Laurette Taylor"[83] He named his daughter after her.

Laurette won the Drama Critics award for best dramatic performance. "We've won it, we've won it!"[84] Laurette exclaimed just before that night's show. "From here on I'm just kicking the clouds around."[85] *Variety* announced that Frank Fay (*Harvey*) and Laurette Taylor were best actor and actress, respectively, on Broadway for 1945. The results were from a poll of 19 New York theater critics.[86] That same year Taylor also won a Page One award from the Newspaper Guild of New York.[87]

Edwin Schallert wrote of a possible Laurette film project in May 1945. "Laurette Taylor is being named as the female lead of Monter-Gray's planned film production of *Never Too Old*, a radio show about young oldsters who find new life in the postwar era. The show thus far has only been optioned, and it's an ambitious project what with Miss Taylor's success in *The Glass Menagerie*."[88] The picture was never made.

Hedda Hopper said "I told you so" in a May 1945 column. "Louis Mayer isn't the only one in New York trying to persuade Laurette Taylor to come west for pictures. I've been shouting about Laurette for years, but the boys had to see her in *The Glass Menagerie* before they'd believe me."[89]

Laurette was so hot in May 1945 that *The Glass Menagerie* producer Louis J. Singer increased her salary to $750 a week; her gross percentage went to 7.5 percent, and her share of the profits to 5 percent.[90] Her money woes were now behind her.

In June 1945 the *New York Times* reported that Laurette was at work on another play. This one was titled *Fun with Stella* and was described as featuring nine characters with settings in London and New York. "The leading character, a London matron of great wealth, shows how a prototype of the famous Mrs. Pat Campbell, whose sharp and witty tongue brought the high and mighty down from their lofty perches, reacts to any given chain of circumstances."[91]

Edwin Schallert mentioned in June 1945 that Laurette had written yet another play. "With Laurette Taylor so much in the spotlight because of *The Glass Menagerie*, a play by this actress becomes more than a mere item. She has written one called *Pin a Rose* and Leonard Sillman is negotiating for the rights, as well as securing one or two other properties."[92]

*Pin a Rose* is an interesting play, probably for all the wrong reasons. Laurette copyrighted the work under a pen name, John Mereson. It is about a sculptor who has two children. In the course of the play she reveals that her husband, long thought dead, actually left her for another woman.[93]

Lloyd Lewis interviewed her around this time and found her charming and likeable. "Miss Taylor is still impish of wit, incredibly gay; her eyes under their heavy lids twinkle and flash, her lips turn up widely at the corners and her words tumble out musically and haltingly — each seemingly to be coined on the spot especially for her listener."

She explained to Lewis why she'd been absent from the stage. "I got to feeling more like acting again, but I couldn't find a play for a time.... It was either acting old mountaineer crones who spit tobacco juice in their son's eye — either that or Ibsen. I couldn't chew tobacco, and I wouldn't be found dead in *A Doll's House*,[94] so I did nothing, till all at once Eddie Dowling sent me the script.... It fascinated me."[95]

Ward Morehouse also interviewed Taylor when she was in *Menagerie*. She drank during the interview. In fact, Morehouse counted three martinis while he talked to her, though he didn't find her to be drunk. "Laurette Taylor took great pride in that performance and she spoke of it with deep humility.... 'In playing Amanda, and when I get on the stage, I become southern. The rest of the time I suppose I'm just American.... I got most of the southern accent that I use from our author, Tennessee Williams. I really don't know any tricks any more. Acting is really so simple and my advice to young actresses is to try not to become a bedroom thinker but wait until you get to the theater to do your acting. I have never felt that playing Amanda was particularly difficult. It's a part in which you're actually riding on an audience's shoulders. There are actually only two parts in the play — the shrew in the old wrapper and the young girl in the faded blue dress. I'd like to go on playing Amanda for as long as they'll let me and I'd enjoy returning to Chicago with the play — it was there that we got off to such a wonderful start — but I don't think I'd want to try any real touring. I haven't even time left in my life for that.'"[96] Laurette concluded by telling Morehouse, "'Until this part of Amanda came along I was offered all the old ladies in the world, but I didn't want a part — I wanted a play. I found it, thank God, in *The Glass Menagerie*.'"[97]

At the end of the year *New York Journal-American* writer Jack O'Brian detailed how "125 gallons of coffee had been consumed, 156 pint jars of Boston baked beans and 250 loaves of bread eaten, while five cartons of cigarettes went up in smoke, mostly inhaled by Mr. Dowling (this was during the war when it was difficult to get cigarettes and envious looks were often cast at the characters onstage as they puffed away). The gentleman caller had chewed

1,300 pieces of gum and Laurette had stuffed 832 powder puffs down Julie's bosom."[98]

In late 1945 a rumor began swirling that MGM was buying the rights to *The Glass Menagerie* and signing Laurette Taylor. Louella Parsons contacted a story editor at MGM to find out the truth. "He says that Laurette will be on the stage for the run of the play and it's such a hit it's bound to go two or three years. As for the play, 'well,' says [Valdemar] Vetlugen, 'Louis B. Mayer is not paying $300,000 or any other fantastic prices for a Broadway play. We told all the Broadway producers we would rather buy books or have our own writers prepare stories and not pay such outlandish prices!'"[99] Hedda Hopper started her own rumor. "I hope it's true that Laurette Taylor and Bing Crosby[100] will make *The Glass Menagerie* under the direction of Leo McCarey."[101] In July Hopper suggested Laurette was campaigning for the role. "Laurette Taylor spurns all movie offers except one — filming of her hit play, *The Glass Menagerie*."[102]

There continued to be rumors that Dowling and Laurette were feuding. Dorothy Kilgallen wrote in her syndicated column, "Sly characters sidle up to me in Shubert Alley and whisper: 'Do you know that Laurette Taylor and Eddie Dowling aren't speaking?' Energetic spies telephone: 'You've heard, of course, that Eddie Dowling and Laurette Taylor are a real Hatfield-McCoy.'" Kilgallen went on to detail a telephone conversation she'd had with Dowling shortly before the play opened. "[H]e went into a rave about Miss Taylor in which the most extravagantly flattering adjectives ... were used to denote that Miss Taylor was the greatest thing since Ben Hur, an actress beside whom Bernhardt was small-time stuff. If that be feuding, I wish Mr. Dowling would feud with me."[103]

In truth, there were difficulties between Dowling and Taylor. Their styles and temperaments were different. One night Taylor thought Dowling, a former song-and-dance man, was too hammy. Without letting the audience know her displeasure, she reined Dowling in with a line she improvised: "You'd better be a good boy."[104] He got the message. Laurette, who'd once been a ham herself, was also said to remind overly emoting performers, "Just say the line."[105]

On the heels of her regained fame, it was announced that Taylor would submit a manuscript to Farrar & Rhinehart. *Stars That Crossed Mine* was an autobiography that was due to the publisher by the end of 1945. Dwight was lined up to do the illustrations. According to Hedda Hopper, "He did a book of his own at 15, and the illustrations in it were charming."[106] The manuscript was never published.

In April 1946 theater critic Robert Garland, who'd seen *The Glass*

*Menagerie* one year before, found that Laurette had actually improved over the year. "Miss Taylor's mother is deeper, richer, and I believe, truer than it was a year ago."[107]

Some noticed that the role took its toll on Taylor. According to Sydney J. Harris, "I remember lunching several times with Laurette Taylor when she was playing the neurotic mother in *The Glass Menagerie*, and much of the role seemed to have carried over into her personal attitudes. Not that she was *like* the mother in the part, but that the mother's burden of anxieties seemed to have settled on her shoulders."[108] Eventually, in June 1946, Laurette was replaced in the play by Margaret Wycherly.

A few weeks later there was talk that Taylor would appear with Cary Grant in *None but the Lonely Heart*. According to Hedda Hopper (again), "Laurette loves the script done by Clifford Odets. She's back in New York now taking off some poundage before making the test. Even the new generation, who never saw her in *Peg o' My Heart*, heard of her charm and wants to see her."[109]

Unfortunately, Laurette's weight gain put an end to this opportunity. Dwight Taylor met her at the Los Angeles train station when she arrived for the test. "When I met her at the station I could barely recognize her. She was as round as a butterball.... When the studio got a look at her, the producer called me and said that they had reluctantly decided to withdraw their offer." Poor Dwight had to break the news to her. "'What do they mean, I'm too fat!' she exploded. "Does one have to be *thin* to be Cary Grant's mother? There are plenty of fat mothers — and a lot of them can't act, either!'

"'She's a poor woman,' I continued. 'She runs a secondhand store — they're practically starving.'"[110] Laurette finally admitted she was too heavy, started seeing a doctor, and finally got her weight under control. Unfortunately, her other health problems worsened.

In October it was reported that Taylor was recovering from a throat ailment. Still, Hedda Hopper announced in November. "Laurette Taylor has plans for doing a new play—adapted from a French story—and also has a picture offer. She hasn't made up her mind which to do first — the play or the picture."[111]

The play was *The Mad Woman of Chaillot*. She'd signed a contract with Randolph Echols and Will Gould to appear in the Paul Bowles adaptation of the Jean Giradoux play.[112]

Laurette died before she could do the role. Just before she died, Sam Wanamaker came up with a genius of an idea. "'I had such a great idea.... I wanted to make a documentary film of all the great performances of our time. I had it all arranged with Laurette Taylor, to go to the theater and take some motion pictures of her in *The Glass Menagerie*, and before she could do it she died. Later, Tennessee Williams ... in a eulogy to her said, 'It is a pity that such a great performance as Laurette Taylor gave, should cease with her death.'"[113]

Burgess Meredith mentioned to Hedda Hopper that Maxwell Anderson had written a short scene for Taylor in a film titled *A Miracle Can Happen*. According to Hopper, "It's tragic that Laurette was taken from us before she could do the part."[114]

Laurette died on Saturday, December 7, 1946, at 7:05 P.M. at the age of 62. She was in her Hotel Fourteen suite (14 East 60th Street) with her private nurse. A private funeral service was held the following Wednesday at the Frank E. Campbell Funeral Home (known as the Funeral Church). The minister was Reverend Arthur L. Charles, the priest from St. Mark's Episcopal Church. Dwight attended, but Marguerite couldn't because she had recently suffered a miscarriage, and her husband advised against it. From the cast of *The Glass Menagerie*, Anthony Ross, understudy Laura Walker, and Julie Haydon were at the service. Celebrities included Raymond Massey, Ina Claire, Burgess Meredith, Florence Reed, Charles MacArthur, Margo Jones, June Walker, and others. Although there was no eulogy, Laurette's favorite songs were played on the organ, including "Kathleen Mavourneen," "Yours Is My Heart Alone," and "Molly Malone."[115] She was buried next to Hartley in Woodlawn Cemetery.[116]

An outpouring of grief and testimonials immediately followed. Syndicated columnist Frank Morriss wrote one of the most poignant ones. He recalled seeing her in *Peg o' My Heart* when he was a child. "[T]he very instant she spoke in that wonderful husky voice of hers I fell in love with her.... And, although I never met her, it was with a deep sense of personal loss that I heard of her death Saturday night.... She was an actress of genius.... Genii don't streak across this planet of ours very often."[117] He realized how fortunate he'd been to see her in New York in *The Glass Menagerie*. "Ten, 20, 30, or perhaps even 40 years from now I shall be able to recall that performance, and savor some of its sweetness and its warmth.... For that characterization of Miss Taylor's had that most precious of theatrical possessions, an inner glow that warmed the imagination and nourished the spirit."

Morriss, like many who had the opportunity to see Taylor on stage, knew he was trying to articulate what couldn't be articulated. "As I write this I realize that not many of you saw Miss Taylor, so it is difficult for me to put into words, and make you realize just how great she was.... She has left me with a great deal to be thankful for. You couldn't buy my memories of her for any price you could offer."

Upon her death, Harold Clurman again attempted to explain her magic. "What distinguished Miss Taylor just as much in her failures as in her successes was the quality of her talent. She expressed a constantly tremulous sensibility that seemed vulnerable to the least breath of vulgarity, coarseness, or cruelty without ever wholly succumbing to the overwhelming presence of all three.... Laurette Taylor seemed to be the victim of a thousand unkind cuts so minute that no word could describe them, no poet make them pathetic. She seemed always to be weeping silent tears, and her slightly bent head or averted eye were unspeakably moving because they were gestures so brief as to appear wholly imperceptible. Her voice was like buried gold whose value we could not guess; her speech flowing and ebbing in strange unequal rhythms was like a graph of her soul in its bursts of tender feeling and recessions of frustration and confusion. A luminous confusion composed her aura. It shone brighter for its ambiguity and its refractions. It warmed us deeply because it was generated from unrhetorical sources of an ordinary woman's being rather than from any studied glamour. There was always something surprising about it, and no one appeared more surprised by what she sensed and experienced than Laurette Taylor herself. Her face was always suffused with a look of startled wonder, at once happy, humorous, frightened, and innocent."[118]

Ward Morehouse believed she was one of the greatest actresses ever. "Laurette Taylor had finesse. She had magic. In 40-odd years of acting she appeared in only three or four plays that were actually worth her time, but at the time of her death, following her great performance in *The Glass Menagerie*, she had so impressed those playgoers who had the great privilege of seeing her upon the stage that the vast majority of them, if called upon to name the finest actress they had ever seen, would have made the instantaneous decision in a single word, 'Taylor!'"[119]

Guthrie McClintic believed her to be one of a kind. "In her entire life in the theater Laurette Taylor appeared in only four plays of any distinction. They were Philip Barry's *In a Garden*, Sutton Vane's *Outward Bound*, J.M. Barrie's *Alice-Sit-by-the-Fire* and *The Glass Menagerie* by Tennessee Williams. But in the English-speaking world I am sure she will be remembered as one of the finest artists this century has produced. Her beginning was vaudeville, where as a child she was billed as 'La Belle Laurette,' doing imitations which were much in vogue then. Her training was cheap melodramatic stock. Her teachers, audiences. The great repertory houses of Europe produced no better. To her, acting was not a passion or a malady, but a joy."[120]

McClintic recalled the shock of seeing her obituary when he and Katharine Cornell were in England where they were staying with Laurence Olivier and Vivien Leigh at their country estate, Notley Abbey. He recalled a story she'd long ago told him. "Laurette once told me of a rehearsal of hers in which a well-known director spoke his piece by saying, 'This is your scene, Miss Taylor, and I feel you should have the center of the stage for it,' to which she replied with that sparkling hesitancy that so often characterized her utterance, 'You know, Mr.-----, this may seem odd to you, but I have always thought that wherever I was—*that* was the center of the stage.' And she was right. When her final curtain fell she was center stage, and that is where she will always be!"[121]

Kenneth Tynan tried to describe the quality Laurette Taylor had. "The Spanish have a word, *duende*. It has no exact English equivalent, but it denotes the quality without which no flamenco singer or bullfighter can conquer the summit of his art. The ability to transmit a profoundly felt emotion to an audience of strangers with the minimum of fuss and the maximum of restraint: that is as near as our language can get to the full meaning of *duende*.... It is the quality that differentiates Laurette Taylor from Lynn Fontanne."[122]

Basil Rathbone, who acted with Katharine Cornell and others, "considered Laurette Taylor the greatest of them all."[123] Tallulah Bankhead admitted that she was unable to impersonate Taylor. "I could never imitate Laurette Taylor. Her superb art came from an inner something I could not snare."[124]

James Cagney believed Pauline Lord, Doris Day, and Laurette Taylor shared a similar quality in their acting styles. "'The touchstone is simplicity, the simple line of performance, directly to you, uncluttered.'"[125]

Ruth Gordon wrote that Pauline Lord, Jeanne Eagles and Laurette were the best twentieth century American actresses, though she singled out Laurette as the "finest."[126] Fredric March also tried to explain Laurette's genius. "There's so much mumbo-jumbo about acting.... Laurette Taylor really explained the way it is for actresses when she told me, 'I just pretend.' Little girls, particularly, know what it's all about. They do Method acting naturally."[127]

Margaret Leighton believed "Laurette Taylor was great. There was no chichi about her. She was a human being who imitated no one."[128]

Tennessee Williams wrote, "I consider her the greatest artist of her profession that I have ever known.... Having created a part for Laurette Taylor is a reward I find sufficient for all the effort that went before and any that may come after."[129]

Laurette's estate wasn't settled until 1949. Her assets, which ended up totaling only $35,386, included ownership of several of Manners' plays, including *Peg o' My Heart*. Her beneficiaries were Dwight and Marguerite.[130]

## Chapter 11

# AFTERLIFE

*"If a critic calls my acting true, that seems to me the highest praise he can possibly give me."*[1]

When it came time to cast the film version of *The Glass Menagerie*, Bette Davis, Helen Hayes, and Pauline Lord were considered for Laurette's role. Irving Rapper admitted that Laurette would never have been cast. "I'll tell you quite frankly ... had Laurette Taylor lived and wanted to do the picture, believe me, she would have been the last person to be asked because those were not the days of originality or experimentation.... It was always a question of distribution. Of name value. Of box office.... I am sure they wouldn't have taken Laurette Taylor"[2] Rapper thought Davis was a good choice though he wondered if she was too young.

Sheilah Graham wrote, "Bette Davis is wanted by Charles Feldman to play the Laurette Taylor role in his *Glass Menagerie*. He says he'd rather have Bette than Helen Hayes. Bette wants to do it, but I doubt whether Warners will loan her. Jennifer Jones, however, is more or less definite for the girl."[3] Of course, "the girl" was ultimately played by Jane Wyman.

Columnist Alice Pardoe West expressed her desire that Lord *not* be signed because she didn't like her stage portrayal. "The significance of the role went over her head, judging from her portrayal on tour. She made comedy, where Laurette Taylor brought tears."[4]

Orson Welles also piped up in a report: "Orson Welles may direct *The Glass Menagerie* for Charles Feldman and possibly play the role created by Eddie Dowling on the stage. After seeing the play 10 times, Orson says, 'There are two actresses who would be wonderful in the Laurette Taylor part: Ethel Barrymore or Helen Hayes.'"[5]

Hedda Hopper, who apparently couldn't make up her mind, also put in a bid for Susan Hayward or Tallulah Bankhead. "Why not Susan Hayward? Incidentally, there seems to be some resistance to Tallulah Bankhead's playing the Laurette Taylor role, but I believe she would knock your eyes out."[6] According to Irving Rapper, Bankhead was thrilled with the idea — and once he saw her he thought they'd found their Amanda. "We tested for three long, suffering, humid days in July in New York City. And in all my experience I never saw a crew so staggered by the impact of a performance as they were by the one that Tallulah gave. But Jack Warner rejected the entire idea because of his fear of her drinking.... With my many experiences with actresses, I can honestly say, with a great deal of conviction, that it was the greatest test I have ever seen or made."[7]

Even Laurette's sister Bessie piped up. Sheilah Graham reported in February 1947 that she wanted producer Charles Feldman to contact her.[8] According to Helen Sheehy, Eva Le Gallienne's turned down the part because the production schedule would have interfered with a tour — and she also didn't think she was right for the role. Irving Rapper approached Ruth Chatterton, but "she was very unhappy about the idea of playing a mother."[9]

Gertrude Lawrence was ultimately chosen. Irving Rapper said she "was a sort of compromise casting."[10] Lawrence saw Laurette perform the role one time. "I don't want to copy her because you know as well as I that no one could do a successful imitation of her.... That would be bad for me and bad for the picture. I want my performance to be a sort of memorial to Laurette, who was a great and distinguished actress."[11] Jane Wyman was chosen for the role of Laura, Kirk Douglas played Jim O'Connor, and Arthur Kennedy was Tom Wingfield.[12] According to Lawrence's biographer Sheridan Morley, the film was deemed "a failure. Tennessee Williams himself thought her casting 'a dismal error' and the film itself the worst he had ever seen of any of his work."[13]

John Ford was one of the first to believe Laurette's life would make a great motion picture. After completing *The Fugitive* in 1947 he and producer Merian C. Cooper were looking for a project for their production company Argosy. "Attracted by its persistent overtones of tragedy — and by alcoholism — Jack [Ford] idly speculated about a film on the life of actress Laurette Taylor.... During the last days of her life she played to an empty house — full of people," he told Hedda Hopper. "Her play [*The Glass Menagerie*] was a great success, but the one guy whom she would have rather have seen it than the rest of the world never came. That was her husband, Hartley Manners, who is dead."[14]

In 1948 Ruth Gordon was appearing in a play she wrote titled *The Leading Lady*. Many thought the lead character was based on Laurette. According to Claudia Cassidy, "Miss Gordon's tale concerns an actress who goes under after the death of her husband ... but comes back to score her greatest triumph."[15] There are certainly similarities to Laurette, but Gordon also seemed to have borrowed life details from the Lunts and even herself.

In 1951 Decca put out a ten-inch vinyl record series titled *Cherished Moments of the Theatre*. In addition to Jane Cowl, Florence Reed, and others, one featured Laurette in *Peg o' My Heart*. This long-out-of-print record provides a rare opportunity to hear Laurette's voice.

In the spring of 1955, *Laurette* was published. Written by daughter Marguerite Courtney, it was the first biography on Laurette. Hedda Hopper had mentioned that the book was in the works in an October 1949 column. Upon publication, reviewers raved about the biography. Marie Blizard called it "a literary event."[16] George Cukor acknowledged that it was "an absolutely first-class theatrical biography."[17] Lewis Nichols wrote, "In the theatre, Mrs. Courtney's [book] would be called a fascinating performance."[18] According to *Time*, "It is to her daughter's uncommon credit that she has not tried to pretty up Laurette's life in a biography that shows the pain of writing on most of its pages."[19] The book indeed stood out because it didn't whitewash Laurette's life. "*Laurette*, by Marguerite Courtney, stood high above all the many books about movie and theater folk. Not only did the tragic story of alcoholic actress Laurette Taylor have more substance that others, it was also told with greater intelligence and in better writing."[20]

Claudia Cassidy, the *Chicago Tribune* drama critic, who wrote so fondly of Laurette in her review of *The Glass Menagerie*, loved the book, though she found it painful to read. "*Laurette* is going to haunt me as I am haunted by her last play. Like the play, it is much gayer, much better company, than I have made it seem, but like that play, too, it is indelible for other reasons. To this day I can shut my eyes and see *The Glass Menagerie* on the dreamstruck stage of the little Civic. Even the backstage bickering, dredged up by the book, is of no importance."[21]

One can only imagine how difficult it must have been for Marguerite to undertake such a task. Laurette herself had once attempted an autobiography but ultimately decided it was impossible. "'It seemed simple enough,' Laurette said. 'But when I got into it, I found the character just too complicated for me to handle.'"[22] Meg Courtney, Marguerite's daughter, said, "I remember her saying it was seven years of her life."[23] She added that Marguerite wrote the book, "Partly, to purge her demons." Laurette and Marguerite had a contentious, difficult relationship which Laurette's alcoholism exacerbated. However, Marguerite successfully purged her demons and went on to have a good life, one full of joy and happiness. According to Meg, she'd come to terms with her mother. One of the first books written from the point of view of a child of an alcoholic, Marguerite's book remains remarkably candid yet tender.

At a July 1955 party hosted by her publisher, Marguerite was asked if she would ever consider playing her mother. She quickly discounted the idea. "I can't act. I never could. I would never dream of it."[24]

Still, Laurette's rich life was thought by many to be a surefire movie hit. "Mindful of the fact that few people could play Miss Taylor, the author [Courtney] is 'exercising the greatest caution' ... in approving the adaptation and especially the title casting — apparently the real hitch to date. Two actresses are out front as contenders.... They are none other than Judy Garland and Barbara Bel Geddes."[25]

In 1956 columnist Mike Connolly reported that Susan Hayward was meeting with producer Sol Siegel to discuss the role.[26] Perhaps the strangest casting suggestion came from director Mervyn LeRoy. He'd directed child actor Patty McCormick in *The Bad Seed* and claimed she was "the greatest dramatic talent he's ever known. Mervyn, a great admirer of the late Laurette Taylor, believes they shouldn't put Laurette's life story, recently written by her daughter, on screen until Patty grows up. She could handle it."[27]

Laurette was one of the reasons Alan J. Pakula went into theatre. He saw her in *The Glass Menagerie*, and according to his biographer Jared Brown, "Pakula was overwhelmed. She wasn't *acting*, he thought, but *behaving*. It was what he would strive for in his work with actors."[28] Pakula and Robert Milligan bought the stage rights to *Laurette* in 1957.[29] At the time they were best known for the film *Fear Strikes Out*, which Pakula produced and Milligan directed.

Pakula first approached playwright Horton Foote to write the play. Foote declined. "'I just didn't feel it would work. I think it's almost impossible because there's going to be that moment when you say, 'Let's see her act.' And there's so much built up about her great acting ability that I just didn't think it would work.'"[30] Indeed, this has been the biggest bugaboo about casting someone to play Laurette. Who's not going to be intimidated playing the woman who's been proclaimed the greatest American actor ever?

Although Stanley Young was hired to write the adaptation, Pakula stayed heavily involved. "On June 4, 1957, for example, he wrote Young a thirty-page letter detailing his conception of the play, his suggestion for the plot structure and the characterizations. Many other memos followed as the script was being developed."[31]

Casting, of course, was key to the play's success. Pakula considered Geraldine Page, Kim Stanley, and others. Columnist Frank Morriss suggested Shirley Booth was a natural fit. "She comes nearest to approaching the greatness of this particular actress."[32] However, Pakula's "first choice was Judy Holliday, the brilliant comic performer who had triumphed in *Born Yesterday* and *Bells Are Ringing*. Beginning in January 1958, Pakula made repeated attempts to persuade Judy Holliday to accept the role. At last, in 1959, she agreed to play the role under Jose Quintero's direction."[33] The original director, Robert Milligan, bowed out, and Quintero signed a contract on November 11, 1959.

As early as February 1957 Judy Holliday had expressed interest in playing Taylor.[34] She'd grown up idolizing her. "I really fell in love with Laurette Taylor when I saw her in a revival of *Outward Bound*. She was the greatest actress of them all. I saw her again, much later, as the faded southern belle of a mother in Tennessee Williams' *Glass Menagerie*. I never knew her, and she never met me. Yet when she died, it was as though I'd suffered a personal tragedy."[35]

Pakula wanted to include Robert Redford in the cast, but it didn't work out. He also approached Laurence Olivier about playing J. Hartley Manners, and Louella O. Parsons reported that there was even talk that Vivien Leigh would play Laurette.[36] Hedda Hopper later reported that the producers hoped to sign Peter Finch to play Hartley.[37]

The cast instead included Holliday, Jack Gwillim, Patrick O'Neal, Joan Hackett, and Nancy Marchand. Advance sales of $500,000 prompted Pakula to write his investors and claim that this represented "one of the largest advance sales for a straight play in the history of the theater." United Artists contacted Pakula about a film version. His budget was $1.5 million, "a rather modest sum for a picture that would feature a large cast, many locations, numerous elaborate costumes, and two distinct time periods."[38]

Newspaper columnist Mike Connolly reported that Holliday was intimidated by the role. "Judy Holliday has never been as nervous as she is about bringing *Laurette* to Broadway."[39] Complications immediately arose during the play's rehearsals. The cast was scheduled to start rehearsing on August 27 at the Forty-sixth Street Theatre, but the producers of *Tenderloin*, Robert Griffith and Harold Prince, refused to leave. Pakula reluctantly found another space. However, it quickly became apparent that the script was weak. Judy Holliday, in particular, was unhappy with "those aspects of the dramatization that put greater emphasis on spectacle than on character development."[40] Pakula unwisely sided with the director and writer. "'I have faith in your intuitions and instincts,' he told them, adding that revisions on the play should be limited to three people: Stanley, Quintero and myself p-e-r-i-o-d,' specifically eliminating Judy Holliday from the process." As might be expected, Holliday pitched a fit. She twice refused to go on in New Haven until the director agreed to changes.

The play began in Laurette's New York apartment. Surrounded by liquor bottles, she is mourning the death of husband J. Hartley Manners. The play concludes with Taylor's comeback in *Outward Bound*. If it sounds hackneyed, it was.

Obviously a troubled production, it opened in New Haven on September 26, 1960. Critics were unkind. The *New Haven Evening Register* critic complained, "*Laurette* is a play in which nothing, for the moment, at least, is quite right."[41]

According to critic Fred Russell, the result was "not too successful.... Despite the efforts of a splendid cast the drama was heavy and slow-moving." He found Holliday, who had been known as an excellent comedienne, awkward as Laurette. "Miss Holliday took a very cautious approach to this switch in characterizations. Maybe too much so. At times her voice was hardly audible. And most of the time she never seemed to appear too happy with the part."[42]

After New Haven the production moved to Philadelphia. Then Pakula announced that the project was being abandoned after the October 6 performance was cancelled an hour and a half before the show's start. The cause was Holliday's illness. In fact, Holliday was soon hospitalized and had surgery to remove a throat tumor. Although this growth was non-cancerous, it was discovered during surgery that she had breast cancer. Holliday appeared in only one additional play after this, *Hot Spot*, and died of cancer on July 7, 1965.

*Laurette* never made it to its scheduled New York opening on October 27 at the Martin Beck Theatre. Pakula referred to the four years he spent working on *Laurette* as "painful."[43] An insurance policy in the case of Holliday's illness paid investors $100,000, but the play still lost money.

It was reported in November 1960 that Kim Stanley would take the play to Broadway. This idea was eventually scrapped, too. Producer Roger Stevens reportedly offered the role to Anne Bancroft, Geraldine Page, and June Lockhart.[44] No one seemed to want to play Laurette. By the end of 1960, Hedda Hopper, who often kept Laurette's name alive in her column, tired of the whole thing. "I wish Roger Stevens would forget about the play *Laurette*. I don't believe the actress has been born who could touch Laurette Taylor."[45]

An Irish production of *Laurette* starred Siobhan McKenna in 1964. Dublin critics hated the Stanley Young play, calling it "banal, a parody of every saccharine Broadway biog. set to music."[46] Seamus Kelly described it as "alien corn."[47]

Judy Garland's name kept popping up for different Laurette projects through the years. In 1961 there was talk about a possible movie version of Judy Holliday's ill-fated stage production starring the gifted but notoriously erratic Garland.[48] Even Hedda Hopper came around. "Friends who saw Judy Garland's rushes on *Judgment at Nuremberg* exclaimed: 'She should play Laurette Taylor's life.' I agree."[49]

George Cukor stated in 1962 that Garland was "the only one who could possibly play the part with all the pathos it requires."[50] Cukor saw something of Laurette in Garland. "When Judy Garland did a very moving scene in *A Star Is Born*, I said: 'That is so wonderful,' as indeed I thought it was. 'It reminded me somehow of Laurette Taylor.' And Judy said, 'Oh, I'm very flattered. I hadn't seen her.'"[51]

This story contrasts with one told by Hedda Hopper in 1950. "Vincente [Minnelli] ... told me about taking her [Judy] to see Laurette Taylor in *The Glass Menagerie*. Her performance gave Judy such an inferiority complex that when they got a note to go back and see Miss Taylor after the play ended, Judy was all set to run away. But they went and before they could get out their words of praise, Laurette took Judy in her arms and said, 'You have the greatest talent ever wrapped up in one little package.' Judy left the room feeling like a queen."[52]

According to Cukor, Marguerite Courtney gave her blessings to Garland. "[I]f the picture is ever done, I can't imagine anybody doing mother but Judy Garland."[53] Pakula had his doubts. "I must admit," he wrote to Courtney, 'that the idea of getting involved with another Judy and other insurance problems leaves me feeling a bit ambivalent. But they say Garland is in good shape and I do think that I have developed some pretty tough scar tissue during the last 'Judy' episode that might make some of the problems easier to face the next time."[54] Ultimately, however, United Artists changed their mind, and there was no film.

Meanwhile, a competing stage production loomed. In 1963 Mary Martin starred in *Jennie*, a play about Taylor's early career.[55] She claimed that she and husband Richard Halliday had thought about the project for 13 years, which duplicated the length of time they'd thought about *Peter Pan*. In this case, 13 turned out to be terribly unlucky.

According to Ken Mandelbaum, the show "had an extremely convoluted history. It was always meant to be about the early life of the legendary actress Laurette Taylor to some degree, but that degree kept changing. First it was to be based on *Laurette*, a book by Marguerite Courtney, Taylor's daughter. When the musical stalled, and Laurette was made into a non-musical for Judy Holliday, which closed after a week in New Haven in 1960, Martin's vehicle was to be based on a book about Laurette and her first husband, the melodrama king Charles A. Taylor, by their son, Dwight. The show, to be called *Blood and Thunder*,[56] was to have had a book by S.N. Behrman, and Martin was to have played seven women (one of them the actress) in Charles' life. Ultimately, it was decided to revert to the Courtney book but to fictionalize its real-life characters, and Arnold Schulman (*A Hole in the Head*) did the adaptation."[57] Sheesh. No wonder it turned out to be a mess.

Marguerite, perhaps thinking about selling the rights, had sent chapters to Martin before the book was published, telling her, "Laurette Taylor would rather share this with Mary Martin than anyone else."[58] According to Richard Halliday, "[I]t was ten years ago that Miss Courtney began to send chapters of her book to Miss Martin. Efforts to bring it to the stage then with Miss Martin were stymied.... *Jennie* will stem from the first 80 pages of Miss Courtney's book. Mr. Schulman's fictionalized treatment will concentrate on an early phase of Miss Taylor's career before she became an established actress. Mr. Schulman's conception will not conflict with Stanley Young's dramatization of *Laurette*, which told the story of the star's later life."[59]

Mary Martin was a huge fan of Laurette's, and Laurette returned the favor. According to Hedda Hopper, Mary was Laurette's "great pet. Laurette saw her in *Lute Song* six times; also in *Annie Get Your Gun*."[60] Dwight Taylor saw similarities between the two actresses. "In many ways she's like mother. She has the same warmth and capacity for fun."[61] Hopper later wrote, "Mary has the same elfin magic of Laurette Taylor."[62]

According to an October 1923 *New York Times* story, Laurette met Martin only one time. Laurette took the cast of *The Glass Menagerie* to see Martin in *Lute Song*. "Afterward she gave a party at her apartment for the star of *Lute Song*, Mary Martin. It was their first and only meeting, and they spent much of it in Miss Taylor's bedroom exchanging stories about their childhood, stories that were remarkably similar despite the fact that Miss Taylor grew up in New York's 125th Street and Miss Martin in Weatherford, Texas. There was theater talk, too. Miss Martin said that she had never believed in studying acting, but she would rather study with Miss Taylor than anyone else. Miss Taylor smiled. Placing her hand on her heart, she said, 'But we have the same teacher. There is nothing I could teach you.'"[63]

According to producer Cheryl Crawford, *she* found the Marguerite Courtenay material and presented it to Mary Martin, who then hired Arthur Schwartz and Howard Dietz "after she fell madly in love with a song of theirs, 'Before I Kiss the World Goodbye.'"[64] Martin accepted Crawford's suggestion for a writer, Arnold Schulman. Crawford, however, came to rue the day she'd agreed to participate. "*Jennie* turned into the toughest production I ever tackled.... The physical production alone was complex and difficult. *Jennie* opened with Mary at the top of a huge waterfall — a real one, too — desperately fighting off an enormous bear. In the nick of time her actor husband's bullet killed the animal, and she managed not to drown. This was for starters."[65]

Martin had misgivings about playing Laurette and sometimes pretended *Jennie* wasn't about the legendary actress. "I'm leery of playing Laurette.... She was the greatest actress in our theater and if I thought I was playing her

I'd never be able to get on the stage. *Jennie* is sort of her life story at the beginning but it's really someone else, I think in terms of myself in projecting the character. But there's a heart and warmth in Jennie that's Laurette Taylor. And her fabulous humor is in *Jennie*, too."[66]

Still, Martin instinctively knew people would see her on stage as Laurette, as did her director. Someone overheard director Victor Donehue remark, "Can't you just see the way Laurette Taylor would do that scene?.... Mary has the key to it." Indeed, Martin admitted, "Laurette must be in the back of my head.... But I try not to let it affect me as Mary Martin playing Laurette Taylor. If the situation were reversed, Laurette would do the same."[67]

As for the name of the play, it was not, at least according to Martin, based on Laurette's character in *Happiness*. She was adamant that the play not be called *Laurette*. "Changing the name of the character and, consequently, of the show was a result of Miss Martin's need to take her mind off Laurette Taylor. She had first wanted to call the character Myra after a friend in Texas. 'Then I saw something in the *New York Times Book Review* about Jenny Jerome, who was Winston Churchill's mother. It's such a beautiful name! I said, 'Let's call her Jenny Jerome.' But they told me you can't do that.'"[68]

Vincent J. Donehue was hand-picked by Mary Martin to direct. He'd directed her in the television version of *Peter Pan* as well as on stage in *Annie Get Your Gun*, *The Skin of Our Teeth*, and *The Sound of Music*. Howard Dietz and Arthur Schwartz provided the music. Dietz and Schwartz had worked together for decades, but this one had to be one of their more bitter experiences. They sued *Boston Globe* critic Kevin Kelly when he accused them of plagiarism, writing that their music "poaches on the melodies of other composers, from Rodgers and Hammerstein to Meredith Willson, Frank Loesser, and Bob Merrill."[69] They feuded with Martin who refused to sing "Before I go to meet my maker/I want to use the salt left in the shaker" because she thought it crude.[70] They feuded with Halliday, who thought it unwise to bring *Jennie* to New York even though advance sales had reached $1.35 million.

The production had other problems, too. Constance Carpenter's role as Jennie's friend was written out; choreographer Matt Mattox was replaced by an uncredited Carol Haney; and Dennis O'Keefe was replaced by George Wallace. According to Cheryl Crawford, after the show opened in Boston "all hell began to break loose between the creators and the management over the writing and the production.... We recast the male lead and replaced the choreographer, but there were no other visible improvements as we limped on to Detroit."[71] Relationships deteriorated further. "Soon I was the only contact among the various parties, spending nights until three A.M. going up and down in elevators to the various rooms trying to effect a compromise about what should be done. Mary was dissatisfied with some of the lyrics. There was a question about which final scene to use.... I was still in the unpleasant position of being the only one to whom the others would talk. It was a dreary, exhausting time for me. Things deteriorated until everyone was in an unbearable state of tension."[72]

The further the production got from Laurette Taylor's life the worse it became. According to Mandelbaum, it ultimately "concerned a romantic triangle involving Jennie Malone, her husband James O'Connor, with whom she has barnstormed across the country in spectacular melodramas, and Englishman Christopher Lawrence Cromwell, a drawing-room playwright who gives Jennie a job when she leaves James. It was a remarkably unexciting book, one of the weakest ever to be accepted by a major star in the fifties and sixties. Neither of the men in Jennie's life were very interesting, and the show had just three things going for it. Martin, as always irresistible to her audiences, an attractive score, and the physical production. *Jennie* offered elaborate and satiric recreations of early-twentieth-century melodramas. The show's high point was its opening, with Martin hanging from the limb of a tree over a working waterfall, struggling to rescue her baby while pursued by a bear and a coolie. There was also the 'Sultan's 50th Bride' sequence, in which Martin, who in other shows had washed her hair and flown onstage, sang upside down, lashed to a torture wheel and rotated while chanting 'Lonely Nights.' This was followed by a simulated fire in which O'Connor's new theatre was destroyed. But these sequences served mainly to rouse the audience from its torpor; *Jennie* was simply a dull show."[73]

Eloise Sheldon thought Martin made a mistake in playing the early days of Laurette as a joke.[74] Another mistake, however, was in the adaptation of Marguerite Courtney's book. There's no question that it's a difficult book to adapt. It's extremely dense in that there are so many stories and themes. It's about the era of melodramas, stock companies, and Broadway. It's also a story about genius, celebrity, fame, comebacks, women's roles, and alcoholism. Unfortunately, the play focused on the most superficial aspects of Laurette's life in cartoon fashion.

Boston critics were harsh. Elliot Norton wrote that the play "was too long, too cultured and sometimes even too solemn for its own good." Kevin Kelly found it "a jerry-built musical ... a shack of a show badly in need of a carpenter, if not a historian."[75]

*New York Times* critic Howard Taubman panned the play. "For more years than a gentleman should mention my heart has belonged to Mary Martin. But *Jennie* does not make it easy to remain faithful.... The trouble is not with Miss Martin but with the soggy saga she has given her heart to.... Although the name is Jennie, the ardent heroine of the story and the story itself reflect Laurette. In the living it was no doubt a touching tale; in the telling by this musical it is as drearily stagy as some of the melodramas of Laurette's and Jennie's early years in show business."[76]

Critic William Glover loved Mary Martin but called the play a "dud." According to him, the story was "just another inane yarn about romantic pathos behind the footlights."[77]

*Time* also panned the play but raved about Martin. "Amid the encircling gloom, only Mary Martin shines with an inextinguishable light.... Whether she is nostalgically sashaying through a cane-and-straw hat routine, or spinning head over heels on a giant Roto-Broil of a torture wheel, or running her voice like a caress over a romantic ballad, she has the star quality that transcends marquees and animates legends. In her bearing, timing, suppleness, versatility, she is a flawless personality. Her only wrong move in *Jennie* is being in *Jennie*."[78]

Cheryl Crawford concluded that "it had all been too much. Everyone was relieved when *Jennie* closed."[79] Despite some great songs, it wasn't successful, closing on December 28 after only 82 performances. Although Richard Halliday said the show made a small profit, that claim is highly suspect.

Guthrie McClintic had presented a lucky rose quartz to Laurette before she went on stage in *The Glass Menagerie*. Taylor passed the quartz down to daughter Marguerite Courtney, who gave the quartz to Mary Martin in her dressing room on opening night.[80] God only knows what happened to this supposed "lucky" charm.

In the ensuing years, Laurette's name and image would occasionally pop up on television. *Hollywood: The Selznick Years* was a TV special in 1969 that featured a rare screen test from Laurette. Reviewers applauded Taylor yet again, with one finding Laurette "in clear command."[81]

In 1975 syndicated columnist Marilyn Beck reported that Joanne Woodward was planning to star in *The Life Story of Laurette Taylor* on CBS. "The project will roll whenever Ms. Woodward sees a script that meets with her complete approval."[82] Later that fall, Quinn Martin Productions reported that they planned to produce a two-hour CBS movie titled *Laurette*. Susan Clark was mentioned as a possible candidate for the lead role in a Lorimar Productions show. Neither project was completed.

Despite the failures of trying to put Laurette's story on stage, film, or television, Laurette's version of *Peg o' My Heart* was shown on television in 1978, part of the Lost & Found series produced in association with the Museum of Modern Art. Reviewer John O'Connor wrote, "It is by no means a great film, but it is extremely valuable because it stars Laurette Taylor.... Miss Taylor ... is remarkably vivacious as the irrepressible girl — tumbling over furniture, chasing her pet dog through a rainstorm, falling through the bleacher seats at a circus."[83]

In 1977 the documentary *That's Acting!* was shown at a benefit for the American Place Theater. Laurette was one of the actors featured in the footage, along with Helen Morgan, George Arliss, Pauline Lord, and others.[84]

In 2005 Bulfinch published *Stars on Stage: Eileen Darby and Broadway's Golden Age*. "None [of the images] is more valuable and unexpected than the series of 12 frames of Taylor in *Menagerie*—a 'key sheet' from which the show's press agent might choose a publicity shot. It records one of Amanda's efforts to earn extra money by selling renewal subscriptions to a 'magazine for matrons' called The Home-maker's Companion."[85]

At least two contemporary plays have been written about Laurette. Carolyn Gage's award-winning play *Leading Ladies: A Cabaret Revue* includes appearances by the ghosts of stage stars Sarah Siddons, Charlotte Cushman, Eleanora Duse, Sarah Bernhardt, Minnie Fiske, and Laurette as they comfort a struggling actress. With music by Teresa Wilhelmi, it is described as "a sparkling all-women cabaret musical incorporating seven separate historical vignettes onto a single set, a backstage dressing room." Gage wrote the play in 1985, and it was given a reading in the Frederick Loewe Room at the Dramatists Guild in New York.

The Laurette character sings a song titled "Old Ingénue." According to Gage, "I wrote about Laurette, because I was intrigued by her biography. What moved me most was the story of her comeback from alcoholism and also the fact that the world underwent so many changes during her lifetime. This was especially true for the world of theatre. The world of *Peg o' My Heart* was light years away, on another galaxy, from *Menagerie*. I use the song 'Old Ingénue' to celebrate the resiliency and stamina of Laurette. I also wanted to show a 'passing of the torch' between her and Julie Haydon. This was a kind of corrective to the *All About Eve* scenario of backbiting, competitive intergenerational rivalries between actresses."[86]

Carl A. Rossi wrote *Yellow to Lavender*, a three-act play set in 1944 in Laurette's New York apartment and in a Chicago theatre dressing room. An earlier one act-version was performed at the Theatre Studio Institute in New York in June 2002 and by Boston Actors' Theatre, Cambridge, Massachusetts, in July 2007. A cold reading of the one-act version was read by Ten Grand Productions in New York, July 2007, as part of its Cold Cuts reading series. The three-act version was given a stage-reading by the Dayton Playhouse, Dayton, Ohio, in July 2008 as part of its FutureFest summer reading series.

Other characters in *Yellow to Lavender* include Eloise Sheldon, Dwight Taylor, Marguerite Courtney, Eddie Dowling, Julie Haydon, Louis Singer, Tennessee Williams, Randy Echols and Tony Ross. Rossi based his play on an anecdote about Laurette dyeing her party-costume from yellow to lavender an hour before *The Glass Menagerie* premiered in Chicago.

Laurette's three films, fortunately, all exist in archives but none are as yet commercially available. However, they are occasionally shown at film festivals. For example, *Happiness* was shown at the 21st Annual Pordenone Silent Film Festival in 2003.

It wasn't exactly what Laurette had in mind when she explained that film would make her immortal. In fact, her three films didn't achieve what she'd intended. Her performances, though likeable, don't convey the magic that critics and audience members described in *Outward Bound* and *The Glass Menagerie*. However, the words of the actors in Rick McKay's documentary, as they struggled to explain what her stage performances meant to them, have made people once again aware of Laurette. It's impossible to say whether the film made her immortal, but the documentary made her famous again.[87]

Dwight Taylor spoke of the ephemeral quality of theatre. "I can see my mother kneeling behind the lighted candles in *The Glass Menagerie* as the shadowy figure of her son at the left of the stage says, 'Blow out your candles, Laura!' At this command, the stage is in darkness, like all stages when the show is over. These images vanish. But where do they go?"[88] Indeed, we must rely on memories which are equally fleeting. Horton Foote wrote, "Last night's performance will never be seen in all of its particulars again. It may be relived in memory, but even then, it will certainly be changed."[89] Laurette's myth is mixed with memorabilia, bits of recordings and films, and inconsistent memories. Those of us who never had the opportunity to see her on stage must rely on these. It's not enough, but it's the only opportunity we have to glimpse Laurette's genius.

# APPENDIX I: FILMOGRAPHY

## Peg o' My Heart (1922)

B&W: Six reels
Directed by King Vidor
Cast: Laurette Taylor [Margaret O'Connell (Peg)], Mahlon Hamilton [Sir Gerald Adair (Jerry), Russell Simpson [Jim O'Connell], Ethel Grey Terry [Ethel Chichester], Nigel Barrie [Christian Brent], Lionel Belmore [Hawks], Vera Lewis [Mrs. Chichester], Sidna Beth Ivins [Mrs. Jim O'Connell], D.R.O. Hatswell (Alaric Chichester], Aileen O'Malley [Margaret O'Connell, as a child], Fred Huntly [Butler], Michael [A dog].

Metro Pictures Corporation production; distributed by Metro Pictures Corporation. / From a play by J. Hartley Manners. Made under the supervision of J. Hartley Manners. Cinematography by George Barnes. Scenario by Mary O'Hara. © October 1, 1923 [LP18736]. Released December 18, 1922.

Survival Status: Print exists. Library of Congress.

Laurette Taylor in what is probably a publicity still for *One Night in Rome* (1919)(photograph courtesy of Mary Pearsall).

## Happiness (1924)

B&W: Eight reels / 7,745 feet
Directed by King Vidor
Cast: Laurette Taylor [Jenny Wreay], Pat O'Malley [Fermoy MacDonough], Hedda Hopper [Mrs. Chrystal Pole], Cyril Chadwick [Philip Chandos], Edith Yorke [Mrs. Wreay], Patterson Dial [Sallie Perkins], Joan Standing [Jenny], Lawrence Grant [Mr. Rosselstein], Charlotte Mineau [supervising saleswoman].

Metro Pictures Corporation production; distributed by Metro Pictures Corporation. From an adaptation by J. Hartley Manners of the play *Happiness* by J. Hartley Manners. Cinematography

by Chester Lyons. © March 5, 1924 [LP20031]. Released March 9, 1924.
Survival Status: Print exists.

## One Night in Rome (1924)

B&W: Eight reels / 7,745 feet
Directed by Clarence G. Badger
Cast: Laurette Taylor [Duchess Mareno/Madame L'Enigme], Tom Moore [Richard Oak], Alan Hale [Duke Mareno], William Humphrey [George Milburne], Joseph Dowling [Prince Danieli], Miss Du Pont [Zephyer Redlynch], Warer Oland [Mario Dorando], Brandon Hurst [Count Beetholde], Edna Tichenor [Italian maid], Ralph Yearsley [Gardener].

Metro Pictures Corporation production; distributed by Metro Pictures Corporation. From an adaptation by J. Hartley Manners of the play *One Night in Rome* by J. Hartley Manners. Cinematography by Rudolph Bergquist. / © October 23, 1924 [LP20744]. Released September 29, 1924.

Survival Status: Print exists.

# Appendix II: Selected Stage Appearances

**The Great John Ganton**. Lyric Theatre. May 3, 1909 – June 19, 1909. Produced by Lee and J.J. Shubert. Written by J. Hartley Manners. Based on the novel by Arthur J. Eddy. Directed by Lucius Henderson. Scenic Design by H. Robert Law.

Cast: George Fawcett, Jack Barnes, R.H. Breese, Josephine Brown, Frederick Burton, Edward Emery, Charles Gay, Lucius Henderson, Jack Leslie, Esther Lyons, H. Frederick Millerton, Jane Peyton, Mona Rank, W.H. Sadler, Laurette Taylor, A.H. Van Burn, Jack Webster.

Notes: The play, originally titled *Ganton & Co.*, was about a Chicago meatpacker. Taylor played May Keating. This was Taylor's first known Broadway appearance. It was also the first Manners' play that she appeared in.

**The Ringmaster**. Maxine Elliott's Theatre. August 9, 1909 – September 19, 1909. Produced by Lee and J.J. Shubert. Written by Olive Porter. Staged by J.C. Huffman.

Cast: Marion Ballou, Ruth Brolaska, Frederick Burton, Arthur Byron, Grant Clarke, Ralph Dean, Edward Emery, Lucius Henderson, George Howell, Willis Martin, Burke Patrick, Charles D. Pitt, George G. Roberts, William Rosell, Laurette Taylor, Oza Waldrop, Vernon Wallace.

Notes: The play was in four acts and set on Wall Street. Taylor played Eleanor Hillary.

**Mrs. Dakon**. Hackett Theatre. December 14, 1909 – December 15, 1909. Produced by C.A. Chandos and Aid of Crippled Children and Association for the Aid of Crippled Children. Written by Kate Jordan.

Cast: P.S. Barrett, William Childs, Dorothy Dorr, George Graham, Ethel Martin, Laurette Taylor, Ann Warrington, Robert Warwick, Anna Wynne.

**Alias Jimmy Valentine**. Wallack's Theatre. January 21, 1910 – June 19, 1910. Produced by Liebler & Co. Written by Paul Armstrong. Based on "A Retrieved Reformation" by O. Henry.

Cast: Edward Bayes (Blinky Davis), Sallie Bergman (Mrs. Moore), Albert Elliott (Smith), Edmund Eton (Bill Avery), Donald Gallaher (Robby), Maude Turner Gordon (Mrs. Webster), Charles E. Graham (Dick the Rat), Harold Hartsell (Handler), Frank Kingdon (Robert Fay, Lieutenant Governor of New York), Louden McCormick (Blickendolfenbach), Frank Monroe (Doyle), Alma Sedley (Kitty Lane), Laurette Taylor (Rose Lane), Joseph Tuohy (Red Joclyn), H.B. Warner (Lee Randall), James E. Wilson (William Lane).

Notes: The play was in four acts. It

Two publicity photographs of a glamorous Laurette Taylor (courtesy of Mary Pearsall).

was first made into a film in 1915 when it was directed by Maurice Tourneur. Ruth Shepley played Rose. The 1920 version was directed by Edmund Mortimer and Arthur Ripley. Vola Vale played Rose. The 1928 remake was directed by Jack Conway with Leila Hyams playing Rose. This version was MGM's first sound film and starred William Haines.

**The Girl in Waiting.** Olympic Theatre. Opened September 4, 1910. Written by J. Hartley Manners. Based on *The Girl in Waiting* by Archibald Eyre.

Cast: Laurette Taylor (Lillian Turner), Wallace Erskine (Joshua Turner, M.P.), Wilfred Draycott (Sir Charles Greville, M.P.), Alice Gale (Mrs. Hemmings), A.H. van Buren (George Hemmings), Julia Ralph (Mrs. Witherspoon), Percy Ames (Montague Witherspoon), E.H. Kelly (Alan Barker), Eliza Mason (Martha Watts), Herbert Budd (Mr. Bland), Charles Laite (Parks), Ada Gilman (Miss Janeway), Mary Keogh (Amy), Geraldine Peck (Rose), Henry Hallam (A Policeman), Arthur Glenmore (A Passer-by), Joseph Rudd (A Footman), E. Warner (A Page Boy), Roy Everett (A Butler), Jess Keppler (A Newsboy), Ernest Bland (A Groom), Marie Caldwell (A Maid).

**Seven Sisters.** Lyceum Theatre. February 20, 1911 – March 1911. Produced by Daniel Frohman. Written by Edith Ellis. Based on a work by Ferencz Herczeg. Translated by Ferike Boros.

Cast: Gaston Bell, Clara T. Bracy, Charles Cherry, Carlotta Doty, Wilfred Draycott, Virginia Hamilton, John B. Hollis, Shelley Hull, Alice John, Orilla Mars, Eva McDonald, Albac Sandor, Gladys Smith, Laurette Taylor, Bernard Thornton.

**Lola.** Lyceum Theatre. March 14, 1911 — Unknown. Written by Owen Davis.

Cast: Laurette Taylor (Lola), Shelley Hull (John Dorris), Sheldon Lewis (Dr. Barnheim), Wilfred Draycott (Dr. Paul Gruzzet), Gaxton Bell (Dick Fenway), Alice John (Mary), Mrs. John Findlay (Mrs. Mooney), Gladys Smith (Nellie), J. Allentown (Ambulance surgeon), Carlotta Doty (Mme. Zeyin), Bernard Thornton (William Barnes), William Carter (Policeman).

**The Bird of Paradise.** Daly's Theatre. January 8, 1912 — January 19, 1912. Maxine Elliott's Theatre. January 22, 1912 — April 13, 1912. Produced by Oliver Morosco. Written by Richard Walton Tully. Featuring songs by Sylvester Kalama and Kapule Kanoa. Staged by Richard Walton Tully. Scenic Design by Ernest Gros. Lighting and storm effect by Kleigl Brothers.

Cast: Laurette Taylor (Luana, a Hawaiian girl), W.B. Aeko (Lanipule, a cane-cutter), Estar Banks (Mrs. Sysonby, Sysonby's wife), Gladys Byers (Miss Kennedy, a debutante), Nance Caldwell (Konia, a woman of the old days), W.J. Constantine (Mr. Sysonby, the missionary), Clyde Crawford (Tomoro, a Japanese), Herbert Farjeon (Kaia), Pamela Gaythorne (Diana Larned, a university graduate), Robert Harrison (Hoheno, a fisherman), S.M. Kaiawe (Naihe, a cane-cutter), A. Kawala (Kuakini, a cane-cutter), Nona Kelly (Hopoe, a hula dancer), W.K. Kolomoku (Kanoa, a cane-cutter), Jane Meredith (Makia, a convert), Craig Miner (Mr. Jameson of the Sugar Company), Margaret Nagele (Mrs. Crothers, a widow), Albert Perry (Hewahewa, a priest of Pele), Guy Bates Post (Dean, a beachcomber), Virginia Reynolds (Liliha, a hula dancer), Theodore Roberts (Captain Hatch, a planter), Lewis S. Stone (Paul Wilson, a young doctor), Van Rensselaer Townsend (Lemule, a graduate), Lenore Ulric (unknown role), B. Waiwaiole (Kapule, a cane-cutter), Ida Waterman (Mahumahu, Luana's foster mother).

Notes: The three-act musical play was set in Hawaii. Songs included Burning Love (Ahi Wela), Farewell to Thee (Aloha Oe), Forget Me Not (Mai Poina oe la'u), Song of the Lonseome Forest (Kumukahi), Hula Shouting Song (Aiaihea), Press Me to Thee (Tomi Tomi), I Love But Thee (Akahi Hoi), My Love Is Like a Blooming Flower (Pua i Mohala), The Sparkling Waters (Waialae), Maui Girl, Honolulu Tom Boy (Sonny Cunha), The Bubbling Spring (Kaua i ka Huahuai), The Drowsy Waters (Wailana), Constancy (Ua Like No a Like), Hawaii Ponoi, Native Plantation Song (Kuu Home), Sacred Dancing Hula Song (Mauna Kea), Maid of Honolulu, The Whirling Waters (Kawiliwiliwai), Hawaiian Hula Dance Song (Moanalua), We Strive to Win (Kokohi), My Honolulu Hula Girl, Fragrance of the Lehua Wreath (Sweet Lei Lehua), Wreath of Carnations (Lei Poni Moi), One-Two-Three-Four, Luana Waltz.

**Peg o' My Heart.** Cort Theatre. December 20, 1912 — May 19, 1914. Produced by Oliver Morosco. Written and directed by J. Hartley Manners.

Cast: Laurette Taylor (Peg, Margaret Connolly), Peter Bassett (Footman), Ruth Gartland (Maud), Reginald Mason (Christian Brant), Emilie Melville (Mrs. Chichester), Christine Norman (Ethel), H. Reeves-Smith (Jerry, Sir Gerald), Hassard Short (Alaric), Michael (Michael).

Notes: The setting is the living room of Regal Villa, Mrs. Chichester's house in Scarborough, England.

**The Day of Dupes: An Allegory.** Cort Theatre. March 6, 1914. Produced by

Oliver Morosco. Written by J. Hartley Manners.

Cast: H. Reeves-Smith (The Artist), Clarence Handyside (The Politician), Reginald Mason (The Financier), Hassard Short (The Litterateur), Emilie Melville (The Attendant), Laurette Taylor (The "Dupe").

**Happiness, a Study.** Cort Theatre. March 6, 1914. Produced by Oliver Morosco. Written by J. Hartley Manners.

Cast: Laurette Taylor (Jenny), H. Reeves-Smith (Philip Chandos), Peter Bassett (Fritz Scowcroft), Violet Kemble-Cooper (Mrs. Chrystal-Pole).

**Just As Well: A Twentieth-Century Romance.** Cort Theatre. March 6, 1914. Produced by Oliver Morosco. Written by J. Hartley Manners.

Cast: Laurette Taylor (Hon. Doleen Sweetmarch, Emilie Melville (Mrs. Carfax), Yvonne Jarrette (Maid), Hassard Short (Captain Trawbridge).

**The Harp of Life.** Globe Theatre. November 27, 1916 — March 1917. Produced by George C. Tyler and Klaw & Erlanger. Written by J. Hartley Manners.

Cast: Lynn Fontanne, Gail Kane, Frank Kemble-Cooper, Philip Merivale, Ffolliott Paget, Laurette Taylor, Dion Titheradge. Hartley dedicated the play: "To the originator of the part of Sylvia: Laurette Taylor I gratefully dedicate this play."

**Out There.** Globe Theatre. March 27, 1917 — June 1917. Produced by George C. Tyler and Klaw & Erlanger. Written by J. Hartley Manners.

 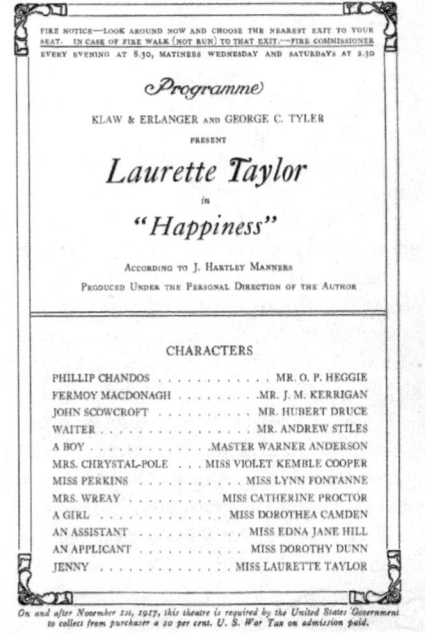

Playbill for *Happiness* (1917) (photograph courtesy of Mary Pearsall).

Cast: Laurette Taylor ('Aunted Annie,' The Help, The Nurse), Daisy Belmore (Old Velvet, Mrs. Hudd), Colin Campbell (Monte, Mr. Montague Marsh), Lewis Edgard ('Erb, Private Herbert Hudd), Lynn Fontanne ("Princess" Lizzie, Miss Elizabeth Hudd), Frank Kemble-Cooper (Dr. Hanwell, The Surgeon), J.M. Kerrigan (The Irishman), Leonard Mudie (The Cockney), George Kemble (A Newcomer), Philip Newman (Another Newcomer), Henry Oxenford (Terence), Catherine Proctor (Gabrielle), Douglas Ross (The Scotchman), A.E. Sproston (The New Zealander), James Archer (Griffin).

**The Wooing of Eve: A Thoroughly Artificial and Sentimental Comedy in Three Acts.** Liberty Theatre. November 26, 1917 — December 1917. Produced by George C. Tyler and Klaw & Erlanger. Written by J. Hartley Manners with A.E.Anson.

Cast: Laurette Taylor (Miss Alverstone), Theresa Maxwell Conover (Mrs. Rodd), Lynn Fontanne (Winifred), Catherine Proctor (Walkley), A.E. Anson (Philip Grafton), Earle Brown (Brice Livingston), Frank Kemble-Cooper (John Rodd), Leonard Mudie (Cyril Dallas Rokeby Parriscourt), Douglas Ross (Reverend Henry Warrender), J.M. Kerrigan (Winch), Basil West (Bates).

**Happiness.** Criterion Theatre. December 31, 1917 — May 1918. Produced by George C. Tyler and Klaw & Erlanger. Written by J. Hartley Manners.

Cast: Warner Anderson (A Boy), Dorothea Camden (A Girl), Hubert Druce (John Scowcroft), Dorothy Dunn (An Applicant), Lynn Fontanne (Miss Perkins), O.P. Heggie (Phillip Chandos), Edna Jane Hill (An Assistant), Violet Kemble-Cooper (Mrs. Chrystal-Pole), J.M. Kerrigan (Fermoy MacDonagh), Catherine Proctor (Mrs. Wreay), Andrew Stiles (Waiter), Laurette Taylor (Jenny).

Notes: This production was a revival.

**Laurette Taylor in Scenes from Shakespeare.** Criterion Theatre. March 5, 1918 — Unknown. Written by William Shakespeare.

*Romeo and Juliet*
Cast: Laurette Taylor (Juliet, daughter to Capulet), Jose Ruben (Romeo, son of Montague).

*The Merchant of Venice*
Cast: Laurette Taylor (Portia), Hubert Druce (The Duke of Venice), Lynn Fontanne (Nerissa), O.P. Heggie (Shylock), Edward Mackay (Antonio), Leonard Mudie (Bassanio), Frederick Perry (Gratiano, friend of Antonio).

*The Taming of the Shrew*
Cast: Laurette Taylor (Katharine), Hubert Druce (Grumia), Lynn Fontanne (Bianca), Shelley Hull (Petruchio), Edward Mackay (Baptista), Frederick Perry (Hortensio), B. Souther (Curtis), Leonard Mudie (Tailor).

**Out There.** Century Theatre. May 17, 1918 — May 1918. Produced by The American Red Cross. Produced by arrangement with George C. Tyler and Klaw & Erlanger. Written by J. Hartley Manners.

Cast: George Arliss, Julia Arthur, George M. Cohan, James K. Hackett, O.P. Heggie, George MacFarlane, Beryl Mercer, Chauncey Olcott, James T. Powers, Laurette Taylor, Helen Ware, H.B. Warner.

**One Night in Rome.** Criterion Theatre. December 2, 1919 — June 1920. Produced by George C. Tyler. Written by J. Hartley Manners.

Cast: Barry Baxter (Denby Wragge), Louise Beaudet (Mrs. Redlynch), Marie Bianchi (La Bambina), Helen Blair

(Zephyr), Valentine Clemow (Aenea), H. Cooper Cliffe (Mr. Justice Millburne), Thomas Coffin Cooke (Gresham), Olin Field (Kiara), Greta Kemble-Cooper (Iola), Giorgio Majeroni (Signor Diranda), Philip Merivale (Richard Oak), Mrs. Felix Morris (Mrs. Oak), John Davenport Seymour (Bikra), Laurette Taylor ('L'Enigme).

Notes: The settings of the three division play included a house in the Great City, and in the heart of a Great Country.

**Peg o' My Heart.** Cort Theatre. February 14, 1921 – October 1922. Produced by A.L. Erlanger. Written by J. Hartley Manners.

Cast: Laurette Taylor (Peg, Margaret Connolly), Percy Ames (Alaric), Thomas A. Braidon (Christian Brant), Greta Kemble-Cooper (Ethel), A.E. Matthews (Jerry, Sir Gerald), Michael (Michael), Maud Milton (Mrs. Chichester), Mildred Post (Maid), George Riddell (Montgomery Hawks), George Sydenham (Jarvis).

**The National Anthem.** Henry Miller's Theatre. January 23, 1922 – April 1922. Produced by A.L. Erlanger and George C. Tyler. Produced under the personal direction of J. Hartley Manners. Written by J. Hartley Manners.

Cast: Laurette Taylor (Marian Hale), William Armstrong (Waiter), Lillian Kemble-Cooper (Madeline Trent), Robert Hudson (Jim Picket), Greta Kemble-Cooper (Etta), Richie Ling (Reuben Hale), J. Hartley Manners (Waiter), Dodson Mitchell (John K. Carlton), Ralph Morgan (Arthur Carlton), Paul Porcasi (Dr. Virande), Frank M. Thomas (Tom Carroll), Jo Wallace (Maud-Ethel), Ray Wilson (Ned Scoofy).

Notes: This was a play in four acts. The settings included Northchester, New York, and Paris.

**Humoresque.** Vanderbilt Theatre. February 27, 1923 – March 1923. Written by Fannie Hurst. Staged by J. Hartley Manners.

Cast: Lutha J. Adler (Leon Kanton, Grown), James H. Bell (Stage Employee), Vera Berliner (Mrs. Finschreiber), Walter Brown (William), Dorothy Burton (Esther Kantor, Grown), Sidney Carlyle (Mannie Kantor), Lillian Garrick (Rosie Ginsburg), Elsa Grey (Gina Berg), Chester Hermann (Isador Kantor), Ada Hewitt (Esther Kantor), Alfred Little (Leon Kanter), Frank Manning (Sol Ginsberg), Charlotte Salkowitz (Ruby Kantor), Sidney Salkowitz (Leon Kantor II), Sam Sidman (Abraham Kantor), Louis Sorin (Isador Kantor, Grown), Laurette Taylor (Sarah Kantor), Hubert Wilke (Max Elsass), Wayne Wilson (Reporter).

Notes: This was a three-act play set in New York City.

**Sweet Nell of Old Drury.** 48th Street Theatre. May 18, 1923 – June 1923. Produced by The Equity Players, Inc. and J. Hartley Manners. Written by Paul Kester.

Cast: Helenka Adamowska (Duchess of Portsmouth), Charner Batson (Second Alderman), George Baxter (Alderman), James Bell (Lord-in-Waiting), Leonard Booker (Lacy), Laura Burt (Tiffin), Lionel Chalmers (Mercer), Lynn Fontanne (Lady Castlemaine), Herbert Grimwood (Lord Jeffreys), Edwin Holland (Captain Clavering), Regan Hughston (Sir Roger Fairfax), Paul Jacchia (Master Bliff), Seymour Jamison (William), Schuyler Ladd (Lord Lovelace), Howard Lindsay (Rollins), Richie Ling (Lord Rochester), Alfred Lunt (Charles II), Marguerite Myers (Lady Olivia Vernon), Leo Stark (Percival), Laurette Taylor (Nell Gwynne).

*Selected Stage Appearances*

# THE PLAYHOUSE

OWNED BY AND UNDER THE DIRECTION OF HARRY FROMKES

EMERGENCY NOTICE: In the event of an alert, remain in your seats. A competent staff has been trained for this emergency. Keep calm. You will receive information and instructions from the stage.   F. H. La GUARDIA, Mayor

FIRE NOTICE: The exit indicated by a red light and sign nearest to the seat you occupy is the shortest route to the street. In the event of fire please do not run—WALK TO THAT EXIT.
Patrick Walsh, Fire Commissioner and Chief of Department

THE · PLAYBILL · A · WEEKLY · PUBLICATION · OF · PLAYBILL · INCORPORATED

Week beginning Sunday, May 6, 1945 • Matinees Wednesday and Saturday

EDDIE DOWLING and LOUIS J. SINGER

present

## LAURETTE TAYLOR and EDDIE DOWLING

in

## THE GLASS MENAGERIE

A New Play

By TENNESSEE WILLIAMS

with

### Julie Haydon and Anthony Ross

Setting designed and lighted by JO MIELZINER

Original music composed by PAUL BOWLES

Staged by MR. DOWLING and MARGO JONES

Try this "*mountain magic*" in your favorite rum drink

Tropical mountain distilling gives Ron Merito delicious, unique flavor which works magic in mixed drinks!

*Ron* MERITO

GOLD AND WHITE LABEL • 86 PROOF • NATIONAL DISTILLERS PRODUCTS CORPORATION, NEW YORK, N.Y.

Playbill for *The Glass Menagerie* (1945) (photograph courtesy of Mary Pearsall).

Notes: This was a play in four acts set in England.

**Pierrot the Prodigal.** 48th Street Theatre. March 6, 1925 — March 1925. Produced by The Actors Theatre. Written by Michel Carre. Directed by Ottokar Bartik.

Cast: Michelette Burani (Madame Pierrot), Clarence Derwent (The Baron), Galina Kopernak (Phrynette), Ivan Lazareff (Mons. Pierrot), Laurette Taylor (Young Pierrot), Jack Thornton (The Negro).

Notes: This was a play in three acts. Settings included Mons. Pierrott's house and Phrynette's boudoir.

**Trelawny of the "Wells."** Knickerbocker Theatre. June 1, 1925 — June 7, 1925. Produced by The Players. Written by Sir Arthur Wing Pinero. Directed by William Seymour.

Cast: Edith Barrett (Miss Brewster), Amelia Bingham (Mrs. Telfer, Miss Violet Sylvester), Charles Coburn (Mr. James Telfer), Theresa Maxwell Conover (Miss Trafalgar Gower), Herbert Corthell (Mr. Augustus Colpoys), William Courtleigh (Mr. Ferdinand Gadd), John Cumberland (O'Dwyer, the Stage Manager), John Drew (Vice Chancellor Sir William Gower), John Evans (Hallkeeper at the Pantheon), Mary Elizabeth Forbes (Miss Adair), Harry Forsman (Charles), Gladys Hanson (Miss Imogen Parrott), O.P. Heggie (Mr. Ablett), Violet Heming (Miss Avonia Bunn), Claude King (Mr. Tom Wrench), Saxon Kling (Mr. Arthur Groves), Ernest Lawford (Captain De Foenix), Patterson McNutt (Mr. Mortimer), Catherine Dale Owen (Clara De Foenix), Molly Pearson (Sarah), John Davenport Seymour (Mr. Denzil), Laurette Taylor (Miss Rose Trelawny), Mrs. Thomas Whiffen (Mrs. Mossop), Douglas Wood (Mr. Hunston).

Notes: This was a play in four acts set in 1860s England.

**In a Garden.** Plymouth Theatre. November 16, 1925 — January 1926. Produced by Arthur Hopkins. Written by Philip Barry. Staged by Arthur Hopkins.

Cast: Marie Bruce (Miss Mabie), Louis Calhern (Norrie Bliss), Cecil Clovelly (Frederic), Frank Conroy (Adrian Terry), Ferdinand Gottschalk (Roger Compton), Laurette Taylor (Lissa Terry).

Notes: This was a play in three acts set in Sutton Place, New York City.

**The Furies.** Shubert Theatre. March 7, 1928 — April 1928. Produced by John Tuerk. Written by Zoe Akins. Directed by George Cukor.

Cast: A.E. Anson (Oliver Bedloe), Alan Campbell (Alan Sands), John Cumberland (Harvey Bell Smith), Clarence Handyside (Hayes), Charles Henderson (Bedloe's Man), Ross Hertz (Bradley), Alfred Kappeler (District Attorney), Greta Kemble-Cooper (Caroline Lee), Ian Maclaren (Dr. Paul Hemmingway), Maurine O'Moor (Theresa), John Parrish (Otis), Ernest Stallard (Bennett), Laurette Taylor (Fifi Sands), Estelle Winwood (Fern Andrews), Frederic Warlock (Owen MacDonald).

Notes: This was a play in three acts set in Harvey Bell Smith's apartment, New York City, the Sands' home on Fifth Avenue and Oliver Bedloe's apartment.

**A Night of Barrie.** Playhouse Theatre. March 7, 1932 — April 1932. Produced by William A. Brady. Produced in arrangement with Charles Frohman, Inc. Written by James M. Barrie. Staged by Stanley Logan. Scenic Design by Livingston Platt.

*Alice Sit-by-the-Fire*

Cast: Laurette Taylor (Mrs. Grey),

Jane Corcoran (Nurse), Charles Dalton (Colonel Gray), Peg Entwistle (Amy Grey), Robert Harrigan (Stephen Rollo), Lucille Lisle (Leonora Dunbar), Nan Sheldon (Richardson), Alice May Tuck (Fanny), Maury Tuckerman (Cosmo Grey).

Notes: This was a three act play set in Grey's apartment and Rollo's chambers.

*The Old Lady Shows Her Medals.*

Cast: Laurette Taylor (Mrs. Dowey), Leslie Austin (Mr. Wilkinson, a clergyman), Jane Corcoran (Mrs. Mickleham), Lawrence Fletcher (Private K. Dowey), Nan Sheldon (Mrs. Haggerty), Alice May Tuck (Mrs. Twymley).

**Outward Bound.** Playhouse Theatre. December 22, 1938 — July 22, 1939. Theatre Owned by Brady Enterprises, Inc. Produced by The Playhouse Company. Written by Sutton Vane. Directed by Otto L. Preminger. Scenic Design by Watson Barratt. Company Manager: M. Healy, Stage Manager: May Marshall. Press Representative: Thomas Barrows. Casting: Briscoe & Goldsmith.

Cast: Florence Reed (Mrs. Clivedon-Banks), Laurette Taylor (Mrs. Midget), Thomas Chalmers (Rev. Frank Thomson), Helen Chandler (Ann), Morgan Farley (Scrubby), Bramwell Fletcher (Mr. Prior), Louis Hector (Mr. Lingley), Alexander Kirkland (Henry), Vincent Price (Rev. William Duke).

Notes: This was a three-act play with two settings: On Board and The Present.

**The Glass Menagerie.** Playhouse Theatre. March 31, 1945 — June 29, 1946. Royale Theatre. July 1, 1946 — August 3, 1946. Theatre Owned and Operated by Harry Fromkes. Produced by Eddie Dowling and Louis J. Singer. Incidental Music by Paul Bowles. Written by Tennessee Williams. Musical Director: Max Marlin. Directed by Eddie Dowling and Margo Jones. Scenic Design and Lighting Design by Jo Mielziner. General Manager: Alex Yokel. Company Manager: Al Lee. Stage Manager: Randolph Echols and Will Gould. Assistant Stage Manager: Mary Jean Copeland. Press Representative: Harry Davies.

Cast: Eddie Dowling (The Son, Tom Wingfield), Julie Haydon (The Daughter, Laura Wingfield), Anthony Ross (The Gentleman Caller, Jim O'Connor), Laurette Taylor (The Mother, Amanda Wingfield). Understudy: Betsy Blair (The Daughter).

Notes: This was a play in two parts.

# Appendix III:
# *THE DYING WIFE*
## by Laurette Taylor*

CHARACTERS

MAURICE FITZ-MAURICE
ARABELLA, *HIS WIFE*

SCENE: *A Boudoir.*

TIME: *The Present.*

*The action takes place in a charmingly-furnished boudoir. A flickering fire is sputtering in the grate, throwing fitful shadows across the darkened room.*

*ARABELLA, a fair, impressionable young woman of perhaps twenty-four or possibly twenty-five is lying on a luxurious couch covered by a Liberty wrapper. But neither the luxury of the couch nor the delicate texture of the wrapper bring her comfort. She is writhing in pain, evidently of an internal nature.*

*Moving slowly about the room, glancing ever and anon at a porcelain banjo-clock, gnawing a somewhat stubby moustache, and occasionally throwing an interrogative and impatient look at the sufferer on the couch, is MAURICE FITZ-MAURICE. He is a tall, uncertain man of middle age. He is evidently under considerable strain which he betrays by his sudden, impulsive movements, noiseless ejaculations and genuine irritation.*

ARABELLA. *(After groaning audibly and breathing heavily for several seconds, calls.)* Maurice! *(Waits; then, louder.)* Morry!
FITZ-MAURICE. *(Goes to her.)* I am here.
ARABELLA. (Groping for him.) Where?
FITZ-MAURICE. Beside you.

---

*The author wishes to express her indebtedness to the Jugo-Slav homily "Knowledge is death when the wronged are instructed thereof."

ARABELLA. It's so dark. I can't feel your hand. *(Clutching his hand.)*
FITZ-MAURICE. *(Eagerly.)* Can't you? Is your sense of touch going?
ARABELLA. I don't think so. This *is* your hand?
FITZ-MAURICE. Take care. You're crushing it. *(Takes his hand away, wrings it, examines it and then puts it carefully inside his vest.)*
ARABELLA. What time is it?
FITZ-MAURICE. *(Triumphantly.)* Eight minutes to eight.
ARABELLA. Why doesn't the doctor come? Why doesn't he come? Why doesn't he —?
FITZ-MAURICE. *(Glowering down at her.)* He will not come.
ARABELLA. Why won't he? Why won't the doctor come?
FITZ-MAURICE. You will not need him.
ARABELLA. But I do need him. I need him terribly. I need him —
FITZ-MAURICE. His coming now would be totally unnecessary.
ARABELLA. Unnecessary! Morry! I'm going to get well. That's why he won't come. I'm going to —
FITZ-MAURICE. You are going to die in seven minutes.
ARABELLA. Die! Die! *(With a loud cry.)* I can't die in seven minutes.
FITZ-MAURICE. When the hour-hand touches eight on the dial of that clock you will breathe for the last time, Arabella.
ARABELLA. *(Cries in fear and pain.)* I can't. Why should I? I'm not ready to die. You won't let me die, will you, Morry?
FITZ-MAURICE. Neither human power nor mine can save you, Arabella. *(ARABELLA moans and sobs.)* Is there anything you wish to say before your spirit passes?
ARABELLA. I can't believe it. I'm too young. Too — Too —
FITZ-MAURICE. Too — *what*, Arabella?
ARABELLA. We've been so happy together. So happy. Haven't we, Morry?
FITZ-MAURICE. *You* have been happy, I *hope*.
ARABELLA. We have been so much to each other.
FITZ-MAURICE. You have been to me.
ARABELLA. *(Gasping.)* I can hardly breathe. Can it really be that I —?
FITZ-MAURICE. In five minutes, Arabella.
ARABELLA. There is one thing I must confess. Confess to you as I would to a priest. You must give me absolution, Morry. You must forgive and absolve me.
FITZ-MAURICE. Confess, Arabella.
ARABELLA. It won't *take* four minutes. Four minutes! All the rest of my life telling you of my shame! The man who climbed with me — I did really climb the Jung-Frau, Morry! *Really* I did. The man — Silvanus Saxon. I

was excited. Everything was so — so — exalted! I felt so — so — above the earth — so spiritual. — And I — he — and he —. We were like children, Morry. Two little children up and up on the Jung-Frau! Alone in the world. And I forgot everything. The cold seemed like fire. The snow melted at the touch as roseleaves. Roseleaves!! In my hair and in my brain. And I — And he — Oh, Morry!! We betrayed you! *(Cries; waits.)* You say nothing. How you must love me! You don't reproach me! You don't even seem surprised that your own Arabella could have —

FITZ-MAURICE. I am not surprised.

ARABELLA. You are not! Morry!... Surely you did not think me capable of deceiving you?

FITZ-MAURICE. I knew you had.

ARABELLA. You knew I had deceived you?

FITZ-MAURICE. Yes, my darling. *That's why I put poison in your coffee.*

*(The clock strikes eight. On the last stroke ARABELLA sinks back on her luxurious couch. MAURICE FITZ-MAURICE frowns down on her, gnawing his extremely stubby moustache. Suddenly he breaks into fiendish laughter.)*

*CURTAIN.*

# Chapter Notes

## Preface

1. Laurette Taylor, www.sheilaomalley.com/archives/010303.html.
2. "Charles Hanson Towne, Flowers for the Living—Laurette Taylor," *The Syracuse Herald*, October 29, 1924.

## Chapter 1

1. Laurette Taylor, "Living and Play-Acting," *McClure's Magazine*, September 1922.
2. Wood Soanes, "Both Fairs Compete with Stage; Attendance Down Here and in the East," *Oakland Tribune*, May 14, 1939.
3. Laurette Taylor, "The Quality Most Needed," in Toby Cole and Helen Krich Chinoy, eds., *Actors on Acting*, pp. 596, 598.
4. "Praises Miss Taylor," *The Indianapolis Star*, February 17, 1923.
5. "Broadway, Peg o' My Heart Returns," *San Antonio Express*, February 26, 1939.
6. Marguerite Courtney, *Laurette*, p. 19.
7. The address is now home to an apartment building that was built in 1910.
8. Lloyd Lewis, "Reminiscing with Peg o' My Heart," *New York Times*, March 25, 1945.
9. "Praises Miss Taylor," *The Indianapolis Star*, February 17, 1923.
10. "Broadway, Peg o' My Heart Returns," *San Antonio Express*, February 26, 1939.
11. Ibid.
12. Laurette Taylor, "From the Player's Point of View," *Chicago Daily Tribune*, September 11, 1910.
13. Lemuel F. Parton, "Who's News Today," *Oakland Tribune*, March 17, 1932.
14. Laurette Taylor, "From the Player's Point of View," *Chicago Daily Tribune*, September 11, 1910.
15. "Broadway, Peg o' My Heart Returns," *San Antonio Express*, February 26, 1939.

## Chapter 2

1. Gladys Hall, "Laurette Taylor as Seen by Gladys Hall," *Motion Picture*, June 1924, p. 24.
2. Dwight Taylor, *Blood-and-Thunder*, p. 5.
3. Courtney, *Laurette*, p. 33.
4. Dwight Taylor, *Blood-and-Thunder*, p. 4.
5. Guthrie McClintic, *Me and Kit*, p. 9.
6. Ibid., pp. 23–24.
7. Laurette Taylor, "The Quality Most Needed," in Cole and Chinoy, eds., *Actors on Acting*, p. 597.
8. Courtney, *Laurette*, p. 43.
9. Dwight Taylor, "My Mother Laurette," *Saturday Evening Post*, December 17, 1960, p. 27. According to Ellen Margolis, Dwight's daughter Audrey Wallace-Taylor told her that her father had tried to write a biography on Laurette. The working title was "After You're Gone." The book was never completed, but the *Saturday Evening Post* article was based on the manuscript. In *Hello, Hollywood!* the editors reprinted an article Dwight wrote for *Screen Writer* in May 1948, titled "You Know How They Are." According to the editors of *Hello, Hollywood!* the title of the book Dwight had written about his mother was *After You've Gone*.
10. Ward Morehouse, *Matinee Tomorrow: Fifty Years of Our Theater*, p. 106.
11. "The 10–20–30 Days of Laurette Taylor," *New York Times*, March 3, 1918.
12. Dwight Taylor, *Blood-and-Thunder*, p. 18.
13. Laurette Taylor, "Living and Play-Acting," *McClure's Magazine*, September 1922.
14. Dwight Taylor, *Blood-and-Thunder*, pp. 23–24.
15. "Deeper Than Greasepaint," *Time*, May 9, 1955.
16. Malcolm Gladwell, *Outliers: The Story of Success*, pp. 39–40.
17. Ibid., p. 40.
18. Sheena Iyengar, *The Art of Choosing*, p. 129.
19. "Empire Gown vs. 'Fig Leaf'; Miss Taylor Favors Latter," *Chicago Daily Tribune*, April 4, 1909.

20. Courtney, *Laurette*, pp. 58–59.
21. Barbara Marinacci, *Leading Ladies*, p. 246.
22. Laurette Taylor, "Living and Play-Acting," *McClure's Magazine*, September 1922.
23. Laurette Taylor, "The Quality Most Needed," in Cole and Chinoy, eds., *Actors on Acting*, p. 598.
24. Frank Carrington, "Voice of Broadway: Visit with the Stars," *Avalanche-Journal* [Lubbock, Texas], September 8, 1960.
25. "About Grandmother and Othess [sic]," *New York Times*, December 22, 1912.
26. Laurette Taylor, "The Quality Most Needed," in Cole and Chinoy, eds., *Actors on Acting*, p. 597.
27. Laurette Taylor, *The Greatest of These—*, p. 44.
28. Dwight Taylor's version was different. In his story the name of the play was *Death Valley Scotty*. The play was probably *Scotty, King of the Desert Mines*, which toured in 1906. It was a disaster. It also featured the debut of Walter Scott, a publicity hound who claimed to have discovered a gold mine. Scott decided he wanted to be an actor. He proved to be unprofessional and unreliable, and the show bombed.
29. "The 10-20-30 Days of Laurette Taylor," *New York Times*, March 3, 1918.
30. Dwight Taylor, *Blood-and-Thunder*, p. 30.
31. Ibid., p. 30.
32. "The 10-20-30 Days of Laurette Taylor," *New York Times*, March 3, 1918.
33. Ibid.
34. Maurice Zolotow, *Stagestruck: The Romance of Alfred Lunt and Lynn Fontanne*, p. 28.
35. Dwight Taylor, *Blood-and-Thunder*, p. 225.
36. Ibid.

# Chapter 3

1. Laurette Taylor, *The Greatest of These—*, p. 32.
2. Preston Wright, "Discoveries in Humans: Dramatic Voice Caught Ear of Stranger and Laurette Taylor Got Chance to Be Star," *The Lincoln Star* [Nebraska], October 4, 1925. Jacott killed himself on May 14, 1914 at the St. James Hotel (137 W. 45th Street) when he jumped down an air shaft.
3. Courtney, *Laurette*, p. 72.
4. Ibid., p. 73.
5. Burns Mantle, "News of the Theatres," *Chicago Daily Tribune*, September 21, 1908.
6. "Belasco—Yosemite Next Week," *Washington Post*, December 17, 1908.
7. "Empire Gown vs. 'Fig Leaf'"; Miss Taylor Favors Latter," *Chicago Daily Tribune*, April 4, 1909.
8. McClintic, *Me and Kit*, pp. 117–118.
9. "Drama," *Life*, May 13, 1909.
10. "Empire Gown vs. 'Fig Leaf'; Miss Taylor Favors Latter," *Chicago Daily Tribune*, April 4, 1909.
11. Ibid.
12. Hortense Saunders, "Laurette Taylor Tells About Her Unusual Romance," *Charleston Daily Mail* [West Virginia], December 2, 1925.
13. "The Death of Hartley Manners," *Morning Herald* [Hagerstown, Maryland], December 26, 1928.
14. Noel Coward, *Present Indicative*, p. 135.
15. Hortense Saunders, "Laurette Taylor Tells About Her Unusual Romance," *Charleston Daily Mail* [West Virginia], December 2, 1925.
16. Courtney, *Laurette*, p. 19.
17. Ibid., p. 136.
18. Laurette Taylor, "Living and Play-Acting," *McClure's Magazine*, September 1922.
19. "Laurette Taylor," in Cole and Chinoy, eds., *Actors on Acting*, p. 595.
20. Julian Johnson, "Profit Here, Prophet There," *Los Angeles Times*, June 23, 1912.
21. George C. Tyler, *Whatever Goes Up—*, p. 272.
22. David Hanna, *Second Chance*, p. 140.
23. Jane Dixon, "At What Age Are Women Most Interesting?" *Oakland Tribune*, January 14, 1920.
24. Courtney, *Laurette*, p. 155.
25. Wood Soanes, "Both Fairs Compete with Stage; Attendance Down Here and in the East," *Oakland Tribune*, May 14, 1939.
26. Laurette Taylor, "Living and Play-Acting," *McClure's Magazine*, September 1922.
27. Noel Coward, *Present Indicative*, p. 135.
28. Artist Clare Sheridan met Laurette and Hartley during a dinner with Ralph Pulitzer. Sheridan wrote about Laurette in her diary describing her as having "great charm, talks well, and seems to have more vision and to be less self-centered than the usual people of the stage—and I like her husky voice."¹
29. Unidentified clipping, Billy Rose Theater Collection, New York Public Library of the Performing Arts at Lincoln Center.
30. Unidentified clipping, Billy Rose Theater Collection, New York Public Library of the Performing Arts at Lincoln Center.
31. Courtney, *Laurette*, p. 248.
32. Coward, pp. 135–136.
33. Courtney, *Laurette*, p. 261.
34. Jared Brown, *The Fabulous Lunts*, p. 49.
35. Leslie Ruth Howard, *A Quite Remarkable Father*, p. 117.
36. Maurice Zolotow, *Stagestruck: The Romance of Alfred Lunt and Lynn Fontanne*, p. 91.

Notes — Chapter 4

37. Ibid., p. 92.
38. Jessie Royce Landis, *You Won't Be So Pretty*, p. 80.
39. Ibid.
40. Howard, p. 87.
41. Courtney, *Laurette*, p. 250.
42. "Alla Nazimova," Axel Madsen, *The Sewing Circle*, p. 117.
43. Axel Madsen also claims that Mercedes De Acosta hosted a 1929 party at a house she was renting with John Colton where the guest list included Alla Nazimova, Katharine Cornell, Laurette, Constance Collier, Diana Wynard — and Greta Garbo. When Garbo called to say she couldn't attend because of a cold, De Acosta left the party and arrived at Garbo's house where she fed her orange and lemon juice, and ultimately spent the night.
44. Gavin Lambert, *Nazimova*, p. 11.
45. Diana McLellan, *The Girls*, p. 14.
46. Leslie Davis, "Hollywood's Golden Age of Lesbian 'Glam,'" http://examiner.com. Retrieved August 28, 2009.
47. Gertrude Lawrence, *A Star Danced*, pp. 132–133.
48. McLellan, *The Girls*, pp. 87–88.
49. Mercedes de Acosta, *Here Lies the Heart*, p. 196.
50. McLellan, *The Girls*, p. 88.
51. Helen Sheehy, *Eva Le Gallienne: A Biography*, p. 65.
52. Ibid., pp. 43–44.
53. Ibid., p. 52.
54. Ibid., p. 54.
55. Courtney, *Laurette*, pp. 257–258.
56. Zolotow, p. 90.
57. Hedda Hopper, *From Under My Hat*, p. 146.
58. Dwight Taylor, "My Mother Laurette," *Saturday Evening Post*, December 17, 1960, p. 64.
59. Ibid.
60. Ibid. Audrey Wallace-Taylor remembered receiving a spontaneous gift from her grandmother, a doll. She was 16 at the time.
61. "Wall Street Fight in *The Ringmaster*," *New York Times*, August 10, 1909. In October Laurette was replaced by Dorothy Bernard.
62. "Amusements," *Logansport Chronicle* [Pennsylvania], September 3, 1910.
63. "Plays and Players," *Des Moines News*, September 5, 1910.
64. Laurette Taylor, "From the Player's Point of View," *Chicago Daily Tribune*, September 11, 1910.
65. Percy Hammond, "Miss Taylor Trifles as The Girl in Waiting," *Chicago Daily Tribune*, September 5, 1910.
66. Laurette Taylor, "From the Player's Point of View," *Chicago Daily Tribune*, September 11, 1910.

67. "New York Likes Miss Taylor, Too," *Washington Post*, December 26, 1909.
68. Morehouse, *Matinee Tomorrow: Fifty Years of Our Theater*, p. 106.
69. "Big Thrill in New Play by Armstrong," *New York Times*, January 21, 1910.
70. "From State Prisons to a New Messiah," *Life*, February 3, 1910.
71. Quoted in Courtney, *Laurette*, pp. 84–85.
72. "Charles Cherry in The Seven Sisters," *Washington Post*, March 26, 1911.
73. Daniel Frohman, *Daniel Frohman Presents*, p. 267.
74. Ibid., p. 268.
75. Ibid.
76. Franklin Fyles, "Adapted from Hungarian in the New Farce *Seven Sisters*," *Chicago Daily Tribune*, February 26, 1911.
77. "Pertinent Data on a Domestic Doctrine," *New York Times*, February 21, 1911.
78. "Laurette Taylor in a Play About a Girl Without a Soul," *New York Daily Tribune*, March 19, 1911.
79. If the play wasn't terrible enough, believe it or not it even resorted to the "it was all a dream" ending.
80. "Offerings at the Local Theaters," *Washington Post*, March 28, 1911.
81. "At the Theaters," *Logansport Journal*, May 19, 1911.
82. Percy Hammond, "Music and the Drama," *Chicago Daily Tribune*, April 18, 1911.

## Chapter 4

1. Mark Feeney, *Lebanon Daily News*, March 25, 2007.
2. Oliver Morosco, "Once Important in Theater, Faces Death After Fall on Stairs of 75-Cent Rooming House," *San Antonio Express*, July 22, 1936.
3. Mary B. Mullett, "Who's Who Among Women," *Lincoln Daily News*, March 30, 1914.
4. Helen Morosco, *The Oracle of Broadway*, p. 185.
5. Ibid.
6. Ibid., p. 186.
7. Ibid., p. 190.
8. Ibid., p. 192.
9. "*Bird of Paradise* Has Scenic Beauty," *New York Times*, January 9, 1912.
10. Adolph Klauber, "Question of Dramatic Values," *New York Times*, January 14, 1912.
11. "*The Bird of Paradise* [review]," *Life*, January 18, 1912.
12. Warren Barton Blake, "Our Un-American Stage," *The Independent*, March 7, 1912.
13. "Laurette Taylor Confesses," *New York Times*, January 14, 1912.

14. Laurette Taylor, "Living and Play-Acting," *McClure's Magazine*, September 1922.

15. According to Jessie Royce Landis, "It seems that Laurette would rather have been a singer than anything else in the world. She nearly drove her daughter, Marguerite, crazy, trying to make her sing, and despite all Hartley could do, Laurette would put a song in every part she played, if it were humanly possible, despite the fact that she couldn't carry a tune — unless it were well wrapped and locked in a suitcase." Despite her desire to sing, Laurette was well aware that she couldn't. In *The Greatest of These* —, she admitted no one wanted to listen to her sing. "Now I'm quite shameless — I'd sing 'Aida' if it would bring money to the Red Cross. (I know it would bring them patients.)"

16. Laurette Taylor, "The Quality Most Needed," in Cole and Chinoy, eds., *Actors on Acting*, pp. 597–598.

17. According to Guthrie McClintic, singer Linnie Love told him that Laurette was paying for her singing lessons in New York. She and Laurette had become acquainted in Seattle where Love was a popular vaudeville child actress. Love went on to have a successful singing career, primarily in a duo ("Lovelee") with Lorna Lea. Love died in 1918 during the flu epidemic. She was stricken when she and Lea were performing at Camp Lewis for World War I soldiers. Love was 25 when she died.

18. McClintic, *Me and Kit*, pp. 67–68.

19. *Racine Journal News*, April 1, 1912.

20. Morosco, p. 198.

21. "Acting Under Difficulties," *Iowa Recorder*, September 3, 1913.

22. *Life*, April 18, 1912. The case was soon solved when a madman was arrested in a Harlem basement with bomb-making materials. When told he was insane, Laurette quipped, "He must have been to think I was too beautiful to live." Marguerite Courtney, *Laurette*, p. 118.

23. "Laurette Taylor, Actress, Quits Job and Vanishes," *Chicago Daily Tribune*, April 6, 1912.

24. *The Bird of Paradise* was a very successful play. However, Morosco and Tully was successfully sued by Grace A. Fendler. She claimed she'd shown Morosco an original play about the Hawaiian Islands. She received damages totaling more than $750,000. See "How the Lucky 'Bird of Paradise' Turned into a Hoodoo," *Ogden Standard-Examiner*, September 9, 1928. Eventually, the award was overturned, and Tully prevailed.

25. Julian Johnson, "From the Mason to the Majestic," *Los Angeles Times*, April 8, 1912.

26. Ibid., April 9, 1912.

27. Morosco, p. 199.

28. Ibid., p. 200. Forrest Stanley became a silent film actor. His best known role was in *The Cat and the Canary* (1927).

29. Morosco, pp. 188–189.

30. Ibid, p. 201.

31. Marguerite Courtney spelled his name Eagan in *Laurette* and wrote that Laurette and Charles Taylor had met him in Seattle.

32. The Egan School of Music & Drama, according to an *LA Times* August 11, 1912, ad, was housed on "The Entire Top Floor of Majestic Theatre Building. Frank Egan wrote *A One Word Play by One Author*. The short play features the characters HE and SHE, and each line of dialogue consists of only one word. In April 1914 Laurette appeared in *One Word* with Cyril Maude, part of a benefit performance for the Relief Fund of Manhattan's theater box office workers. The entire play was printed in the *New York Times* on April 19, 1914. The title of the article is "No Wasted Dialogue in This Play. It is officially credited to Frank C. Egan. Laurette often used this short piece for benefits. For example, in 1932 she performed it at the Casino Theatre for an Actors' Dinner Club benefit. See "Actors' Dinner Club Nearly Ends Deficit," *New York Times*, October 10, 1932.

33. "Reception to Taylor," *Los Angeles Times*, May 19, 1912. The ad also included a letter from Laurette Taylor: "Who knows your school better than I? Let me heartily urge those contemplating entering our profession to receive a thorough stage education, and I most certainly approve of your clever method of teaching. Lots of good cheer and luck. Sincerely yours, Laurette Taylor." The ad included additional letters from Richard Bennett and James K. Hackett.

34. "Laurette on Platform," *Los Angeles Times*, May 26, 1912.

35. Courtney, *Laurette*, p. 141.

36. "Taylor in Child Play," *Los Angeles Times*, June 2, 1912.

37. Laurette Taylor, "Living and Play-Acting," *McClure's Magazine*, September 1922.

38. Gardner Bradford, "Peg Comes Home Again," *Los Angeles Times*, May 24, 1914.

39. Hedda Hopper, "Hedda Hopper's Hollywood," *Los Angeles Times*, August 7, 1941. To add to the confusion, according to Hopper, in 1941 Collier had a hit with a play written by Ivor Novello and titled *Curtain Going Up*. The original title was *Comedienne*, but Laurette asked that the title be changed because that was the same title as a different Hartley play.

40. Harry Carr, "The Lancer," *Los Angeles Times*, October 13, 1925.

41. E.V. Durling, *Tucson Daily Citizen*, August 2, 1946.

42. Lloyd Lewis, "Reminiscing with Peg o' My Heart," *New York Times*, March 25, 1945.

43. "Taylor in Manners' Play," *Los Angeles Times*, May 26, 1912.

44. Morosco, p. 202.

45. Otheman Stevens, *Los Angeles Examiner*, May 26, 1912.
46. Johnson, "Peg, Little Genre-Piece," *Los Angeles Times*, May 27, 1912.
47. Johnson, "Wee Walker for Belasco," *Los Angeles Times*, June 14, 1912.
48. Johnson, "In the Big Play-World," *Los Angeles Times*, July 12, 1912.
49. Ibid.
50. Courtney, *Laurette*, p. 121.
51. Ibid., p. 131.
52. Grace Kingsley, "Tailoring This Town," *Los Angeles Times*, July 28, 1912.
53. Ibid.
54. "Out of the Past," *Time*, July 7, 1947.
55. "This Girl Sprints a Mile in Just Nine Minutes Time," *Des Moines Daily News*, August 31, 1912.
56. Morosco, p. 208.
57. Johnson, "From the Mason to the Majestic," June 17, 1912.
58. Johnson, "Peg Taylor's [sic] Sixty Thousand," *Los Angeles Times*, August 3, 1912.
59. Johnson estimated that Hartley Manners was probably earning about a thousand a week from royalties derived from *Peg* as well as other plays.
60. Johnson, "Peg Taylor's [sic] Sixty Thousand," *Los Angeles Times*, August 3, 1912.
61. Johnson, "Peg's Father Gives Way to Lauretta's [sic] Grandma," *Los Angeles Times*, September 15, 1912.
62. Ibid. Much of the remaining article consists of a pack of lies Laurette told Johnson. She claimed she was born in Newark, New Jersey with the name Lauretta Nellie and was sent to convent schools by her parents. Johnson left newspaper writing to become a film editor and screenwriter. His credits included *Wings* (1927) and *Interference* (1928). Johnson was married to vaudeville performer (and speakeasy hostess) Texas Guinan from 1910 to 1920, so he knew a thing or two about strong-willed women.
63. "Burbank," *Los Angeles Times*, September 29, 1912.
64. Johnson, "Virtuosa of the Emotions," *Los Angeles Times*, September 23, 1912.
65. Ward Morehouse, *Matinee Tomorrow*, p. 117.
66. Ibid.
67. Years later when Frances Marion was a renowned screenwriter, William Randolph Hearst came to her to write a screenplay for mistress Marion Davies — an adaptation of *Peg o' My Heart*. Frances, who hated the play, worked on the adaptation but gladly turned the scenario writing over to Frank R. Adams. According to Marion, Hearst told her, "'I've seen Laurette Taylor in her silent film and she was excellent. But the talking picture really calls for a pretty young girl and Marion just fits the part. We already have a cute little dog picked out for her.'" Marion, *Off With Their Heads!*, p. 236.
68. Marion, *Off With Their Heads!*, pp. 4–5.
69. Morosco, p. 217.
70. Ibid., p. 218.
71. Ibid.
72. Ibid., p. 219. Frankly, Morosco comes off as a braggart and egomaniac in this book, so many of his statements should be taken with a grain of salt.
73. Ibid, p. 220.
74. Vanderheyden Fyles, "New Plays Are Seen in Gotham," *Indianapolis Star*, December 29, 1912.
75. "*Peg o' My Heart* Charms at Cort," *New York Times*, December 21, 1912.
76. "*Peg o' My Heart* [review]," *Life*, January 2, 1913.
77. Sheldon Cheney, "The American Playwright and the Drama of Sincerity," *Forum*, April 1914.
78. "Echoes of the Stage," *Town and Country*, January 4, 1913.
79. Johnson, "Laurette Taylor to Be Stellar Summer Visitor," *Los Angeles Times*, February 19, 1912.
80. Johnson, "Morosco, the Silent Noise," *Los Angeles Times*, March 31, 1912.
81. "About Grandmother and Othess [sic]," *New York Times*, December 22, 1912.
82. Ibid.
83. Morosco, p. 231.
84. Ibid., p. 232.
85. Courtney estimated that from the road companies alone, Hartley was earning $10,000 per week in royalties.
86. Morosco, p. 233.
87. Ibid., p. 218.
88. Gardner Bradford, "Peg Comes Home Again," *Los Angeles Times*, May 24, 1914. Bradford named Elsa Ryan, Peggy O'Neill, Blanche Hall, Florence Martin, and Lois Meredith as other successful Pegs.
89. Lloyd Lewis, "Reminiscing with Peg o' My Heart," *New York Times*, March 25, 1945.
90. Edwin Schallert, "Joan Evans Brightens Dated Peg o' My Heart," *Los Angeles Times*, July 6, 1951. See also "Joan Evans Will Star in Peg o' My Heart," *Los Angeles Times*, July 1, 1951.
91. Lawrence Christon, "The Resurrection of Peg," *Los Angeles Times*, September 6, 1974.
92. Dan Sullivan, "Peg o' My Heart at the Staircase," *Los Angeles Times*, September 19, 1974.
93. Richard F. Shepard, "A 'Peg' for All Our Hearts," *New York Times*, February 18, 1977.
94. McClintic, *Me and Kit*, pp. 50–51.
95. "Bernhardt Praise Has Proved Aid," *Los Angeles Times*, September 14, 1924.

96. Ibid.
97. "Praises Miss Taylor," *The Indianapolis Star*, February 17, 1923.
98. Hopper, *From Under My Hat*, p. 146.
99. Ibid.
100. Emory B. Calvert, "Peg o' My Heart Tops Off Year's Run," *Lincoln Daily Star*, December 28, 1913.
101. Courtney, *Laurette*, p. 106.
102. "Broadway, Peg o' My Heart Returns," *San Antonio Express*, February 26, 1939.
103. "About Grandmother and Othess [sic]," *New York Times*, December 22, 1912.
104. "Seen and Heard," *Lowell Sun* [Massachusetts], September 16, 1925.
105. Mary B. Mullett, "Who's Who Among Women," *Lincoln Daily News*, March 30, 1914.
106. Morosco, p. 239.
107. "In Our Set," *New York Times*, May 31, 1914.
108. "Theatrical Notes," *New York Times*, February 28, 1913.
109. "Not So Many Inventions in the London Theaters," *New York Times*, April 4, 1915.
110. Ibid, June 21, 1914.
111. Ibid.
112. Ibid.
113. Morosco, p. 239.
114. Ibid, p. 241.
115. Ibid., p. 243.
116. "Miss Taylor Thinks it a 'Shabby Trick,'" *Chicago Daily Tribune*, June 22, 1914.
117. Morosco, pp. 248–249. See also "Star's Whims Lead to Court," *Chicago Daily Tribune*, June 12, 1914.
118. "Peg's London Triumph," *Washington Post*, October 25, 1914.
119. Ibid.
120. Zolotow, p. 18.
121. Ibid. Most agree that Laurette had appallingly bad taste in clothing. Helen Hayes admitted that her own wasn't that great, "but I am the Duchess of Windsor and Jacqueline Kennedy combined compared to Laurette Taylor. One cannot describe her getups." Helen Hayes, *On Reflection*, pp. 122–123.
122. Zolotow, p. 18.
123. Ibid., p. 19.
124. Ibid., p. 90.
125. Ibid., p. 20.
126. "Brilliant American Stars of Stage Take London Theater Public by Storm," *Washington Post*, April 15, 1915.
127. William M. Drew, *Speaking of Silents: First Ladies of the Screen*. New York: Vestal Press, 1989, p. 241.
128. Drew, "Broadway, Peg o' My Heart Returns," *San Antonio Express*, February 26, 1939.
129. Quoted in Ellen Marie Margolis, *Recoveries*, pp. 124–125.

130. Unidentified clipping, Billy Rose Theater Collection, New York Public Library of the Performing Arts at Lincoln Center.
131. "Laurette Taylor May Return from London," *Lincoln Daily Star*, June 20, 1915.
132. "News and Gossip of the Theatrical World," *Washington Post*, November 7, 1915.
133. "Peg in the Cellar," *New York Times*, October 31, 1915.
134. "Miss Taylor on Zeppelins," *New York Times*, December 9, 1915.
135. Peg Comes Home Ambitious," *New York Times*, December 12, 1915.

## Chapter 5

1. "Laurette Taylor at Work and at Play," *Middletown Times-Press*, December 31, 1917.
2. "Laurette Taylor Returns Today," *Washington Post*, December 5, 1915.
3. "Peg Comes Home Ambitious," *New York Times*, December 12, 1915.
4. "Laurette Taylor, "Living and Play-Acting," *McClure's Magazine*, September 1922.
5. Maurice Zolotow, *Stagestruck: The Romance of Alfred Lunt and Lynn Fontanne*, p. 21.
6. George C. Tyler, *Whatever Goes Up—*, p. 272.
7. Zolotow, Ibid., p. 22.
8. Ibid., p. 23.
9. "Laurette Taylor and Eve's Wooing," *New York Times*, November 10, 1917.
10. [no title], *Life*, November 22, 1917.
11. Zolotow, Ibid., p. 23.
12. Quoted in Ellen Marie Margolis, *Recoveries*, pp. 158–159.
13. Ibid., p. 159.
14. "Beauty and Truth in *The Harp of Life*," *New York Times*, November 28, 1916.
15. "Her performance was beguiling," McClintic, *Me and Kit*, p. 157.
16. "*The Harp of Life* [review]," *Life*, December 14, 1916.
17. "Coming Attractions," *Syracuse Herald*, October 22, 1916.
18. "The New Plays," *The Independent*, January 15, 1917.
19. Anna Steese Richardson, "Old Faces for Young," *McClure's Magazine*, March 1917.
20. Alan Dale, "Plays and Players," *Puck*, December 23, 1916.
21. "Society," *Fort Wayne Journal-Gazette*, April 26, 1917.
22. Laurette Taylor, "The Quality Most Needed," in Cole and Chinoy, eds., *Actors on Acting*, p. 597.
23. Alexander Woollcott, "Second Thoughts on First Nights," *New York Times*, March 11, 1917. According to Woollcott's biographer Howard Te-

ichmann, "Woollcott's critiques were always honest, though they were, as Burns Mantle had cautioned him, prejudiced in favor of those he liked. In addition to Ada Rehan and Laurette Taylor, the Barrymore family — Lionel, John, and eventually Ethel — became his pets. He lavished praise with a heavy, sugary hand" (*Smart Aleck*, p. 69).

24. Zolotow, Ibid, p. 25.
25. Ibid., p. 24.
26. "Between Seasons," *New York Times*, July 22, 1917.
27. Quoted in Ellen Marie Margolis, *Recoveries*, p. 160.
28. *Oakland Tribune*, September 30, 1917. See also "Movies Boom Liberty Loan," *New York Times*, September 19, 1917.
29. "Laurette Taylor at Work and at Play, " *Middletown Times-Press*, December 31, 1917.
30. Ibid.
31. Ibid.
32. Ibid.
33. Ibid.
34. Ibid.
35. "The Girl on Our Cover," *Puck*, July 5, 1917.
36. Laurette Taylor, "The Quality Most Needed," in Cole and Chinoy, eds., *Actors on Acting*, p. 598.
37. "The New Plays," *New York Times*, March 11, 1917.
38. "The Comedies of Manners," *New York Times*, November 11, 1917. This article provided one of the best biographies on the former actor.
39. "Written and Staged in Just Four Weeks," *New York Times*, April 1, 1917.
40. Laurette Taylor, "Living and Play-Acting," *McClure's Magazine*, September 1922.
41. "*Out There* Proves Most Appealing," *New York Times*, March 28, 1917.
42. Alan Dale, "Plays and Players," *Puck*, April 21, 1917.
43. Woollcott, "Second Thoughts on First Nights," *New York Times*, April 8, 1917.
44. "Music and Drama," *Current Opinion*, May 1917. A large excerpt of *Out There* is included in the review.
45. "Drama," *Life*, April 12, 1917.
46. Zolotow, p. 27.
47. "The Death of Hartley Manners," *Morning Herald* [Hagerstown, Maryland], December 26, 1928.
48. "Up and Down Broadway," *New York Times*, September 30, 1917.
49. "Laurette Taylor in Shakespeare," *New York Times*, March 17, 1918.
50. Ibid.
51. Jared Brown, *The Fabulous Lunts*, p. 50.
52. "Laurette Taylor in Shakespeare," *New York Times*, March 17, 1918.

53. *Life*, April 18, 1918.
54. McClintic, *Me and Kit*, p. 170.
55. Helen Hayes, *On Reflection*, p. 122.
56. C. Courtenay Savage, "The Theatre in Review," *Forum*, June 1918.
57. Wood Soanes, "Curtain Calls," *Oakland Tribune*, June 26, 1934.
58. "Laurette Taylor Replies," *New York Times*, April 14, 1918.
59. Ibid.
60. "How *Out There* Started," *New York Times*, July 14, 1918.
61. George C. Tyler, *Whatever Goes Up—*, p. 275.
62. Ibid.. p. 276.
63. ,Ibid., p. 277.
64. Ibid., p. 278.
65. Ibid.
66. Laurette Taylor, *The Greatest of These—*, p. 36.
67. Hedda Hopper, *San Francisco Chronicle*, December 20, 1941.
68. Laurette Taylor, *The Greatest of These—*, p. 22.
69. Ibid., p. 27.
70. Ibid., p. 36.
71. Percy Hammond, "Your Get Your Money's Worth at *Out There*," *Chicago Daily Tribune*, May 25, 1918.
72. "Laurette Taylor an Author," *Syracuse Herald*, October 27, 1918.
73. Gordon Ray Young, "*The Greatest of These* [review]," *Los Angeles Times*, November 17, 1918.
74. "*The Greatest of These—*[review]," *New York Times*, October 20, 1918.
75. "Playing to $32,000 a Night," *The Independent*, December 21, 1918.
76. Laurette Taylor, *The Greatest of These—*, p. 17.
77. Laurette Taylor, "Living and Play-Acting," *McClure's Magazine*, September 1922.
78. Ibid.
79. "Notable Books in Brief Review," *New York Times*, July 14, 1918.
80. Walter Prichard Eaton, "Some Plays in Print," *The Bookman: A Review of Books and Life*, August 1918.
81. "*Out There* [review]," *The Independent*, August 31, 1918.
82. "The Ambitions of Laurette Taylor," *New York Times*, January 6, 1918.
83. "Up and Down Broadway," *New York Times*, October 7, 1917.
84. It was also performed as a London benefit in April 1915.
85. Burns Mantle, "Laurette Taylor Recreates in Three Plays," *Chicago Daily Tribune*, March 15, 1914.
86. Metcalfe, *Life*, March 19, 1914.

87. "Laurette Taylor in One-Act Plays," *New York Times*, March 7, 1914.
88. "*Happiness* is a Cheer-Up Play, With a *Peg* Comedy Part," *New York Times*, January 1, 1918.
89. Percy Hammond, "Another Good One," *Chicago Daily Tribune*, November 4, 1918.
90. "J. Hartley Manners, The Freedom of the Dramatist: A Defense and a Plea," *New York Times*, January 13, 1918.
91. Zolotow, p. 28.
92. Brown, *The Fabulous Lunts*, p. 49.
93. Ibid., p. 45.
94. Zolotow, p. 90.
95. "The 10–20–30 Days of Laurette Taylor," *New York Times*, March 3, 1918.
96. "Miss Taylor's Record," *New York Times*, April 28, 1918.
97. Both quotes are from "Laurette Taylor: A Big Hit in Chicago," *Fort Wayne News and Sentinel*, December 2, 1918.
98. At the Hartman, *Newark Advocate*, February 7, 1919.
99. Woollcott, "The Play," *New York Times*, December 3, 1919.
100. Woollcott, "Second Thoughts on First Nights," *New York Times*, December 7, 1919.
101. "Season for Benefits in New York City," *Galveston Daily News*, February 1, 1920.
102. Savage, "The Theatre in Review," *Forum*, January 1920.
103. "Stage Plays That Are Worth While, " *Motion Picture Classic*, April/May 1920, p. 6.
104. Grace Kingsley, "Our 'Peg' Grown Up Now," *Los Angeles Times*, September 14, 1924.
105. Ibid.106. "Deep-Fringed Cape Spanish Inspiration," *Charleston Daily Mail*, March 22, 1920.
107. Zolotow, p. 65.
108. Ibid., p. 66.
109. *The Indianapolis Star*, May 4, 1920.
110. "Encore!" *Janesville Daily Gazette* [Wisconsin], May 5, 1920.
111. James Douglas, "How David Belasco Knelt and Soothed Laurette Taylor After Theater Riot," *Washington Post*, June 6, 1920.
112. "British Boors Broke Up Play," *The Mansfield News* [Ohio], April 30, 1920.
113. Cochran wrote, "I firmly believe that English girls with the right temperament and natural qualifications are to be found but they do not get the right schooling. The British theatre is a hot-bed of snobbery. Our leading actors and actresses think more of a nod from a duchess or a tea party with Lady 'X' than proficiency in their art." If you think that's bad, consider this statement from producer J.L. Sacks on why he cast American Edith Day in *Irene*: "English actresses … are dead lazy." See "Laurette Taylor Razzing Result of Many Causes," *New York Clipper*, May 5, 1920.

114. "London Stirred by Theater Riot," *Bridgeport Telegram*, May 1, 1920. See "British Actors Accused of Snobbery," *San Antonio Evening News*, June 18, 1920.
115. Marguerite Courtney, *Laurette*, p. 216.
116. "On Some London Hoodlums," *Fort Wayne Journal-Gazette*, May 3, 1920. Politics entered into the incident as well. John W. Davis, American ambassador to Great Britain, was roundly criticized for not speaking out more vehemently against the riot. At the time Davis was a Democratic contender for president, and his inaction may have hurt his chances for the nomination. See "Nomination is Acceptable to John W. Davis," *Anniston Star*, June 16, 1920.
117. "Laurette Taylor Will Again Face London House," *Janesville Daily Gazette* [Wisconsin], May 3, 1920.
118. "Miss Laurette Taylor's Reappearance," *London Times*, May 3, 1920.
119. "Encore!" *Janesville Daily Gazette* [Wisconsin], May 5, 1920.
120. "One Night in Rome [review]," *London Times*, May 4, 1920.
121. Ibid. .
122. "Laurette Taylor Will Again Face London House,' *Janesville Daily Gazette* [Wisconsin], May 3, 1920.
123. "Peg o' My Heart," *London Times*, July 17, 1920.
124. Ibid.
125. "To Revive Peg," The *Mansfield News* [Ohio], January 23, 1921.
126. Harry Carr, "'Peg' Reborn on Gotham Stage," *Los Angeles Times*, February 20, 1921.
127. Woollcott, "The Play," *New York Times*, February 15, 1921.
128. "Remarkable Remarks," *The Independent*, March 5, 1921.
129. "Robert C. Benchley, Drama," *Life*, March 3, 1921.
130. Woollcott, "Seconds Thoughts on First Nights," *New York Times*, February 20, 1921.
131. Carr, "Benefit Has Too Many Aces," *Los Angeles Times*, March 20, 1921.
132. "Percy Hammond's Letter," *Fort Wayne Journal-Gazette*, July 9, 1922.
133. "New York Letter," *Brownsville Daily Herald*, February 1, 1922.
134. Laurette Taylor, "Living and Play-Acting," *McClure's Magazine*, September 1922.
135. Laurette Taylor, "Living and Play-Acting," *McClure's Magazine*, September 1922.
136. Helen Hayes, *On Reflection*, p. 123.
137. Woollcott, "The Play," *New York Times*, January 24, 1922.
138. Benchley, "Sacred and Profane Dancing," *Life*, February 9, 1922.
139. Woollcott, "Seconds Thoughts on First Nights," *New York Times*, February 5, 1922.

140. Kenneth Andrews, "Broadway, Our Literary Signpost," *The Bookman: A Review of Books and Life*, April 1922.
141. Margaret O'Leary, "More Ado About the Flapper," *New York Times*, April 16, 1922.
142. "Laurette Taylor Finds Jazz a Bane," *New York Times*, February 20, 1922.
143. Westbrook Pegler, "Jazz Denounced by Galli-Curci as Evil Influence," *Atlanta Constitution*, February 6, 1922. For more on the evils of jazz see Mrs. Martha Lee, "Jazz Drags Its Blinded Addicts Back Toward the Mental and Emotional State of the Savage," *Atlanta Constitution*, February 26, 1922.
144. Ellen Marie Margolis, *Recoveries*, p. 212.
145. "Hartley Manners Writes," *Los Angeles Times*, October 15, 1924.

## Chapter 6

1. James Card, *Seductive Cinema*, p. 255.
2. Gladys Hall, "Laurette Taylor As Seen By Gladys Hall," *Motion Picture*, June 1924, pp. 24, 93.
3. Gardiner Carroll, "Why: Jane Cowl, Norma Talmadge and Laurette Taylor Explain Their Preference for Screen and Stage," *Photoplay*, July 1924, p. 73.
4. Hall, *Motion Picture*, June 1924, p. 93.
5. Frances Marion, *Off With Their Heads!*, p. 4.
6. "Calls 'Highbrows' Drama's Enemies," *New York Times*, February 27, 1916.
7. "Laurette Taylor and the Movies," *New York Times*, March 31, 1918.
8. Janet Gaynor also expressed interest in playing Peg.
9. "Laurette Taylor and the Movies," Ibid.
10. "Peg o' My Heart Will Be Put On Screen," *Billings Gazette*, July 13, 1919.
11. Emma-Lindsay Squier, "Peg Writes Her Epitaph," *Picture-Play Magazine*, p. 54.
12. Wanda Hawley was a big star at the time the film was made. However, her career fizzled once sound films arrived. It has been rumored that she became so desperate she turned to prostitution after her career failed.
13. "Peg at Last!" *Oakland Tribune*, June 11, 1922.
14. "Written on the Screen," *New York Times*, April 18, 1920.
15. "Among the Movies," *Nebraska State Journal* [Lincoln], June 4, 1922.
16. Emma-Lindsay Squier, "Peg Writes Her Epitaph," *Picture-Play Magazine*, pp. 54, 95.
17. Carroll, "Why: Jane Cowl, Norma Talmadge and Laurette Taylor Explain Their Preference for Screen and Stage," *Photoplay*, July 1924, p. 72. Cowl appeared in *The Spreading Dawn* (1917) but dismissed it in the same article. "I am glad that the picture as released was unsuccessful, for it suffered all the defects we have been discussing and I would not have my ability as an actress judged by it." Cowl later appeared as herself in *Stage Door Canteen* (1943) and had small roles in *Once More, My Darling* (1949), *The Secret Fury* (1950), *No Man of Her Own* (1950), and *Payment on Demand* (1951). Born in 1884, she died in 1950.
18. Squier, "Peg Writes Her Epitaph," *Picture-Play Magazine*, p. 54.
19. Ibid., p. 95.
20. "Laurette Taylor Here for Films," *Los Angeles Examiner*, August 1, 1922.
21. Unidentified clipping, Billy Rose Theater Collection, New York Public Library of the Performing Arts at Lincoln Center.
22. "Laurette Taylor Sees No Stars in Hollywood Streets," *Logansport Pharos-Tribune* [Indiana], February 14, 1923.
23. "Laurette Taylor in Film Debut," *Capital Times*, October 13, 1922.
24. "Camera Chatter," *Oakland Tribune*, November 5, 1922.
25. Harry Carr, "Laurette Does Her Stuff," *Motion Picture Classic*, p. 25.
26. King Vidor, *A Tree Is a Tree*, p. 93.
27. "This was a new adventure for me," Nancy Dowd, *King Vidor*, p. 33.
28. Vidor, p. 93.
29. Ibid.
30. Edwin Schallert, "Right from the Front," *Los Angeles Times*, October 1, 1922.
31. Vidor, pp. 93–94.
32. Emma-Lindsay Squier, Peg Writes Her Epitaph, *Picture-Play Magazine*, p. 95.
33. Vidor, p. 94.
34. Nancy Dowd, *King Vidor*, p. 34.
35. Vidor, pp. 94–95.
36. Ibid., p. 95.
37. Dowd, *King Vidor*, p. 34.
38. Ibid., pp. 34–35.
39. Unidentified clipping, Billy Rose Theater Collection, New York Public Library of the Performing Arts at Lincoln Center.
40. Carr, "Laurette Does Her Stuff," *Motion Picture Classic*, p. 25.
41. George Oppenheimer, *The Great Days of Broadway*, p. 114.
42. Axel Madsen, *The Sewing Circle*, p. 115.
43. Vidor, p. 96. According to the *Los Angeles Times* (June 16, 1929), one of the set's buildings had become a home for a Hollywood art director. "Overlooking Hollywood, the residence of an art director, is a house finished from a set originally built for Laurette Taylor's home in *Peg o' My Heart*."
44. Vidor, p. 96.

45. Ibid., p. 97.
46. Ibid., p. 98.
47. Ibid.
48. Ibid.
49. Carr, "Laurette Does Her Stuff," *Motion Picture Classic*, p. 25.
50. "It Looked Different on Screen," *Los Angeles Times*, June 1, 1924.
51. Unidentified clipping, Billy Rose Theater Collection, New York Public Library of the Performing Arts at Lincoln Center.
52. Unidentified clipping, Billy Rose Theater Collection, New York Public Library of the Performing Arts at Lincoln Center.
53. Unidentified clipping, Billy Rose Theater Collection, New York Public Library of the Performing Arts at Lincoln Center.
54. Carroll, "Why: Jane Cowl, Norma Talmadge and Laurette Taylor Explain Their Preference for Screen and Stage," *Photoplay*, July 1924, p. 72.
55. Ibid., p. 73.
56. Ibid.
57. Unidentified clipping, Billy Rose Theater Collection, New York Public Library of the Performing Arts at Lincoln Center.
58. Unidentified clipping, Billy Rose Theater Collection, New York Public Library of the Performing Arts at Lincoln Center.
59. "Screen Acting Hard, Says Laurette Taylor," *The Billings Gazette* [Montana], December 23, 1923.
60. Squier, "Peg Writes Her Epitaph," *Picture-Play Magazine*, p. 54.
61. Dowd, *King Vidor*, p. 36.
62. Vidor, pp. 95–96.
63. Screen Siftings, *The Lincoln Star* [Nebraska], November 26, 1922.
64. "Peg Stage Gowns Used in Star's Gowns, " *Logansport Press*, February 10, 1923.
65. Unidentified clipping, Billy Rose Theater Collection, New York Public Library of the Performing Arts at Lincoln Center.
66. Unidentified clipping, Billy Rose Theater Collection, New York Public Library of the Performing Arts at Lincoln Center.
67. "Here's Peg Again," *New York Times*, January 22, 1923.
68. Charles Hanson Towne, "Flowers for the Living—Laurette Taylor," *The Syracuse Herald*, October 29, 1924.
69. Unidentified clipping, Billy Rose Theater Collection, New York Public Library of the Performing Arts at Lincoln Center.
70. "*Peg o' My Heart* [review]," *Life*, February 15, 1923.
71. Unidentified clipping, Billy Rose Theater Collection, New York Public Library of the Performing Arts at Lincoln Center.
72. Unidentified clipping, Billy Rose Theater Collection, New York Public Library of the Performing Arts at Lincoln Center.
73. Carr, "Art vs. Youth Adjudged Draw," *Los Angeles Times*, January 14, 1923.
74. Helen Klumph, "Valentino Is Still Rage," *Los Angeles Times*, January 25, 1923.
75. Unidentified clipping, Billy Rose Theater Collection, New York Public Library of the Performing Arts at Lincoln Center.
76. Unidentified clipping, Billy Rose Theater Collection, New York Public Library of the Performing Arts at Lincoln Center.
77. "Peg o' My Heart [review]," *Variety*, January 1, 1923.
78. Unidentified clipping, Billy Rose Theater Collection, New York Public Library of the Performing Arts at Lincoln Center.
79. "Laurette Taylor a Delight in Adaptation of Her Stage Success," *Film Daily*, December 17, 1922.
80. Eugene O'Brien was considered for Jerry's role.
81. "Atmosphere of *Peg* Realistic," *Los Angeles Examiner*, October 17, 1922.
82. Edwin Schallert, "'Peg' Begins Today," *Los Angeles Times*, August 17, 1922.
83. Card, *Seductive Cinema*, p. 254.
84. Baxter, *King Vidor*, p. 16.
85. Unidentified clipping, Billy Rose Theater Collection, New York Public Library of the Performing Arts at Lincoln Center.
86. Vidor, p. 98.
87. Grace Kingsley, "Our 'Peg' Grown Up Now," *Los Angeles Times*, September 14, 1924.
88. "'Miss Barrymore accepts with pleasure,'" Baxter, *King Vidor*, pp. 16–17.
89. "Another of the happy memories," Ethel Barrymore, *Memories*, p. 256.
90. "Laurette Taylor Makes Some Significant Remarks About Ruts," *The La Crosse Tribune* [Wisconsin], April 8, 1943.
91. Laurette wanted Paul Muni to play her son. However, she was late for his appointment, and he refused to wait. "He was there before the time set. Five minutes after the hour of the appointment he walked out." According to Muni, "Perhaps Miss Taylor was detained unavoidably. I do not know. If I were the star I would have been ten minutes early. I did not get the role, and honestly, I did not care." In "Don't Call Me Lon Chaney," *Photoplay Magazine*, January 1930, p. 116.
92. "News and Gossip of the Rialto," *New York Times*, March 13, 1921.
93. "Calls the Managers 'Glorified Janitors,'" *New York Times*, February 12, 1923. The Lotos Club was located at 110 W. 57th Street. This dinner for Laurette represented only the second time the club had hosted a woman. More than 300 people attended. Speakers included Alexander Woollcott,

Chester S. Lord, James M. Beck, Clayton Hamilton, and W. Bourke Cockran.
94. E.M. Kelley, "Odd Motif in New Drama," *Los Angeles Times*, March 11, 1923.
95. Unidentified clipping, Billy Rose Theater Collection, New York Public Library of the Performing Arts at Lincoln Center.
96. John Corbin, "The Play," *New York Times*, February 28, 1923.
97. Robert C. Benchley, "Drama," *Life*, March 22, 1923.
98. "First Nights," *Time*, March 10, 1923.
99. Burns Mantle, "Laurette Taylor Scores Success in First Invasion of Character Field," *Chicago Daily Tribune*, March 11, 1923.
100. "Laurette Taylor Candid," *New York Times*, March 19, 1923.
101. *The Nebraska State Journal* [Lincoln], March 22, 1923.
102. "The Cold Gray Dawn," *New York Times*, March 25, 1923.
103. "Notes," *Time*, March 17, 1923.
104. "Betsy Blair," *The Memory of All That*, p. 121.
105. Quoted by Horton Foote in Ben Hodge, ed., *The American Theatre Wing Presents the Play That Changed My Life*, p. 41.
106. Unidentified clipping, Billy Rose Theater Collection, New York Public Library of the Performing Arts at Lincoln Center.
107. *Time*, October 15, 1923.
108. Jared Brown, *The Fabulous Lunts*, p. 107. Brown also reports a rumor that J. Hartley Manners supposedly helped write the play in 1900, though he received no credit.
109. Sheppard Butler, "The Actor at Play: A Person We Miss," *Chicago Daily Tribune*, July 8, 1923.
110. "New York Letter," *The Brownsville Daily Herald* [Texas], May 26, 1923.
111. "New Plays," *Time*, May 28, 1923.
112. John Corbin, "The Play, " *New York Times*, May 19, 1923.
113. Corbin, "A Final Use for *Peg*—With Some Statistics," *New York Times*, May 18, 1924.
114. Daniel Carb, "To See or Not to See," *The Bookman: A Review of Books and Life*, July 1924.
115. "New Plays," *Time*, May 19, 1924.
116. Benchley, "Drama," *Life*, May 29, 1924.
117. Anthony Slide researched Metro's payroll ledger at the Margaret Herrick Library and found that Laurette received payments of $5,000 on September 2, 1922, December 1, 1923, June 4, 1924, and July 2, 1924. There was no indication as to which film or films the payments were for (personal letter from Anthony Slide, May 15, 2006).
118. "Laurette Taylor," *Atlanta Constitution*, December 30, 1923.
119. Carr, "Laurette Does Her Stuff," *Motion Picture Classic*, p. 25.
120. "Hall, *Motion Picture*, June 1924, p. 23.
121. "Studio Gossip," *Sunday State Journal* [Lincoln, Nebraska], July 20, 1924.
122. Carr, "Laurette Does Her Stuff," *Motion Picture Classic*, p. 25..
123. "Studio Gossip," *Sunday State Journal* [Lincoln, Nebraska], July 20, 1924.
124. Myrtle Gebhart, "New Cinema Will Depict Quest for Happiness," *Los Angeles Times*, January 6, 1924.
125. "Inexpensive Costume," *Los Angeles Times*, December 9, 1923.
126. Katherine Lipke, "The Magic of the Cameraman," *Los Angeles Times*, January 21, 1925.
127. "Laurette Taylor Gives Her Secret of Beauty," *Billings Gazette*, June 1, 1924.
128. According to Anthony Slide's excellent *Silent Players*, Gilbert had proposed to Ruth Clifford in 1923 — the same year he married Leatrice. Clifford claimed Gilbert asked for her hand in marriage via a written note, but she declined because he was divorced. Gilbert had been married to Olivia Burwell from 1917 to 1922.
129. Fountain, *Dark Star*, p. 95.
130. William M. Drew, *Speaking of Silents: First Ladies of the Screen*. New York: Vestal Press, 1989, p. 79.
131. Fountain, *Dark Star*, p. 96.
132. Drew, *Speaking of Silents: First Ladies of the Screen*. p. 79
133. Fountain, *Dark Star*, p. 96.
134. "Their Lighter Moments," *Sunday State Journal* [Lincoln, Nebraska], August 3, 1924.
135. Grace Kingsley, "Star Returns," *Los Angeles Times*, July 9, 1924.
136. Fountain, *Dark Star*, p. 98.
137. Ibid., p. 99.
138. Ibid..
139. Ibid., p. 101.
140. Ibid., p. 171.
141. Ibid., p. 242.
142. Hedda Hopper, *From Under My Hat*, pp. 146–147.
143. Ibid., p. 147.
144. Unidentified clipping, Billy Rose Theater Collection, New York Public Library of the Performing Arts at Lincoln Center.
145. *Chillicothe Constitution* [Missouri], March 14, 1925.
146. Advertisement, *Chillicothe Constitution* [Missouri], March 16, 1925.
147. *Happiness* [advertisement], *Hayward Review*, June 22, 1925.
148. Myrtle Gebhart, "New Cinema Will Depict Quest for Happiness," *Los Angeles Times*, January 6, 1924.
149. Ibid.

150. Nancy Dowd, *King Vidor*, p. 42.
151. Ibid., p. 43.
152. Ibid.
153. "The Screen," *New York Times*, March 11, 1924.
154. Unidentified clipping, Billy Rose Theater Collection, New York Public Library of the Performing Arts at Lincoln Center.
155. Unidentified clipping, Billy Rose Theater Collection, New York Public Library of the Performing Arts at Lincoln Center.
156. Unidentified clipping, Billy Rose Theater Collection, New York Public Library of the Performing Arts at Lincoln Center.
157. Unidentified clipping, Billy Rose Theater Collection, New York Public Library of the Performing Arts at Lincoln Center.
158. Unidentified clipping, Billy Rose Theater Collection, New York Public Library of the Performing Arts at Lincoln Center.
159. Unidentified clipping, Billy Rose Theater Collection, New York Public Library of the Performing Arts at Lincoln Center.
160. Unidentified clipping, Billy Rose Theater Collection, New York Public Library of the Performing Arts at Lincoln Center.
161. Unidentified clipping, Billy Rose Theater Collection, New York Public Library of the Performing Arts at Lincoln Center.
162. Mae Tinnee, "*Happiness* is All That With Miss Taylor," *Chicago Daily Tribune*, April 15, 1924.
163. Carr, "Laurette Does Her Stuff," *Motion Picture Classic*, p. 25.
164. Robert E. Sherwood, "The Silent Drama," *Life*, March 27, 1924.
165. Grace Kingsley, "Honors for Star," *Los Angeles Times*, June 2, 1924.
166. Personal letter from Kevin Brownlow, August 21, 2006.
167. Baxter, *King Vidor*, p. 17.
168.<en Card, *Seductive Cinema*, p. 256.
169. Dowd, *King Vidor*, p. 43.
170. "Laurette Quits Pollyanna Roles," *Middletown Daily Herald*, November 18, 1924.
171. "Players Should Not Enact Same Role Very Long," *Charleston Gazette* [West Virginia], October 5, 1924.
172. Kingsley, "Our 'Peg' Grown Up Now," *Los Angeles Times*, September 14, 1924.
173. Unidentified clipping, Billy Rose Theater Collection, New York Public Library of the Performing Arts at Lincoln Center.
174. Unidentified clipping, Billy Rose Theater Collection, New York Public Library of the Performing Arts at Lincoln Center.
175. *Lima News*, February 22, 1925.
176. Kingsley, "Our 'Peg' Grown Up Now," *Los Angeles Times*, September 14, 1924.
177. Ibid.
178. Ibid.
179. "The Death of Hartley Manners," *Morning Herald* [Hagerstown, Maryland], December 26, 1928.
180. Edwin Schallert, "*One Night in Rome* Is Interesting," *Los Angeles Times*, September 15, 1924.
181. Roberta Nangle, "Cast Is Much Better Than This Picture," *Chicago Daily Tribune*, October 9, 1924.
182. "One Night in Rome,'" unidentified clipping, Billy Rose Theater Collection, New York Public Library of the Performing Arts at Lincoln Center.
183. Unidentified clipping, Billy Rose Theater Collection, New York Public Library of the Performing Arts at Lincoln Center.
184. Marguerite Courtney, *Laurette*, p. 269.
185. "Author of 'Peg o' My Heart' Dies," *Syracuse Herald*, December 20, 1928.
186. "Hartley Manners Writers," *Los Angeles Times*, October 15, 1924.

## Chapter 7

1. "What Tracy Wants Most is 'Days Off,'" *Lincoln Evening Journal* [Nebraska], December 13, 1959.
2. "Miss Taylor Turns to Pantomime," *New York Times*, March 8, 1925.
3. Clarence Derwent, *The Derwent Story: My First Fifty Years in the Theatre in England and America*, p. 145.
4. Stark Young, "The Play," *New York Times*, March 7, 1925.
5. Helen Hayes, *On Reflection*, p. 122.
6. "New Plays," *Time*, March 16, 1924.
7. Derwent, p. 145.
8. Ibid., pp. 145–146.
9. Ibid., p. 146.
10. Ibid.
11. Ibid.
12. Ibid, pp. 147–148.
13. "Pinero Comedy Rich in Stage Lore of Past," *Los Angeles Times*, May 26, 1927.
14. Burns Mantle, "Notables of Stage Revive *Trelawny*," *Chicago Daily Tribune*, June 7, 1925.
15. Charles Belmont Davis, "Percy Hammond's Letter," *Ogden Standard-Examiner* [Utah], June 14, 1925.
16. Brett Page, "Players Club is Outstanding for Annual Revival," *The Lincoln Sunday Star* [Nebraska], June 14, 1925.
17. Stark Young, "The Play," *New York Times*, June 2, 1925.
18. "New Plays," *Time*, June 15, 1925.
19. Helen Hayes, *On Reflection*, p. 122.
20. Hortense Saunders, "Laurette Taylor

Tells About Her Unusual Romance," *Charleston Daily Mail* [West Virginia], December 2, 1925.
21. Patrick McGilligan, *George Cukor: A Double Life*, p. 48.
22. "The Play," *New York Times*, November 17, 1925.
23. Alexander Woollcott, "Second Thoughts on First Nights," *Oakland Tribune*, November 29, 1925.
24. "New Plays," *Time*, November 30, 1925.
25. "NEA Play Jury, New Play Questions Secret Romance of Married Life," *The Ogden Standard-Examiner* [Utah], December 9, 1925.
26. "Percy Hammond's Letter," *The Ogden Standard-Examiner* [Utah], November 22, 1925.
27. Mantle, "Laurette Taylor Minus Her Humor," *Chicago Daily Tribune*, November 22, 1925.
28. Gilbert Seldes, "The Theatre," *The Dial*, January-June, 1926, Vol. LXXX, p. 73.
29. R. Dana Skinner, "Mid-Season," *The Independent*, January 9, 1926.
30. Larry Barretto, "The New Yorker," *The Bookman: A Review of Books and Life*, February 1926.
31. Marguerite Courtney, *Laurette*, pp. 286-287.
32. Wood Soanes, "Curtain Call," *Oakland Tribune*, February 9, 1926.
33. Other authors included Augustus Thomas, William Gillette, Rachel Crothers, William C. De Mille, Arthur Hopkins, Clare Kummer, Zoe Akins, Arthur Pinero, and A.A. Milne. Hartley's play was titled *Hanging and Wiving* and concerned a couple who are on the verge of marrying when the husband-to-be's current wife shows up to thwart their plans.
34. Laurette Taylor, "The Dying Wife," *One Act Plays for Stage and Study*, p. 190.
35. Marguerite Courtney, *Laurette*, p. 294.
36. "Manners and Wife Not in Accord On Sex Plays," *Fresno Bee*, July 17, 1926.
37. Patrick McGilligan, *George Cukor: A Double Life*, p. 53.
38. Ibid.
39. Ibid., pp. 53-54.
40. "Gossip of the Rialto," *New York Times*, October 10, 1926.
41. "Leslie Ruth Howard," *A Quite Remarkable Father*, p. 116.
42. Ibid., p. 117.
43. Ibid., p. 118.
44. Ibid., p. 122.
45. Ibid. , p. 123.
46. Robert Emmet Long, ed., *George Cukor Interviews*, p. 82.
47. Howard, p. 127.
48. Alexander Woollcott, "What's Doing in New York," *Los Angeles Times*, March 27, 1927.

49. "$4,000 Verdict Given to Laurette Taylor," *New York Times*, January 16, 1927.
50. James Bowers, "'Dark Horses' Rule Theatre This Season," *Lowell Sun* [Massachusetts], March 28, 1927.
51. "Laurette Taylor Acts an Actress at Palace," *New York Times*, December 28, 1926.
52. "What News on the Rialto?" *New York Times*, February 13, 1927.
53. "*The Comedienne* [review]," *Chicago Daily Tribune*, February 15, 1927.
54. Wood Soanes, "Curtain Calls," *Oakland Tribune*, February 22, 1927.
55. Ibid., March 22, 1927.
56. Marguerite Courtney, *Laurette*, p. 307.
57. Chester B. Bahn, "Laurette Taylor in New Manners Play," *Syracuse Herald*, October 12, 1927.
58. "Exits and Entrances," *Oakland Tribune*, December 18, 1927.
59. Jessie Royce Landis, *You Won't Be So Pretty*, p. 78.
60. Ibid., pp. 78-79.
61. Laurette Taylor, "Living and Play-Acting," *McClure's Magazine*, September 1922.
62. Landis, p. 79.
63. "In Feature Broadcast," *Lowell Sun* [Massachusetts], November 1, 1927.
64. "Actor Scorns Radio as Theatre's Rival," *New York Times*, January 31, 1925.
65. Harry Carr, "The Lancer in Hollywood," *Los Angeles Times*, November 11, 1928.
66. "What News on the Rialto?" *New York Times*, February 20, 1927.
67. "Laurette Taylor Returns to Stage," *San Antonio Express*, March 13, 1932.
68. Patrick McGilligan, *George Cukor: A Double Life*, p. 57.
69. Courtney, *Laurette*, p. 313.
70. Jessie Royce Landis, *You Won't Be So Pretty*, p. 90.
71. Ibid.
72. Ibid.
73. Ibid., p. 91.
74. Ibid., p. 92.
75. Alan Kreizenbeck, *Zoe Akins: Broadway Playwright*, p. 107. Akins' previous original play, *Thou Desperate Pilot*, ran for only eight performances in 1927.
76. J. Brooks Atkinson, "The Play," *New York Times*, March 8, 1928.
77. "New Plays in Manhattan," *Time*, March 19, 1928.
78. "Albert Carroll in Impersonations," *New York Times*, April 12, 1928.
79. "New Plays in Manhattan," *Time*, June 11, 1928.
80. "Albert Carroll as Mimic," *New York Times*, April 23, 1928.
81. Ernest Boyd, "Sights and Sounds," *The

*Bookman: A Review of Books and Life*, August 1928.
82. Robert Benchley, "The Theatre," *Life*, June 21, 1928.
83. "Mimics from Grand Street, and Their Methods," *New York Times*, June 10, 1928.
84. "Keating and Carroll Open Holiday Run," *New York Times*, December 23, 1929.
85. Courtney, *Laurette*, p. 316.
86. "Television Thrills Radio Show Crowd," *New York Times*, September 21, 1928.
87. Landis, p. 102.

## Chapter 8

1. Marguerite Courtney, *Laurette*, p. 329.
2. Jessie Royce Landis, *You Won't Be So Pretty*, p. 102.
3. "Author of Peg o' My Heart Dies," *Syracuse Herald*, December 20, 1928. See also "Hartley Manners, Playwright, Dies," *New York Times*, December 20, 1928.
4. "Author of Peg o' My Heart Dies," *Syracuse Herald*, December 20, 1928.
5. "Peg o' My Heart," *The Buffalo Center Tribune* [Iowa], October 17, 1929.
6. Courtney, *Laurette*, pp. 329–330.
7. Landis, p. 102.
8. Genevieve Parkhurst, "Poison for Ladies," *San Antonio Light*, October 28, 1945.
9. Ibid.
10. Helen Hayes, *My Life in Three Acts*, p. 165.
11. Courtney, *Laurette*, p. 175.
12. Talbot Lake, "Laurette Taylor Returns to Stage After 10 Years," *San Mateo Times* [California], January 18, 1939.
13. Wood Soanes, "Both Fairs Compete with Stage; Attendance Down Here and in the East," *Oakland Tribune*, May 14, 1939.
14. Hedda Hopper, *From Under My Hat*, p. 147.
15. Ward Morehouse and Ward Morehouse III, *Broadway After Dark*, p. 9.
16. "Writer's Will Fans Memory of War Hates," *Oakland Tribune*, March 12, 1929.
17. Soanes, "Curtain Calls," *Oakland Tribune*, November 19, 1929.
18. Carl A. Rossi, Interview with Eloise Sheldon Armen, Stamford, Connecticut, October 7, 2007.
19. Pat McGilligan, *Backstory*, p. 318.
20. Percy Hammond, "List of Best Actresses and Actors on the Stage Is Given Out," *Charleston Daily Mail*, November 30, 1930.
21. "Actresses Win Over Albany Legislators to Repeal of Theatre Arrest Provision," *New York Times*, February 5, 1930. The other actors included Frank Gillmore, Margalo Gillmore, June Walker, Vivian Tobin, and Genevieve Rubelle.
22. Soanes, "Curtain Call," *Oakland Tribune*, September 18, 1931.
23. James Aswell, "My New York," *Evening Independent* [Massillon, Ohio], October 1, 1931. See also "$1,000 Found in Bank by Laurette Taylor," *New York Times*, September 24, 1931.
24. "Dreadful Thing," *Time*, October 5, 1931. The bank was the Union Dime Savings Back in Manhattan.
25. Richard Massock, "Seen and Heard in New York," *Appleton Post-Crescent* [Wisconsin], June 24, 1931.
26. "Laurette Taylor Plays Barrie on Return to Stage," *Oakland Tribune*, March 20, 1932.
27. Ibid.
28. Ibid.
29. Hammond, "Reappearance Real Pleasure," *Los Angeles Times*, March 13, 1932.
30. Sam Love, "New York Inside Out," *Daily News* [Huntingdon, Pennsylvania], March 22, 1932.
31. Gilbert Swan, "Hollywood Rushes in Where Play Angels Fear to Tread," *The Piqua Daily Call* [Piqua, Ohio], April 11, 1932.
32. "Laurette Taylor Returns to Stage," *San Antonio Express*, March 13, 1932.
33. Ibid.
34. J Brooks Atkinson, "The Play," *New York Times*, March 8, 1932. One of Laurette's cast members was Peg Entwistle, who ended her life by jumping off the "Hollywood" sign in September 1932.
35. "Revivals," *Time*, March 21, 1932.
36. "Actress Ill, Plays Close," *Los Angeles Times*, April 7, 1932.
37. News and Comment of Stage and Screen, *Fitchburg Sentinel* [Massachusetts], April 23, 1932.
38. "*Hay Fever* Suspends," *New York Times*, April 19, 1932.
39. "Laurette Taylor to Star at Berkshire Playhouse," *North Adams Transcript*, August 13, 1932.
40. Eileen Percy, *Los Angeles Evening Herald Express*, December 18, 1931. See also "To Star in Hay Fever," *New York Times*, April 16, 1932.
41. "Peg o' My Heart Fulfills Dream for Marion Davies," *Los Angeles Evening Herald Express*, June 9, 1933. MGM considered remaking Peg in 1940 with Katherine Grayson.
42. Muriel Babcock, "Old Favorite to be Filmed," *Los Angeles Times*, August 20, 1931. Personally, I would have paid a lot of money to see Garbo as Peg, probably for all the wrong reasons.
43. "Marion Davies' Wish Granted," *The Times Recorder* [Zanesville, Ohio], June 20, 1933. Director Robert Z. Leonard was a good choice

to helm the picture. He appeared with Taylor in the premiere of *Peg o' My Heart* as the butler, Jarvis.
44. Louella O. Parsons, "Movie Go Round," *San Antonio Light*, July 2, 1933.
45. Unidentified clipping, Billy Rose Theater Collection, New York Public Library of the Performing Arts at Lincoln Center.
46. "Laurette Taylor, Sickened Thoughts," *New York Times*, May 7, 1922.
47. Ellen Marie Margolis, *Recoveries*, p. 11. Margolis' doctoral dissertation provides much in-depth description and analysis of Laurette's plays as well as plays written by others for Laurette.
48. Ibid., p. 223.
49. "Theatrical Notes," *New York Times*, April 1, 1933.
50. "*Enchantment* Deferred," *New York Times*, April 17, 1933.
51. Louella O. Parsons, *Los Angeles Examiner*, February 10, 1933.
52. John Scott, "Whispers in the Wings," *Los Angeles Times*, March 28, 1933.
53. Parsons, "Marion Davies Is To Play in Robert Chambers' Novel," *Charleston Gazette* [West Virginia], November 18, 1933.
54. "Universal Preparing Ambitious Schedule," *Evening Gazette* [Xenia, Ohio], December 1, 1933.
55. Lloyd Pantages, "I Cover Hollywood," *Los Angeles Examiner*, February 16, 1935.
56. "News of the Stage," *New York Times*, February 28, 1935.
57. "Laurette Taylor Appears in Own Play," *New York Times*, August 14, 1934.
58. Margolis, p. 224.
59. Courtney, *Laurette*, p. 355.
60. "News of the Stage," *New York Times*, August 21, 1935.
61. "Capacity Audience at Casino Theatre," *Newport Mercury and Weekly News* [Rhode Island], August 9, 1935.
62. Ibid.
63. Ibid.
64. Edwin Schallert, "Laurette Taylor Seriously Considers Return to Motion Picture Medium," *Los Angeles Times*, October 9, 1935. Schallert followed up his report on October 19, 1935 by stating that Laurette didn't accept the role, and the picture was facing casting difficulties.
65. "News of the Stage," *New York Times*, December 3, 1935.
66. Gavin Lambert, *Nazimova*, p. 352.
67. "Tennis Meet in Florida," *New York Times*, January 5, 1936.
68. "News of the Stage," *New York Times*, February 3, 1936. The two other shows Hartwig produced that season were *Daisy Mayme* and *Kind Lady*.
69. Courtney, *Laurette*, p. 260.

70. Helen Sheehy, *Eva Le Gallienne: A Biography*, p. 371.
71. Courtney, *Laurette*, p. 368.
72. "Gordon Seeks Play," *Los Angeles Times*, September 30, 1936.
73. "Laurette Taylor Returning to Stage in *Promise*," *Los Angeles Times*, November 24, 1936.
74. "*Promise* Postponed Until December 30 on Broadway," *Los Angeles Times*, December 19, 1936.
75. Mark Barron, "Many New Plays Being Tested for 1937 Season," *Florence Morning News* [South Carolina], August 9, 1937.
76. "Miss Taylor to Appear," *New York Times*, March 21, 1938.
77. "Laurette Taylor Appears," *New York Times*, March 22, 1938.
78. . Parsons, "Dorothy Gish Prospect No. 5 for Role of Miss Fortune in Young in Heart," *Waterloo Daily Courier* [Iowa], May 13, 1938.
79. "News of the Stage," *New York Times*, August 12, 1938.
80. Brooks Atkinson, *New York Times*, August 31, 1938.
81. Robert Lewis, *Advice to the Players*, p. 149.
82. Lewis, *Slings and Arrows*, p. 348.
83. Larry Moss, *The Intent to Live*, p. 180.
84. Ibid., p. 180.
85. "Gossip of the Rialto," *New York Times*, October 30, 1938.

# Chapter 9

1. "Broadway, Peg o' My Heart Returns," *San Antonio Express*, February 26, 1939.
2. Otto Preminger, *Preminger: An Autobiography*, p. 49.
3. Foster Hirsch, *Otto Preminger*, pp. 68–69.
4. Preminger, p. 49.
5. Ibid., p. 50.
6. Willi Frischauer, *Behind the Scenes of Otto Preminger*, p. 76.
7. Preminger, p. 50.
8. Hirsch, p. 69.
9. Preminger, p. 50.
10. Ibid., pp. 50–51.
11. Hirsch, p. 69.
12. Frischauer, p. 78.
13. Ibid.
14. Preminger, p. 51.
15. Hirsch, p. 70.
16. Barbara Bladen, "The Marquee," *San Mateo Times*, October 18, 1965.
17. Victoria Price, *Vincent Price: A Daughter's Biography*, p. 98.
18. "Broadway, Peg o' My Heart Returns," *San Antonio Express*, February 26, 1939.

19. Talbot Lake, "Laurette Taylor Returns to Stage After 10 Years," *San Mateo Times* [California], January 18, 1939.
20. Ibid.
21. "Broadway, Peg o' My Heart Returns," *San Antonio Express*, February 26, 1939. The "secret" play was *Pin a Rose*.
22. David Hanna, *Second Chance*, p. 145.
23. Paul Shinkman, "Stars Shine Again on Broadway as Yesterday's Stage Favorites Tread Board in Today's Hits," *The Hammond Times* [Louisiana], June 26, 1939.
24. "Walter Winchell on Broadway," *The Daily Times News* [Burlington, North Carolina], January 20, 1939.
25. Richard Watts, Jr., "*Outward Bound* Revived; Called Best of Plays Dealing with Death," *Oakland Tribune*, January 8, 1939.
26. Preminger, p. 51.
27. George Ross, "The Stage," *Gastonia Daily Gazette* [North Carolina], April 29, 1939.
28. Diana Barrymore, *Too Much, Too Soon*, p. 125.
29. Ibid., pp. 128–129.
30. Ibid., p. 130.
31. Preminger, p. 51. Barrymore and Fletcher married in 1942 and divorced in 1946.
32. Barrymore, p. 129.
33. Ibid., p. 133.
34. Uta Hagen, *Respect for Acting*, p. 101.
35. Robert Lewis, *Slings and Arrows*, p. 127.
36. Helen Hayes, *My Life in Three Acts*, p. 34.
37. "Old Play in Manhattan," *Time*, January 2, 1939.
38. Brooks Atkinson, "Laurette Taylor, Player," *New York Times*, January 1, 1939. See also Atkinson, "The Play," *New York Times*, December 23, 1938.
39. Jennifer Dunning, "Barnard Hughes Offers Advice on Craft of Acting," *New York Times*, July 25, 1979.
40. Ben Hodges, *The American Theatre Wing Presents the Play That Changed My Life*, p. 38.
41. Maurice Zolotow, *Stagestruck: The Romance of Alfred Lunt and Lynn Fontanne*, p. 92.
42. "First Lady Called a Force in Theatre," *New York Times*, May 9, 1939.
43. Leonard Lyon, "Story of Her Comeback: She's 'In the Sun Again,'" *The Salt Lake Tribune*, October 19, 1963.
44. "Viennese to Open in Refugee Revue," *New York Times*, May 24, 1939.
45. Sheilah Graham, *San Francisco Chronicle*, February 23, 1940. Graham mentioned that Julie Haydon was already signed for the film, though she was not in the final credits. She also suggested Vincent Price would appear in the film, but he also received no credit.
46. Hedda Hopper, "Hedda Hopper's Hollywood," *Los Angeles Times*, June 9, 1939.
47. Preminger, p. 51.
48. "Broadway, Peg o' My Heart Returns," *San Antonio Express*, February 26, 1939.
49. Hopper, "Hedda Hopper's Hollywood," *Los Angeles Times*, August 16, 1939.
50. Pauline Lord also turned it down. Aline MacMahon ended up with the role.
51. Robert Lewis, *Slings and Arrows*, p. 127.
52. Hopper, "Hedda Hopper's Hollywood," *Los Angeles Times*, April 6, 1940.
53. Edwin Schallert, "Paramount Campaigns for Laurette Taylor," *Los Angeles Times*, July 11, 1940.
54. Hopper, "Hedda Hopper's Hollywood," *Lowell Sun and Citizen-Leader* [Massachusetts], November 1, 1941.
55. Scott Eyman, *Print the Legend: The Life and Times of John Ford*, p. 194.
56. "Taylor Funeral Set for Tomorrow," *Los Angeles Times*, March 22, 1942.
57. "Gossip of the Rialto," *New York Times*, March 29, 1942.
58. Courtney, *Laurette*, p. 389.
59. Hopper, *The Salt Lake Tribune*, January 22, 1944.
60. Dorothy Kilgallen, *Lowell Sun* [Massachusetts], June 7, 1945.
61. Hopper, "Hedda Looking at Hollywood," *Los Angeles Times*, March 4, 1944.

## Chapter 10

1. Quoted in Laurette Taylor obituary, *Time*, December 16, 1946.
2. "Alice Pardoe West, Behind the Scenes," *Ogden Standard-Examiner* [Utah], December 21, 1945.
3. Ibid.
4. Mary C. Henderson, *Theatre in America*, p. 1988.
5. Edwina Dakin Williams, *Remember Me to Tom*, p. 143.
6. Sam Zolotow, "Script for Dowling," *The Glass Menagerie*, October 18, 1944.
7. Williams, p. 145.
8. Claudia Cassidy, "On the Aisle," *Chicago Daily Tribune*, January 8, 1945.
9. Jessie Royce Landis, *You Won't Be So Pretty*, p. 142.
10. Ward Morehouse, *Matinee Tomorrow*, p. 281.
11. George Oppenheimer, "Stars Glitter in Minor Plays," *Winnipeg Free Press*, July 17, 1974.
12. Leonard Lyon, Story of Her Comeback: She's 'In the Sun Again,' *The Salt Lake Tribune*, October 19, 1963.
13. Williams, p. 145.

14. Ibid., p. 146.
15. Mike Steen, *A Look at Tennessee Williams*, p. 48.
16. Donald Windham, *Tennessee Williams' Letters to Donald Windham*, p. 155.
17. Claudia Cassidy, "On the Aisle," *Chicago Daily Tribune*, May 1, 1955.
18. Mike Steen, *A Look at Tennessee Williams*, p. 145.
19. Williams, *Remember Me to Tom*, p. 146.
20. Ibid., pp. 146–147.
21. Ibid., p. 148.
22. Ibid., p. 149. The documentary *Amanda* features a film clip of Laurette meeting Mrs. Williams backstage. *Amanda* was shown on the television show *Character Studies* in 2005.
23. Williams, p. 149.
24. Claudia Cassidy, "Fragile Drama Holds Theater in Tight Spell," *Chicago Daily Tribune*, December 27, 1944.
25. Cassidy, "On the Aisle," *Chicago Daily Tribune*, January 7, 1945.
26. Leonard Lyon, "Story of Her Comeback: She's 'In the Sun Again,'" *The Salt Lake Tribune*, October 19, 1963. Geraldine Page later appeared in Tennessee Williams' *Summer and Smoke*. She was thrilled when he told her, "'Yours is the best portrayal of one of my female roles since Laurette Taylor.'" Understandably flattered, Page repeated the comment to a friend who informed her, "'He says that to everyone!'" Cited in Walter Winchell's column, *Nevada State Journal*, May 2, 1963. In fact, Hermione Baddeley was also thrilled when Tennessee told her, too, that she reminded him of Laurette. "I was overjoyed and oddly enough I knew he was right." See Mike Steen, *A Look at Tennessee Williams*, p. 83.
27. Mike Steen, *A Look at Tennessee Williams*, pp. 249–250.
28. Hedda Hopper, "Looking at Hollywood," *Los Angeles Times*, September 12, 1945.
29. Courtney, *Laurette*, p. 400.
30. Donald Windham, *Tennessee Williams' Letters to Donald Windham*, p. 155.
31. Ibid., p. 160.
32. Mel Gussow panned Haydon's performance. "Affecting the air of a duchess and an otherwordly tone of voice, Miss Haydon offers a studied, mannered and not always audible Amanda. In her most dramatic scenes, she strikes poses, as if acting for a silent-movie camera." See "Stage: Julie Haydon Plays Mother in *Glass Menagerie*," *New York Times*, November 6, 1980.
33. Eleanor Blau, "Julie Haydon at 70: Same Menagerie, Different Role," *New York Times*, October 30, 1980.
34. Ibid.
35. Ibid.
36. Betsy Blair, *The Memory of All That*, pp. 118–119.
37. Ibid., p. 119.
38. Ibid., p. 121. Taylor gave Blair the rabbit's foot she used to apply blush. Some twenty years later Blair gave it to a budding, unnamed actress who apparently lost it.
39. Windham, pp. 155–156.
40. Hayes, *On Reflection*, p. 123.
41. Ibid., pp. 123–124.
42. Hayes, *My Life in Three Acts*, p. 165.
43. Ibid., p. 166.
44. Ibid., p. 169.
45. Windham, *Tennessee Williams' Letters to Donald Windham*, p. 157.
46. Ibid., p. 156.
47. Ibid., p. 166.
48. Claudia Cassidy, "On the Aisle," *Chicago Daily Tribune*, February 18, 1945.
49. Diana McLellan, *The Girls*, p. 320. Ticket prices for the New York premiere ranged from $1.80 to $7.20. After the premiere tickets were priced between $1.20 and $4.20. See "*Glass Menagerie* Arriving Tonight," *New York Times*, March 31, 1945.
50. Helen Sheehy, *Eva Le Gallienne: A Biography*, p. 279.
51. Mike Steen, *A Look at Tennessee Williams*, p. 145.
52. Cecil Smith, "Hepburn Stars in Definitive Production of *Glass Menagerie*," *Los Angeles Times*, December 16, 1973.
53. David Hanna, *Second Chance*, p. 137.
54. "Katie Becomes Talkative," *Chronicle-Telegram* [Ohio], July 18, 1982.
55. Lloyd Lewis, "Memo from Chicago," *New York Times*, January 14, 1945.
56. "New Play in Manhattan," *Time*, April 9, 1945.
57. Lewis Nichols, "The Play in Review," *New York Times*, April 2, 1945. See also Nichols, "*Glass Menagerie*," *New York Times*, April 8, 1945.
58. Courtney, *Laurette*, p. 409.
59. Frank Morriss, "Here, There and Hollywood," *Winnipeg Free Press*, March 22, 1946.
60. Ward Morehouse and Ward Morehouse III, *Broadway After Dark*, p. 85.
61. Robert Lewis, *Advice to the Players*, p. 67.
62. Harold Clurman, "The Ideal Audience!" in Loggia and Young, eds., *The Collected Works of Harold Clurman*, p. 305.
63. Clurman, "Mysterious Rites of the Rehearsal," in Loggia and Young, eds., *The Collected Works of Harold Clurman*, p. 437.
64. Quoted in "Laurette Taylor," in Cole and Chinoy, eds., *Actors on Acting*, p. 595.
65. Stephen Adly Guirgis, "The Communion of Plays," *Los Angeles Times*, August 14, 2009.
66. Hanna, *Second Chance*, p. 137.
67. Mike Steen, *A Look at Tennessee Williams*, p. 97.

68. Morriss, "Here, There and Hollywood," *Winnipeg Free Press*, December 10, 1946.
69. Cynthia Lowry, "Burr May Snub New Law Role," *Robesonian*, August 16, 1966. Booth later told columnist Mike Connolly that Tallulah Bankhead (apparently in a drunken moment) said to her, "'You're *much* more talented than Laurette Taylor, darling...but without her charm!'" Cited in Mike Connolly, "Notes from Hollywood," *The Independent* [Pasadena], December 31, 1963.
70. Lillian and Helen Ross, *The Player: A Profile of an Art*, p. 65.
71. Philip K. Scheuer, "Acting Can Be Too Real, Star Declares," *Los Angeles Times*, April 10, 1962.
72. John Garfield, "Lecture on Film Acting," *The Drama Review*, Winter 1984, p. 76. Laurette was also a fan of Garfield's. She told Robert Lewis his eyes were remarkable: "It's as if he's looking inside himself." Robert Lewis, *Slings and Arrows*, p. 61.
73. Sheena Iyengar, *The Art of Choosing*, p. 214.
74. Larry Moss, *The Intent to Live*, p. 68.
75. Muriel Rockhauser, "Gazzara Meets Alter Ego in TV Series," *Berkshire Eagle*, September 18, 1965.
76. Lillian and Helen Ross, *The Player: A Profile of an Art*, p. 347.
77. Ben Brantley, "Broadway Babies, 58 Years Apart," *New York Times*, June 6, 2004.
78. Hedda Hopper, "Fame Fails to Affect Greg Peck's Humility," *Los Angeles Times*, August 26, 1951.
79. Maureen Stapleton, *A Hell of a Life*, p. 51.
80. David Kaufman, "When It's a Hard Act to Follow," *New York Times*, June 14, 1987.
81. Stapleton, *A Hell of a Life*, p. 262.
82. Hedda Hopper, "David Wayne Believes Occasional Work on Stage Will 'Enrich' Actors," *Los Angeles Times*, July 9, 1950.
83. Hopper, "Serious Roles Springboard for Comedian Tony Randall," *Los Angeles Times*, January 3, 1960.
84. Edwina Dakin Williams, *Remember Me To Tom*, p. 155.
85. Ibid., pp. 154–155.
86. Frank Fay, "Laurette Taylor Voted 'Tops' By Papers," *The Nebraska State Journal*, May 31, 1945.
87. "Outstanding Writers, Entertainers Honored," *Morning Avalanche* [Lubbock, Texas], December 8, 1945.
88. Edwin Schallert, "Donlevy as City Editor Stepping Up Socially," *Los Angeles Times*, May 5, 1945.
89. Hopper, "Looking at Hollywood," *Los Angeles Times*, May 22, 1945.
90. Zolotow, *New York Times*, May 15, 1945.
91. Zolotow, "Barry Play Plans to Close Saturday," *New York Times*, June 4, 1945.
92. Schallert, "Sillman Negotiates for Laurette Taylor Play," *Los Angeles Times*, June 14, 1945.
93. Ellen Marie Margolis, *Recoveries*, p. 253.
94. On April 22, 1928, Laurette appeared in a program celebrating the 100th anniversary of Ibsen's birth. She did a scene from *The Lady from the Sea*. Other participants in the program at the Hudson Theater included Eva Le Gallienne, Helen Chandler, Helen Hayes, Lionel Atwill, and others. See "Ibsen Memorial Plans," *New York Times*, April 8, 1928.
95. Lloyd Lewis, "Reminiscing with Peg o' My Heart," *New York Times*, March 25, 1945.
96. Ward Morehouse and Ward Morehouse III, *Broadway After Dark*, p. 8.
97. Ibid., p. 9.
98. Williams, pp. 155–156.
99. Louella Parsons, *Lowell Sun* [Massachusetts], June 1, 1945.
100. Early in the Chicago production there was talk about Gary Cooper appearing in a film version. See Claudia Cassidy, "On the Aisle," *Chicago Daily Tribune*, January 8, 1945.
101. Hopper, "Looking at Hollywood," *Los Angeles Times*, May 17, 1946.
102. Ibid., July 25, 1946.
103. Dorothy Kilgallen, *Lowell Sun* [Massachusetts], April 16, 1945.
104. Morriss, "Here, There and Hollywood," *Winnipeg Free Press*, December 10, 1946.
105. The Stephen Mosher Blog, "Listen Up: The Christmas Music Part Two," December 19, 2009. Retrieved December 22, 2009.
106. Hopper, "Hedda Hopper Looking at Hollywood," *Los Angeles Times*, December 7, 1945. See also "Books and Authors," *New York Times*, June 29, 1945. The New York Public Library has a copy of the manuscript in its collection.
107. Robert Garland, "Eddie Dowling Has His Own Way," *San Antonio Light*, April 14, 1946.
108. Sydney J. Harris, "Strictly Personal," *Waterloo Daily Courier* [Iowa], February 24, 1956.
109. Hopper, *The Salt Lake Tribune*, February 1, 1944.
110. Dwight Taylor, "My Mother Laurette," *Saturday Evening Post*, December 17, 1960, p. 64.
111. Hopper, "Looking at Hollywood," *Los Angeles Times*, November 11, 1946.
112. Zolotow, "Miss Segal Quits Role in *Toplitzky*," *New York Times*, December 9, 1946. Martita Hunt took over Laurette's role when the play was finally produced in December 1948.

113. Parsons, "Sam Wanamaker Sheds Natty Mustache for Screen Debut," *Charleston Gazette* [West Virginia], July 20, 1947.
114. Hopper, *The Salt Lake Tribune*, January 20, 1944.
115. "Stage Folk Mourn at Taylor Funeral," *New York Times*, December 12, 1946.
116. Laurette's grave has no headstone. In 2004 Rick McKay was reportedly soliciting donations to purchase a headstone for her. See http://www.broadwaytovegas.com/November14,2004.html. Retrieved January 10, 2010.
117. Morriss, "Here, There and Hollywood," *Winnipeg Free Press*, December 10, 1946.
118. Clurman, "Death by Entertainment," in *The Collected Works of Harold Clurman*, p. 101.
119. Ward Morehouse and Ward Morehouse III, *Broadway After Dark*, pp. 7–8.
120. McClintic, *Me and Kit*, p. 56.
121. Ibid., p. 262. Other sources indicate that the director was Sir Cedric Hardwicke.
122. http://annyballardini.blogspot.com/2009/04/duende-again.html. Retrieved October 19, 2009.
123. "Basil Rathbone is Dead at 75," *Waterloo Daily Courier* [Iowa], July 23, 1967.
124. Tallulah Bankhead, "Acting is Form of Confession," *Waterloo Daily Courier* [Iowa], February 18, 1953.
125. "Doris Day Follows Suit," *The Advocate* [Newark, Ohio], February 2, 1976.
126. Clurman, "Ruth Gordon's Special Sort of Self-Portrait," *Los Angeles Times Book Review*, May 23, 1971.
127. Lillian and Helen Ross, *The Player: A Profile of an Art*, pp. 361–362.
128. Ibid., p. 393.
129. "Tennessee Williams, An Appreciation," *New York Times*, December 15, 1946.
130. "Estate of Actress Finally Determined," *Amarillo Daily News*, February 21, 1949.

# Chapter 11

1. Walter Winchell, *Wisconsin State Journal* [Madison], June 17, 1947.
2. Mike Steen, *A Look at Tennessee Williams*, pp. 20, 22.
3. Sheilah Graham, *Hollywood Citizen News*, November 15, 1947.
4. Alice Pardoe West, "Behind the Scenes," *Ogden Standard-Examiner* [Utah], August 7, 1949.
5. Hedda Hopper, "Looking at Hollywood," *Los Angeles Times*, May 14, 1947. On May 23, 1947 Hopper reported that ZaSu Pitts wanted to do Laurette's part in a summer stock production of *The Glass Menagerie*.
6. Hopper, "Clifton Webb Will Portray Murderer," *Los Angeles Times*, February 26, 1949.
7. Steen, *A Look at Tennessee Williams*, p. 22.
8. Graham, *Hollywood Citizen News*, February 5, 1947.
9. Steen, p. 21.
10. Ibid., p. 23.
11. Louella O. Parsons, "Gertie Lawrence, Making First Movie, Praises Hollywood," *Galveston Daily News*, December 11, 1949.
12. Parsons, *Charleston Gazette* [West Virginia], June 28, 1949. At one time Jack Carson was considered for Eddie Dowling's stage role.
13. Sheridan Morley, *A Bright Particular Star: A Biography of Gertrude Lawrence*, p. 181.
14. Scott Eyman, *Print the Legend: The Life and Times of John Ford*, p. 327. See also Hopper, "John Ford Pictures May Tumble More Traditions," *Los Angeles Times*, February 22, 1948.
15. Claudia Cassidy, "On the Aisle," *Chicago Daily Tribune*, April 26, 1948.
16. Marie Blizard, "Legend of an Actress' Tragedy and Trumph [review of *Laurette*]," *The Bridgeport Post*, May 8, 1955.
17. Long, ed., *George Cukor Interviews*, p. 90.
18. Lewis Nichols, "Clouds and a Star," *New York Times*, May 1, 1955.
19. "Deeper Than Greasepaint," *Time*, May 9, 1955.
20. *Time*, December 26, 1955. According to Ellen Marie Margolis, Marguerite had started working on a second book, tentatively titled *Here I Come, Ready or Not*.
21. Claudia Cassidy, "On the Aisle," *Chicago Daily Tribune*, May 1, 1955.
22. Leonard Jennewein, "Complex Life of Former Star Revealed in Book By Daughter," *The Huronite and The Daily Plainsman* [South Dakota], August 7, 1955.
23. Telephone interview with Meg Courtney, August 4, 2009.
24. Harvey Breit, "In and Out of Books," *New York Times*, July 10, 1955. In fact, Marguerite had acted when she was younger but quickly decided on a writing career instead.
25. Howard Thompson, "By Way of Report," *New York Times*, July 17, 1955.
26. Mike Connolly, *The Independent* [Pasadena], April 2, 1956.
27. Hopper, "Astaire Will Star in Non-Dancing Role," *Los Angeles Times*, November 28, 1955.
28. Jared Brown, *Alan J. Pakula: His Films and His Life*, p. 20.
29. According to a blurb in the *New York Times* on January 15, 1960, Pakula purchased the rights to Dwight Taylor's *Blood-and-Thunder*. The book at that time was still unpublished.

Pakula, according to the blurb, planned to make a musical from the book.
30. Brown, *Alan J. Pakula: His Films and His Life*, p. 34.
31. Ibid.
32. "Here There and Hollywood with Frank Morriss," *Winnipeg Free Press*, November 7, 1956.
33. Brown, *Ibid*, pp. 34–35.
34. Parsons, "Judy Holliday Talking About New Stage Play," *San Antonio Light*, February 19, 1957.
35. Frank Rasky, "The Smartest Dumb Blonde in Showbusiness," *New Liberty*, April 1952.
36. Parsons, "Louella's Movie-Go-'Round," *Albuquerque Journal*, December 30, 1958.
37. Hopper, "Judy Holliday Will Enact Laurette," *Los Angeles Times*, June 23, 1959.
38. Brown, Ibid., p. 35.
39. Mike Connolly, *Star-News* [Pasadena], September 14, 1960.
40. Brown, Ibid., p. 36.
41. Ibid.
42. Fred Russell, "Passing Show," *The Bridgeport Post*, September 27, 1960.
43. Brown, Ibid., p. 37.
44. Connolly, *Pasadena Independent*, January 6, 1961.
45. Hopper, "Tryon Will Star in Marine Drama," *Los Angeles Times*, December 24, 1960.
46. "Little Old New York," *The Morning Herald* [Uniontown, Pennsylvania], October 1, 1964.
47. Robert Goode Hogan, *After the Irish Renaissance: A Critical History of Irish Drama Since the Plough and the Stars*, p. 184.
48. Connolly, "Notes from Hollywood," *Star-News* [Pasadena, California], December 12, 1964.
49. Hopper, "Holden Will Star in *China Story*," *Los Angeles Times*, March 30, 1961.
50. Connolly, "Notes from Hollywood and Television," *Star-News* [Pasadena], February 6, 1962.
51. Long, ed., *George Cukor Interviews*, p. 90.
52. Hopper, "Columnist Reports on Metro Studio Tour," *Los Angeles Times*, September 16, 1950.
53. Long, ed., *George Cukor Interviews*, p. 91.
54. Brown, p. 37.
55. A play about Laurette Taylor's first husband, Charles, was also planned. Titled *Come One, Come All*, it apparently never made it to Broadway.
56. Dwight Taylor's book *Blood-and-Thunder* was published in 1962. It is an affectionate and entertaining biography of his father Charles Taylor. Though Laurette is included, especially in the early chapters, the book focuses on the "Master of Melodrama."

57. Ken Mandelbaum, *Not Since Carrie: Forty Years of Broadway Musical Flops*, p. 53. At one time it was thought that Dwight Taylor might write the adaptation. Also, one of the working titles was *Come One, Come All*.
58. John S. Wilson, "The Life of *Jennie*," *New York Times*, October 13, 1963.
59. Sam Zolotow, "Martin Musical to Wait a Season," *New York Times*, September 24, 1962.
60. Hopper, "Buckner Schedules Religious Subject," *Los Angeles Times*, December 15, 1949.
61. Ibid. Dwight Taylor also saw similarities between Laurette and Shirley MacLaine. "The comparison is irresistible.... There are only a few over the years who can say 'I'm going out to buy a can of pork and beans' and find you choking up. Judy Holliday has a lot of that. And Shirley Booth's voice has some of it. But if I had a choice of a performance I'd want my mother to see — if she could come back for 80 minutes — I'd pick Shirley's in *Some Came Running*." "The Ring-a-Ding Girl," *Time*, June 22, 1959.
62. Hopper, "Anastasia Likely for Jennifer Jones," *Los Angeles Times*, July 8, 1955. Dwight Taylor died in January 1987 at the age of 84. He was living at the Motion Picture and Television Hospital.
63. Wilson, "The Life of *Jennie*," *New York Times*, October 13, 1963.
64. Cheryl Crawford, *One Naked Individual: My Fifty Years in the Theatre*, pp. 180–181. Crawford, a lesbian, says remarkably little about Laurette Taylor in her autobiography. She mentions her own friendship with a "lonely" Alla Nazimova and then wrote, "Nazimova wasn't the only one who needed friendship. I also spent evenings with Pauline Lord, Fanny Brice, Alice Brady and Laurette Taylor." (p. 47)
65. Ibid., p. 181.
66. Wilson, The Life of *Jennie*, New York Times, October 13, 1963.
67. Ibid.
68. Ibid.
69. Mandelbaum, *Not Since Carrie: Forty Years of Broadway Musical Flops*, p. 53. See also "Song Writer Suing Boston Stage Critic," *New York Times*, August 14, 1963.
70. Mandelbaum, Ibid., p. 53.
71. Crawford, *One Naked Individual: My Fifty Years in the Theatre*, p. 181.
72. Ibid.
73. Mandelbaum, *Not Since Carrie: Forty Years of Broadway Musical Flops*, p. 55.
74. Carl A. Rossi Interview with Eloise Sheldon Armen, Stamford, Connecticut, October 7, 2007.
75. Both quotes are from Mary Martin Shines in Overlong Musical, *Los Angeles Times*, August 2, 1963.
76. Howard Taubman, "Theatre: Mary

Martin Stars in *Jennie*," *New York Times*, October 18, 1963.
77. William Glover, "Mary Martin is Great, but Jennie is Held Dud," *The Fresno Bee Republican*, October 20, 1963.
78. "Disenchanted Evening," *Time*, October 25, 1963.
79. Crawford, *One Naked Individual: My Fifty Years in the Theatre*, p. 181.
80. Leonard Lyon, "Quartz as Good Luck Charm," *The Evening Standard*, October 23, 1963.
81. "TV Previews," *The Bridgeport Telegram* [Connecticut], March 21, 1969.
82. Marilyn Beck, *Albuquerque Tribune*, June 17, 1975.
83. John O'Connor, "TV Weekend," *New York Times*, July 7, 1978.
84. "Films of Bygone Stars to Aid American Place," *New York Times*, September 20, 1977.
85. Jesse Green, "The Face That Says *Glass Menagerie*, Frame by Frame," *New York Times*, May 8, 2005.
86. E-mail correspondence with Carolyn Gage, December 1, 2009.
87. On July 20, 2009, Theatre East gave the first Laurette Taylor Award to Tom Oppenheim and the Stella Adler Studio of Acting. Theatre East's Inaugural Benefit was held at the Sage Theatre. The presenter was Tovah Feldshuh.
88. Dwight Taylor, "My Mother Laurette," *Saturday Evening Post*, December 17, 1960, p. 64.
89. Ben Hodge, ed., *The American Theatre Wing Presents the Play That Changed My Life*, p. 41.

# BIBLIOGRAPHY

Barrymore, Diana. *Too Much, Too Soon.* New York: Henry Holt, 1957.

Barrymore, Ethel. *Memories: An Autobiography.* New York: Harper & Brothers, 1955.

Baxter, John. *King Vidor.* New York: Monarch Press, 1976.

Blair, Betsy. *The Memory of All That: Love and Politics in New York, Hollywood, and Paris.* New York: Knopf, 2003.

*Broadway: The Golden Age, By the Legends Who Were There.* DVD, directed by Rick McKay, 2004.

Brown, Jared. *Alan J. Pakula: His Films and His Life.* New York: Back Stage Books, 2005.

———. *The Fabulous Lunts.* New York: Atheneum, 1986.

Card, James. *Seductive Cinema: The Art of Silent Film.* Minneapolis: University of Minnesota Press, 1994.

Carr, Harry. Laurette does her stuff. *Motion Picture Classic*, August, 1924, pp. 24–25.

Carroll, Gardiner. "Why: Jane Cowl, Norma Talmadge and Laurette Taylor Explain Their Preference for Screen and Stage." *Photoplay*, July 1924, pp. 72–73.

———. "Why Jane Cowl Avoids the Screen, Norma Talmadge Avoids the Stage, Laurette Taylor Appears on Both." *Photoplay*, July 1924, pp. 72–73.

Cole, Toby, and Helen Krich Chinoy, eds. *Actors on Acting: The Theories, Techniques, and Practices of the World's Great Actors, As Told in Their Own Words.* New York: Three Rivers Press, 1995.

Courtney, Marguerite. *Laurette: The Intimate Biography of Laurette Taylor.* New York: Limelight Editions, 1984.

Coward, Noel. *Present Indicative.* Garden City, NY: Doubleday, Doran, 1937.

Crawford, Cheryl. *One Naked Individual: My Fifty Years in the Theatre.* New York: Bobbs-Merrill, 1977.

Curtis, Anthony, ed. *The Rise and Fall of the Matinee Idol.* New York: St. Martin's Press, 1974.

De Acosta, Mercedes. *Here Lies the Heart.* New York: Reynal, 1960.

Derwent, Clarence. *The Derwent Story: My First Fifty Years in the Theatre in England and America.* New York: Henry Schuman, 1953.

Dooley, Roger. *From Scarface to Scarlett: American Films in the 1930s.* New York: Harcourt Brace Jovanovich, 1979.

Dowd, Nancy, and David Shepard. *King Vidor.* Metuchen, NJ: Scarecrow Press, 1988.

Eyman, Scott. *Print the Legend: The Life and Times of John Ford.* New York: Simon & Schuster, 1999.

Fontanne, Lynn. "Thoughts on Acting," in Toby Cole and Helen Krich Chinoy, eds., *Actors on Acting: The Theories, Techniques, and Practices of the World's Great Actors, Told in Their Own Words.* New York: Crown Publishers, 1970, pp. 610–612.

Fountain, Leatrice Gilbert. *Dark Star.* New York: St. Martin's Press, 1985.

Frischauer, Willi. *Behind the Scenes of Otto Preminger: An Unauthorized Biography.* New York: William Morrow, 1974.

Frohman, Daniel. *Daniel Frohman Presents: An Autobiography.* New York: Claude Kendall & Willoughby Sharp, 1935.

Gladwell, Malcolm. *Outliers: The Story of Success.* New York: Little, Brown, 2008.

Green, Abel, and Joe Laurie, Jr. *Show Biz: From Vaude to Video.* New York: Henry Holt, 1951.

Hagen, Uta. *Respect for Acting.* New York: Wiley, 2008.

Hall, Gladys. "Laurette Taylor as seen by Gladys Hall." *Motion Picture*, June 1924, pp. 23–24, 93.
Hanna, David. *Second Chance*. New York: Belmont Tower Books, 1976.
Hayes, Helen. *My Life in Three Acts*. New York: Harcourt Brace Jovanovich, 1990.
———. *On Reflection: An Autobiography*. New York: M. Evans, 1968.
Henderson, Mary C. *Theater in America*. New York: Harry N. Abrams, 1968.
Hirsch, Foster. *Otto Preminger: The Man Who Would Be King*. New York: Knopf, 2007.
Hodges, Ben, ed. *The American Theatre Wing Presents the Play That Changed My Life: America's Foremost Playwrights on the Plays That Influenced Them*. New York: Applause Books, 2009.
Hogan, Robert Goode. *After the Irish Renaissance A Critical History of Irish Drama Since the Plough and the Stars*. Minneapolis: University of Minnesota Press, 1967.
Hopper, Hedda. *From Under My Hat*. Garden City, NY: Doubleday, 1952.
Howard, Leslie Ruth. *A Quite Remarkable Father*. New York: Harcourt, Brace, 1959.
Iyengar, Sheena. *The Art of Choosing*. New York: Twelve, 2010.
Kreizenbeck, Alan. *Zoe Akins: Broadway Playwright*. Westport, CT: Praeger, 2004.
Lambert, Gavin. *Nazimova: A Biography*. New York: Knopf, 1997.
Landis, Jessie Royce. *You Won't Be So Pretty (But You'll Know More)*. London: W.H. Allen, 1954.
"Laurette Taylor a Delight in Adaptation of her Stage Success." *Film Daily*, December 17, 1922.
Lawrence, Gertrude. *Gertrude Lawrence: A Star Danced*. Garden City, NY: Doubleday, Doran, 1945.
Lewis, Robert. *Advice to the Players*. New York: Theatre Communications Group, 1993.
———. *Slings and Arrows: Theater in My Life*. New York: Applause Books, 2002.
Loggia, Marjorie, and Glenn Young, eds. *The Collected Works of Harold Clurman: Six Decades of Commentary on Theatre, Dance, Music, Film, Arts and Letters*. New York: Applause Books, 1994.
Long, Robert Emmet, ed. *George Cukor Interviews*. Jackson: University Press of Mississippi, 2001.

Madsen, Axel. *The Sewing Circle*. Secaucus, NJ: Birch Lane Press, 1995.
Mandelbaum, Ken. *Not Since Carrie: Forty Years of Broadway Musical Flops*. New York: St. Martin's Press, 1991.
Manners, J. Hartley. *The Girl in Waiting: A Comedy in Four Acts*. Boston: Walter H. Baker, 1922.
———. *Happiness and Other Plays*. New York: Dodd, Mead, 1917.
———. *The Harp of Life: A Play*. New York: George H. Doran, 1921.
———. *Out There: A Dramatic Composition in Three Parts*. New York: Dodd, Mead, 1918.
———. *The Wooing of Eve: An Entirely Artificial and Sentimental Comedy in Three Acts*. New York: Samuel French, 1920.
Marinacci, Barbara. *Leading Ladies: A Gallery of Famous Actresses*. New York: Dodd, Mead, 1961.
Marion, Frances. *Off with Their Heads! A Serio-Comic Tale of Hollywood*. New York: Macmillan, 1972.
McClintic, Guthrie. *Me and Kit*. Boston: Little, Brown, 1955.
McGilligan, Pat. *Backstory: Interviews with Screenwriters of Hollywood's Golden Age*. Berkeley: University of California Press, 1986.
McGilligan, Patrick. *George Cukor: A Double Life*. New York: St. Martin's Press, 1991.
McLellan, Diana. "The Girls: Sappho Goes to Hollywood." New York: *LA Weekly* Books, 2000.
Menefee, David W. *The First Female Stars: Women of the Silent Film*. Westport, CT: Praeger, 2004.
Margolis, Ellen Marie. *Recoveries: A History of Laurette Taylor*. Santa Barbara: University of California, 1997.
Morehouse, Ward. *Matinee Tomorrow: Fifty Years of Our Theater*. New York: McGraw-Hill, 1949.
———, and Ward Morehouse III. *Broadway after Dark*. Albany, GA: Bear Manor Media, 2007.
Morley, Sheridan. *A Bright Particular Star: A Biography of Gertrude Lawrence*. London: Pavilion Books, 1986.
Morley, Sheridan. *The Great Stage Stars: Distinguished Theatrical Careers of the Past and Present*. London: Angus & Robertson, 1986.

Morosco, Helen M., and Leonard Paul Dugger. *The Oracle of Broadway: Life of Oliver Morosco.* Caldwell, ID: The Caxton Printers, 1944.

Mosel, Tad. *Leading Lady: The World and Theatre of Katharine Cornell.* Boston: Little, Brown, 1978.

Moss, Larry. *The Intent to Live: Achieving Your True Potential as an Actor.* New York: Bantam, 2005.

*One Act Plays for Stage and Study (First Series): A Collection of Twenty-five Plays by Well-known Dramatists, American, English and Irish.* New York: Samuel French, 1925.

Oppenheimer, George. "The great days of Broadway," in Anthony Curtis, ed., *The Rise and Fall of the Matinee Idol.* New York: St. Martin's Press, 1974, pp. 108–121.

"Peg o' My Heart." *Photoplay*, February 1923.

\_\_\_\_\_ *Variety*, January 25, 1923.

Peters, Margot. *Design for Living: Alfred Lunt and Lynn Fontanne: A Biography.* New York: Knopf, 2003.

Preminger, Otto. *Preminger: An Autobiography.* Garden City, NY: Doubleday, 1977.

Price, Victoria. *Vincent Price: A Daughter's Biography.* New York: St. Martin's Press, 1999.

Rivkin, Allen, and Laura Kerr, eds. *Hello, Hollywood!* New York: Doubleday, 1962.

Ross, Lillian, and Helen Ross. *The Player: A Profile of an Art.* New York: Simon & Schuster, 1962.

Schanke, Robert A. *Shattered Applause: The Lives of Eva Le Gallienne.* Carbondale, IL: Southern Illinois University Press, 1992.

Sheehy, Helen. *Eva Le Gallienne: A Biography.* New York: Knopf, 1996.

Slide, Anthony. *Silent Players: A Biographical and Autobiographical Study of 100 Silent Film Actors and Actresses.* Lexington: University Press of Kentucky, 2002.

Squier, Emma-Lindsay. "Peg Writers Her Epitaph." *Picture-Play Magazine*, January 1923, pp. 54, 95.

Stapleton, Maureen, and Jane Scovell. *A Hell of a Life.* New York: Simon & Schuster, 1995.

Steen, Mike. *A Look at Tennessee Williams.* New York: Hawthorn Books, 1969.

Taylor, Dwight. *Blood-And-Thunder.* New York: Atheneum, 1962.

\_\_\_\_\_. My mother Laurette. *Saturday Evening Post*, December 17, 1960, pp. 26–27, 62, 64.

Taylor, Laurette. "The Dying Wife," in *One Act Plays for Stage and Study (First Series): A Collection of Twenty-five Plays by Well-known Dramatists, American, English and Irish.* New York: Samuel French, 1925, pp. 186–190.

\_\_\_\_\_. *The Greatest of These—.* New York: George H. Doran, 1918.

\_\_\_\_\_. "The Quality Most Needed," in Toby Cole and Helen Krich Chinoy, eds., *Actors on Acting: The Theories, Techniques, and Practices of the World's Great Actors, Told in Their Own Words.* New York: Crown, 1970, pp. 595–598.

Teichmann, Howard. *Smart Aleck: The Wit, World and Life of Alexander Woollcott.* New York: William Morrow, 1976.

Tyler, George C. *Whatever Goes Up—The Hazardous Fortunes of a Natural Born Gambler.* Indianapolis: Bobbs-Merrill, 1934.

Vidor, King. *A Tree Is a Tree.* New York: Harcourt, Brace, 1953.

Williams, Edwina Dakin. *Remember Me to Tom.* New York: G.P. Putnam's Sons, 1963.

Wyndham, Donald, ed. *Tennessee Williams' Letters to Donald Windham 1940–1965.* New York: Holt, Rinehart and Winston, 1977.

Zeist, Joshua. *Flapper: A Madcap Story of Sex, Style, Celebrity, and the Women Who Made America Modern.* New York: Crown, 2006.

Zolotow, Maurice. *Stagestruck: The Romance of Alfred Lunt and Lynn Fontanne.* New York: Harcourt, Brace & World, 1964.

# INDEX

*Abie's Irish Rose* 170
Abrams, Hiram 116
Adams, Frank R. 247
Adams, Maude 51, 85, 99, 175, 180, 182
Adams, Samuel Hopkins 33
Adler, Lutha J. 236
*After You're Gone (After You've Gone)* 243
Akins, Zoe 166, 167, 175, 238, 255
Alexandria Hotel 48
*Alias Jimmy Valentine* 37, 61, 231
*Alice-Sit-by-the-Fire* 174, 175–176, 190, 214, 238–239
*All About Eve* 227
*All Clear* 172
Allgood, Sara 191
*Amanda* 259
Ames, Percy 118, 232, 236
Ames, Sybil 170
Anderson, Judith 31, 119, 193
Anderson, Maxwell 213
Anderson, Warner 235
Anglin, Margaret 50
*Anna Christie* 193
*Annie Get Your Gun* 223, 224
Argosy 217
Arliss, George 90, 92, 93, 227, 235
Armstrong, Paul 37
Arthur, Julia 90, 92, 235
Arto, Florence 120
Arzner, Dorothy 30, 31
*At Marian's* 179, 180, 181, 187
Atkinson, Brooks 167, 175, 183, 190
Atwill, Lionel 260
*The Awful Truth* 173

Babcock, Muriel 177
Bacon, Frank 107, 108
*The Bad Seed* 219
Baddeley, Hermione 259
Badger, Clarence 149–150, 151, 230
Baker, Carrol 207
Ballard, Kaye 2
Bancroft, Anne 221
Bankhead, Tallulah 30, 31, 119, 187, 215, 216–217, 260
*Barbaraza* 56, 57

*Barbary Coast* 173
Barnes, George 118, 119, 121, 122, 128, 229
Barnes, Jack 231
Barratt, Watson 239
Barrett, Edith 186, 238
Barretto, Larry 159
Barrie, James M. (J.M.) 174, 175, 176, 214, 238
Barrie, Nigel 129, 229
Barriscale, Bessie 42
Barry, Phillip 157, 158, 159, 174–175, 214, 238
Barrymore, Diana 187–188, 189
Barrymore, Ethel 28, 30, 83, 129, 130, 134, 156, 166, 168, 173, 216, 249
Barrymore, John 139, 168, 179, 249
Barrymore, Lionel 249
Barter Theater's Laymen's Committee Award 191
Barthelmess, Richard 31
Bartik, Ottokar 154, 238
Baxter, John 130, 148
Bayes, Edward 231
Bayes, Nora 92
Beck, James M. 253
Beck, Marilyn 226
Beecher, Janet 134
*Behind the Verdict* 179–180
Behrman, S.N. 222
Bel Geddes, Barbara 179, 219
Belasco, David 103
Bell, Monte 143
*Bells Are Ringing* 219
Belmore, Daisy 235
Belmore, Lionel 129, 229
Benchley, Robert 107, 109, 132, 135, 168
Bennett, James O'Donnell 37
Bennett, Richard 246
Bentham, Max 155
Bergdorf Goodman 108
Bergman, Ingrid 193
Berlin, Irving 31, 111
Bernard Sisters 8
Bernhardt, Sarah 64–65, 81, 112, 156, 211, 227
Berquist, Rudolph 230
*Between Two Worlds* 191
*The Bicycle Thief* 130

*Bird of Paradise* 40, 42, 43, 44, 45, 46, 47, 48, 49, 61, 165, 246, 233
*Birth of a Nation* 117
Bitzer, Billy 117
Blair, Betsy 133, 201–222, 239, 259
Blinn, Holbrook 108
Blizard, Marie 218
Blondell, Joan 118
*Blood-and-Thunder* 16, 222, 261–262
Boardman, Eleanor 139, 143, 144–145
Boland, Mary 180
Booth, Shirley 207, 219, 260, 262
*Born Yesterday* 219
Bowles, Paul 198, 212
Boyd, Ernest 168
Bradford, Gardner 63
Brady, Alice 166, 262
Brady, William A. (Bill) 104, 174–175, 176, 185
Brando, Marlon 208
Brice, Fanny 31, 262
*The Bridge Tender's Daughter* 17
*Broadway Brevities* 134
*Broadway: The Golden Age, By the Legends Who Were There* 1–2, 228
Broun, Heywood 134
Brown, Jared 28, 98, 102, 134, 219, 253
Brown, Tom 180
Browne, Irene 177, 182
Brownlow, Kevin 148
Bruce, Virginia 143
Bryan, Alfred 55
Bryan, William Jennings 172
Buchanan, Jack 30
Bulfinch 227
Burani, Michellette 154, 238
Burke, Billie 166, 169
Burton, Frederick 231
Burwell, Olivia 139, 253
Byrne, Edmund 82

Cagney, James 215
Calhern, Louis 158, 159, 173, 238
Calvert, Emory B. 66
*Camille* 98
Campbell, Alan 238
Campbell, Mrs. Patrick 32, 33, 193, 209
*Candida* 183
*The Captive* 33
Carb, David 135
Card, James 129–130, 148–149
*Carmen* 14, 16
Carpenter, Constance 224
Carr, Harry 127, 147, 166
Carre, Michel 238
Carrington, Frank 16
Carroll, Albert 167–168
Carroll, Leo G. 176
Carson, Jack 261
Caruso, Enrico 112
Cassidy, Claudia 198, 199–200, 204, 217, 218

Castle, Irene 31, 132
Chadwick, Cyril 229
Chandler, Helen 239, 260
*Chantecler* 85
Chaplin, Charlie 115, 126, 137, 146, 148
*Character Studies* 259
Charles, Arthur L. 213
*Charlot's Revue* 31
Chatterton, Ruth 217
Chekov, Anton 30
Cheney, Sheldon 61
Cher 149
*Cherished Moments of the Theatre* 218
Cherry, Charles 37–38, 232
*The Cherry Orchard* 32
*Child Wife* 10
Churchill, Winston 224
*Cinderella* 51, 147
Claire, Ina 142–143, 168, 213
Clark, Susan 226
Clarke, Marguerite 64
Clifford, Ruth 253
Clow, Stephen G. 134
Clurman, Harold 206, 214
Coburn, Charles 108, 238
Cochran, C.B. 103–104, 250
Cockran, W. Bourke 253
Cohan, George M. 7, 43, 90, 92, 93, 235
Collier, Constance 32, 33, 51, 176, 246
Colton, John 245
*Come One, Come All* 262
*The Comedienne* 163
Comegys, Kathleen 176
Compton, Juliette 177
Connolly, Mike 219, 220, 260
Connolly, Walter 173
Considine, John, Jr. 179
*The Constant Wife* 166
Converse, Thelma Morgan 141
Coogan, Jackie 147
Cook, Joe 173
Coolidge, Calvin 156
Cooney, Edward 6, 8, 9, 174
Cooney, Elizabeth (Bessie) 6, 8, 9, 217
Cooney, Elizabeth Dorsey 5, 6, 7, 8, 9, 20, 23, 25, 72, 77
Cooney, James 6, 7, 8
Cooper, Gary 260
Cooper, Merian C. 217
Copeland, George 154
*Coquette* 32
Corcoran, Jane 239
Cornell, Katharine 10, 31, 32, 208, 214, 215, 245
Cort, John 55, 59
Coulouris, George 176
Courtney, Marguerite 2, 6, 9, 11, 12, 13, 14, 19, 25–26, 27, 28, 30, 33, 35, 46, 48, 50, 54, 72, 73, 104, 149, 157, 159, 160, 163–164, 169, 173, 179, 181, 192, 193, 195, 200, 205,

213, 215, 218–219, 222, 223, 225, 226, 228, 246, 261
Courtney, Meg 218
Coward, Noël 22–23, 26, 27, 28, 30, 193
Cowl, Jane 64, 114, 134, 193, 197, 208, 218, 251
Crawford, Cheryl 204, 223, 224–225, 226
Crawford, Joan 177
Crews, Laura Hope 178
Crooker, Herbert 152
Crosby, Bing 211
Cukor, George 30, 158, 160, 161, 166, 178, 180, 218, 221–222, 238
*Curtain Going Up* (also known as *Comedienne*) 246
Cushman, Charlotte 227

*Dakon's Daughter* see *Mrs. Dakon*
Dale, Alan 80–81, 86
Dale, Duchess 63
Dale, James 164
Daly, Augustin 59
Davies, Marion 148, 177, 247
Davis, Bette 216
Davis, John W. 250
Davis, Leslie 31
Davis, Owen 39, 233
Davis, Tyrell 177
Day, Doris 215
Day, Edith 250
*The Day of Dupes* 96, 97, 233–234
De Acosta, Mercedes 31, 32, 33, 179, 245
*Death Valley Scotty* 244
Decca 218
de Cesneros, Eleanor 92
*Delicate Justice* 164–165
DeMille, Cecil B. 137, 139
de Mille, William 113
Dentler, Marion 62, 63
*The Derby Mascot* 12
Derwent, Clarence 154, 155, 238
De Sica, Vittorio 130
Deval, Jacques 160, 161
*The Devil* 20–21
Devol, Dr. 170
de Wolfe, Elsie 31
Dial, Patterson 229
Dickens, Charles 24
Dietrich, Marlene 30, 143
Dietz, Howard 31, 223, 224
Digges, Dudley 173
*The Distaff Side* 180
*Dr. Jekyll and Mr. Hyde* 7
*A Doll's House* 166, 209
Donehue, Victor 224
Dorr, Dorothy 231
Dorsey, Bridgett 6, 7, 67, 191
Doty, Carlotta 232, 233
Douglas, James 102–103
Douglas, Kirk 217
Dowd, Nancy 117

Dowling, Eddie 196, 197, 200, 201, 202, 203, 205, 210, 211, 216, 228, 239, 261
Dowling, Joseph 230
*Downstairs* 143
Dressler, Marie 193, 195
Drew, John 238
Druce, Hubert 235
*duende* 215
Dunne, Irene 178
Du Pont, Miss 230
Dupree, Minnie 183
Durning, Charles 1
Duse, Eleanora 61, 66, 112, 156, 227
*The Dying Wife* 3, 159–160, 177, 240–242

Eagan, Frank see Egan, Frank
Eagels, Jeanne 31, 32, 161, 163, 166, 215
*East Lynne* 98
Eaton, Walter Prichard 95
Ebb, Fred 2
Echols, Randolph (Randy) 212, 228, 239
Eddy, Arthur J. 231
Edison, Thomas
Egan, Frank 50, 51, 182, 246
Egan School of Music & Drama 50, 51, 246
Ellis, Edith 232
Emery, Edward 231
*Enchantment* 177, 178, 187
Entwistle, Peg 239, 256
*Escape* 193
*Escape the Night* 209
*Escapes from the Harem* 12
Evans, Joan 63
*The Eveready Hour* 165–166
Eyre, Archibald 35, 232

Fabray, Nanette 2
Fairbanks, Douglas 27, 83, 115, 130, 140, 141
Famous Players–Lasky 113
*Faust* 16
Fawcett, George 22, 231
Fay, Frank 209
Fazenda, Louise 127
*Fear Strikes Out* 219
Feldman, Charles 216, 217
Feldshuh, Tovah 263
*The Female Detectives* 12
Fendler, Grace A. 246
Ferguson, Elsie 32, 128
Ferrers, Helen 118
Fields, Lew 88
50 Riverside Drive 26–27, 28, 30, 83, 101, 130, 144, 169, 170, 171
*Finale* 176, 178, 179
Finch, Peter 220
Fisher, Fred 55
Fiske, Minnie Maddern 91, 92, 93–94, 112, 134, 157, 168, 190, 227
Fletcher, Bramwell 184, 188, 239
Fletcher, Lawrence 239

Fontanne, Lynn 18, 28, 33, 72–73, 78–79, 81, 82, 92, 97–98, 100, 101–102, 111, 134, 173, 174, 181, 190–191, 193, 215, 217, 234, 235, 236
Foote, Horton 190, 219, 228
Ford, John 193, 217
Ford, Wallace 180
Foster, Lillian 182
Fountain, Leatrice Gilbert 139, 141–142
*The Fox* 54
Francis, Kay 2
Frankau, Ethel 108–109
Frawley, T. Daniel 62
Frederick, Pauline 83
Frischauer, Willi 185
Frohman, Daniel 38
*From Rags to Riches* 12, 19
*The Fugitive* 217
*Fun with Stella* 209
*The Furies* 166–167, 168, 175, 238
Furness, Thelma 143
Fyles, Franklin 39

Gage, Carolyn 227
*Ganton & Co.* see *The Great John Ganton*
Garbo, Greta 142, 177, 204, 245, 256
Garfield, John 191, 192, 207, 260
Garland, Judy 219, 221–222
Garland, Robert 211–212
Gates, Larry 191
*The Gay Divorcee* 173
Gaynor, Janet 251
Gazzara, Ben 1, 208
Gebhart, Myrtle 144
*The Gentleman Caller* 196
George, Grace 156, 182, 185
Gershwin, George 31
Gershwin, Ira 31
Gilbert, John 138, 139–143, 160, 253
Gilbert, Susan Ann 143
Girardoux, Jean 212
*The Girl in Waiting* (aka *Miss Brown, Burglar*) 35–36, 232
Gish, Dorothy 127, 136, 166, 182–183
Gish, Lillian 183, 193
Gladwell, Malcolm 14
*Glass Menagerie* 1, 2, 6, 18, 52, 171–172, 194, 196–207, 208–209, 210, 211–212, 213, 214, 216, 217, 218, 219, 220, 222, 223, 226, 227, 228, 237, 239, 259, 260, 261
Glazer, Alice 140
Glazer, Barney 140
Glover, William 226
Glyn, Elinor 141
*God of My Fathers* 172
Goldman, Emma 30
*Gone with the Wind* 178
Gordon, Maude Turner 231
Gordon, Max 181
Gordon, Ruth 215, 217

Gottschalk, Ferdinand 238
Gould, Will 212
Goulding, Edward (Eddie) 31
Graham, Sheilah 216, 217, 258
*The Grand Street Follies* 167
Grant, Cary 212
Grant, Lawrence 229
Gray, Elsa 178
Grayson, Katherine 256
*The Great John Ganton* 14, 22, 35, 231
*The Greatest of These—* 16, 91, 92, 94–95, 177, 246
*The Green Book Magazine* 16
Griffith, Corinne 111
Griffith, D.W. 30, 117
Griffith, Robert 220
*The Guardsman* 100
Guinan, Texas 247
Guirgis, Stephen Adly 207
Gussow, Mel 259
Gwillim, Jack 220

Hackett, James K. 90, 92, 235, 246
Hackett, Joan 220
Hagen, Uta 1, 189, 202, 208
Haggin, Ben Ali 173
*The Hairy Ape* 133
Hale, Alan 148, 230
Hall, Blanche 48, 63
Halliday, Richard 222, 223, 224, 226
Hamilton, Clayton 253
Hamilton, Mahlon 129, 229
*Hamlet* 133
Hammerstein, Oscar 31, 224
Hammond, Percy 36, 41, 94, 97, 99, 158, 173, 175
Haney, Carol 224
*Hanging and Wiving* 255
Hanna, David 207
*Happiness* 5, 75, 77, 95–97, 98, 99, 112, 120, 135–136, 137, 139, 144, 145–149, 150, 162, 163, 165, 224, 228, 229, 234
*The Happy Man* see *In a Garden*
Hardwicke, Cedric 181, 184, 261
Harlem, New York 5, 6
Harlem Opera House 7
*The Harp of Life* 46, 79–80, 81–82, 172, 178, 234
*Harriet* 202
Harris, Sam 43
Harris, Sydney J. 212
Hart, Kitty Carlisle 208
Hart, Lorenz 31
Hartwig, Walter 181, 257
*Harvey* 209
Hatswell, D.R.O. 129, 229
Hawley, Wanda 113, 114, 251
*Hay Fever* 27, 176
Haydon, Julie 180, 198, 199, 200–201, 202, 203, 211, 213, 227, 228, 239, 258, 259

# Index

Hayes, Helen 32, 90, 108–109, 132, 155, 157, 171, 173, 177, 189–190, 202–203, 216, 248, 260
Hayward, Susan 216, 219
Hearst, William Randolph 247
*Heavenly Express* 192, 258
Heggie, O.P. 90, 92, 235, 238
Heifetz, Jascha 31
Helburn, Theresa 204
Held, Anna 7, 8
Henderson, Lucius 231
Henderson, Mary C. 196
Hepburn, Katharine 204
*Her Cardboard Lover* 32, 160, 161, 163, 166
Herczeg, Ferencz 232
*Here I Come, Ready or Not* 261
Herne, James A. 24
Hitchcock, Raymond 83
Hitler, Adolf 191
*A Hole in the Head* 222
Holliday, Judy 207, 219–220, 221, 222, 262
*Hollywood: The Selznick Years* 226
Hopkins, Arthur 158, 238
Hopper, De Wolf 83, 92
Hopper, Hedda 33, 35, 65, 93, 143, 171, 191, 192, 193, 195, 209, 211, 212, 213, 216, 217, 218, 220, 221, 222, 223, 229
*Hot Spot* 221
Houghton, Norris 206–207
*House of Women* 32
Howard, Leslie 28, 30, 161, 163
Howard, Ruth 28, 30
Howard, Sidney 181
Howard, W.K. 179
Hoyt, Julia 178
Huffman, J.C. 231
Hughes, Barnard 190
Hull, Shelley 232, 233, 235
*Humoresque* 115, 130, 131, 132–133, 134, 236
Humphrey, William 230
Hunt, Martita 260
Hunter, Helen 12
Huntly, Fred 129, 229
Hurst, Brandon 230
Hurst, Fannie 130, 131, 236

Ibsen, Henrik 210, 260
*An Ideal Husband* 32
*I'll Know My Love* 193
*I'm Over 39 see Finale*
*In a Garden* 157–159, 214, 238
Inge, William 207
Ingram, Rex 146
*Intolerance* 117
*An Irish Fable* 191–192
*It Happened One Day* 179
Ivens, Sidna Beth 229
Iyengar, Sheena 14, 207–208

Jacott, Howard 20, 244

Jaffee, Sam 173
*Jailbreak* 173
Janis, Elsie 33, 68, 73, 83
Jefferson, Joe 107
*Jennie* 222–226
Jerome, Jenny 224
Johnson, Julian 48, 53, 54, 56–57, 61, 247
Jones, Cherry 42
Jones, Jennifer 216
Jones, Margo 202, 213, 239
Jones, Robert Edmond 178
Jordan, Kate 36, 231
Joy, Leatrice 139, 141, 142, 143, 253
Joy, Leatrice II *see* Fountain, Leatrice Gilbert Fountain
*Judgment at Nuremberg* 221
*Just as Well* 96, 97, 234

Kane, Gail 82, 234
Keane, Doris 32, 166
Keating, Fred 168
Keaton, Buster 126
Kelley, E.M. 131
Kelly, Kevin 224, 225
Kelly, Seamus 221
Kemble, George 235
Kemble-Cooper, Frank 79, 234, 235
Kemble-Cooper, Greta 236, 238
Kemble-Cooper, Lillian 236
Kemble-Cooper, Violet 58, 118, 234, 235
Kennedy, Arthur 217
Kern, Jerome 31
Kerrigan, J.M. 235
Kester, Paul 135, 236
Kibbee, Guy 173
Kilgallen, Dorothy 195, 211
King, Claude 238
King, Edith 155
*King of the Opium Ring* 9, 12
Kingsley, Grace 148
Kirkland, Alexander 239
Klauber, Adolph 44
Klumph, Helen 128
Kopernak, Galina 154, 238

*The Lady from the Sea* 260
*The Lady of the Slipper* 68
La Marr, Barbara 149
Lambert, Gavin 30
Landau, Martin 2
Landis, Jessie Royce 28, 164–165, 166–167, 169, 170, 171, 196–197, 246
Langtry, Lillie 112
Lauren, S.K. 176, 179
*Laurette* 219–221, 223
Laurette Taylor Award 263
*Laurette Taylor in Scenes from Shakespeare* 235
*Laurette: The Intimate Biography of Laurette Taylor* 2, 205, 218, 219, 222, 223, 225
Law, H. Robert 231

Lawford, Ernest 238
Lawrence, Gertrude 30, 31, 217
Lawton, Frank 181
Lazareff, Ivan 154, 238
Lea, Lorna 246
*Leading Ladies: A Cabaret Revue* 227
*The Leading Lady* 217
Lee, Lovey 135
Lee, Martha 251
Le Gallienne, Eva 31, 32, 33, 173, 181, 204, 217, 260
Leigh, Vivien 214, 220
Leighton, Margaret 215
Leonard, Robert Z. 256–257
LeRoy, Mervyn 219
*The Letter* 32
Levitin, Daniel 14
Lewis, Lloyd 204–205, 210
Lewis, Robert 183, 189, 192, 206, 260
Lewis, Vera 229
Leyser, Billy 127
*The Life Story of Laurette Taylor* 226
Lillie, Beatrice 31
Lindsay, Howard 236
Ling, Richie 236
*Little Women* 177
Lloyd, Harold 126
*La Locandiera* 133
Lockhart, June 221
Loesser, Frank 224
Logan, Stanley 238
Lohr, Marie 33, 105
*Lola* 39, 41, 233
Lonsdale, Frederick (Freddie) 30
Loos, Anita 132
Lord, Chester S. 253
Lord, Pauline 134, 180, 190, 215, 216, 227, 258, 262
Lorimar Productions 226
Lotos Club 131, 133, 173, 252–253
Love, Linnie 46, 246
*Love Never Dies* 118–119
Lubitsch, Ernst 146
Lunt, Alfred 28, 72, 100, 101, 134, 173, 217, 236
*Lute Song* 223
Lyons, Chester 137, 145, 230
Lytell, Bert 115

MacArthur, Charles 213
MacFarlane, George 90, 92, 235
MacKay, Edward 235
Mackaye, Dorothy 62
MacLaine, Shirley 262
MacMahon, Aline 258
*The Mad Woman of Chaillot* 212, 260
Madsen, Axel 30, 245
Mandelbaum, Ken 222, 225
Mannering, Mary 156
Manners, J. Hartley 1, 3, 5, 20, 21–30, 33, 35, 36, 41, 42, 43, 44, 45, 46, 48, 49, 50, 51, 52, 53, 54, 56, 57, 58, 59, 62, 63, 66–67, 70, 73, 75, 76, 77, 78, 79, 80, 81, 82, 85–86, 87, 88, 90, 91, 94, 95, 96, 98, 99, 101, 105, 106, 107, 108, 109, 110, 111, 113–114, 115, 116, 117, 119, 120, 121, 125, 126, 129, 130, 131, 133, 134, 135, 137, 139, 140, 141, 143–144, 146, 149, 152–153, 155, 157, 159, 160, 161, 163, 164, 165, 168–169, 170–171, 172, 173, 179, 190, 191, 197, 213, 217, 220, 229, 230, 231, 232, 233, 234, 235, 236, 246, 249, 253, 255
Mansfield, Richard 7, 45
Mantle, Burns 20–21, 96, 132, 156, 158, 249
Marbury, Elisabeth (Bessie) 31
March, Fredric 215
Marchand, Nancy 220
Margolis, Ellen Marie 111, 159, 178, 179, 243, 257, 261
Marion, Frances 58, 112, 195, 247
Marlowe, Julia 89
Marsalis, Wynton 207–208
Martin, Florence 63
Martin, Mary 222–226
Martin, Rhea 63
Marx, Harpo 209
Mason, Reginald 57, 233, 234
Massey, Raymond 213
Massock, Richard 174
Matthews, A.E. 28–30, 60, 236
Mattox, Matt 224
Maude, Cyril 246
May, Aileen 10, 11
Mayer, Levy 70
Mayer, Louis B. (L.B.) 143, 195, 209, 211
McCarey, Leo 211
McClintic, Guthrie 10–11, 45–46, 80, 89, 214–215, 226, 246
McCormick, Patty 219
McCrea, Joel 178
McCreary, Allen 170
McGilligan, Patrick 160, 166
McIntosh, Burr 92
McKay, Rick 1–2, 228, 261
McKenna, Emma 193
McKenna, Siobhan 221
McLellan, Diana 30, 31–32, 33
McNein, Neysa 31
Megrue, Roi Cooper 113
Meighan, Thomas 113
*The Melody of Youth* 33
Melville, Emilie 54, 233, 234
Menken, Helen 32
Mercer, Beryl 90, 92, 175, 235
*The Merchant of Venice* 90, 183, 235
Meredith, Burgess 213
Meredith, George 24
Mereson, John 210
Merivale, Philip 79, 81, 234, 236
Merrill, Bob 224

Metro 113, 115, 120, 121, 122, 130, 135, 137, 143, 144, 229, 230
MGM 143, 173, 177, 178, 179, 193, 195, 196, 211, 256
Michael (dog) 27, 52, 54, 55, 107, 120, 121, 229, 233, 236
Mielziner, Jo 239
Miller, Alice Duer 132
Miller, Gilbert 160, 161, 181, 182, 184–185
Milligan, Robert 219, 220
Mineau, Charlotte 229
Minnelli, Vincente 183, 222
*A Miracle Can Happen* 213
*Miss Brown, Burglar* 35
*Miss Susie Slagle's* 193
Mitchell, Maggie 7, 66
Mitchell, Thomas 193
Moissi, Alexander 168
Monnette, Helen Hull 105
Monnette, Orra Eugene 105
Monter-Gray 209
Montmartre 137
*Moonstruck* 149
Moore, Alex 93
Moore, Colleen 143, 150
Moore, Tom 230
Mooser, George 62
Morehouse, Ward 12, 37, 197, 205–206, 210, 214
Morgan, Anne 31
Morgan, Edward J. 156
Morgan, Helen 227
Morgan, J.P. 31
Morgan, Ralph 236
Morley, Sheridan 217
Morosco, Annie 42, 49, 54
Morosco, Oliver 42–43, 46, 48, 49, 53, 54, 55, 56, 58, 59, 61–62, 63, 67, 68, 70, 113–114, 116, 246, 247
Morris, Clara 96
Morriss, Frank 205, 213, 219
Moss, Larry 183
Mostel, Zero 207
*Mother of Christ* 179
Motherwell, Hiram 173
Mount Vernon, New York 12
*Mrs. Dakon* (aka *Dakon's Daughter*) 36–37, 80, 231
Mudie, Leonard 235
Muni, Paul 252
Museum of Modern Art 226

Nagel, Conrad 173
Nathan, George Jean 196–197, 204
*The National Anthem* 108, 109–111, 172, 179, 191, 236
Nazimova, Alla 30, 31, 32, 33, 99, 131, 166, 181, 193, 245, 262
Neal, Patricia 2
Negri, Pola 127

Neilan, Marshall 116
*Never Too Old* 209
Nichols, Dudley 193
Nichols, Lewis 218
*The Nick of Time Baby* 149
*A Night of Barrie* 174–176, 238–239
Nilsson, Anna Q. 150
*None but the Lonely Heart* 212
Norman, Christine 57, 233
Normand, Mabel 126, 127, 136, 148
Norton, Elliot 225
Novello, Ivor 246
*Numbered Men* 173
Nye, Gene 64

O. Henry 37
O'Brian, Jack 210
O'Brien, Eugene 156
O'Connor, John 226–227
Odets, Clifford 212
*Of the Theatre* 181, 182, 187
O'Hara, Mary 115, 229
O'Keefe, Dennis 224
Oland, Warner 230
Olcott, Chauncey 90, 92, 235
*The Old Lady Shows Her Medals* 174, 175, 176, 195, 239
Olivier, Laurence 214, 220
O'Malley, Aileen 229
O'Malley, Pat 147, 229
*One Act Plays for Stage and Study* 159, 255
*One Night in Rome* 99, 101, 102, 103, 104, 105, 106, 148, 149, 150–152, 153, 229, 230, 235–236
*One Word Sketch* (also known as *A One Word Play by One Author*) 182, 246
O'Neal, Patrick 220
O'Neil, Nance 83
O'Neill, Eugene 30
O'Neill, James 24
O'Neill, Peggy 62, 63, 70, 104
Oppenheim, Tom 263
Oppenheimer, George 119, 197
*Our Dancing Daughters* 118
*Our Mutual Girl* 83
*Out There* 84, 85–88, 90, 91–95, 98, 234–235
*Outliers: The Story of Success* 14
*Outward Bound* 1, 171, 172, 182, 184–189, 190, 191, 192, 196, 214, 220, 228, 239
Owen, Catherine Dale 238

Page, Brett 156
Page, Geraldine 200, 219, 221, 259
Paget, Ffolliet 79, 234
Pakula, Alan J. 219–220, 221, 222, 261–262
Pantages, Lloyd 179
Paramount 193
Parker, Dorothy 31
Parker, Eleanor 191

Parkhurst, Genevieve 171
Parsons, Louella O. 178, 211, 220
Parsons, Schuyler 31
Pavlova, Anna 168
Peck, Gregory 208
*Peg o' My Dreams* 135
*Peg o' My Heart* 1, 2, 6, 18, 22, 23, 25, 29, 31, 32, 33, 34, 37, 41, 42, 43, 45, 49, 50, 51–56, 57–59, 60, 61–64, 65, 66–68, 69, 70, 72, 73, 74, 75, 76, 77, 78, 79, 80, 88, 90, 96, 97, 99, 102, 105, 106, 107, 108, 111, 112, 113, 114–121, 124–129, 130, 131, 132, 135, 137, 144, 145, 146, 149, 150, 151, 152, 159, 160, 161, 163, 165, 166, 167, 170, 172, 174, 175, 176–177, 193, 196, 200, 204, 205, 212, 213, 215, 218, 226–227, 229, 233, 236, 247, 251, 256–257, 259
Pelswick, Rose 147
Perkins, Osgood 173
Perry, Frederick 235
*Peter Pan* 51, 175, 222, 224
Peyton, Jane 22, 33, 231
Phillips, Norma 83
Pickfair 139, 140, 141
Pickford, Mary 27, 83, 113, 115, 127, 128, 136, 140, 141, 149, 182
*Pierrot the Prodigal* 154–155, 238
*Pin a Rose* 209–210
Pinero, Arthur W. 156, 238
*The Piper* 51
Pitts, ZaSu 261
Platt, Livingston 238
Players Club 156
Playhouse Company 184
Poole, Abram 32
Porcasi, Paul 236
Porter, Olive 231
Post, Guy Bates 233
Powers, James T. 90, 92, 235
Preminger, Otto 184–186, 187, 188, 239
Prevost, Marie 150
Price, Vincent 119, 181, 186, 239, 258
Prince, Harold (Hal) 2, 220
Proctor, Catherine 92, 235
*Promise (L'Espoir)* 181–182, 184–185
Pulitzer, Ralph 244
Putnam, George Haven 104
*Pygmalion* 32

*The Queen of the Highway* 12, 13
*Queen of the White Slaves* 12
Quinn Martin Productions 226
Quintero, Jose 220

Randall, Tony 209
Rapf, Harry 151
Rapper, Irving 198, 216–217
Rathbone, Basil 215
Reagan, Nancy 30
*Rebecca* 118

Red Cross 91, 92, 93, 94, 246
Redford, Robert 220
Reed, Florence 187, 188, 213, 218, 239
Reeves-Smith, H. 57, 233, 234
Rehan, Ada 59, 249
Reinhardt, Max 183
*Remember Me to Tom* 199
"A Retrieved Reformation" 37
*The Ringmaster* 35, 231
RKO 178
Rodgers, Richard 31, 224
Rodney, Jean 184
Rogers, Will 83, 150
*Romance* 32, 166
*Romeo and Juliet* 90, 235
Roosevelt, Eleanor 191
Roosevelt, Franklin 191
Roosevelt, Theodore 172
Ross, Anthony (Tony) 200, 203, 213, 228, 239
Ross, Douglas 235
Rossi, Carl A. 173, 227–228
Rowlands, Gena 1
*The Royal Family* 168
Royal General Theatrical Guild of England 172–173
Ruben, Jose 178, 235
Ruman, Sigfried 173
Russell, Fred 221
Russell, Lillian 93
Ryan, Elsa (Elsie) 62, 63

Sacks, J.L. 250
*Sadie Thompson* 118
St. Denis, Ruth 168
*Samson and Delilah* 118
Sands, Dorothy 168
Santley, Joseph 12, 98
Sarg, Tony 135
*Saturday Night Live* 133
Savage, Courtenay 90
Schallert, Edwin 63, 116, 151, 209, 257
Schulman, Arnold 222, 223
Schwartz, Arthur 31, 223, 224
Scott, Allan 173
Scott, Walter 244
*Scotty, King of the Desert Mines* 244
Seldes, Gilbert 158
Seldes, Marian 2
Selznick, David O. 178, 182
Sennett, Mack 149
*The Seven Sisters* 37–39, 41, 48, 49–50, 232
Sewell, C.S. 152
Seymour, William 238
Shakespeare, William 82, 87, 88–91, 99, 154, 195, 235
*Shanghai Gesture* 187
Shaw, George Bernard 24, 32, 183
*She* 14, 17
Shearer, Norma 177

Sheehy, Helen 33, 217
Sheldon, Edward 32
Sheldon, Eloise 173, 181, 182, 188, 225, 228
Sheldon, Nan 239
Sheridan, Clare 226, 244
Sherwood, Robert (Bob) 31, 147
Shinkman, Paul 187
*The Shooting of Dan McGrew* 149
Short, Hassard 57, 58, 233, 234
Shubert, Lee 20, 21–22, 184
"Sickened Thoughts" 178
Siddons, Sarah 227
Siegel, Sol 219
Sillman, Leonard 209
*The Silver Cord* 178
Simpson, Russell 120, 229
Singer, Louis J. 196, 209, 228
*The Skin of Our Teeth* 224
Skinner, R. Dana 158
*Slants on Famous Personalities* 167
Slide, Anthony 253
*Smiling Through* 107
Smith, Chester J. 146
Smith, Gladys 232, 233
Smith, Winchell 66
Soanes, Wood 173, 174
Sommer, Edith 191
*A Son Comes Home* 180, 257
*The Sound of Music* 224
*Spellbound* 118
Standing, Joan 229
Stanford, Henry 52
Stanislavsky, Constantin 30, 82, 133–134
Stanley, Forrest 49, 246
Stanley, Kim 202, 208, 219, 221
Stapleton, Maureen 2, 202, 208–209
*A Star Is Born* 222
Starr, Muriel 179–180
*Stars on Stage: Eileen Darby and Broadway's Golden Age* 227
*Stars That Crossed Mine* 211, 260
Stella (astrologer) 177
Stella Adler School of Acting 263
Stevens, Ashton 99, 158
Stevens, Onslow 177
Stevens, Otheman 53
Stevens, Roger 221
Stewart, Jimmy 195
*Stolen by the Gypsies (Yosemite)* 10–11, 22, 42
Stone, Lewis 40, 233
*The Sultan's Wife* 149
Swanson, Gloria 149
Swanson, Marcella 176
Sweeney, Joseph 173
Sweet, Blanche 73
*Sweet Nell of Old Drury* 134–135, 236, 238, 253

Talmadge, Norma 149
*Taming of the Shrew* 90, 235

Taubman, Howard 225
Taylor, Charles 8, 9–19, 20, 21, 25, 192, 193, 222, 246, 262
Taylor, Charles E. 193
Taylor, Dwight 9, 12, 13, 17, 19, 27, 35, 46, 48, 67, 73, 160, 173, 192, 193, 195, 211, 212, 213, 215, 222, 223, 228, 243, 244, 261–262
Taylor, Marguerite *see* Courtney, Marguerite
*Teddy at the Throttle* 149
Teichmann, Howard 248–249
*Ten Commandments* 137
*Ten Nights in a Bar Room* 98
*Tenderloin* 220
Terry, Ellen 30, 72, 82, 105
Terry, Ethel Grey 229
Thackeray, William Makepeace 24
*That's Acting* 227
Third Avenue Theatre (Seattle) 12–14, 16–18, 98
Thorndyke, Sybil 31
Thornton, Jack 154, 238
*Three Billion Dollars in Four Weeks* 83
*Through Fire and Water* 12
*Thy Name Is Woman* 146
Tichenor, Edna 230
Tinnee, Mae 147
Titheradge, Dion 79, 80, 81
Toland, Gregg 193
*Top Hat* 173
*Tosca* 98
*Town and Country* 193
Towne, Charles Hanson 1, 126
Tracy, Lee 173
Tracy, Spencer 204
*Trelawny of the Wells* 156–157, 238
Tuck, Alice May 239
Tully, Richard Walton 42, 43, 44, 45, 233, 246
Tumulty, Joseph 156
*Twelfth Night* 180
Tyler, George C. 24, 74, 75, 78, 85, 91, 164, 190
Tynan, Kenneth 215

Ulric, Lenore 31, 233
*Uncle Tom's Cabin* 98
United Artists 116, 220, 222

Valentino, Rudolph 30, 115
Van Burn, A.H. 231, 232
Vanbrugh, Irene 105
Vanbrugh, Violet 105
Vanderbilt, Anne 31
Vane, Sutton 184, 187, 191, 214, 239
Velez, Lupe 143
Vernon, Bobby (Bobbie) 149
Vetlugen, Valdemar 211
*Victor Regina* 181
Vidor, King 110, 112, 116–121, 122, 124–125, 126, 128, 129–130, 131, 135, 136, 137, 139, 141, 143, 144–145, 146, 148–149, 229

Vitak, Albertina 135
Vonnegut, Ruth 178

Walker, June 31, 213
Walker, Laura 203, 213
Wallace, George 224
Wallace-Taylor, Audrey 195, 243, 245
Wanamaker, Sam 212–213
Wardwell, Geoffrey 176
Ware, Helen 90, 235
Warfield, David 93
Warlock, Frederick 164, 238
Warner, H.B. 90, 92, 231, 235
Warner, Jack 217
Warner Bros. 191, 216
Watts, Richard, Jr. 187
Wayne, David 209
Wayne, John 193
Webb, Clifton 31
Weber & Fields Music Hall 57
Weber and Fields 88
*The Well of Loneliness* 33
Welles, Orson 216
West, Alice Pardoe 216
Westley, Helen 173
*The White Tigress of Japan* 12
Whittington, Ida (Miss Whitty) 7, 8, 9
Wilhelmi, Teresa 227
Williams, Edwina Dakin 197, 198, 199, 259
Williams, Tennessee 172, 196, 197–199, 201, 202, 203–204, 205, 206, 210, 213, 214, 215, 217, 220, 228, 239, 259
Willson, Meredith 224
Wilson, Edith 92
Wilson, Lois 167
Wilson, Woodrow 83, 92, 156, 172
Winchell, Walter 187
Windham, Donald 198, 203–204
Winters, Shelley 200
Winwood, Estelle 31, 166–167, 238
Wolheim, Louis 166
Wong, Anna May 173
Wood, Audrey 196
Woodlawn Cemetery 213, 261
Woods, Donald 180
Woodward, 226
*The Wooing of Eve* 77, 78–79, 235
Woollcott, Alexander 27, 31, 81, 99, 107, 109, 154, 158, 163, 178, 248–249, 252
Wright, Haidee 168
Wycherly, Margaret 212
Wyman, Jane 216, 217
Wynard, Diana 245
Wyndham, Charles 72
Wyngate, Valerie 160, 161

Yearsley, Ralph 230
*Yellow to Lavender* 227–228
Yorke, Edith 229
*Yosemite* see *Stolen by the Gypsies*
Young, Stanley 219, 220, 221, 223
Young, Stark 154, 156–157
*Young in Heart* 182–183
*Young Love* 166
Ysu, Y.Y. 173

Zolotow, Maurice 33, 72, 78, 87–88, 98, 101

www.ingramcontent.com/pod-product-compliance
Lightning Source LLC
Chambersburg PA
CBHW021349300426
44114CB00012B/1143